R. N. Schwab

EUROPEAN INTELLECTUAL
HISTORY SINCE 1789

ROLAND N. STROMBERG

UNIVERSITY OF WISCONSIN-MILWAUKEE

EUROPEAN INTELLECTUAL
HISTORY SINCE 1789

NEW YORK

APPLETON-CENTURY-CROFTS

DIVISION OF MEREDITH CORPORATION

PRINTED IN THE UNITED STATES OF AMERICA
E 85411

One Cannot Live Without Ideas; Every Step One Takes Is Directed, If Not By A Conscious, At Least By An Unconscious Or Sub-conscious Idea.

ARNOLD HOTTINGER

Preface

This book owes most to the author's students, having grown largely out of a course he has inflicted upon some of the hardier among them for the past several years. There seemed to be an urgent need for a basic book around which to organize such a course in Modern European Intellectual History. Obviously one would want to supplement such a book with various readings in the sources, and in the rich literature of more specialized secondary works. But when all is said and done, the textbook remains an essential skeleton of the course. It should be fairly concise, well-informed, attractively written, well-organized—no mere outline, but worth reading in itself; full enough to raise the issues and introduce the topics that need to be introduced, above all able to stimulate the student to more exact investigations, and supply him with the references he needs to carry on these; yet not so long as to become tedious, and to drown the beginning student in detail. Suggestive essays have been written in this field, and several good source books compiled, for example by F. L. Baumer, Eugene C. Black, and Eugen Weber. But it is difficult to think of many coherently arranged accounts covering the modern period, that is, from the "dawn of modern thought" in the seventeenth century to the present, the period covered by *An Intellectual History of Modern Europe* (published in 1966), of which this volume is approximately the latter half. The author can at least say, then, that an urgently felt need impelled this attempt to fulfill the requirements of such a book. Others operating in this area have felt the same need. Intellectual History is growing in popularity, and for excellent reasons. It is not merely that the historian feels the need to understand the background of ideas in order to interpret the processes of social change and political incident at any given time, but that those concerned with literature, philosophy, and other disciplines also need this background. The tendency of scholarship in these fields to abandon the historical approach throws a larger burden upon the historian of ideas. And, more important, the average citizen wants to know about his heritage of civilization, which is contained in a fabric of thought so old and so complex that guides are urgently needed. There are some additional remarks on the subject of intellectual history in the Introduction.

This portion of the larger work has been published separately in response to a number of requests. These requests frequently have come from instructors of courses dealing with European or Western Civilization since 1789 or 1815, who wish to supplement political, social, and economic history with material on intellectual history. In certain respects modern Western man's culture of the mind, his intellectual furnishings and his basic structure of thought, date from the great Scientific Revolution of the seventeenth century, and it is here—following a brief general comment on the earlier ages of ideas—that the larger book begins. The first of the two parts into which that book is divided also covers that extraordinary chapter of intellectual history, the eighteenth century Enlightenment. But 1789 is a landmark of unrivalled significance on the scene of history, and this is no less true of intellectual history than political or social. It is possible to argue that our specifically modern world began in 1500, or in 1600, or in 1700, or at various times in between, as in various ways it did; but no one questions the importance of the years around 1800 as a decisive turning point. In what ways this was as true of the literary and philosophical realms as it was of the political, the first chapter attempts to make clear. This book, then, though representing only a little more than half of the original one, can stand on its own feet as a self-contained unit. A few minor changes have been made in the original edition.

A book of this sort must, of course, rest on the labors of innumerable scholars who have been at work supplying the building blocks for it in the form of detailed research in the history of ideas. These are too numerous to mention; a glance at the additional readings at the end of the book will suggest the dimensions. Professors John C. Rule and Peter Gay read the manuscript of this book at various stages and contributed many suggestions which greatly improved it, though for the faults which remain they can bear no responsibility. Every academic author owes something to the institution that employs him and sometimes gives him unusual research opportunities in the form of favorable or reduced teaching schedules. One comes back, however, to the students, whose interest and intelligence sustains one's faith in the worth of the serious study of ideas and of history.

R. N. S.

Contents

EUROPEAN INTELLECTUAL HISTORY SINCE 1789

Introduction

To "trace the history of the human mind," said Hume, is the task of the historian, as distinct from the chronicler. Voltaire added that "it is better to know how men thought in former times than how they acted." A great deal of intellectual history has crept, willy-nilly, into History, it being impossible to keep out the men of ideas. A current collection of readings offered to students of the beginning college course in Western civilization includes selections from Plato, Aristotle, the Bible, Cicero, Augustine, Aquinas, Machiavelli, Rabelais, Luther, Calvin, Bodin, Descartes, Locke, Bossuet, Rousseau, Burke, Tocqueville, Marx, Nietzsche, Sartre, and Camus. Obviously it would be difficult to justify their exclusion from such a course. One wonders, though, to what extent most freshmen are equipped to grapple with these formidable adversaries.

We no longer restrict history to politics or public events, if for no other reason than that these cannot be "understood" without reference to the climate of opinion in which they took place. The deeds of Charlemagne cannot be understood apart from the peculiar mixture of ideas and values that made up the mind of his age, a mind quite different from ours. Nor, to come closer to home in both space and time, can the deeds of Thomas Jefferson be understood except in the context of the Enlightenment—a "lost world," as one Jefferson student has cogently argued. Some men of ideas "made history" directly—Luther, for example. Others, who did not, contributed so much to those who did that we cannot leave them out: Robespierre had his Rousseau, Lenin his Marx. "If ideas in politics more than elsewhere are the children of practical needs," J. N. Figgis has written, "none the less is it true, that the actual world is the result of men's thought. The existing arrangement of political forces is dependent at least as much upon ideas, as it is upon men's perceptions of their

1

interests." Here is not the place to go into the troublesome question of just how *ideas* and *interests* act together in history. It is enough to observe that they do interact, that they are the "two faces of reality," in Jean Lhomme's expression, which one sees in all the great issues of mankind. Ideas are quite commonly found first in the mind of some unworldly person, a recluse like Bentham, an obscure pauper like Marx, a poor vagabond like Rousseau; then they are taken up by men of affairs, who, as John Maynard Keynes observed, snatch them from the air perhaps without knowing that they came from some scribbler of yesterday.

The interaction of historically important ideas with the social milieu from which they emerge and which they in turn influence—this is, broadly, the domain of intellectual history. The separate disciplines, such as philosophy, the sciences, or political theory, insofar as they study their past ideas tend to do so unhistorically, treating them substantively and as if they arose in a vacuum. It must remain for the intellectual historian to show how these ideas interacted with social reality, with past ideas, and with each other. At any particular time and place there is a specific set of influences on the human mind, which includes (1) the legacy of past ideas available to men at that time, (2) a social context, consisting of all sorts of phenomena prominent in the environment of the times, political, economic, etc., and, (3) other contemporary strains of thought and expression. If, for example, we wish to grasp the thought of Nietzsche, we have to know the older thinkers who influenced him (a great many reaching back to the Greeks), some more than others, such as his immediate predecessor Schopenhauer, also his social atmosphere, of nineteenth-century bourgeois culture, together with such events as the Franco-Prussian War and the Bismarckian supremacy; and finally other significant intellectual movements of his time, among them French estheticism, Darwinism, socialism, etc. A recent European scholar has remarked, "There is room for a discipline whose aim is to assess the factors which influence the human mind in one period or in one region," this being his definition of the realm of intellectual history.

What validates or testifies to the importance of intellectual systems? Few of them, if any, can stand the test of absolute logic: the great philosophies have all turned out to be postulates at bottom, mere assertions, fiats, resting on something assumed to be true without proof. This is quite as true of allegedly "scientific" structures such as Marxism, Newtonian physics, or logical positivism as it is of more patently "metaphysical" ones. The reason they appear and are adopted, become popular and influential, is related to factors other than the merely immanent laws of thought. These factors, it may be suggested, are historical and social; historical, in that ideas evolve in time as one generation hands down its thoughts to others who take them up and use them as a point of departure—the endless dialectic of intellectual history; social, in that the selection of some ideas rather than others for emphasis and discussion has to do with the structure of social reality at a given time—the issues, atmosphere, and great events of the day. Even genius must create with reference to the external social world it finds to hand; it cannot just create, in a vacuum.

Intellectual history as an academic discipline is fairly new and probably has yet to complete the task of clarifying its scope, methods, and content.

Clearly the subject matter is intensely interesting, for those with a flair for ideas. Some do not have this taste and should probably avoid the subject. Indeed, other historians, fact-minded, often lack it, which is perhaps a reason why they suspect intellectual history. Defined as the study of the role of *ideas* in historical events and processes, intellectual history is admittedly a difficult art. In this connection a recent student observes that historical writing of the usual sort "often fails to apprehend the slow subterranean movements which minds inclined to be too matter-of-fact find intangible"[1]—those movements of the mind, of ideas and ideologies and tides of taste, which never appear overtly in history until one day, perchance, they explode in a French Revolution. While the details of politics and administrations and wars are studied in the most minute detail, because they are neatly documented in archives and can be grasped by the matter-of-fact mind, the role of ideas may be dismissed in a vague phrase or two. The need for careful and precise studies in intellectual history is now recognized and is being met.[2] But much work remains to be done.

Writing some years ago, that philosopher so celebrated in the "history of ideas," Arthur O. Lovejoy, approaching the subject from the vantage point not of the historian but of the student of thought as such, noted the unnatural fragmentation of the study of ideas, apportioned out among at least twelve "disciplines."[3] While students of literature, of the arts, of science, theology, education, social thought, etc., each cart away a portion of the body of Western thought, to dissect it minutely in the privacy of their chambers in isolation from each other, the whole organism perishes of this process, and there is no one to restore it to life unless a discipline called "history of ideas" can do so. The specialist work done by the various departments of learning is extensive and valuable, but badly needs to be collated. And a service may be rendered to these various departments themselves, for Milton's poetry cannot be understood apart from the poet's store of general ideas, nor can Darwin's science be fully grasped without this context.

As an introductory textbook, in a difficult domain of study still far from mature, this volume need offer no apology for its defects. Introductory textbooks are intended for the important function of introducing the as yet fairly unsophisticated student to fields which it is hoped he will further explore, with the aid of the suggestions for additional reading supplied. This book should of course also be supplemented by outside readings in the sources of intellectual history. Asked what to read, Walter Pater advised students to "read the great authors whole; read Plato whole; read Kant whole; read Mill whole." Excellent advice, but a little impractical for many students. This textbook is not meant to substitute for the reading of the great thinkers, but rather to prepare for or supplement that task. It is, indeed, not meant to be more than a serviceable text for college courses. It has arisen from a number of years of experience in teaching such a course in modern European intellectual history. Intellectual history, as it seems to us, should provide an introduction to the most important

---

[1] Henri Peyre, "The Influence of Eighteenth Century Ideas on the French Revolution," *Journal of the History of Ideas*, January, 1949.

[2] See some apposite remarks in the introduction to Walter M. Simon's recent book, *European Positivism in the Nineteenth Century*, 1963.

[3] "The Historiography of Ideas," in *Essays in the History of Ideas*, 1948.

—from a general cultural viewpoint[4]—"ideas" (intellectual systems, movements of the mind) in the cultural heritage; it should relate these ideas to the social and political background so far as possible; it should show the continuity and lineage of thought; it should indicate the relevance of the ideas to general culture.

Most especially, perhaps, as a *history* of ideas, a presentation of this sort should provide a sense of history. That means a sense of the living context of reality, and it means a sense of the flow and movement of things. Too often the great thinkers and the great ideas are drained of life by being presented as disembodied abstractions. The historian wants to see Kepler in his classroom at the moment when he stumbled upon what seemed to him a great truth, and which really was not, but which launched him on a lifelong quest destined to alter the mind of the West. He wants Kepler's unhappy childhood and restless adolescence. (Arthur Koestler, that great contemporary writer, has done this in *The Sleepwalkers*.) He wants Voltaire's misspent youth and Rousseau's neuroticism and Marx's proud poverty; Locke's bourgeois prudence and Nietzsche's madness—all the human story of the great thinkers.

Nor should they, intellectual historians feel, deal only with the great thinkers, for Croce was right in observing that the spirit of an age is sometimes better found in the second-rate thinkers, and the spirit of the age must always be close to what the historian of ideas seeks. It is the general direction of the movement of thought that concerns him. From earliest times to the present, the great army of thought has marched—some individuals ahead, some in the rear, a large straggling army—steadily past one milestone after another, leaving behind some ideas, fashioning new ones, transforming old ones. We do not know the ultimate destination of the long trek, if it has any. But where we have been and what we have learned is worth knowing, for each of us is a part of the army, anxiously searching for signposts and wondering where, in the endless chaos of things, we are. History orients us.

It also equips us to live. To understand the past is to be able to live fully in the present. To be acquainted with the intellectual heritage of our long and rich Western civilization is to be a civilized person and to be prepared for constructive thinking. The object of this book is to present the most important general ideas in modern European history, not in isolation but as part of the stream of history. As Dr. Johnson said, "There is no part of history so generally useful as that which relates to the progress [?] of the human mind, the successive advances of science, the vicissitudes of learning and ignorance, the extension and resuscitation of arts and the revolution of the intellectual world."

---

4 Philosophy students, attuned to the analytical mood, often do not find the intellectual history course satisfying because it is not much interested in the truth or falsity, consistency or inconsistency, of intellectual systems or philosophies and is therefore prone to linger over some not interesting from this point of view, while ignoring others that are. Rousseau and Marx are not great philosophers and the essentially analytical mind soon grows impatient with their cloudy terms and vague ideas; they are historically and existentially of the highest importance, that is, they posed questions relevant to their age and of deepest significance for the human situation of modern times. It has been noted that specialists in whatever field, from economics to theology, will choose figures different from those selected by historians for their general cultural interest.

THE MODERN EPOCH

No one denies that the French Revolution ushered in the specifically modern epoch of history. The Revolution in some measure looked to the eighteenth century "philosophers," to Rousseau and Voltaire and Montesquieu and Diderot, for its inspiration and ideas; but it soon swept beyond their prescriptions (which were hardly in agreement with each other) to explore political frontiers previously unheard of. Recent examinations of the role of Rousseau's and Voltaire's ideas in the Revolution impressively document both the extensive nature of this role and its amazingly chameleon-like character: the revolutionaries constantly quoted the Enlightenment giants but just as constantly made these words mean entirely different things. Apart from its specific content of novel political ideas, including equality, individualism, democracy, nationalism, and socialism, the Revolution was so massive that men could not help thinking of it as ushering in a new epoch in every department of life. Then the reaction to its violent excesses entailed opposition to all those ideas that had presumably inspired it, and a kind of intellectual counter-revolution against the Enlightenment, associated with Edmund Burke, took place. The titanic struggles of the twenty-five years after 1789 left the entire civilization forever altered, socially, politically, and intellectually. This era of revolutions dominates the early part of the nineteenth century.

The nineteenth century falls rather naturally into three parts, from the viewpoint of *Zeitgeist* and history of ideas. The morning is the Romantic and Revolutionary age, lasting from about 1789 to 1832 or perhaps 1848. It is marked by convulsions both political and moral, an intellectual revolution, and a great deal of creativity, emerging from its storm and stress. Its heroes of thought are Kant and Fichte and Hegel; Burke, Chateaubriand, Saint-Simon, Fourier; the Romantic poets; the renovators of political philosophy; the creators of new social doctrines. It is an age in which men felt old moorings give way and wondered where the storm would blow them.

Then, during the noonday of the century, calm returns and there is time to take soundings. Doubts and tensions remain, but this Victorian period is marked by relative stability, and by the undertaking of extraordinary efforts at synthesis. This is the time of Comte, Marx, Darwin, and Mill. Realism replaces Romanticism in literature and the arts; science, the ultimate realism, mounts the pedestal as the modern god; visions of utopia in politics and society suffer a severe blow with the failure of the revolutions of 1848. There is disenchantment, but there is also success, on solid if pedestrian foundations, the kind of success and solidity the adjective "mid-Victorian" conveys.

The evening brings its gloom and uncertainties; unquestionably a darker mood strikes Europe late in the century, from about 1885 down to the stunning collapse of 1914. If the average man remained complacent and hopeful, post-Darwinian and post-Marxist Europe produced a crop of amazingly insightful thinkers who were exploring domains never heretofore much known, zones of fearful nonsymmetry. The unconscious irrational, or the prerational, interested the men who dominate this epoch—Nietzsche, Freud, Bergson, Sorel, Max Weber. In part, this mirrored the experiences of an epoch which brought vast movements of population from farm to city, vast increases in population with the accompanying problem of "mass," almost terrifying technological "advances." In this period the artist and intellectual tends to be estranged or alienated from society, yet become creative as never before.

Of all watersheds, 1914 is rivalled only by 1789 in the modern world; nothing after the terrible World War could be the same. Shattered visions of infinite progress littered the postwar landscape, and Western man suddenly found that he had no other values to fall back on. He tried to invent new ones, tried even to recover old ones, but watched his world descend into even lower depths of war and degradation. The response of thought to the challenge of "decline and fall" was at times nothing less than heroic, if likewise nothing less than desperate. If the future does not call it the age of Lenin and Hitler, it may decide to know it as the age of Toynbee and Sartre. Withal, it was the age of Le Corbusier and Picasso, Lawrence and Joyce, and others who have expressed the contemporary idiom. We are midstream of it and can hardly evaluate it, but because its waters are our own, to swim around in them and try to sense which way the current goes is one of our greatest pleasures and needs.

This volume, then, tries to take European man from the French Revolution through the nineteenth century and into his current fix. It begins with him emerging from the Enlightenment into Romanticism, from an aristocratic into a democratic society, from an agrarian and commercial era into the industrial-technological one. It leaves him perhaps a confused and buffeted creature, the victim in part of too much knowledge, too many ideas; but at the same time needing to rethink and put to use his manifold inheritance of thought and expression.

What is the good of curbing sensuality, shaping the intellect, securing the supremacy of
reason? Imagination lies in wait as the most
powerful enemy.

GOETHE

I have seen the beginning and the end of a
world.

CHATEAUBRIAND

Romanticism and Revolution: 1789–1815

1

At least three revolutions, the French, the Romantic, and the Kantian, The Three
occurred in the 1780s, with their direct impact carrying on through the Revolutions
next several decades to leave a deep mark on the entire modern world.
To these, general history must perhaps add the Industrial Revolution.
Contemporaries were prone to regard them as but different aspects of a
single revolution. Thus the conservative Francis Jeffrey in 1816, discussing "the revolution in our literature," attributed it to "the agitations
of the French revolution . . . the hopes and terrors to which it gave occasion." (Some recent scholarly students of Romanticism have been inclined
to endorse this verdict.) And the German poet Heine, speaking of Immanuel Kant, remarked that "with this book (*The Critique of Pure Reason*) an intellectual revolution began in Germany which offers the
strangest analogies with the material revolution in France . . ."—and,
he added, to the reflective mind is of equal importance. This judgment
was endorsed by Karl Marx who observed that the Kantian revolution in
philosophy was the intellectual counterpart of the French revolution in
politics. It only remains to connect Kant with Romanticism, and of course
that is a common juxtaposition—not that the two things were quite the
same, but that Kant's successors and disciples, Fichte and Schelling, provided philosophical grounding for the Romantic poets.

Clearly these three important developments, in pure philosophy,
literature, and politics respectively, did interact and sometimes blend. It

is not clear that they were of similar origin. Kant was working on problems bequeathed to philosophy by Locke, Berkeley, Leibniz, and especially Hume; he wrote his chief books before the Revolution, and his basic position does not seem to have been affected by that event, though it stirred him deeply even in his ivory tower at Königsberg. (But Jean-Jacques Rousseau demonstrably influenced both Kant and the French Revolution.) The Revolution, needless to say, owed nothing directly to the German philosopher on the shores of the Baltic, whose abstruse speculations were unknown in 1789 to all but a few. As for Romanticism, which also can be traced back to Rousseau, it most clearly announced its arrival in Germany around 1781, with the writings of Schiller and the young Goethe, in a context that seems neither politically revolutionary nor at all interested in technical philosophy. The young Goethe was mostly interested in mystical religion. Schiller's *William Tell* was to inspire many a revolutionary, but it was not written until 1804.

Causation in history is a tricky problem, never simple. Monistic dogmas which assert the invariable priority of one factor, such as technological change or the rise of a social class, do not stand the test of careful criticism. Material, social, and intellectual factors continually interact on each other. It is not clear that they do so within the matrix of a single system, so that one can speak of the unity of an historical epoch. Any historical period contains within itself many processes and themes, not necessarily all knit together in a seamless web; there are always loose ends.

One can say with assurance that there was restlessness and malaise in the 1780s. The American Revolution, an event of the profoundest significance for Europe, not least France, concluded successfully. The French monarchy was in deep trouble before 1789, reeling toward bankruptcy, apparently unable, since the failure of the Turgot reform effort in 1776, wherein new king Louis XVI began bravely only to fall back, to install necessary reforms. In Great Britain, a political organism weakened by the American defeat faced impending great changes, as reformers demanded a more democratic and representative Parliament. In the realm of literature and thought, there were some equally disturbing signs. The German drama of *Sturm und Drang* (storm and stress) was a strong reaction against Enlightenment Classicism, while the turn toward mysticism and religion expressed itself in France in such figures as the popular *philosophe inconnu*, Saint-Martin. (Hamann, Swedenborg, and Blake are other examples in diverse quarters of Europe.) The 1780s was a glorious decade that gave us Mozart and the American Constitution as well as Kant, in many ways the climax of the Enlightenment. But the leaders of the great *philosophe* era were falling away. Voltaire died in 1778, Rousseau in the same year, Hume in 1776, Diderot in 1784, d'Alembert in 1783, Condillac in 1780, Frederick the Great in 1786, etc. Buffon and

Franklin were octogenarians. These illustrious passings signalled the demise of an age. Many sensed change in the air—even before the French Revolution arrived to confirm it.

Though Enlightenment strains continued on, to be seen in such prominent schools as British Utilitarianism and Political Economy, the Revolution ended by discrediting much of it. It was accused, by the important conservative manifesto of Edmund Burke, of having led France to disaster through its simplistic and abstract conception of man, its utopian quest for a perfect social order. It was now said to have been metaphysical, a charge it had once itself levelled at the past. It had invented fantasies and called them Reason. It had thrown out the really important things in life, such as religion and tradition and concrete human ties, in favor of slogans about the rights of man which, in practice, only invited godless men to slaughter each other. Europe, the conservative foes of revolutionary France believed, would have to purge herself of this disease which, erupting in the Terror, had its roots in the sick cynicism of Voltaire, the wild dreams of Rousseau. In Burke and his numerous followers strains of Romanticism interacted with the reaction against the Revolution that affected most of Europe's major intellectual figures by 1798, continuing on through the Napoleonic wars and into the post-Napoleonic Restoration.

THE FRENCH REVOLUTION

Recent historians of the French Revolution tell us that we should not speak of a *French* Revolution. "In fact, the French revolution was only one aspect of a Western, or more exactly an Atlantic revolution, which began in the English colonies in America shortly after 1763, extended through revolutions in Switzerland, the Low Countries, and Ireland, before reaching France between 1787 and 1789" (Jacques Godechot). From France, it bounced over to Germany, Switzerland, Italy, and other parts of Europe. One might object that it is foolish to compare the rumblings in Holland or Ireland with the French Revolution for significance and scope, and that the later revolutions came about precisely because France's had done so. But it is certainly true that the French Revolution from the beginning exerted a worldwide influence, and, if this was because of French prestige and influence throughout Europe, it was also because the Revolution produced ideas for which the whole Western world was ready.

A Western Revolution

What were the great ideas of the Revolution? Some of them seem self-evident and therefore pedestrian today, but they were not so familiar then, and they were given vibrant new meaning by the marvelous events of 1789: popular sovereignty, self-determination of peoples, equality of rights. And nationalism. Frenchmen joyously toasted "la patrie" of which they were all, equally, the children now: no more Bretons, Angevins or

The Revolutionary Ideas

Dauphinards, any more than nobles and commoners. The whole conception of the political society changed. The king could no longer be king of France, he must (if he stayed) be king of the French, for he owed his power to the people. The special privileges and rights of the nobility, renounced by the nobles themselves in an orgy of ideological altruism, were no more; all citizens were equal before the law, with equal access to office, equal liability to taxation. Much of the Revolution's mystique went into that word *citoyen.* The Nation, then, was born—a community of men sharing equally in rights and duties, not a class hierarchy. If people did not like the government they had, they should have a right to change it. And they had a right to speak up freely, according to the Declaration of the Rights of Man and Citizen, that great manifesto of the Revolution.

Those who alleged a certain vagueness and utopian character in the ideology of the Revolution would of course be right. It was an apocalyptic moment, and all kinds of millennial ideals came forth. Universal peace was one of them, ironically enough in view of what the Revolution in fact soon brought to Europe. Numerous orators repudiated the very right to make war, and the Assembly solemnly adopted a resolution of this sort in 1790. Two years later, France was at war with the monarchies of Europe and only that incurable ideologist, Maximilien Robespierre, was still (for the time being) a pacifist. It had been expected that all mankind would be brothers. In fact, "popular sovereignty" or "self-determination" entailed war, because Europe's political order did not correspond to this principle. Nor would it have been possible to decide what this slogan meant exactly, in practice, in many parts of Europe.

Different Veins of Revolutionary Thought

Faced with the need to transform the largely negative character of the initial revolution (the first Constitution resounds with "il n'y a plus"— "there no longer exists"), men fell back in good part on eighteenth-century ideas. Rousseau especially was to be quoted incessantly by leaders of the Revolution. Enlightenment political theory tended to be vague and utopian. Nor was it all of a piece. Montesquieu disagreed with Voltaire, Voltaire with Rousseau, and Rousseau, if not with himself, at least with some of his followers. It is easy to identify as least three major strains in the Revolution, perhaps more. The first period of the Revolution was in the hands of moderate men, who did not wish drastic change; the intellectual idol of this phase was Montesquieu, the goal a limited, constitutional monarchy on the English model. Then, in terms of the chief Revolutionary factions, came the Girondin, Jacobin or *Montagnard,* and *sans culotte* or perhaps Babeuvist forces[1]—in broader ideological terms, roughly liberal, democratic, socialist.

[1] These terms are often used loosely, because the lines of distinction were not always clear in the frenetic course of the Revolution. The Girondins, so named because most of their leaders seemed to come from the region of Gironde in France,

The Girondins admired Voltaire, his disciple Condorcet being one of their brains trust. Not lacking in revolutionary zeal, the party of Brissot, Condorcet and Mme. Roland was anticlerical, antiaristocratic, and inclined to a doctrinaire liberalism, based on Montesquieu and Locke along with Voltaire (though Mme. Roland also admired Rousseau, an ambivalent figure, as we know). These were the upper bourgeoisie, insofar as a class label might be roughly pinned on them. They believed in natural rights of the individual and were suspicious of excessive state power. Constitutional government with "checks and balances" but not too much democracy appealed to this group, who perhaps betrayed their bourgeois outlook as much in their deistic anticlericalism as in the law against workers' associations passed in 1791. Anglophile admirers of the British constitutional system, they bequeathed much to nineteenth-century French liberalism, always weaker than in Britain but not without its influence. They lost out in the struggle that developed, were destroyed, and sent to the guillotine by their enemies on the Left. It is significant that under the impact of events they moved toward democracy. Initially hostile to universal suffrage, some of them came around to it. Condorcet's constitution of 1793, which never went into effect, included universal suffrage and a single legislative assembly, ideas approved by the American friend of this group, Benjamin Franklin. But executive and judicial checks on the will of this assembly were to exist. If the Gironde moved close to a type of democracy under the pressure of events during the Revolution, its position should be distinguished from Jacobin democracy.

Girondin Liberalism

The left-wing Jacobins developed an unusual conception of democracy based on Rousseau's social contract and general will, or their construal of these concepts. Their goal was equality, and the idea of the general will together with the mass or mob action on which their power often depended caused them to glorify the people *en masse*. Robespierre and Saint-Just accepted a dictatorship of reason, with themselves representing the "people." This strain of thought had relatively little regard for individual rights or parliamentary institutions, which seemed to it selfish and corrupt. The Jacobin constitution of 1793 provided for no separation of powers, no limit on the power of the state, no guarantees of individual liberties. It sanctioned a plebescitary or democratic dictatorship, based on the popular will but with power delegated to a small number of men. Jacobin democracy with its frank worship of the mob

Jacobin Democracy

---

were technically one branch of the widely based Jacobin Society. The term *Montagnard* is often used to mean the left-wing Jacobins because this was where the leftists sat in the Assembly (on the slope of the hall rather than on the floor where the "Plain" was.) But the term *Jacobin* came to be used popularly for any partisan of the *sans culottes* (poor people of Paris) or extreme left-wing cause. Jacobins of the "Mountain" like Saint-Just and Robespierre clearly did not approve of some even farther to the Left of them—"enragés" or socialists.

spirit is difficult for Anglo-Saxons to grasp, but it has been a potent tradition in France. Democratic in a deep sense, with a feeling for the common man *en masse,* a desire to bring the people directly into government (Robespierre wished to build a stadium holding twelve thousand people to allow the crowd to watch the legislators), and a passion for equality, its disregard of legal processes and individual rights may have been reflected in the Reign of Terror, though that abnormal episode ought not to be charged to ideology alone. (Later Jacobins showed a keen concern for individual justice: consider the glorious fight of Georges Clemenceau, a century later, on behalf of Captain Dreyfus.)

Robespierre

Robespierre was the great ideologist of the Revolution and leading personality during the hectic bloody days of the Republic of Virtue. It is significant for his love of Jean Jacques that he believed in the worship of a Supreme Being; atheism, he declared, is aristocratic. He was a believer, but his true God was a kind of abstract conception of the People. Effective mass orator, he was coldly unhappy in most of his relationships with concrete, real people. With a sensitivity that caused him to tremble at the sight of blood, he could order the death of thousands in the name of Humanity. All that Edmund Burke meant when he accused the Revolution of abstract theorizing and a want of practical judgment is embodied in Robespierre, the man of austere principle who hated the intrigues of practical politics and ended a bloody dictator because he would not compromise.

Robespierre was not the most radical product of the French Revolution. Jacobinism was not socialistic though it accepted the supremacy of community over individual, in the spirit of Rousseau's social contract. Danton, Robespierre, and Saint-Just assumed a right to regulate property in any way necessary, but the social order they believed to be best was one in which every citizen held a little property, as Rousseau had suggested. This might well be designated as a petty-bourgeois or artisan-workman utopia.

Pioneer Socialists

Socialism did appear in the French Revolution though it did not get far. Babeuf and Buonarrotti, revolutionary socialists, attempted an insurrection in 1795 (the Conspiracy of the Equals) but failed badly. Nevertheless they began a powerful tradition. Their thought was crude, but their feelings strong; somewhat inarticulately they hated property, commerce, luxury, while extolling the virtues of poverty, equality, honest labor. They, too, took their inspiration chiefly from aspects of the writings of Jean Jacques, which partially articulated their natural class feelings. Morelly, an obscure writer, had developed Rousseau's thought in a more socialistic direction just before the Revolution. Mably and Holbach also wrote in a similar vein and reached large audiences. These were mostly poor men and their words are significant as among the first sounds from the lower depths. Like the Levellers and Diggers of the English Revolution, the left-wing Jacobins and the Equals spoke briefly for classes of men hardly yet represented at all in literate thought; the revolution had stirred the pot sufficiently to bring them momentarily to the top, then they subsided. But this time their voices were not forgotten. Buonarroti survived to become a link with the socialism of the 1840s, and Parisian revolutionary radicalism lived on in other workingmen such as Blanqui. This *sans culotte* socialism spread over Europe quickly, making an appeal to doctrinaire representatives of the poorer classes. It was, after all, close to elemental Christianity. Russo, the Italian Babeuvist, echoed Savonarola's medieval call to the rich to throw away their jewels.

These extremes tended to discredit the Revolution. The initial joy with which it was greeted all over Europe turned to disillusionment as the 1790s wore on and the Revolution led to civil war, persecution, terror, international war. At first all the intellectuals of Europe were enchanted by it, including dozens who later became its bitter foes. "Bliss was it in that dawn to be alive." Not only Wordsworth but Maistre, Chateaubriand, Kant, Fichte, Novalis, Goethe, Coleridge, Southey, and many others felt this. Rousseau had passionate admirers in England, like the father of Thomas Malthus, who asked only to be known as "the friend of Rousseau." Gilbert Wakefield, a Rousseau disciple, was imprisoned in 1799 for allegedly expressing a wish that the French would invade and conquer Britain. Everyone at this time, too, was reading Gibbon, whose *Decline and Fall of the Roman Empire*, which he had finished in 1787 after more than twenty years of labor, radiated a republican spirit—or did it only seem so in the atmosphere of 1789? The Roman state had begun its collapse with the very first emperor, and Christianity had finished it off, the great historian seemed to be saying.

But the Revolution seemed to lose its way and turn to violence, rapine, and injustice. It ended with the Reign of Terror and the awesome spectacle of the revolution devouring its own children. The result was a reexamination of the premises of the Age of Reason, and a rejection of them that aided the turn toward Romanticism.

Reaction against the Revolution

The Revolutionaries had seemed to cling to eighteenth-century rationalism. It was not the Romantic Rousseau they worshipped, but the utopian rationalist of *The Social Contract*. Before his suicide in a revolutionary prison, Condorcet, the disciple of Voltaire, wrote his hymn to unlimited human progress under reason. The Republic of Virtue and of Terror paraded the Goddess of Reason through the streets. Volney (*The Ruins*, 1791) theorized that empires fall from an insufficiency of natural religion and too many priests. Robespierre, in his meteoric path upward to grand inquisitor and then downward to victim of the Terror he had instituted, carried Rousseau's words with him everywhere. Little wonder that some who watched turned away in disgust from eighteenth-century thought, holding it responsible for the failure of the Revolution.

Edmund Burke's great indictment of the Revolution stood out above all others. It was eloquently answered by Tom Paine and others; the conservative reaction did not entirely sweep the field. But it tended to dominate. Historians still debate the element of validity in Burke's charges against the Revolution, but it would probably be generally agreed that he was right in holding that *philosophe* thought on politics was both too vague and too doctrinaire, in an area where these qualities are peculiarly dangerous. (See the discussion earlier in this book, on pages 180–182). A recent scholar has observed concerning the thought of Helvétius and Holbach that they "must answer for the fact that they ultimately offered nothing beyond pious wishes" for an enlightened despot, ignoring "institutional structure" altogether.[2] One can readily find fantasies in which it was simply assumed that revolution would somehow install good government and do away with all evils—crime, hatred, deceit, envy, lawsuits, prisons, poverty, etc.—presumably by a sweep of the pen. No more monumentally innocent thought can be imagined. It can still be found in the Revolution of 1848.

The Rights of Man

The famous Declaration of the Rights of Man and of Citizen, manifesto of the Revolution, is a case in point. Attempting to reduce the formula for political justice to a few axioms, it revealed considerable confusion and subsequently was completely ignored. It might mean everything or nothing. "Men are born and remain free and equal in rights." "The purpose of the state is to secure the citizen in enjoyment of his rights." What exactly were these rights, and how could the state maintain them? They were said to include "the unrestrained communication of thought and opinions," as well as "a sacred and inviolable right to property"; but in both cases there might be exceptions, "in cases of evident public necessity." Similarly equivocal were statements that "the law ought to prohibit only actions hurtful to society" and "ought to impose no other penalties but such as are absolutely and evidently necessary." Would anyone disagree about the principle, but could any two people agree on the all-important matter of just what these actions and penalties are?

Critics of the "natural rights of man" school (Hobbes, Bentham) have claimed that such rights are either equivocations or tautologies—meaningless slogans. But clearly they have an emotional value. At this time, their concrete referents were real enough. For example, Robespierre in his younger days attacked the law that "inflicted civil infamy upon the innocent family of a convicted criminal" (John Morley) as well as another that denied civil rights to children born out of wedlock. Such remnants of irrational barbarity fell before this wave of political reform. The reforms of the Revolutionary era were real enough, though stated in

[2] Everett C. Ladd, Jr., "Helvétius and D'Holbach," *Journal of the History of Ideas*, April-June, 1962.

an abstract way. And had they not been so stated, they might never have been secured. In their attempt to bring about the final perfect state of mankind, the Revolutionary ideologists overstated their case and spoiled it, but en route to its ultimate failure as an apocalyptic movement the Revolution achieved all sorts of useful changes in the lot of mankind. The old order of inequality, with its relics of the seigneurial system in the countryside, its unequal taxation and denial of equal economic opportunity, its unjust and arbitrary laws, disappeared forever. This is what the Revolution meant, and why it has always been celebrated joyously in France.

But it meant something else in England—something suggested by that cartoon in which an ugly assassin armed with faggot and dagger is offering to give "liberty" to Brittania. Secure (as most Englishmen thought) in their own liberties, the work of history and experience not slogans and theories, Brittania looked with horror on the bloody and turbulent French scene, and found herself at war with revolutionary imperialism. From this position she produced the leading works of the counterrevolution, most notably that of Burke.

Edmund Burke's renowned book of 1790 is as famous as any tract in the history of politics, and about as controversial as any. *The Reflections on the Revolution in France* has been and probably always will be the subject of violent disagreement. But its distinction is usually admitted even by those whose ideology forces them to be its foe on principle. Burke claimed that the revolution went wrong because its leaders tried to scrap an entire political system and put a new one in its place overnight; he related this mistake to the outlook of the *philosophes,* the political rationalists whose method lacked realism in an era where abstractness is fatal and the nondoctrinaire approach is vitally necessary. On neither of these points has he lacked adversaries, then and later. But he made a strong case on both scores, though it may be hard to see how the mistakes could have been avoided. It is true that the wholesale abolition of an entire order in France in 1789 created immense confusion during the transformation period. "Feudalism" was declared at an end, which meant the dissolution of such institutions as the army, local government, the judicial system, the clergy. As for the *philosophe* political ideology, it did indeed consist in good part of general maxims without careful attention to detail and so was more helpful in tearing down than in building back up.

Whether Burke's analysis of the Revolution was right or wrong, the events in France stimulated him to formulate his political philosophy. A soaring eloquence and dazzling sense of the subtle texture of actual politics lent to Burke's book a memorable quality; as a piece of literature, it is one of the pioneer works of the new school of Romanticism. The leading idea emerging from this eloquence and this subtlety was that

Burke's Attack on the Revolution

society is a vast and complicated historical product which may not be tinkered with at will like a machine; it is a repository of collective human wisdom to be regarded with reverence, and if reformed at all it must be with due respect for the continuity of its traditions. There were other related ideas: that a political community is something made by history, an unanalyzable bond between men which makes free government possible; that the social organism has its "natural aristocracy" which the commoner sort of men must and do, in a healthy society, respect; that general rules and abstract principles are no help in politics.

With a disdain for the "abstract rights" proclaimed by the French, he tried to make clear the real rights of man: Burke certainly believed in rights, but he stressed the degree to which men in entering civil society must give up some of their liberties in order to gain the advantages of government. He distrusted the restless innovators who had no patience to search out the wisdom of their ancestors but must draw amateur blueprints for the total reconstruction of society, as if they were the first to think. The science of government is not for these, whose visionary schemes "in proportion as they are metaphysically true, are morally and politically false." These "smugglers of adulterated metaphysics" knew not man—or God. Burke was pious and felt that political society was sound only on Christian foundations.

There is irony, and perhaps confusion, in the fact that Burke accused the *philosophes* of being "metaphysicians," they whose banner always bore the motto "Down with metaphysics." He turns their own weapon against themselves. It seems that Burke is right, if we think of some of the cruder post-Rousseau political pamphleteers. They were, as indicated, utopian fantasists without the least practical knowledge of politics. But Burke's own empiricism has roots in the better sort of Enlightenment political thought, Hume and Montesquieu especially.

The Irish politician deeply influenced all subsequent conservative political thought. Edition followed edition of the *Reflections,* all over Europe. Louis XVI personally translated it into French. For this popularity, its timeliness, and what seemed an uncanny prophetic quality (Burke announced the failure of the Revolution before it had failed, it seemed) were partly responsible along with the richness and color of the style. Stripped of its rhetoric, Burke's though may not appear extraordinary, but its phrases would echo long afterward.

Perhaps it was not necessarily "conservative" in the most obvious sense of this word. In suggesting an empirical approach to the enormous complexity of human affairs, in place of the vague sloganizing of the *philosophes,* Burke may well be viewed as the founder of a real science of social reform, rather than as a hidebound conservative. He was certainly not opposed to change, if properly carried out, and his own career, that of a person of humble birth, consisted of one passionate crusade after another. His biographer, Philip Magnus, identifies many; the more famous were his crusades on behalf of American independence, Ireland, India (the Warren Hastings affair), and against the French Revolution. "The most urgent need of his nature was always some great cause to serve—some monstrous injustice to repair." This tempestuous Irishman was temperamentally as little a conservative as well can be.

But there was of course the conservative Burke, or, since he almost created the school, the Burke traits that came to be thought of as Conservative. The feeling of piety for the social order, the mistrust of hare-brained reformers with a one-shot plan, the organic conception of social growth, these were the foundations of the conservative faith.

Insofar as he was trying to defend tradition and "prescription" as the "guardians of authority," Burke was swimming against the tide of the times. Despite its excesses and horrors, the French Revolution happened and, as Lord Acton later remarked, "it taught the people to regard their wishes and wants as the supreme criterion of right"; it accustomed men to change and swept away the old order beyond hope of recovery. Even Burke did not imagine, realist that he was, that it would be possible to restore the *status quo ante* in France. Soon the troops of France spread the Revolution all over Europe. The dictatorship of Napoleon (1800–1814) turned most of thinking Europe, even thinking France, against the Revolution, but the Bonapartist victories continued to overturn the old arrangements of Europe.

Against the rule of Napoleon, a good many of France's leading men of letters protested and went into exile, though some (like Bonald) came back now that the anarchy was over and order had been restored by a vigorous ruler. Benjamin Constant, Mme. de Staël, and Chateaubriand headed the brilliant crowd of refugees, to whom Bonapartism was purely and simply tyranny. There were others, like Goethe, who never lost faith in Napoleon, seeing in him the man of destiny whose mission it was to unite Europe under a single progressive law. In France, beginning in the period just before Napoleon (the Directory), the so-called "Ideologues" reacted against political failure and disillusion by becoming severely objective, seeking to study the human mind as strict scientists. (They were perhaps the ancestors of those antiseptic moderns, the "behavioral scientists.") This was the time of Laplace, Lamarck, Cuvier, and other great French scientists, indicating that the more detached subjects could flourish under Bonaparte. Laplace crowned the "classical mechanics," perfecting Newton, and was the author of a famous *Système du monde* which undertook to explain the operations and evolution of the universe without recourse to Newton's *deus ex machina*. ("Sire, I have no need of that hypothesis," he responded when Napoleon asked him about God.) Cuvier and Lamarck began the controversy over evolution. The Italians,

The
Bonapartist
Era

Galvani and Volta, were installing the age of electricity. Napoleon did admire the sciences and thought it important to encourage them in every way possible.

The Mind of
Napoleon

Within France, however, political controversy could hardly exist and freedom of speculation was limited. Not that Bonaparte was, personally, anything other than the most emancipated of thinkers. Enormously cynical, he delighted in shocking people with his atheism in private conversation; but, believing that "only religion gives the state firm and lasting support," he would not tolerate any public irreligion. "You must form believers, not reasoners," he told the teachers of a state school for girls. Since "the stability of marriages serves the interest of social morality," the Code Napóleon was severe on adultery, but privately Napoleon called it "a mere peccadillo, an incident at a masked ball . . . a most common occurrence." Women he regarded as "mere machines to make children," and intellectuals and artists he affected to despise; therefore Mme. de Staël, an intellectual and artistic woman, was his *bête noire*. But many of Napoleon's outrageous opinions were, as they so often are, a kind of defense mechanism of an ego unsure of itself in this domain, and cannot quite be taken seriously. He claimed, for example, to be "insensitive to what is called style," but he obviously was not. An omnivorous reader, he missed little that went on in the world of art, science, and philosophy and often commented on it shrewdly. Nevertheless we feel he was sincere when he wrote that "the statistics of my army are, as far as I am concerned, the most enjoyable literary works in my library and those which I read with the most pleasure in my moments of relaxation!" But one should not be unjust to this remarkable man; in some ways his insatiable curiosity especially about scientific matters was hardly less than epochal. On his expedition to Egypt in 1798 he took along two hundred scholars to investigate that fascinating but still largely unknown land of antiquity. He shared and advanced the historical and orientalist interests of the times. He did not, however, admire the new literary fashion of Romanticism that belonged to his foes, Mme. de Staël and Chateaubriand. Speculative thought and letters did not flourish in France in the years of Napoleon.

Impact of
French
Revolution-
ary Ideas
on Britain

Abroad, the leading theme was a rallying of forces against Bonapartism. The *mystique* of the French Revolution gradually lost what force it had had in England. In 1794, Tom Paine's reply to Burke (the *Reflections* did not lack answers), *The Rights of Man*, sold like hot cakes and the London Correspondence Society caused a fear of the French Revolution happening in Great Britain. William Godwin's *Enquiry concerning Social Justice* was very much in the French spirit, a rationalist utopia based on the ideal perfection of individuals. Though repeating Rousseau's indictment of existing property relations as theft, Godwin's utopia differed significantly from most of the French in being antistatist. In Britain, the idea of a natural order of society took the laissez-faire form: society will run itself if left free from interference. The Physiocrats also believed this, but the idea took deeper root in the Whiggish environment of England. Tom Paine claimed that "the common consent of society, without government" can perform all the necessary functions heretofore discharged by government. The rest ought to be dispensed with, and would be as men approached perfection: "government, like dress, is a badge of lost innocence." Laws regulating property and morality are, as Godwin observed, useless if men are not virtuous, and unnecessary if they are.

The combination of Smith, Rousseau, and the spacious fields of America with her sturdy, self-reliant citizens brewed this heady dogma in the mind of Paine. That it was not exclusively American was indicated by Godwin, father-in-law of the poet Shelley and husband of the women's rights author, Mary Wollstonecraft—a group around which much of the political Left in Great Britain revolved. Godwin was so suspicious of the state and indeed of all forms of institutional organization that he attacked public education, among other things. "Did we leave individuals to the progress of their own minds," Godwin believed, "without endeavoring to regulate them by any species of public foundation, mankind would in no very long period convert to the obedience of truth." This was the ultimate laissez-faire. Godwin believed, as H. N. Brailsford once remarked, that all men are as rational and virtuous as Swift's Houyhnhnms.

William Godwin

England was to be the land of liberalism, and Godwin no doubt is significant for the British bent of mind. But after some initial popularity he was regarded as a crank, and was the only man ever known to have caused Coleridge to lose his temper. British opinion turned fully away from the French Revolution and all radical thoughts during the long wars with France. Coleridge was among those who, earlier enthusiastic for the Revolution, "threw away his squeaking baby-trumpet of sedition" and combatted the revolutionary heresy with all his strength. Coleridge ranks with Burke, to whom he owed much, as a founding father of English conservatism. But the sometime radical journalist, William Cobbett, joined the anti-Jacobin cause too, indicating that this mood was well-nigh universal in Britain. The Evangelical movement within the Church of England, led by William Wilberforce, was a reaction against the deistic laxities of the eighteenth-century church, thus a reproach to the infidel French.

Germany gave birth to nationalism, in reaction against humiliation by the French. Herder and Fichte, giants of German thought, preached it along with humbler writers and organizers of youth (Arndt, Jahn, Kleist). The Enlightenment had been cosmopolitan. Fichte became convinced that this was another one of the errors made by that now politically dis-

Germany and Nationalism

credited era. If France gave the world the Enlightenment and the Revolution, did not Germany have something to give? Every nation has its day, and the German day might be the greater for being so long postponed. Defeated in war by Napoleon, the Germans were assuming the cultural and intellectual leadership of the world in this time of Goethe, Schiller, Kant, Beethoven. A cultural people should have a great state. Germany must wake up politically as she had done artistically and culturally. (*Addresses to the German Nation*, 1807.)

Herder
    J. G. Herder's contribution to nationalism stands out in the intellectual career of a many-sided genius. Romanticism blended with nationalism in his thought. It was a humane and liberal nationalism, by comparison with some manifestations of that spirit; it meant, to Herder, the self-fulfillment of peoples who thereby make their contribution to the brotherhood of man. He glorified the people, the *Volk*, exaggerating a strain already met with in Burke (there is wisdom in the collective consciousness of the people, that is, in traditions). Herder went seeking the songs of the people "on the streets, in alleys and fish markets, in the simple roundelay of the peasant folk." He has been compared to the American poet Walt Whitman in this respect, and indeed he deeply influenced Whitman. Mystical adulation of the national genius could lead in dangerous directions, perhaps, but at least Herder did not suggest them. He simply believed that nations exist, that peoples have their national cultures, and that these should be developed as the source of a valuable literature and art. The democratic element in this romantic nationalism is apparent.

    Napoleon I met his downfall in 1814–1815, and conservative Europe gathered at Vienna to try as far as possible to restore order based on principles of tradition, prescription, monarchy. But forces had been set in motion which could not be halted though they might be slowed or deflected. Between 1815 and 1830, Restoration France and conservative Europe produced some notable attempts to develop the conservative ideology, but it also saw the elaboration of the liberal, democratic, and socialist political philosophies. These political "isms" will be dealt with in the next chapter. Meanwhile we may note that of all these, the most potent "ism" in the nineteenth century was to be nationalism, affecting even the smaller and lesser peoples of Europe. The English and the French had long suspected they were nations, the Germans were finding it out, the Italian soon would discover it; but also we catch a glimpse of the Danes, who previously had had no inkling of their separate nationhood, seeking to restore the ancient Danish tongue and old Danish customs, while Gothicism in Sweden represents a similar impulse. The Belgians will find that they cannot live under a Dutch king, no matter how beneficent his rule and how logical and beneficial the larger political unit is, for they are different. Nietzsche, in a characteristically impatient moment, burst out that Napoleon had tried to unite Europe but reactionary nationalism had interfered to botch his plans. For better or worse, Europe was to divide into numerous national cultures in the nineteenth century—a process accompanied by disruptions and upheavals. This vast and epochal process was in part a movement of the mind. More will be said about it later. Certainly that other of our three revolutions, the Romantic, had much to do with it.

IMMANUEL KANT AND THE REVOLUTION IN PHILOSOPHY

Born in 1724, the man who became the greatest of modern philosophers did his most creative work in the 1780s, against the background of the crisis in Enlightenment thought. Rousseau made a deep impression on Immanuel Kant, as he did on so many of this generation. Indeed little that was discussed during the Enlightenment escaped the attention of the omniscient little professor of Königsberg. The young Kant, brought up in the reigning German philosophical school of Leibniz as systematized by Christian Wolff, showed strong scientific interests and entered into some of the typical *philosophe* controversies: thus, we find him contributing his bit to the Lisbon Earthquake argument. But it was particularly the work done by Berkeley and Hume to undermine the confident certainties of rationalism that engaged his attention. It was only in his middle age that Hume awakened him from his "dogmatical slumber." He found Hume's scepticism most unsatisfactory and, like the Scottish "common sense" philosophers (but more effectively than those simpler souls, whom he ridiculed), determined to rescue men from it, restoring their confidence and vitality. Kant was an *Aufklärer*, a spokesman of the Enlightenment. But his powerful mind in attempting to refute Hume penetrated into ground beyond the frontiers of that movement. He made what he called a "copernican revolution" in philosophy and was, in later years, compared to the French Revolution in his impact on thought: "With this book (*The Critique of Pure Reason*) an intellectual revolution began in Germany which offers the strangest analogies with the material revolution in France, and, to a more reflective mind, appears to be of equal importance. . . . On both banks of the Rhine we see the same break with the past, all respect for tradition is revoked" (Heinrich Heine).

One of Kant's major objectives, then, was to rescue science from Humean scepticism. Hume, it will be recalled, took his departure from Locke's empiricism, which held that the only real knowledge comes from sense experience, and there is nothing in the mind except what comes to it from the senses. He demonstrated—and Kant accepted his demonstration as "irrefutable"—that through the senses alone the human mind cannot encounter reality at all, nor can it have a science founded on anything

Kant's
Answer
to Hume

but "opinion." We have only an unrelated sequence of sense impressions. The principle of cause-and-effect cannot be derived from experience; we simply assume it arbitrarily; it may only be an accident of our mental processes.

Kant's reply was roughly as follows: the mind or intellect, so far from being passive or negative, contains the organizing principles which *impose order on experience.* The mind contains forms and categories, which are the basic concepts that give meaning to experience. These "fundamental conditions of thought itself" are a priori, that is, not derived from experience. Kant, in what he describes as the hardest metaphysical work ever done, specified these forms and categories: two forms of perception (space and time), twelve categories of the understanding (for example, cause and effect).[3] (These correspond to the types of judgment of Aristotelian logic, that is, the types of quantity, quality, relation, modality.) All minds contain these categories, thus mind is a fundamental unity.

Thus our minds condition and indeed determine knowledge by being as they are. Agreeing with Leibniz, Kant denied that there is nothing in the mind except what the senses bring in: there is the mind itself, which sorts out, classifies, relates this raw material, making it intelligible. We will not here, of course, follow Kant in all his arguments and terminology. From his powerful analysis, it is enough to say, emerged a picture of mind as creative, not passive, and of reason as something a priori, thus rescued from the scepticism of an empiricist approach. Goethe interpreted Kant to mean that "had I not borne the world in myself by anticipation, I would have remained blind even with eyes that see." It is not our senses that enable us to experience reality, but a preformed structure within the mind that prepares us to receive and understand sensory impressions. It is not the "solid" data of sense which provide the basic cement of science, it is something given within the mind, something like those "innate ideas" Locke had sought to banish as too mysterious or occult.

Because of a debate that arose, it must be added that Kant was evidently not an "Idealist" in the sense that some of his followers were. He does not say that reality is a creation of the mind. Things are out there, and in striking our senses they provide the indispensable, primary data of knowledge. The point is that we could not "understand" them if we did not have minds equipped with a rational structure. Kant is pointing out that the world outside must appear to us in a certain way because of the kind of mind, as well as the kind of senses, that we have. If we put on

---

[3] Kant's categories are: quantity: unity, plurality, totality; quality: reality, negation, limitation; relation: substance and accident, cause and effect, community; modality: possibility, existence, necessity. It is usually held today that Kant's categories, too dependent on the logic of his day, do not hold up; but this is not to say that basic categories of the understanding do not exist.

red-tinted glasses, things look red, though they really are not all red; and we have also our built-in sensory apparatus, so that colors, odors, etc., appear to us as they do because of the way that apparatus works. Kant adds the important point that things appear rational—classifiable and subject to order, such as cause and effect, identity, comparison—not because of the way *they* are but because of the way our minds are. The mind makes sense out of experience; it would be senseless without mind. But the external world exists; Kant is not denying that, nor that we must have its stimuli for the mind to work on in the knowing process.

This was only part of Kant's examination of the knowing process, and it must be added immediately that the sort of knowledge we have been talking about—scientific knowledge, taken from experience as worked on by the categorizing intellect—was not, to him, knowledge of ultimate reality. This domain of science is perfectly valid; Kant's goal was to rescue science from scepticism, and to represent him as a foe of science (the view is not uncommon) is a gross error. He himself made some contributions to the sciences, in which he was always interested. But it is a particular sort of knowledge, appropriate to the practical or useful realm only; it is knowledge of appearances, not of substance. In the famous Kantian language, it is the *phenomenal,* as opposed to the *noumenal,* world. It relates to the properties of things, not the "thing-in-itself." Kant's other great objective, the inspiration for which he perhaps derived from Rousseau, was to rescue the realm of *value* from the scientists. Thus he sets up two sharply different categories. The realm of science, which is useful knowledge, deals with the phenomenal world, the world of appearances. The realm of value, of moral and esthetic experience, is intuitive and deals with the noumenal world, the world of substantive reality. Kant thinks that the two realms must not be confused. One of his achievements was to riddle the proofs of God's existence derived from the facts of physical nature—arguments extremely popular during the eighteenth century, especially the "argument from design." From ontological argument to argument from design, Kant devastated all these venerable "proofs" with such effectiveness that few have dared revive them since. The proofs appropriate to science have nothing to do with God, Kant believed. For they can never give us values.

There is nevertheless the noumenal realm. It is a valid realm, but Kant was not quite sure whether we can know it at all. He seemed to think that in moments of moral or esthetic experience we can glimpse it fleetingly, and these hints were to be built upon by the Romantics who followed him. The human soul, a thing-in-itself, by quite other roads than the analytical reason may make contact with other things-in-themselves. Kant seems ambiguously poised between the Enlightenment and Romanticism here. On the one hand he said that he "had to deny knowledge to make room for faith," which he clearly much wanted to do. His

The Kantian Dualism

most widely quoted sentence is that in which he proclaims the equal wonders of the two realms, the starry heavens and the moral law. On the other hand Kant seldom departed from his Enlightenment hard-headedness, was certainly no mystic by temperament, and was not at all sure about our being able to make contact with the noumena at all. Perhaps we are condemned to live in the phenomenal world as far as intellectual activity is concerned, while being aware that there is another world, the real world, which we can never know at least in this life. Each of Kant's realms is flawed for man. From the scientific, phenomenal one we can get clear and useful knowledge, but it is knowledge of appearances only. From the spiritual, noumenal realm we could get ultimate truth if we could reach it, but ordinarily we cannot do so.

Kant nevertheless at times put great stress on his rescuing of religion from the clammy grip of science so as to restore faith to its true estate. The existence of God, freedom of the will, the soul, these things cannot be proved by scientific argument. But when we move from "pure reason" to the "practical" or moral reason we are in a realm which is in its own ways quite valid though different. Pascal's "the heart has its reasons" was close to Kant's meaning. Man's moral consciousness exists and is entitled to great respect though its knowledge is not the kind appropriate to science.

It is interesting to compare the dualism of Kant with the other great dualisms of Western thought—Plato's, Ockham's, Descartes'. To Plato, the realm of essences or ideas alone is real and knowable; to Kant, it is alone real, even more so, but it is scarcely knowable, certainly not knowable by the reasoning intellect as Plato thought. To Descartes, there are two realms, the physical and mental, one the domain of necessity and the other of freedom; there is something of this in Kant but, again, Descartes felt the physical world to be perfectly knowable in a way that Kant could not. Kant is closer to William of Ockham, and to Pascal. Science is one thing, religion another; two wholly different kinds of cognition are appropriate to them; we cannot pass from one to the other.

Kant's successors tended to quarrel about what he meant, and it is **Post-Kantian** plain that with but a slight twist his "critical philosophy" might be made **Developments** the foundation of several different systems. Some Kantians forgot about the thing-in-itself and became either Idealists, arguing that the world is completely a mental construct, or Positivists (phenomenalists), urging that we do not and cannot know what ultimate reality is and had better remain content with the orderly arrangement of our observations. Others developed Kantian noumenalism in a Romantic or mystical direction, stressing the role of the poetic or religious intuition in touching the deepest reality by nonscientific methods. Kant himself, as we have said, was hardly a Romantic by temperament; but the Romantic era was beginning as he wrote and his immediate followers in Germany tended to be either

Idealists or Romantics, sometimes blending the two. There is no doubt a sense in which Kant is the uncle if not the father of Romanticism. But we ought not to forget that the bulk of his work was directed towards clarifying scientific philosophy and that his contribution here was enormous. It is part of the wonder of the Königsberg philosopher that he greatly advanced both of those different domains of the mind which he so sharply separated, the scientific and the esthetic-religious.

Kant's dualism nevertheless was unsatisfactory for many who had been accustomed by the Enlightenment to clear and final conclusions. Phenomena and noumena, pure reason and practical reason, seemed completely divorced, a situation not felt to be satisfactory. Fichte and Schelling, his immediate successors in German philosophy, sought for a unifying principle that would weld the divided self and divided world of thought together. Impressed by Kant's "transcendent" structure of reason, they wished to broaden it so as to bring pure and practical reason together under one roof. Kant stimulated future philosophy by the problems he left, as every great philosopher does.

But in both of Kant's two realms, the "copernican revolution" is evident: the human mind is creative, not passive, whether it is working as scientist or as seer. It is an active agent, far from the wax of Condillac; it imposes order on nature, even in the scientific process. Kant reminded scientists that Galileo had understood the necessity of hypothesis, asking questions of nature; pure empiricism is poor scientific method. The creative mind is as much a necessity in science as in poetry. This is well understood today; Kant probably more than any other modern thinker established it firmly. *The "Copernican Revolution"*

Kant made significant contributions to political and ethical thought, too. For our purposes it will be sufficient to note the *liberal* implications of these. The Kantian ethical rule or "categorical imperative" (an objective, necessary command) included the principle that persons must be treated "as an end, and never as a means." In making *duty* a linchpin of his system, Kant may have betrayed his Prussianism; but his political thought was generally liberal. It stressed individual freedom, the moral autonomy of the person, human beings as ends. There were even a few Kantian socialists in the nineteenth century, who pointed out that the rule of treating people as ends and not as means, as persons not as things, invalidates the labor system of capitalism, which makes the workingman a commodity. *Kant's Political Ideas*

These liberal features, along with the attack on rational proofs of God's existence, caused Kant's writings to be banned for a time in his native country. But his political thought also stressed the reign of law, obedience to duly constituted authority; it sought to resolve the dilemma of liberty and authority (a dilemma of which Kant was very conscious) through just and general laws. History is the story of the education of mankind toward freedom under law. Thought should be free. Kant was one of those who "wished to be warmed by the fire of the French Revolution but not burnt up by it," he was a moderate liberal with a horror of violent revolution. But he believed a republic to be the best form of government and his thought worked in a liberal-democratic direction. It has been argued otherwise; but if Kant stresses authority, he also believes in liberty. His political thought is perhaps a little trite; his well-known essay on universal peace does not take us much farther than the usual utopian exhortations. But Kant's deep respect for the individual was rooted in his great Critical Philosophy: one can readily see that he made the human mind and the inner self more important and sacred than did the Lockeans. They would have it determined, passive, dictated to by external conditions; to Kant it is hub and focus of all, it is self-determining and free insofar as noumenal, and even in its phenomenal aspects it dictates to nature rather than being dictated to. The final purpose of all creation, Kant suggests, is the full realization of man as a moral being.

Kant came soon to be regarded as the greatest of modern philosophers (Hegel disputed the title with him in the nineteenth century, but clearly Kant made Hegel possible) as well as a notable contributor to moral and political ideas. It seemed that he brought an end to the typical Enlightenment philosophy by rejecting both its empiricism and confused scepticism in favor of a new form of rationalism. The peculiar Enlightenment formula of common-sense empiricism was not tenable after his criticisms and reconstructions. He also gave hints to both the Romanticists and the Liberals, to whose influence the next generations largely belonged. The intellectual revolution of this era was bigger than Kant, but he was somehow an integral part of it.

Fichte   The grand lineage of German philosophy in its golden age began with Kant and ended with Hegel, a half century later. In between lay several others, most significantly Johann Gottlieb Fichte and Friedrich Wilhelm Joseph von Schelling. Here a very brief summary will suffice. Fichte, brought up on the writings of the French *philosophes,* praised the French Revolution and subsequently wrote much of significance on political, social, and economic subjects—especially his famous *Addresses to the German Nation* (1807), inspired by the Prussian defeat at the hands of Napoleon, which we have mentioned. He also had a good deal to say about religion, and was in fact dismissed from the University of Jena in 1799 largely because of his excursions into this arena, bringing on him the charge of atheism. (A sort of pantheism would, of course, be closer.) He was not very romantic in temperament; philosophy, he thought, should be a science. But he adopted and preached a philosophy of Idealism, believing that anything else leads to determinism and materialism, which destroy human dignity. According to the vision of reality that Fichte developed, the universe consists of an absolute Ego which is like our own consciousness, a unique, free activity which strives to realize itself in perfect self-awareness and is the foundation of all nature. Leaving aside the technical jargon, which probably mystified all but a few, this vision of reality dramatized the human will or consciousness as hub and center of the universe because an expression of the absolute spirit of which the universe consists. Spirit or idea makes up reality, and our spirits, represented by our basic consciousness, an indescribable but intuitively certain thing,[4] are the concrete manifestations of this world spirit. One might say without too much distortion that according to Fichte each of us is God, or a part of God—if we equate the "absolute" or "world spirit" with God. So, if Fichte was technically not a "Romantic," he introduced an intoxicating idea which in the broader sense was very romantic: that the world is spiritual, that we are a part of that spiritual world, and that in moral experience especially we can touch the uttermost sublimities of the universe.

Schelling, a disciple of Fichte and friend and collaborator of Hegel, **Schelling** whom he influenced, produced a stream of writings, especially between 1797 and 1802, which developed the Idealist outlook into what he called Transcendental Idealism. He put greater stress than Fichte on physical nature as the objective form of the Absolute and pointed out the road Hegel was to follow in many respects. Perhaps the most striking feature of his thought was its representation of the artistic creation, the act of esthetic intuition, as the supreme achievement. In it the unconscious and the conscious forces, representing the two forms of the Absolute, are fused in synthesis; it is in art that the infinite manifests itself in finite form.[5] Coleridge and all the Romantic poets absorbed Schelling eagerly, for understandable reasons; he provided a metaphysical basis for the artist such as had never before been known. Romanticism's glorification of the poet as seer, as "unacknowledged legislator of the human race," as discoverer and purveyor of loftier truths than the merely logical, relates closely to Schelling's thought. Much later in his career, Schelling opposed Hegel's excessively abstract rationalism by offering a kind of foreshadowing of Existentialism; he influenced Kierkegaard, who listened to his

---

[4] Consciousness is the foundation of all thought and experience, yet we cannot find it in thought or experience because it cannot be objectified, cannot be made an object of thought or experience, Fichte pointed out. This seems to be true and resembles the point made in recent times by Sartre and the Existentialists.

[5] To further explain, the unconscious is the real, or objective, physical world, the conscious the realm of the ideal and subjective. Both are parts of the Absolute. Their destiny is to be merged in one, the objective becoming merged in the subjective and vice versa. This happens when the artist shapes nature, or cooperates with it, as Michelangelo carving a statue.

lectures at Berlin in the 1840s. He came to reject all abstract, conceptual thinking as "negative philosophy," inferior to concrete, existent realities. He showed a keen interest in the history of religious mythologies, like Jung in our time. In this his earlier preference for art may perhaps be seen continuing.

Fichte and Schelling may seem to have travelled a long way from Kant, who so far as he lived to meet their ideas evidently repudiated them. But Kant had started them off. This extraordinary spate of German philosophizing concluded with the titanic figure of Hegel, consideration of whom we shall postpone for a moment. The whole of it cut a wide swath in intellectual Europe in the first half of the nineteenth century. It combined keen and searching thought with daring speculation and a good deal of moral sublimity. Later, especially in the non-German world, it seemed excessively "metaphysical" and might be dismissed as empty bombast. From another point of view, it revealed about as radical a perspective as Europe had seen. For it may be noted that Fichte, Schelling, and subsequently Hegel offered a philosophical alternative to religion, substituting their "Absolute" for the Christian conception of God. A prominent feature of this metaphysical faith was man's place in it as almost the equivalent of God. The Absolute was not quite just the individual human Ego writ large, but it came close to being that, at least in the popular interpretation of these philosophies. The human consciousness reflects and participates in the divine. Man's art and moral experience are in effect cosmic forces working in and through him. German Idealism united with Romanticism to deify the mysterious forces working in the human soul and so to introduce that theme of "titanism" so marked in the nineteenth century, and according to some so dangerous. "Glory to Man in the highest," as the poet Swinburne sang.

At any rate the lofty and searching inquiries of the great German philosophers of the Kantian age captured mankind's imagination. Near the end of the century the South African, General Jan Smuts, having made his fortune and reputation by the age of thirty, decided to retire. "I prefer to sit still, to water my orange trees, and to study Kant's 'Critical Philosophy,'" he said. It could have been any thinking man's dream. Kant —together with his children—came close to meaning *philosophy* for the nineteenth century.

The Germans soon found their way to England, chiefly by way of Coleridge. They were less well known in France until around 1850; the Enlightenment carried on more strongly there, represented by Condillac's empirical psychology. But eventually the impact on French thought, and on Italian, was to be strong. Meanwhile another German export, closely related to the German philosophy, was Romanticism, which swept over all Europe in the first years of the century.

ROMANTICISM

Romanticism is often said to have begun with Rousseau, and particu- larly with that amazingly successful novel *La Nouvelle Héloise,* which had all Europe weeping in 1762. Certain Romantic affinities can be found in other eighteenth-century writers, notably the English poet James Thomson (d. 1748), while the poets Gray and Cowper are often classi- fied as "pre-Romantics" bridging the gap between Dryden and Pope on the one end and Wordsworth and Coleridge on the other.[6] (And, indeed, it is possible for Geoffrey Clive to separate out a whole "Romantic En- lightenment.") Rousseau strongly influenced practically all the Romantics of the next generation or two; it is hardly too much to say that in France the figure of Jean-Jacques, shrouded in mists of legend, became deified. Before long the German writers Goethe and Schiller took up the Romantic manner, the former's *Sorrows of Werther* rivalling *La Nouvelle Héloise* in its ability to reduce all manner of people to tears, while the *Sturm und Drang* (storm and stress) plays of the early Schiller were to be show pieces of Romanticism for many years. (*The Robbers* was written in 1781.) The chief disciples of Rousseau at first seem to have been the Germans; in France the influence of the rationalist Enlightenment con- tinued, with Voltaire getting his tremendous triumph in Paris near the end of his life in 1778. But the restless decade of the 1780s, with its Saint-Martin mood, has been mentioned.

Then came the Revolution, which tended to halt literary and intel- lectual life, diverting all attention to the political melodrama being en- acted at Paris. Some Frenchmen for a time suspected Romanticism as too German to be patriotic. But in 1801 to 1805 French Romanticism asserted itself with the powerful figure of Chateaubriand, the leading literary personality of his day. With *Atala* and *René* a new mode of literature had arrived, it was widely recognized. Chateaubriand was the father, as Rousseau was the grandfather, of all subsequent French romantic litera- ture.

Meanwhile in England the young poets Coleridge and Wordsworth were experimenting with a new poetry they rightly felt to be nothing less than revolutionary. They along with the poet-seer William Blake began English Romanticism in the years just before the turn of the century, but it remained obscure for some time. Blake printed his own books *Songs of Innocence* (1789) and *Songs of Experience* (1794), but they were neither noticed nor understood for a number of years. He was known slightly as designer and engraver, but evidently not at all as poet, until well into the nineteenth century.

Origins of Romanticism

---

[6] It may be questioned, though, whether "pre-Romanticism" is a very useful concept. The criterion is passion or emotion, but this is not really the right one, as will be seen.

The Revolutionary and Napoleonic wars were going on; Chateaubriand became an exile from Bonaparte's dictatorship and even Coleridge and Wordsworth took up political pamphleteering. In Germany, Romanticism continued to flourish uniquely: a group that included Frederick Schlegel and his brother August in Berlin, Novalis and Schelling at Dresden and Jena, called themselves Romantic and threw out ideas important to the philosophy of the movement, to which it is necessary to add the theology of Schleiermacher (1799) and the music of Beethoven (1800). All this was in the years 1798–1801—Romanticism's moment of creative fruition. But its popular triumphs lay ahead.

Period of Romantic Zenith

Picking up momentum, Romanticism reached its maximum of influence in the years 1810-1830. Wordsworth and Coleridge began to achieve fame and were joined by Shelley, Byron, and Keats to make up the most renowned group of poets in England's history, all of whom, with the possible exception of Byron, are customarily labelled "Romantic." In 1813 the Swiss-born Mme. de Staël, a glamorous figure who wrote, made love, and fought Napoleon with equal verve, popularized the Germans in France with her celebrated work *D'Allemagne*. France succumbed to Romanticism between 1820, when Schiller's *Maria Stuart* (composed in 1801) took Paris by storm, and 1830, when Victor Hugo's *Hernani* caused the wildest tumult in the history of the French theatre but emerged triumphant. Hugo and Lamartine, along with the novelist Alexander Dumas, the avowed leaders of the Romantic movement, were the most popular and distinguished writers of their age. At the same time the painter Eugene Delacroix headed a school which called itself Romantic.

Opposition to Romanticism

In the 1830s a "Romantic" influence may be seen in many directions, and indeed for the rest of the century that influence never ceased to exist, being so absorbed into the texture of thought and expression that "nothing after it could be the same." But it became diffused. A partial reaction against it set in. We must not think of Romanticism as ever quite sweeping away all opposition. In France, where a strong Classical tradition existed, Hugo was denied admission to the Academy five times, the last time in 1836, and warfare between Romantic and Classic never ceased to enliven the theatrical season, at least. (In 1829 the Academy denounced Romanticism as that which "puts in disorder all our rules, insults our masterpieces, and perverts mass opinion.")[7] In England, embittered literary reactionaries helped bring on Keats' early death, his friends believed. The greatest German literary figure in history, Goethe, who contributed to Romanticism early in his career, eventually declared that Classicism is healthy and Romanticism diseased. Unconverted "classicists" always existed and indeed there was something of a classical

[7] S. O. Simches, *Le Romantisme et le goût esthétique du XVIIIᵉ siècle*, 1964, documents the extensive survival of eighteenth-century taste, classical, rococo, at the high tide of the Romantic.

rerevival contemporary with Romanticism. If we grant that the Romantics had carried away most of the prizes by 1830, they were under attack from the younger generation of the forties and fifties as too pompous and theatrical. Broadly speaking this next generation preferred to absorb its Romanticism, if at all, in carefully filtered form (see pages 355 ff.).

Yet between 1760 and 1840—to take the widest time span (the crea- **Definitions**
tive zenith coming then in the middle of it)—Europe had been hit by **of Romanticism**
something new, exciting, and controversial. We have yet to define what this was, having only named its landmarks. What was Romanticism? The question has puzzled the more literal-minded for a century. A definition is elusive. It is possible to declare that this inability to define Romanticism is the scandal of the century. The word took on many meanings. The Romanticism of Chateaubriand was Catholic, reacted against the Revolution, became Royalist; but the Romanticism of Victor Hugo was (eventually—Hugo began as a conservative) republican, liberal, even revolutionary. It was romantic to suffer, to pray, to fight (as Byron did for Greece), to venture on far voyages, to commune with nature, to have a sense of history. It was romantic to love passionately and transcend the conventional moral boundaries, but the eighteenth century, now old hat, had done this too, like all other centuries. It was romantic to read about the Middle Ages, and to admire that pseudoprimitive bard Ossian,[8] but also to adore the days of classical antiquity—"fair Greece, sad relic." Fate was romantic; so was soul-baring. What was not, if done with the proper spirit? Romanticism was a mood and a style much more than a doctrine; moods and styles are hard to define.

Romanticism "has become a label for half a dozen different things that have only an accidental connection" (Christopher Dawson). He instanced the following: expressing one's emotions, love of nature, intuition as a source of truth, the quest for new experience, the view of society as organism rather than machine. This is not an exhaustive list. In drama it meant departing from the classical "rules," to the great indignation of the traditionalists; in poetry it meant, to Wordsworth at least, using simple rather than "literary" language and writing about plain people rather than fancy ones.[9] In a clever essay Arthur O. Lovejoy once showed that

---

[8] Between 1760 and 1763 the Scotsman James MacPherson published three volumes purporting to be literal translations from the legendary ancient Gallic poet Ossian, a sort of Celtic Homer of the third century A.D. Suspected by a few at the time and confirmed by later scholarship was the fact that little if any of this material really came from such a source, most of it being made up by MacPherson himself. But this "romantic" verse enjoyed wide popularity throughout Europe, much though Johnson inveighed against it ("Sir, a man might write such stuff for ever, if he would abandon his mind to it").

[9] The word *Romantic* derives from the medieval "romances" so named because written in the vernacular (French) rather than in classical Latin. Thus in returning to popular speech, and trying to find folk themes, Romantics were loyal to the basic meaning of their movement.

these various meanings can be made to seem flatly contradictory, and suggested that we must speak of romanticism*s*—not one thing, but a number, that happened to coincide in roughly a single period and have sometimes gotten badly confused. Romanticism, Lovejoy pointed out, has meant a belief in progress and a spirit of reaction; a return to Christianity and a naturalistic humanism; also various other philosophies arrantly at odds with each other. In concluding that "the word 'romantic' has come to mean so many things that, by itself, it means nothing," Lovejoy came near the truth; and yet of course we must not conclude that therefore it did not exist at all. The mood of an age may be nonetheless real for being illogical. Future historians will find it as difficult to say exactly what Existentialism was as present ones do to define Renaissance, Enlightenment, or Romanticism. Historical phenomena take on many accretions as they pass through society; they become involved with other phenomena and eventually lose themselves in the common stream. Any major movement of the mind inevitably accumulates a crowd of different associations and meanings as it spreads. It becomes rather like our political parties: too big to stand for any one creed on which all its followers might agree, except the vaguest sort of generalities. But we do not for this reason infer the nonexistence or meaninglessness of Democrats and Republicans. It is, in fact, possible to argue the reverse: that whenever we find a doctrine that everyone knows about but no one can quite define we are in the presence of a major intellectual revolution.

Without question Romanticism was such a revolution. We are in danger of losing this truth if we seek too narrow or precise a definition. Behind the *forms* of Romanticism, which were various, lay a deep spiritual change, often vague but nonetheless mighty. Critics of Romanticism, then and later, charged that it was a fever which rejected all discipline and, by being out of proportion with nature, refusing to accept boundaries, became a dangerous malady. To them it was nothing less than the destruction of the sense of balance on which European civilization had rested ever since the Greeks invented Classicism with its message of nothing in excess, everything in proper proportion, each element in its due place. On the other side, friends of the new spirit believed that it had for the first time emancipated Europe from a timid orthodoxy and opened minds and hearts to poetry, to real religion, to true philosophy, to sincerity rather than artificiality. It was, said Sismondi, a "Protestantism in letters and the arts," a demand for liberty against authority in style; some have added that it was nothing less than an ultimate Protestantism (without dogma) in all ranges of life—a defiant, Promethean rejection of all constraints on the free spirit of the individual man.

Leaving such sweeping claims aside for the moment, we may try more precisely to state the range of Romantic attitudes. First, Romanticism began in *reaction against* the eighteenth century, that is, against rationalism, mechanistic materialism, Classicism, all the dominant ingredients of the Enlightenment. There comes a time when youth tires of the orthodoxy of its elders which, once itself revolutionary and exciting, has come to seem pallid and dull. Youth looked for new ideas and found them in Rousseau, subsequently in Kant, Fichte, Burke. A chief weakness in the Enlightenment was its neglect of the imagination, its externalism and absence of anything inward or deeply esthetic. It denied religious emotion; it ignored the mystery and terror of existence in its effort to make all things clear. All common sense and broad daylight, it became uninspiring and unthrilling. It lacked what the French call *frissons* or thrills, and its literary style was, or came to seem, flat, conventional, unenterprising. Likewise its ethic of selfish hedonism, along with its mechanical and materialistic view of the universe, could appear as ignoble or dull.

Consequently the Romantic era is filled with cries of rejection. "I, for my share, declare the world to be no machine!" exclaimed Thomas Carlyle, repeating the German Idealists. The eighteenth century had said that it was. Burke speaks of reason being "but a part, and by no means the greatest part," of human nature, while Coleridge says that the "calculating faculty" is inferior to the "creative faculty." This rejection of the analytical reason in favor of an intuitive "eliciting of truth at a flash" was very close to the heart of Romanticism and represented, in good part, another reaction against the Enlightenment. In literary form, Romanticism rebelled against the "rules" imposed on drama or poetry by the classical formula, and against Classicism's preference for the general rather than the concrete. "We are not to number the streaks of the tulip," Classicism had pronounced. Romantics wanted to do just that. Romantics sought religion —a source of *frissons,* if nothing more—because rationalists scorned it. Chateaubriand declared that nothing is pleasing except the mysterious; the mysterious had been the great common enemy of all the *philosophes.* So, too, with "enthusiasm."

That which had been sensible moderation now seemed like torpor, or worse. The eighteenth century, "soul extinct but stomach well alive" in Carlyle's phrase, became a byword for crass materialism; Thackeray called it an age of gluttony. "The man of Locke" was to be scorned. "I mistrust Locke," Schelling announced; virtually all the Romantics shared this contempt for that earthbound philosophy.[10] "Unable to believe but terrified of scepticism," the peculiar "heavenly city" of the eighteenth-century philosophers with its "faith of reason" was now seen to be uninhabitable. Carlyle spoke for the Romantic generations in repudiating its hedonistic

---

[10] Some Romantics made use of Locke (compare the young Hugo), but if so they read him as meaning that the senses, that is, the feelings, and immediate experience, are to be trusted above the abstract reason. Ernest Tuveson, in *The Imagination as a Means of Grace: Locke and the Aesthetics of Romanticism,* 1960, has explored this line of Lockean development in the eighteenth century.

ethic or pleasure-seeking spirit as unworthy of man: "the pig philosophy" he called it. (It was still vigorously alive in Carlyle's Britain in the guise of Jeremy Bentham's Utilitarianism; the two schools could not abide each other.) This reaction against "the pursuit of happiness" as swinish sensualism pushed the Romantics into some very lofty poses: man was once again to be Promethean hero, world-conquering adventurer, sublime sage or saint—anything except that simpering courtier of the eighteenth century whose only goal in life was to satisfy his creature comforts. Keats, who certainly celebrated the sensual pleasures, regarded them as the doorway to transcendental realms of knowledge, not as ends in themselves.

The Poetic Imagination

The Age of Reason had been an Age of Prose; and so Romanticism meant poetry, or a new kind of poetic prose such as Chateaubriand wrote. Romanticism was after all primarily a literary movement, though it spilled over into all branches of life. Eighteenth-century poetry had become on the whole unsatisfactory. "Crushed by rules, and weakened as refined," this polite literature usually failed to communicate sincere feeling, was overly formalized and abstract; it was Dr. Samuel Johnson, no Romantic,[11] who noticed this much:

> From bard to bard the frigid caution crept
> While declamation roar'd and passion slept.

In revenge, the Romantic poets gave full vent to what Locke had disparaged as "the conceits of a warmed or overweening brain." For a later taste as well as an earlier, they sought too many "grand effects," they bared their souls overly and gushed too much. Still, few would deny the mighty debt to literature owed to the poets of the Romantic generation. They revitalized language, and, among other things, brought poetry to the people. Too vast to be estimated is the force exerted on millions of people, heretofore hardly reached by the printed word, by Romantic literature: think of Musset and Hugo in France, Shelley and Wordsworth in England, Goethe and Kleist in Germany, Emerson and Longfellow in the United States. These and their imitators molded the consciousness of the nineteenth century, it is not too much to say. They made poetry something more than rhymed reason; as image and symbol, haunting the imagination, it shaped the feeling for life in its own unique way.

Nature's Role in Romanticism

Among the affirmations of Romanticism a number were notable and original. One was an interest in "nature." When an American tourist drives a thousand miles to exult in the scenery of the mountains, he is, perhaps without knowing it, a Romantic: *echt* neoclassical taste thought

---

[11] From his famous Dictionary, definition of "Romantick":
1 Resembling the tales of romance; wild. . . .
2 Improbable; false.
3 Fanciful; full of wild scenery. . . .

the Alps hideously unkempt and would have gone some distance out of the way to avoid them.[12] "Nature" was a word much on eighteenth-century lips, but it did not usually mean the woodlands wild. Rousseau's *Reveries of a Solitary Walker* passed down to Chateaubriand and to Lamartine's *Meditations;* and everyone knows how important Nature was to Wordsworth and Thoreau. This attachment to the trees and flowers and hills had, or came to have, a metaphysical foundation which, forming a link to philosophical Idealism, is one of the leading ideas of the age. Rousseau believed vaguely that nature soothes and calms us, returning us to fundamentals and reminding us of deeper truths than those of human society. Wordsworth, without much philosophy, felt keenly

> . . . a sense sublime
> Of something far more deeply interfused,
> Whose dwelling is the light of setting suns
> And the round ocean and the living air,
> And the blue sky, and in the mind of man;
> A motion and a spirit that impels
> All thinking things, all objects of all thought,
> And rolls through all things.

In Germany, where philosophy had been stimulated by Kant, and where Romanticism from the first interacted with it, this pantheistic sense of spirit in nature, "rolling through all things," received explicit formulation. How Kant's critical philosophy created a revolution in philosophy, and how this led on to the other great German philosophers (Fichte, Schelling, Hegel) has already been pointed out. There were philosophers who specifically called themselves "Romantic"; and there were Idealists, like Fichte, who contributed to the popular conception of Romanticism in certain ways. Broadly speaking, the result was to present a vision of reality as basically spiritual, and to suggest in some sense a unity of this world spirit linking man to nature. The post-Kantians in various ways postulated a fundamental knowable unity, spiritual in nature—a mind-stuff underlying and giving form to the appearances, corresponding to the mind-stuff we have in us, and which we contact when we are using our minds creatively. Fichte called it the Ego, adopting an Idealist position in which thought is the basic reality and stressing moral experience; Schelling spoke of the Absolute, of the union of object and subject in the human consciousness, and of the paramountcy of esthetic experience. All this might seem rather Teutonically mystifying to most people; on any

---

[12] Despite neoclassical preference for neat symmetry, the eighteenth century had permitted a place for much that was not "beautiful" but nevertheless somehow impressive, under the title of "the sublime." Romantics—*cf.* the young Burke's notable essay on the Sublime—developed this concept. Especially was this true in England, never as orthodox neoclassical as France. "Mountain gloom and mountain glory" (Marjorie Nicolson) was celebrated by some eighteenth-century sublimists.

showing it was difficult and academic, for these worthies of German philosophy were all University professors. But it got outside the class-room, as the poets Novalis and Hölderlin and Richter transformed its abstract words into concrete poetic symbols. And as esthetic doctrine it was tremendously influential.

Pantheism   Many people came to hold, more or less loosely, something like this Idealist-Romantic position, meaning that we can see God or a higher reality in Nature, actually commune with it, feel its basic kinship to our own souls. Nontechnical, semipopular romantic idealism may be found in Thomas Carlyle's first book, *Sartor Resartus*, wherein this vivid writer gave expression to the idea that "the external world known to our senses and explored by our sciences is mere Appearance. Reality is its divine, unseen counterpart, standing to Appearance as Soul stands to Body" (D. C. Somervell). "Transcendentalism" became a byword among both French and American literary men of the period 1820–1840; the name of Ralph Waldo Emerson is enough to remind Americans of its potency. This heady doctrine might persuade men that all the appearances, social conventions, for example, are a fraud, and that each of us can be godlike if only he dares to search his own soul. It was close to mystical pantheism, a heresy long known to Christianity, whereby the god-intoxicated man felt that he might communicate directly with Deity. Often it had explicit roots in neo-Platonism; William Blake's mysticism has been traced to this source, and these writings were also prominent in the omnivorous reading of Coleridge, who claimed that he had found mysticism in many of the ancients before he read the Germans. There was also a discovery of the Indian religiophilosophical tradition at this time. "The pantheism of the Orient, transformed by Germany," E. Quinet wrote in 1841, was respon-sible for what he called a *"renaissance orientale."* (But the discovery and translation of the Hindu classics owed most to an Englishman, Sir William Jones, and a Frenchman, M. Anquetil-Duperron.)

The Romantics added the thought that it is above all the Artist, the Poet, who feels the Infinite Spirit in him when he creates. Working intui-tively, he "elicits truth as at a flash" (Coleridge), truth deeper than the experimental or analytical. His poetic images are symbols of nature, keys to reality. The visionary-religious element in Romanticism is perhaps to be found in its most remarkable state in the works of William Blake, the English artist-seer-poet. Taking quite seriously the identification of his own thoughts with the soul of the universe,[13] Blake believed it was the mission of the poet and artist to be a religious prophet, endowing the old religious truths with new meaning. A "symbolist" before the French school that was to bear this name later in the nineteenth century, a discoverer of the "archetypes of the unconscious" before Jung, Blake

---

[13] Compare Gerard de Nerval, the French Romantic poet: "The human imagina-tion has invented nothing that is not true, either in this world or the next."

gave new names to the gods and spoke of building a "new Jerusalem" in England. His haunting, childlike songs touch closely on perennial religious and moral experience.

The Church called the New Jerusalem was associated not with Blake but with the writings of the eighteenth-century Swedish seer Emanuel Swedenborg (d. 1772), whose visionary writings interpreting the Christian scriptures became popular, especially in England, in the early nineteenth century. There is still a Swedenborgian society in England; there was considerable American interest, too. The German Romantic theologian Friedrich Schleiermacher (*Discourses on Religion,* 1799) sought to transpose Christianity from dogma to interior experience—a faith experimentally true, true to the meaning and purpose of life when its doctrines are transformed into concrete human terms. This idea grew familiar in the nineteenth century and merged with the "liberal" Christianity which dismissed Biblical literalism arguing that the "essential" truths of Christianity are deeper and broader, and often absorbed such secular goals as liberty or social justice. Romantic theology stressed inward emotional experience as a criterion of faith, and interacted with a revival of evangelical, pietistic Christianity. Already begun by the Wesleyans in the eighteenth century, this movement was quite popular from about 1780 to 1825. Various fervent if unorthodox sects arose. Alexander of Russia succumbed to one and tried to write it into the Holy Alliance of 1815; the socialist Saint-Simon (see pages 60-62) preached a "new Christianity" to go with his Enlightenment social science. The Evangelical movement within the Church of England, beginning at the end of the eighteenth century, greatly influenced the whole Victorian era. Within Catholicism, the celebrated "Oxford Movement" produced John Newman and others in England in the 1830s; in rebellion against materialism and utilitarianism, these apostate Anglicans shared with the Romantics a poetic and spiritual emotionalism, a sense of history, a medievalism. Some Oxonians stayed within Anglicanism but revived the "high church" tradition.

Evangelical Christianity

Oxford Movement

Politically, Romanticism was ambiguous. Coinciding with the French Revolution, it could not help but interact with it. At first, the Romantics hailed the Revolution with delight, joining figuratively with the young Wordsworth as he danced with the French people. Then they turned against it listening to Burke's great indictment, which is charged with many feelings close to the heart of Romanticism. The Revolution stood for eighteenth-century rationalism and failed for that reason; it was, in fact, reactionary. Most Romantics distinguished between the French Revolution as a particular historic event and the broader movement of history it imperfectly embodied. They did not doubt that humanity was on the march, seldom wanted to go back to the eighteenth-century "old regime," but agreed that the French Revolution had degenerated in a cynical and vulgar imperialism, because of its false groundings in Enlightenment

Political Romanticism

materialism. In his famed history of the Revolution, Thomas Carlyle regarded it as having failed because it did not (until Bonaparte) produce any "great man." But the advocate of hero worship condemned the Old Regime also for having failed to provide inspired leadership, a sure sign of decadence. Romantics might, like Wordsworth, retain a rather naive Godwinian faith in human perfectibility, believing however that this utopia would come through man realizing his *inner* powers of consciousness, something not to be attained by changes in forms of government.

Coleridge's political odyssey may be taken as typical: interested in politics and at first enthusiastic for the Revolution, he wrote an ode on the storming of the Bastille; his *Ode to France*, 1798, records his disillusion and despair. "In Mr. Burke's writings the germs of almost all political truths may be found," he thought, but he also thought Burke had gone too far in his hatred of the Revolution. There must be a moral basis of policy; Kant's categorical imperative, that persons are not to be treated as things, is the great foundation. Coleridge was a staunch foe of economic individualism and of the pseudoscience of political economy, which he regarded as "solemn humbug." The mystic bonds that tie men together shape the almost sacred entity of Society, which is a reflection of the divine, as much so as physical nature. This *organic* view of society, opposed to the eighteenth century's alleged atomistic individualism, was a marked Romantic trait. Coleridge's political insights are deep, but he failed to communicate any very coherent platform; he had too much awareness of the complexity of things, and felt the great need was not for a program but for human understanding.

At any rate the great events of Revolution and war wove themselves through the texture of feelings of all the writers. Stendhal, in his essay on "Racine and Shakespeare," remarked that those who had lived through such times, who had experienced the Terror and marched with bloody feet through Russian snows with Napoleon, could no longer be moved by the chaste tragedies of Classicism. The blood stirred by these mighty happenings, and warmed by revolutionary slogans, simply could not be aroused by the older proprieties. It demanded stronger meat and drink. The political thought of Romanticism was diverse, but whatever it was it demanded and created excitement. The young Hugo, worshipping Chateaubriand and abhorring the Revolution, was royalist, conservative, and even reactionary, but it was out of strong emotions and also a love of liberty. He simply thought that a false liberty and democracy had led to despotism, the enslavement of the people in the name of slogans about equality. Later he became a liberal, radical, or revolutionary (reversing the conventional picture of men growing more conservative with age). The fact is that Hugo was always passionate, always idealistic, always libertarian; the modes in which he expressed this spirit changed with the times, that was all.

Nevertheless the confusion in Romanticism is amply evident in its political thought. We have only to observe that an organic view of society is widely regarded as most typical of it, but how are we to adjust this vision of collectivism with the spirit of revolt and individual self-expression, even alienation, also obviously a Romantic attitude? Between Coleridge opposing the English reform bill of 1832 and Hugo on the barricades there seems a decided gulf. No doubt German philosophy could provide a shaky bridge between the ego and the cosmos, but there seems little to be gained by trying to cover positions so various with a single term.

A century of scholarship and criticism has sought in vain for a single definition of Romanticism. From this, some have drawn the conclusion that the term is useless, that no such thing existed, rather a number of different things that somehow got lumped together owing to sloppy thinking or "label-itis." In any case, was Romanticism the same in Germany, France, Great Britain, Spain? Plainly it took on regional variations. Should not one study the concrete—this Spanish poet, that German philosopher, Wordsworth, Keats, Coleridge—and forget about the elusive general? This has almost been the direction of literature studies in recent decades. Still, the term *Romanticism* survives despite all efforts to kill it. It survives because it *is* a useful term to cover a number of striking if not identical cultural phenomena of the period around 1780–1830. Large terms are needed, though they are necessarily imprecise. The philosophy, literature, and general *Zeitgeist* of this period had enough in common over large areas to justify the use of some general word to describe it. Possibly we should use several terms; but we can, if we like, choose to subdivide the one term, qualify it, mark the exceptions—but retain it.

Can Romanticism be Defined?

All kinds of definitions, divisions, and distinctions have been offered. Of these, it seems useful to distinguish the *negative* Romanticism which was a reaction against the Enlightenment, against neoclassicism, materialism, hedonism, etc., from the positive Romanticism which was largely a gift of German philosophy—the philosophy of subjective and intuitive truth, spiritual nature, and the poet's role in bringing the two realms together in conscious creative experience. It may be useful, too, to sort out things which got interlocked with Romanticism but were not essentially of it such as the political explosions of the times, nationalism, democracy, the reaction against the French Revolution. It is also helpful to sort out things which while characteristic of numerous Romantics were not at all new, such as Byron's sexual morals. And the careful student will take note of national differences. Thus the English Romantics, despite Byron and Keats, were a much more chaste and prudent lot than the Germans, as a recent scholar has pointed out, reflecting the stability of English life and its strong bourgeois morality. French Romanticism wore

Distinctions between Romanticisms

the badge of anti-Revolution with special prominence. Romanticism was weakest in Spain and Italy, especially in the latter, perhaps because of the pervasive influence of Classicism on the Italian landscape. (The Gothic had been weakest there too.)

Subjectivism When all is said, the Romantic Revolution must be linked to the French Revolution as a vital aspect of what was perhaps the most exciting and creative period of modern times. If one wishes to hazard a definition of the basic factor in this intellectual revolution, it would be *subjectivism* or the participation of mind in shaping reality. It has been said that no one previously had conceived the knowing process except in terms of the object known; now the subject came into the picture. The mind partly creates the external reality it grasps. Coleridge objected that "Newton was a mere materialist. Mind, in his system, is always passive—a lazy looker-on in an external world. . . . *Any system built on the passiveness of mind must be false.*" This was the central insight of the Romantics, and it will be seen, then, how important Kant was. And in this sense Romanticism, though many aspects of it went out of fashion after a time, has left its stamp on the contemporary Western world. For, as the later portions of this book will amply suggest, subjectivism is the leading theme of the West.

Genius Subjectivism worked itself out in the unique Romantic conception of the free individual, freed from the rules, from moral conventions, from all external restraints because he is the Creative Genius. In the concept of genius, Romanticists found their central literary conception. Bound by no rules, he makes his own. By no means everyone is a genius, but conceivably all *might* be. At any rate they do arise—a Homer, a Shakespeare, a Goethe—and they make the pattern for others to follow. In the last analysis we follow and should worship the actions of genius. Carlyle, in his famous *Sartor Resartus,* repeated the message of Goethe as an antidote to scepticism and lethargy: arise, WORK, do what thou canst do. Hero worship, and the gospel of work, affected people in all walks of life in the nineteenth century; they were Romantics without knowing it.

Individualism It may be suggested then that Romanticism was a literary and intellectual counterpart of the new principle of individualism in society— and this despite the fact that Romantics often inveighed against individualism. The Old Regime had been corporative and organic, a society of estates and classes; after the French Revolution, one had a society of equal individuals. The literature of the eighteenth century, as we earlier noted, was a social literature which sought essentially not to express the personal soul but to communicate the common ideas. Romanticism was the former. Men had begun their modern fate of loneliness in the crowd, or their modern privilege of individual self-development, as one may choose to put it. It is true that the family remained, and was to be all the more stressed in Victorian times; but classes were dissolving (in

France, and to a lesser degree in England), free competition in the market place was becoming the arbiter of success, the church was fading, the stable order of countryside would soon be challenged and overcome by the city's anonymity. A collection of individuals replaced "society," as Jeremy Bentham and the Utilitarians divined. One stood or fell by one's own unaided efforts. Romanticism was a literary retreat to the individual Ego which, seen or not as part of a larger world soul, remained as the one solid basis of life.

Arthur O. Lovejoy, that great student of ideas, found the fundamental Romantic trait to be diversity, as over against Enlightenment standardization and simplification—the search for unique particulars, rather than universals and generals.[14] So stated, the change embraces a great deal of this age of Revolution, Counterrevolution, and Romanticism. The French Revolution, seen as the climax of the eighteenth-century desire to simplify and generalize, encountered Burke's opposition based on the complexity of political life, which must be handled concretely. Kant, faced with the choice between naive materialism and straightforward scepticism, fashioned a philosophical fabric that was far more intricately woven. Nationalist diversity replaced cosmopolitanism. All were interconnected. *The Concrete versus the General*

Romanticism's stress on diversity relates to some general features of nineteenth-century civilization. That civilization was in many ways more diverse and less unified than the older one. Aristocratic and cosmopolitan, the eighteenth century had *a* style, even though one might note exceptions to it. The nineteenth was to be eclectic in its architecture, pillaging the past for borrowed styles; it was to offer a "generous confusion" of modes in the arts and in ideas; it divided into separate national cultures. It was a much more pluralistic civilization. Man was parcelled out in men, as the poet Rossetti put it—which he, looking backward nostalgically, took to be a sign of the decadence of Europe. Unconsciously perhaps, Romanticism reflected the atomization of European society.

[14] In *The Great Chain of Being,* 1936 written after the essay "On the Discrimination of Romanticisms" quoted earlier, and suggesting that Lovejoy found his way to more unity in Romanticism than he had once seen. See also his paper, in a symposium on "The Romantic Movement," *Journal of the History of Ideas,* June, 1941.

From the thunder of Napoleon battles, to the jabbering of Open-vestry in St. Mary Axe, all things announce democracy. Democracy is everywhere the inexorable demand of these ages, swift fulfilling itself.

THOMAS CARLYLE

I alone shall have confounded twenty generations of political imbecility and it is to me alone that present and future generations will owe the beginning of their boundless happiness.

CHARLES FOURIER

The Birth of Ideologies: 1815–1848

2

THE EUROPEAN SITUATION 1815–1848

The Crisis of 1815

The profusion of political and social "isms" in Europe after 1815 was a consequence of the situation men faced in that year. Especially acute in France, the crisis affected all Europe, for none of it had been untouched by the Revolution and Napoleon, and much of it had been as profoundly altered as France herself. Bonaparte had destroyed the old order in Italy and Germany and had brought sweeping innovations wherever his legions marched. Now the Revolution and its great leader were vanquished. But was it possible to go back to the old regime of 1789 as if nothing had happened? Even the most reactionary did not really believe that. If one could not believe in either the old order or the new, what lay ahead? All over Europe, men felt the need to take soundings and mark out some course. Europe seemed to be rushing into a yawning void. Clearly the old Europe was dead—ten centuries of civilization washed out. The new Europe had failed, morally and now physically, from the Reign of Terror to the coup d'état of Bonaparte and so to his military defeat after a terrible war. But Europe was going on, filled with all kinds of half-understood dynamisms such as democracy, industrialization, etc. Did they portend destruction or creation, rebirth or decadence?

In France, the impulse to order showed itself strongly. Laissez-faire liberty did not appeal to the rationalist French mind. Both Conservatives and Socialists shared a desire to define and shape the reconstruction of a positive social order. But this must be done in a new way, and there was widespread realization that science and fact, not metaphysics and dogma, had to form the foundation. In Great Britain, liberal individualism was much more prominent. In both countries, political and social ideologies constituted the leading intellectual interest. Even in Germany is that true; for while the great Hegel reigned as the last of the classical lineage of German philosophy, and produced a system some found too metaphysical, Hegel's chief interest was in human history and its political order; his disciples included critical historians such as David Strauss and social ideologists such as Karl Marx.

For the greatest need in Europe after 1815 was for political and social reorganization following the destruction of the old order by the French Revolution. The peace settlement at Vienna in 1815 tried to do this in the arena of practical politics; it partly succeeded and partly failed. Popular movements such as nationalism in Germany and Italy, or working-class radicalism in Britain and France, reflected the deep disturbances of a society undergoing rapid economic change along with political uncertainty.

Socially, one marked the decline of the old aristocracy and the rise of a new class, an upper bourgeoisie of commerce, finance, and industry. The period of a few years from 1815 to 1830 witnessed a generally conservative spirit, the product of the reactionary victors of the long war against Bonapartism; in France, it is the time of the attempted Bourbon restoration, in England the Tories continued their power, and in Germany Prince Metternich's Austrian conservatism controlled affairs. But the underlying social realities defeated the attempt to preserve aristocratic domination. The revolution of 1830 sweeps aside the restored monarchy in France; the great reform act of 1832 signals the demise of old-fashioned toryism in Britain. *From 1815 to 1830*

The middle classes had begun their long reign. There was at this time considerable class consciousness among spokesmen for this group. Power must be transferred from the landed oligarchy to the "intelligent middle and industrious classes," said Richard Cobden, an oracle of British Liberalism. These classes distinguished themselves from the "mob" below as carefully as from the aristocracy, or what was left of it, above—from both of which they differed in possessing the traits of industriousness, sobriety, and morality, they thought. They were serious, frugal, upright, hard-working and, according to some critics, hard-hearted. Certainly they were builders of wealth in this vigorous morning of the Industrial Revolution, very proud of their achievements, inclined to be scornful of those who contributed less, as they believed. Distinctions must be noted within the "bourgeoisie"; the term is too broad to be meaningful. In France, at least, the "grande bourgeoisie," who dominated the 1830–1848 Orleanist *Dominance of Middle Classes* *The Bourgeoisie*

Monarchy, was a haughty coterie of rich bankers and industrialists who were "political liberals but social conservatives," having little regard for their social inferiors and absolutely no taste for democracy. In France, the 1830 revolution brought a "liberalization" of the suffrage to the degree that perhaps 1 in 40 adult male Frenchmen voted as compared to 1 in 75 before. In Great Britain, after the great Reform Bill of 1832, 1 in 8 had the vote. In the Continental revolutions of 1848 a lower bourgeoisie joined with workers in demanding universal suffrage. Britain escaped that revolution because to a much greater extent her lower as well as upper bourgeoisie were enfranchised.

The word *bourgeois* became an epithet in two circles: the socialists and the literary men. It was alleged that the middle classes were indifferent to the arts as well as to the sufferings of the poor. The stereotype of the bourgeois (as he appears in a Daumier caricature, for example) had some basis in reality. It is true, for example, that the Benthamite *Westminister Review* regarded literature as inappropriate to civilization, while the liberal *Economist* along with Herbert Spencer coolly considered it better to starve the poor than to administer public charity. But we must remember the strength of this "industrious and intelligent" bourgeoisie. By and large, they *were* in possession of a large share of those not altogether contemptible characteristics, industry and intelligence. They were creating wealth as it had never been created before. If their natural habitat was the bourse or the factory rather than university or parliament, they did produce powerful spokesmen in this age: not merely Samuel Smiles with his propaganda of self-help, but such as Cobden, Bright, Thiers, Guizot.

Threat of Lower-class Revolution

It is necessary also to keep in mind the point once made by Balzac, the astute French novelist and observer of the "human comedy": if the bourgeoisie destroyed the nobility, a combat would immediately ensue between the bourgeoisie and the people beneath them. The weapons with which the bourgeoisie had brought down the aristocracy—charges of special privilege and unearned income, demands for more democracy and equality—could obviously be turned on them by the others. Coleridge, opposing the extension of the suffrage in 1832, warned the middle class that they would be unable to stop by giving the vote just to themselves, but would eventually have to give it to all. Carlyle warned them that by refusing to look after their workers they would drive them to social revolution; for the feudal landlords had at least given protection to their serfs, whereas the new factory owners gave them no human sympathy, only an inadequate wage. So the "social question" arose early and socialism became a factor, though unable to overturn the rule of the bourgeoisie. Few serious thinkers were ever quite happy with the new organization of society, or lack of it, under middle-class industrialism.

If the bourgeois leaders could sometimes give expression to feelings of disdain for the lower classes, they did not entirely neglect their welfare. Rejecting most plans of state assistance in accordance with their approval of the "night watchman" state which only "prevented crime and preserved contracts," bourgeois liberals could not deny that their maxim of "a fair field and no favors" required some social services. Education was perhaps the leading case of this sort. "The schoolmaster was abroad" in these years, in Europe as well as in the United States, where the name of Horace Mann became a household word. Guizot, who scorned the multitude, nevertheless put through the educational reform of 1833, called the charter of French primary education. It was far from installing free and universal elementary education, but by requiring every commune to maintain a public primary school it began the movement that led in this direction. Probably the nineteenth-century bourgeoisie have been overly blamed for their alleged callousness toward the poor and the workers. Still, their creed did not allow for much social welfare legislation by modern standards. The political economists wrote their basic textbooks. The great nineteenth-century economists were engaged in developing a highly specialized, formidably exacting branch of knowledge, with rare success; they were arbiters of public policy and beacons of light to the powerful industrial bourgeoisie.

Beginnings of Popular Education

Writing in 1831 on "The Spirit of the Age," young John Stuart Mill remarked that "a change has taken place in the human mind. . . . The conviction is already not far from being universal that the times are pregnant with change, and that the nineteenth century will be known to posterity as the era of one of the greatest revolutions of which history has preserved the remembrance, in the human mind, and in the whole constitution of human society." In 1830 France had a revolution, sweeping aside the restored Bourbons and establishing a constitutional monarchy; in 1832 Great Britain, too, entered into the Liberal era with the passing of the great Reform Bill after a severe political struggle. But with the progress of the so-called industrial revolution, the rise of what Carlyle named the "social question," and a steady trend towards popular democracy, there was to be no stability on the basis of the 1830–1832 settlements, which provided for neither a democratic suffrage nor a welfare state. They were in fact political and social orders dominated by the upper classes and offered little to either the workers or the lower middle class, who were to join in making the revolutions of 1848, proving, however, incompatible allies. The 1830s witnessed a rise of interest in socialism and related ideas, brought violent insurrection to some districts (for example Lyons in 1831) and then gave way to the "hungry forties," at the end of which major revolutions swept Europe from one end to the other.

Further Revolutions

An unprecedented ferment of social and political thought prepared the way for the revolutions of the year 1848, a secondary tremor hardly less earth-shaking than the first quake of 1789. Various sorts of socialism, democracy, social democracy, liberalism, mingled in another apocalyptic moment, when many expected the deferred social millennium. Again came apparent failure and disillusion. But in fact 1848 marked the permanent arrival, if not the absolute victory, of both democracy and socialism; after that they dominated the European scene for a century. The ideas that grew up in this 1815–1848 period are the political and social ideas or ideologies on which the Western world has been living ever since. They are, then, of the utmost importance.

CONSERVATISM

Burke

The rise of a conservative ideology began with Edmund Burke, and all subsequent members of this school were basically indebted to his *Reflections on the Revolution* (see pages 193–195). To Burke two human needs were evident above all: history, and religion. Man is a religious animal who, if he did not have Christianity, would turn perforce to some other, and probably less satisfactory faith—not a bad prediction of what has actually happened in recent times. He is a social animal, who would be no more than a beast if he were cut off from the fabric of ancient custom and tradition that sustains him. Reverence toward God and toward the social order are therefore the two great duties, and they are linked, for history is the revelation of God's purpose. This idea, developed into an elaborate system by the German philosopher Hegel, was a familiar Jewish-Christian conception; but in the eighteenth century, the spirit of the times had been entirely against it. Neither History nor Christianity had been much in fashion. Voltaire and Gibbon had regarded the former as a melancholy record of "crimes, follies, and misfortunes"; how they looked upon the latter is well known.

Coleridge

Coleridge, as we have noted, built on Burke's foundations in England, though his political thought was somewhat scattered. Writing under the impact of his own later (1798) disillusionment with the French cause, he did not go as far as Burke in rejecting all rationalism in politics; he joined him in the respect for tradition, the organic sense of society, and the feeling for a moral order in history (see page 38). His influence flowed down through the nineteenth century as a strong philosophic source of British enlightened Toryism; John Stuart Mill declared that Coleridge and Jeremy Bentham, the Utilitarian, were the two opposing seminal figures in nineteenth-century British thought. The contrast must be noted, for American students: British and European conservatism has been an enemy of laissez-faire. Coleridge believed in government regulation of manufacturers, government aid to education, the duty of the state to enhance the moral and intellectual capabilities of its citizens in all sorts of positive ways. Conservatism abhorred, and was set over

against, the individualism of the "liberals," who preached free competition and no state intervention in the economic order. It can be related
to the rural squirearchy, was certainly not equalitarian or levelling (Coleridge opposed the reform bill of 1832), but was deeply humanistic and
more likely than Liberalism to support governmental welfare measures
for the poor. The leading hero of factory reform and other humanitarian
measures in early industrial England was the Tory, Lord Shaftesbury.

It was in France, though, that the conservative ideology developed
most prominently, in the Restoration period after 1815. There were a few
liberals in post-Napoleonic France (1815–1830), for example Benjamin
Constant and Mme. de Staël, those old foes of Bonaparte; they stressed
constitutionalism, civil liberties, a limited monarchy, parliamentarianism.
In this camp too one might put Chateaubriand, his career now turned to
statesmanship as he struggled to make the system of parliamentary monarchy work. But even these French "liberals" do not seem to have had
much of the spirit of Benthamite individualism, then becoming dominant
in Britain. Nor were they the dominant voices, distinguished though the
thought of Constant was. France in the 1820s produced two brilliant
streams of thought from opposite directions: Right and Left. These were
the conservatives and the socialists. The conservative camp included
Joseph de Maistre and the Vicomte de Bonald as its chief ornaments.

Born in 1753, of aristocratic Savoyard family, the first of these was   The
early a follower of Rousseau. In the 1780s he became interested in the   Conservative
occult Christianity pursued in the circle of the Marquess de Saint-Martin,   School
"the unknown philosopher" as he signed himself, but dropped the attachment when the Church pronounced against it. A provincial senator, happily married, Maistre would never have made himself a famous figure in
the history of thought had it not been for the French Revolution. Initially,
he was known as a liberal or even a Jacobin. But he fell afoul of the
Revolution in 1793 and went into exile. At Lausanne in Switzerland, he
frequented the society of M. Necker and his celebrated daughter, Mme.
de Staël, and met Gibbon the historian. At that time he began to put
together his thoughts on the origins of the Revolution, the reasons for
its failure, and the means of reconstructing France. These were themes
to which the thoughts of many men turned in these dramatic years.

Bonald was in exile in Heidelberg at the same time, and Maistre   Joseph
wrote to him in 1796 that "your spirit and mine are in perfect accord."   de Maistre
They had to wait out the Napoleonic years; Bonaparte, though he read
and admired a book of Maistre's in 1797, could not secure the loyalty of
the man who had made himself the spokesman of French royalism.
Maistre worked as diplomatist for the King of Sardinia, going to St.
Petersburg as ambassador in 1803. The rugged integrity of this Savoyard
(a people noted for this trait), who separated himself from his family

whom he deeply loved, whose faith in France did not waver through the darkest days, added to the eloquence of his prose and the charm of his personality. He was a writer of genius and a scholar of great learning, as even his foes conceded. In St. Petersburg he wrote his chief works: *On the Pope, On the Gallican Church, Evenings in St. Petersburg*. After the fall of Napoleon and the restoration of Louis XVIII, Maistre returned to France to receive considerable acclaim, and his books, now published in France, earned him the reputation of chief theoretician of the Bourbon restoration; he died in 1821 just as he was gaining this long-deferred but well-earned recognition. Bonald, whose ideas were quite similar (he lacked Maistre's grace of style but was rather more systematic), lived on to reign as the high priest of the monarchists, joined among others by the youthful and fiery La Mennais, who would later take up a different crusade. But of these Maistre's writings are the best known.

Negatively, Maistre's thought was marked by a cold fury against the whole *philosophe* school. He wished to "absolutely kill the spirit of the eighteenth century." In this sense these "Ultraists," as they were known, were reactionaries. The lucid intellect of Maistre concluded that the *philosophes* had introduced the poison that had induced the sickness of the Revolution; the poison must be purged from France's body before she could be restored to health. Maistre would not even allow Voltaire and company the virtue of common honesty. They were great criminals; to like Voltaire is the sign of a corrupt soul; the very visage of the great satirist bespoke his service of the Devil. Locke, Hume, Voltaire, Rousseau were all evil or at the very least horribly misguided men. Here Maistre was simply a polemicist, a vigorous and eloquent one, turning Voltaire's weapons against himself and assailing the mockers as they had once assailed the church.

However, once the poison had been cast out, these "reactionaries" saw the additional task of reconstructing society and tried to show how it might be done. Here they proved immensely stimulating and influenced many who did not at all share their ideological preconceptions; they even, and most notably, influenced the socialists, Saint-Simon being the best example.[1] Counterrevolutionaries, royalists, Catholics, conservatives, these men cannot be written off as sterile reactionaries. They combined keen intelligence with penetrating insights into the weaknesses of the liberal or democratic order, while also contributing some fruitful ideas about methodology in the social sciences. They were aware that one could not go back to 1789, much though they may have regretted the

[1] John Morley in his essay on Maistre commented at length on the fact that pretty obviously the great reactionary valued religion and the church less for their inherent truth than for their social utility. The stress of analysis is on the part that such institutions must play in stabilizing society. In this sense, Maistre himself is almost a "utilitarian."

Revolution, which Maistre could only explain as having been sent by God to punish France for her sins! Maistre was not the "prophet of the past" as a wit dubbed him. It was necessary to establish a new political philosophy; this was the age of ideology, with mere habit no longer sufficing; "the intellectual principle has taken priority over the moral principle in the direction of society," as Maistre put it. Living in a France which had seen the failure of the Republic and then (defeated in frightful war) the collapse of the dictatorship that succeeded it, and which now found itself trying the uncertain experiment of a restored Bourbon monarchy, Maistre and Bonald hoped to explain clearly why republics always failed and only monarchies could provide political security. The task stimulated them to a wide-ranging investigation of political and sociological phenomena.

Their argument made extensive use of the idea that the natural order of society is historical and traditional, while individualism and democracy are diseases resulting in social anarchy. Take away the discipline imposed by church, monarchy, nobility, each in its proper place in the orbit that is natural to France (nations have character; each has a form of government suitable to it; you must not tamper with this truth by an arid rationalistic universalism), take this away, and the result will be disorder, corruption, decay. Written constitutions are crude and artificial; the true constitution of a people is written in the hearts of its people and expressed in its ancestral customs. The school of Maistre, Savigny, and Haller[2] was historical; they held that wisdom in politics comes from experience only, that is, from a discriminating study of the past, and from the understanding of national character as revealed in history. Abstract theory had caused much damage, they believed, ignorance of and contempt for history being the prime source of political error.

Their arguments in favor of absolute monarchy may now make tedious reading, but the conservative school had a considerable influence on nineteenth-century thought. Bonald has been called the founder of sociology; he certainly influenced Comte, who is more frequently granted that title. Alexis de Tocqueville's famous *Democracy in America,* which might be called the pioneer work of sociological analysis, was much influenced by these writers. (See La Mennais' comments on democracy in his 1825 book, *De la religion considerée dans ses rapports avec l'ordre politique et civil,* volume I. It looks as if Tocqueville were testing the hypotheses of La Mennais: that democracy leads to despotism, enshrines mediocrity, causes people to be restless, rootless, and godless, and makes money the only idol.) Whereas their recommendations for the good

[2] Savigny was spokesman for the historical school of jurisprudence in Germany, Burkean in its stress on the organic evolution of the law rooted in tradition. Haller, a German Swiss, held similar views. The latter's nostalgia for the Old Regime in its corporate, organic, and inequalitarian aspects was especially strong.

society came to little, their critical analysis of the social changes over-taking France, their investigations of such matters as what effect the loss of religious faith or of social hierarchy will have on politics and society, were truly stimulating. Their appeal from the abstract theories of the rationalists to positive historical facts and careful sociological investiga-tion bore fruit in many students after them, who admired their methods while not necessarily sharing their political prejudices.

A deep awareness of the tragic aspects of the human situation marks Maistre's thought, and is deserving of respect. It will hardly do to banish Maistre because he points out that the plight of humanity is not a con-soling one. In politics he was a conservative, yet not illiberal; he wished to see the monarch checked by tradition and by local institutions in a "pluralistic" society, as in the Old Regime. His recent editor, Jack Lively, has pointed out how close he was after all to Rousseau, whom he thought he hated. Like Bossuet, Maistre distinguished an "absolute" monarchy from an unlimited or despotic one. In a notable argument set forth in *Du Pape,* he argued that the Papacy might mediate between the sover-eignty of the state and the liberty of the individual. The argument im-pressed few, least of all the Pope; but it indicates Maistre's desire to mitigate the authority of the state (which he felt necessary) in some way lest it become tyranny. He did not think democracy the answer, not at least for France (he conceded that England had it in her national char-acter to live as a republic). It would only lead to a new Bonapartism. How accurate that prophecy was the events of 1848–1851 would reveal. Too much the polemicist, and marred by corroding hatreds, Maistre remains a major figure because of his flashes of rare insight.

A recent writer (Benjamin N. Nelson) has observed that "a society founded on sheer egoism . . . will undergo atomization, anomic loss of a sense of belonging." It then leads to totalitarianism by reaction, modern totalitarianism being an effort to substitute for "subtle and satisfying forms of organic solidarity" by "imposing the yoke of mechanism." In other words, a natural community being absent there is flight from the intolerable rootlessness and anonymity of modern urban life, towards some kind of statism. The case for the conservatives of nineteenth-century France must rest on some such point as this, and it would seem to be one of enduring pertinence.

British Utilitarianism and Political Economy postulated the free, self-reliant individual, the "mainspring of social progress" because his energies were released by the knowledge that what he gained would be his own, capable of enriching himself, and thereby also enriching the nation, capable also of enlightening and educating himself. But an accom-paniment of this far from unworthy idea was the loss of a social sense. The market was an impersonal force, though it regulated the relationships of society—impersonal and selfish. Society became only a collection of individuals, and thus something necessary to man was lost; for though he likes to assert his individuality he cannot do without membership in a community. The conservatives whatever their sins in other respects surely performed a valuable service to modern Europe in defending the community against atomization.

Moreover the conservatives typically disliked industrialism as well as mass democracy, and they had a deep sense of human dignity. Their values tended to be rooted in the stable society of the countryside where everybody knows everybody else and the impersonality of the city is abhorrent. In both England and France there were "Tory radicals" throughout the century who sided with the working class against the capitalists on matters of social reform. They produced a strong vein of social criticism. Coleridge, Carlyle, Disraeli, and perhaps Ruskin might be put into this category in England—a distinguished heritage of social thought, by no means reactionary, holding up the ideal of a society that was aristocratic but not plutocratic, socially responsible rather than irresponsible, opposing the social neglect of laissez-faire with a paternalism of the upper class.

Saint-Simon, the socialist, acknowledged his debt to Bonald who taught him that society is "an organic machine whose every part contributes to the movement of the whole," it is not a mere collection of separate and unconnected individuals. The conservatives and the socialists had something in common, and that, an important idea: the social principle. But the conservatives saw society as the will of God, favored obedience to political authority, believed religion to be a necessity, abhorred revolution, and could scarcely accept either equality or democracy. Agreeing in the conviction that society must be ordered and organized, wherein they both differed from the nineteenth-century liberals, conservatives and socialists disagreed about the nature of that organization, and its source. For the socialists held to an Enlightenment faith that human reason might contrive an ideal organization and establish it all at once. Conservatives, with a wisdom they thought they had learned from the melancholy experiment of the Revolution, held this to be impossible, and disastrous. They would rely on the allegedly natural social order, which seemed to mean just the *status quo*. Their defect was that the age was seething with change, and there was no stable order of things.

Conservatism and Socialism

LIBERALISM

The Great Britain out of which had come Adam Smith, which had not known absolute monarchy and had been living under the freest of European governments since 1688, proved to be incorrigibly individualist. Most striking and significant here, in the 1815–1830 period, was the movement known as Utilitarianism, of which the prophet was Jeremy

Utilitarianism

Bentham. Bentham had been writing as early as the 1770s and was an old man in 1810 when his school suddenly became prominent; he belonged to the later Enlightenment and never departed from it in essential spirit. What he did do was offer certain revisions designed to make scientific social reform palatable to Englishmen at this time, and to make it practical.

Decidedly no Romantic, Bentham was a thoroughgoing rationalist, a scoffer at religion, a man without poetic instincts and almost, it seems, without emotions. John Stuart Mill, son of Bentham's leading disciple, described in his famous autobiography the inhuman regimen under which he was raised, and which finally caused him to have something like a breakdown, his relief coming only when he found consolation in poetry and philosophy. After this dramatic and symbolic experience, Mill wrote a series of essays in which he presented Bentham and Coleridge as the two seminal influences of the century. The Romantic Conservative and the Utilitarian Liberal, rivals and opposites, sent forth two different strains of thought and feeling which even Mill's wise and catholic mind could not quite reconcile though he strove to do so.

Origins of
the Utilitarian
School

The lineage of Utilitarianism can be traced back to various earlier sources. Helvétius, the French *philosophe*, had announced as a momentous discovery the apparently trite idea that good government is that which secures the greatest happiness of the people. He also shared, if somewhat confusedly, the Physiocratic idea that about the best thing government could do to this end was to leave men alone—certainly, to leave trade alone. The recipe for maximum happiness was left somewhat vague in the pages of Helvétius' *Treatise on Man*. In Britain Francis Hutcheson had used the phrase "greatest happiness of the greatest numbers," and David Hume had arrived at a form of "utilitarianism" when in his criticism of the social contract he had concluded that it was a fiction that might be dispensed with: "It is therefore on opinion only that government is founded." That is to say, there is no sort of sanction for government, on rational analysis, except the usefulness of that government in the eyes of its citizens. (Hume could scarcely have supported Bentham's view that an objective, rational standard of utility is possible, however.) William Paley, in his influential textbook *Principles of Moral and Political Philosophy* (1785), accepts this and defines utility as the sum of happiness. A law is good or bad accordingly as it increases or lessens this total of well-being.

Based on Enlightenment hedonism, Utilitarianism was severely rationalistic, sweeping aside claims of sentiment or habit in government (the charismatic, customary, and bureaucratic forms of authority, as we might say today, following Max Weber) and requiring laws and institutions to justify themselves on the practical grounds of welfare achieved. But how measure welfare or happiness? Individualistic, atomistic by its birthright, Utilitarianism assumed that the sum of individual happiness is the social optimum. One had, somehow, to measure this, seemingly a difficult task. What is happiness, and how does one count it up? Further, how could one calculate the effects of a law, which might have an infinite number of ramifications, reaching far into the future and affecting all manner of men differently?

Utility is thus a very large tent which might cover a multitude of programs. Paley himself granted favoring nods to both socialism and democracy but came to rest in a defence of the rotten-borough system, which undoubtedly had its usefulness! Approving democracy in principle, he saw greater inconveniences in establishing it. Burke was also a utilitarian in the sense that he based his case against revolution on the unhappiness that it ultimately brings in its disregard of real social forces. Bentham, however, thought that he could perform the herculean task of providing an objective measuring-stick for happiness on which all might agree. He invented a "felicific calculus."

The Benthamite principle of social welfare as the sum total of units of individual happiness, a total which could in principle be measured rather exactly thus providing the basis for a science of welfare, lasted a long time; as late as 1920 A. C. Pigou, British economics professor, claimed to have solved the problem of finding this exact science (*The Economics of Welfare*). The effort to make an exact science of welfare economics must nevertheless be regarded as a failure and illusion. Bentham's notion of it certainly was inadequate and received many criticisms and subsequent restatements. But for all his extravagances Bentham had a genius for practical reform. From his tireless pen flowed a series of projects for the practical reform of everything: schools, prisons, courts, laws. Some of them were fanciful, some ingenious. By sheer energy and perseverance, Bentham and his followers (James Mill being the first and chief) forced upon the public constant consideration of the questions, "What good is it? Can it be improved?" There were many things in the British Isles in obvious need of reform by these standards. On the eve of the French Revolution, basic reforms such as redistricting, extension and regularization of the suffrage, and poor law reform, had seemed near; then the shock of the earthquake in France caused a reaction against all change. Now the Utilitarians offered a hard-headed approach to it, refreshingly different from the Jacobin variety. For Bentham despised the vacuity of the French theorists; "natural rights" he declared to be nonsense, nothing counting except the practical. Utilitarianism, which was the driving force behind a series of liberal acts culminating in the great political Reform Bill of 1832, brought to Great Britain the equivalent of the French Revolution, by peaceful means.

Utilitarianism and laissez-faire were closely associated, though not necessarily logically linked. The Physiocratic-Adam Smith idea that "the

Reforms

Utilitarian-
ism and
Laissez-
faire

world goes of itself" if left alone, that men are the best judges of their own interest and that there is a natural harmony of interests, was one of the most exciting new ideas of the later eighteenth century, one which apparently bore the authoritative stamp of science. The Utilitarians had an affinity for Political Economy, Bentham and especially James Mill actively working in the latter field as well as the former. David Ricardo, the heir of Adam Smith, was close to Utilitarian circles. Taken together, Political Economy and Utilitarianism formed a creed often called Philosophical Radicalism. Bentham's instincts were in part to be a more active, positive reformer than the laissez-faire credo indicated, but he went a good way with it. "The whole art of government," Smith had written, "lies in the liberty of men and things." Utilitarian reformers could agree with those who thought this way, because a good deal of reform at this time consisted in getting rid of special privileges and inequalities. The vote was not held by all; let it be, let each man count as one and be able to defend his own interests, said Bentham. There were religious discriminations, monopolies, special subsidies, nests of privilege. To banish these and substitute a uniform set of laws which would treat all exactly alike, and leave them maximum liberty, seemed highly useful reform. Thus did Utilitarianism contribute to the development of what was soon to be known as Liberalism. Bentham, however, did not completely subscribe to the dogma of natural and automatic harmony of interests, we should stress; he thought that in many areas this would have to be brought about through legislative action.

The influence of the recluse Bentham, sent down from his lonely eminence through a chain that included James Mill and such loyal grassroots workers as Francis Place, the tailor of Charing Cross, spread rapidly. Though the school was too radical as yet in the 1810s and 1820s for most of the members of Parliament, there were always a few spokesmen there and through organs of opinion (the *Westminster Review* and the *Edinburgh Review*) Utilitarianism permeated the educated public mind. It would work steadily on Britain all through the century, encouraging piecemeal reform, especially in law and administration. It was democratic in its Benthamite phase and contributed greatly to the hard-won victory of 1832 when the vote was extended and made more representative of population, the decisive victory for the principle of democratic suffrage in British history.

Utilitarianism spread beyond its native shores to exert an influence in other countries, as far afield as Russia, Spain, and Latin America. It offered a simple and rational rule for reform and had the merit of avoiding nebulous sloganizing as well as revolutionary radicalism; it was hardheaded and practical. But its individualistic foundations rendered it less acceptable in France. There the key social theorists of this period, whether conservatives like Maistre, socialists like Saint-Simon, or bourgeois thinkers like August Comte, stressed the social principle and were more statist.

One other notable Benthamite contribution lay in a vigorous revival of the Hobbean theory of law as "positive" rather than "natural." Bentham and his follower John Austin rejected natural law arguments as ultimately meaningless. All that counts is the law that the state is willing to enforce; law is the command of the sovereign. We cannot appeal beyond it to a natural law that is somewhere up in the sky or written in the hearts of men. Bentham tended toward an Enlightenment materialism and atheism. He wished to get rid of metaphysical rubbish in politics and law, bringing everything back to the touchstone of measurable human happiness.

Austinian Sovereignty

Legal reform was to enjoy considerable popularity in the nineteenth century, and the Utilitarians more than any other group attached themselves to the central goal of this reform: to make the law both clearer and more adaptable to human needs. In Germany, the "Germanists" opposed the proponents of the old Roman law in the name of greater flexibility and better adjustment to the customs of the times. By contrast, Bentham's followers hoped to codify the English Common Law, reducing its luxuriant confusion to some order (they never succeeded entirely in this, of course.) But they also wished to make a law that would be suited to human needs by being flexible. They did not solve the problem, but bequeathed their interest, which they had inherited from the eighteenth century (Montesquieu, Beccaria, Blackstone) to later legal reformers and philosophers. It was no slight contribution.

It was this school of Utility that Carlyle attacked as piggish and which sent the amiable Coleridge into a rage. Bentham and James Mill cared nothing for the arts, dismissing poetry as nonsense in the best or worst tradition of the Enlightenment; they cared nothing for "society," seeing in it nothing more than a group of individuals. Selfishness and hedonism seemed enshrined in their utterly unheroic ethics. The Romantic-conservative, Coleridge-Carlyle temperament could not understand them. Nor, indeed, were they anywhere popular at first; they were radicals, as Lord Brougham remarked in 1827, "in their religion intolerable atheists, in their politics bloody-minded republicans. . . ." Bentham's immense body of writing (of which the best known was *Principles of Morals and Legislation,* 1789) is marked by few if any graces of style. It is rather more prolix and formless than the works of his forerunners in the English tradition, Hobbes and Locke; but it does swarm with ideas for practical reform. Bentham's creed of self-interest has doubtless gone out of style in the twentieth century, but it appealed mightily to the nineteenth-century bourgeoisie and was conceivably a suitable polity for that day—witness the enormous growth of wealth in Great Britain. His method of attacking social reform piecemeal, assailing it with factual research and avoiding large nebulous slogans, continued on in the Fabian Social-

Reactions to Bentham

ists later, the goal being rather different but the method similar. It seemed to suit the English genius—individualistic, hard-headed, empirical, mistrustful of general ideas and metaphysics. And it can be interpreted as a creed for the English bourgeoisie in particular.

The Political Economists

Closely related to and allied with Utilitarians in the camp of British liberalism were the Political Economists. In the early nineteenth century the brilliant beginnings in economic thought made by the French Physiocrats and Adam Smith reached maturity in the writings of such men as Thomas Malthus, David Ricardo, J. B. Say, and Nassau Senior. Say along with Sismondi kept up the French contribution, but in the main the British took over this subject. Perhaps this was because its determined individualism suited the British temperament, tradition, and experience. It is significant that Sismondi defected to socialism, while in Germany there were "Romantic" economists such as List and Mueller who rejected the individualistic premises of the British "classical" economists. In Britain, too, the great Scottish writer Thomas Carlyle joined Coleridge and other poets and moralists, dismissed as mere amateurs and sentimentalists by the economists,[3] in deploring the "dismal science." But it flourished and developed influence uniquely in the British Isles.

In some ways Malthus and Ricardo continued Adam Smith's thought; in other ways they wrought changes. Smith had posited the "economic man," seeking his own advantage, and made this self-seeking individual the key to his system; so did Ricardo, perhaps even more. That every man wishes to obtain additional wealth, as efficiently as possible, Senior made his starting point. It should be noted that the supremacy of individual desires was a keystone of the whole structure of liberal economics. Suppose the state to direct men to produce something they are not producing. The view of the classical economists was that this must mean a diversion from what is desired to what is not; and this was a sufficient refutation in their eyes. Some Romantic economists protested that the nation might wish to elevate itself by choosing a standard of production other than just what people want: it might wish, for example, to create more musical instruments and fewer evening dresses for wealthy women. This cannot be refuted by the classical economists, except that they would simply dismiss it as "uneconomic," that is, going beyond their system. They would add that a directed economy must burden itself with an expensive bureaucratic system whereas the undirected one is largely self-running. But in large measure they identified efficiency with meeting the desires of individuals.

[3] John Stuart Mill in his discriminating and appreciative essay on Coleridge said that "in political economy he writes like an arrant driveler, and it would have been well for his reputation had he never meddled with the subject." In turn Coleridge regarded Political Economy as "solemn humbug."

Smith and the Physiocrats had claimed that in accordance with a law of nature the "invisible hand" causes individual and social objectives to coincide, the rule of laissez-faire generally sufficing, via competition and the profit incentive, to secure the most efficient production and distribution of wealth. His successors may have moralized less, but they continued to assume that the free competitive system is the best and that state intervention seldom serves a useful purpose. It now became a mark of ignorance not to recognize as much; Ricardo was more cocksure and dogmatic on this than Smith. "Mercantilism" was well on its way to becoming a synonym for the dark ages of economic thought. Merchants and statesmen began to accept free trade, which had by about 1820 (witness Baring's petition from the London merchants to Parliament in that year) become business orthodoxy.

There were some apparent differences, at least of stress, between Smith and his successors. It was generally felt that the later economists were more pessimistic. There is an air of roseate eighteenth-century optimism about Smith; things do come out for the best, we are assured, and such unpleasantries as the subsistence theory of wages are glossed over. Certainly, by contrast, both Thomas Malthus and David Ricardo earned a reputation for almost delighting in the grimmer inferences of economic theory. (This is not fair to them, but we find indignant opinions of this sort frequently expressed.) Malthus became famous for his theory that population will always increase up to the limit of the food supply, thus ensuring perpetual poverty. The only remedy is birth control or "moral restraint" checking the procreation of children. Ricardo declared that "the natural price of labour is that price which is necessary to enable the labourers, one with another, to subsist and perpetuate their race, without either increase or dimunition." (That these economic ideas were not new may be seen by comparing Turgot, the eighteenth-century statesman and economist: "It cannot fail to happen . . . that the wages of the workman are limited to what is necessary to procure him his subsistence.") Both Ricardo and Malthus somewhat modified these statements; it was the socialists, anxious to convict them of heartlessness, who spoke of the "iron law" of wages. It would be difficult, too, to surpass for severity the opinions of Defoe and of Arthur Young, expressed in the eighteenth century, that the poor must be kept poor or they will not work, and that charity only encouraged idleness. But so humane a man as Francis Place, the Utilitarian reformer, agreed with the latter opinion as did most Utilitarians and Political Economists.

Ricardo, too, was known for his attacks on the landlord class as economically parasitic on the industrial segment. James Mill observed that capital tends to increase less rapidly than population, nor can the growth of capital be forced; it must make its own pace. The classical economists would certainly have listened with bewilderment or perhaps amusement

Pessimism of Political Economy

to the recent debate about just how you go about "creating economic growth" by the activities of various governmental agencies. Their world was strictly bounded by the limitations of nature, they saw the laws of diminishing returns and increasing population as probable barriers to any great improvement in the overall lot of the human race. They permitted themselves only an occasional hint of a brighter future.

Yet they became the respected arbiters of policy. This was a triumph not only for their obvious intelligence but also for the readiness of the middle classes to receive the message of hard work and austerity. Classical political economy appealed to the Puritan spirit of the industrious small manufacturers and businessmen who were climbing from poverty to riches in the favorable economic climate of England during and soon after the Napoleonic War. The slogan of the industrial middle class was self-help. The creed which Carlyle thought a monstrous, inhuman "gospel of mammon" seemed to them the law of life and of progress. As Great Britain assumed the leadership in industrialization, it was the presence and the power of this class, more perhaps than any other single factor, that was responsible for her success. They had energy, and the system of laissez-faire capitalism provided them with incentive.

The British economists were both much admired and cordially disliked, and excited a vigorous countermovement. Socialism took its point of departure from the economic inequalitarianism as well as the economic individualism or selfishness of their teachings. Bentham, who had supported political and legal equality, accepted economic inequality. There must be, he wrote, equality in the sense that each man is entitled to the just fruits of his own labor. But since men have unequal talents and energies this will mean unequal rewards. Compelling people to share the fruits of their labors with others, the only practical way of securing economic equality, not only violates justice but will prove disastrous. Coleridge reached exactly the same conclusion—a rare example of agreement between the two leaders of rival schools. It is difficult to overstate the importance for the nineteenth century of this apparent truth that you must choose between civil and economic equality, you cannot have both; as students of ethics would put it, the problem of personal versus distributive justice.

Legal Equality as Leading to Economic Inequality

The great Utilitarian admitted that on other grounds equal distribution of wealth was desirable as contributing to the greatest happiness of the greatest number. (The principle of diminishing utility, he pointed out, means that the addition of a unit of wealth to one who already has a good deal of it brings less pleasure than it does to one with less of it.) Thus was posed the dilemma: in the name of social justice and economic efficiency one sanctioned inequality and hence unhappiness.

Other facets of Political Economy, especially the labor theory of value and the theory of profits, also exposed it to counterattack (see the next section below). Socialism, Harold Laski has written, was based on "the realization that the liberal ideal secured to the middle class its full share of privilege, while it left the proletariat in its chains." With allowance for rhetorical embellishment, the statement comes close to expressing the essence of the matter. Liberty—the liberty of everyone to prosper or fail in accordance with his energies, abilities, and luck, the law maintaining a scrupulous impartiality and the state refusing in any way to intervene to protect the weaker or less fortunate—meant inequality, and even injustice. It meant that those who succeeded had both the protection of the law and the accolades of society, while those who failed, for whatever reason, might expect to hear only that most ancient of cries, *vae victis.*

SOCIALISM

At about the same time as conservatism and liberalism, socialism entered vigorously upon the scene. In 1822 Charles Fourier, son of a Besançon merchant, published his *Traité de l'association,* a work not exactly greeted with wild acclaim when it appeared, one among multitudes of strange schemes for the total reconstruction of society, but destined in time to a greater fame than any of these. Between 1814 and 1822 the eccentric Count Saint-Simon, who modestly called himself a combination of Bacon, Newton, and Locke, sent forth a spate of books on the basis of which his claim to be the first important socialist has usually been approved. Meanwhile in Britain, Robert Owen, the Scottish factory owner, was popularizing by example his plan for a more social organization of industry; thousands came to New Lanark to inspect it. Sismondi had broken with the laissez-faire economists, repelled by their selfish atomism and apparently callous disregard of human beings. The word *socialism* does not seem to have come into use until the 1830s, but the idea itself was forming, clearly, in the 1820s. "Associationalism" was a term then in use.

Naturally, it had earlier roots. Leaving aside the strong tradition of communalism in both Platonism, the Church, and medieval feudalism, and such examples of Christian millenarianism as earlier observed in Gerrard Winstanley, we can find strands of socialism in the Enlightenment, along with the stronger element of laissez-faire individualism. By no means consistently a socialist (indeed, he sometimes called private property "sacred"), Rousseau in one memorable passage, which shocked Voltaire, regretted the origins of private property in an initial act of usurpation. Someone said, "This is mine!" and got away with it, ending the idyll of primitive communism and ushering in greed, civilization, and all their accompaniments. From Rousseau's concept of the General Will—the will of society as a whole, something more than the sum of individual wills—

Varieties of Socialism

Rousseau and Eighteenth-Century Socialism

many of his disciples derived a strong statism. Rousseau's *Social Contract* taught that all rights are derived from society, without which they could not exist; the state therefore is justified in regulating property; there is no absolute right of property; if property exists it is at the sufferance of society. Rousseau believed that private property should be permitted to exist but should be approximately equal and represent only what one earned with one's labor. Moreover he considered the pursuit of wealth an evil, a source of modern society's ills. Though to describe Rousseau as a socialist would be to commit an anachronism, some of his attitudes fed into the nineteenth-century stream of this school. His influence did not encourage the kind of socialism that stressed greater productivity and wealth, for he thought the good life was one of Spartan simplicity.

Babeuf and the Equals

Morelly, called "the only consistent communist among the eighteenth-century thinkers," combined Rousseau's General Will with his attack on private property to arrive at a crude socialist theory. Equally crude, yet fervently sincere, was the thought of those who backed "Gracchus" Babeuf in his rather pathetic Conspiracy of the Equals in the latter days of the French Revolution (1795). Robespierre, that "child of the ideas of Rousseau," had been willing to use the power of the state ruthlessly in accordance with the General Will concept, but had basically been a Jacobin democrat who did not wish to abolish private property. Babeuf, however, advocated a "distributive socialism," a common pool of property, to which everyone brings what he earns and which is then carved up equally. "Nature has given to every man an equal right to the enjoyment of all goods." The same nature that provided the basis for bourgeois property rights might be turned in another direction. A passion for equality and a belief that private property creates inequality moved these simple, poor people.

Like Romanticism, socialism is a large word covering a multitude of rather different things. There have been various sorts of socialism, though one may link them all by certain common denominators. Sismondi, in 1819, attacked laissez-faire economics, urging that the state intervene to regulate the use of property for the well-being of the community; he had been impressed, for reasons not difficult to understand, by the dubious character of the economists' assumption that private desires add up to public welfare. Whereas it was the poor man's passion for equalizing himself with the rich that seemingly inspired Babeuf, the central idea of Sismondi and of Saint-Simon was that of *planning* the economy.

Saint-Simon

Saint-Simon did not suggest equality, but rather a hierarchy. He looked upon society as one great workshop whose efficient organization was the main task of modern times. Science could surely answer this need, Saint-Simon thought, and he proposed an elite of social engineers planning and running society on scientific principles. He rejected democracy; the crowd cannot govern. He added, later, the need for a new public religion, a "new (rationalized) Christianity," also presided over by a priestly elite. One can see why this eccentric nobleman has appealed to the present Communists of the Soviet Union, who grant him a place with Marx and Lenin among the makers of modern communism. On the other hand, Saint-Simon did not suggest class war or the dominance of the "proletariat." The new elite should seemingly be drawn from the industrialists and engineers. "Technocracy," a later scheme which enjoyed a brief vogue in the 1920s and 1930s, expressed more nearly what was in Saint-Simon's mind than Marxism. Perhaps, indeed, this is the way the world is going, whether in the West or in the Communist world today.

Rather like Jeremy Bentham in England, Saint-Simon was an eccentric who succeeded in planting an idea that percolated down through the nineteenth century in his native France. The Emperor Louis Napoleon (1851–1870) was one of his influential disciples, even writing a book on *The Extinction of Poverty*. Certain aspects of his thought were carried on by August Comte (see below, pages 87–93). Saint-Simonianism was not necessarily "radical," as noted; its "captains of industry" might be industrialists, and Saint-Simon was quite willing to accept even the Bourbon monarchy if this regime would back his plan. Like the Physiocrats of the preceding century, Saint-Simon preferred enlightened despotism to democracy. He announced a new epoch marked by industrialism and the power of scientific and technological knowledge, and he called for a new aristocracy, to replace the defunct orders of church and nobility. He stressed increased productivity, to satisfy material wants, agreeing with Bentham that the social goal is "happiness," which he defined largely as the satisfaction of physical wants. All this could be as attractive to a businessman as to a proletarian, perhaps, though the element of state compulsion might repel him. As a matter of fact, Saint-Simon inspired most notably a number of public-spirited administrators who wanted to impose a rational plan on the disorderly economy of laissez-faire. The French down to the present have pretty steadily shown less enthusiasm for the free, unregulated economy and society than have the English. It is possible to see at work here the urge toward order and lucidity of the French mind, always influenced by classicism and rationalism. It might be added in regard to Saint-Simon that he was not a nationalist, but advocated and predicted a European society and economy.

Saint-Simon, and Thomas Carlyle who owed much to him, reiterated their message that Europe had entered the industrial age, the "mechanical age," a new epoch calling for wholly new methods of government and thought; they called attention to the fact that the "social question" (Carlyle) was the burning issue of modern times and would not be solved by laissez-faire negativism. They did not have any exact blueprint for this new order but were sure that the "captains of industry" would have to assert leadership rather than content themselves with profits; they were sure that society needed a plan. These ideas, vigorously expressed, exerted an incalculable influence in Europe. It is impossible to imagine Marx and the other later socialists without this background. Saint-Simon, who lived in direst poverty and was laughed at as a crank, takes on great stature as one of the seminal minds of modern times, as we view the nineteenth century in perspective. Perhaps the modern society will turn out to look more like his vision than any one else's, including Bentham or Marx.

Fourier

Charles Fourier, a sweet and saintly sort of person, thought in terms of social harmony, cooperation, "association." He may be regarded as the prototype of that variety of socialist to whom these things are values in themselves. In him it is easy, though, to detect the continued influence of the eighteenth century. Like the Physiocrats, he presumes a preordained harmony and a perfect plan for society; only, unlike them, he does not believe in the separateness of the individual atoms but thinks they must be placed in association according to an exact formula. Everybody has his precise niche in Fourier's carefully constructed plans. Science, speaking through Fourier, has determined the organization of the community down to the last detail. The ideal community must contain between sixteen hundred and eighteen hundred people, with a certain proportion of each occupation and age group; they are to be housed in certain types of buildings; they rise at specified hours, etc. There are communal dining-halls; no one is to be left—or let—alone. It is rather monastic (Fourier was a religious man) and rather depressing. It had the attraction of being a precise plan, where others had been vague. It suggested the perhaps enduringly important idea of a balanced society. And Fourier promised the elimination of all vice, crime, unhappiness. The state will become unnecessary. Fourier declared that his scheme was completely voluntary. He hoped by setting up model communities to demonstrate by example the superiority of his cooperative system to the competitive anarchy of the economists, against whom he launched violent diatribes. He wished to make labor enjoyable instead of unpleasant. Many experimental communities did indeed come into being inspired by the pages of the *Treatise on Association;* most of them were not very successful, as we might guess. There were some rather unusual features of the Fourierist community, such as polygamy.

We can smile at Fourier, but we may be surprised at the number of people who took him seriously enough to try out his scheme. Harriet Martineau, the liberal Englishwoman who may be supposed to have had no special love for socialists (Coleridge regarded her as an incorrigible social atomist), wrote that the principle of cooperation "will now never rest till it has been made a matter of experiment." It was. Numbers of the sturdy individualists of New England founded Brook Farm on Fourierist lines, with predictable results. The fad for socialist communities, to which Robert Owen and his son also contributed, died down after a while but was tremendously popular in the 1830s and 1840s, many being established on the virgin soil of North America. They did much to popularize the idea of socialism, though also ultimately to discredit it in this form, since they usually failed. From this many would conclude socialism to be impractical, but Karl Marx thought only that this was an impractical form of socialism.

Étienne Cabet, author of the utopian romance *Voyage to Icaria* in 1839, was a slightly later specimen of French socialism. He was a "communist" in the sense of vesting total ownership and absolute power in the community—a veritable police state, suppressing all freedom of thought, in the name of an ideal society where economic efficiency was joined to perfect social harmony. The "Icarians" joined the Owenites and the Fourierists in establishing socialist communities in the New World (Illinois, Iowa, Texas), one of which survived until 1898 though in general the utopian ideal was not realized in practice.

Thus there were various kinds of socialism. Agreeing in their desire for some sort of social control over private property and individual rights, the socialists differed in the degree of control they would exercise, in its manner, and in its institutionalization. In the thought of Saint-Simon, Fourier, and Cabet, socialism is sometimes vague and often foolish; but it was an exciting beginning.

Modern socialism and Communism have lain so heavily under the influence of Karl Marx that his predecessors in this field sometimes are forgotten. A recent and quite good book on Marxism does not even mention Saint-Simon, Fourier, and their numerous offshoots; it says that Marx is the "heir of Jan Hus, Thomas Moore (*sic*), Thomas Paine, and Jean-Jacques Rousseau." Doubtless he was, but in a much more meaningful sense he was the heir of the numerous socialists who had filled the press of Europe with their schemes and debates all through the years when Marx and Engels were growing up. Marx had more theoretical and philosophical talent than most of them; he syncretized a great many of their systems, marrying revolutionary Babeuvist communism to Saint-Simonian and Fourierist conceptions in a Hegelian ceremony. But he really created few if any of the various ideas he strung together so ingeniously. To a large extent this creativity belonged to the half-mad Saint-Simon and the eccentric Fourier, along with their whole generation of (mostly French) messiahs of "social science."

Many of them appeared; the names of Jones and Owen in Great Britain, of Rodbertus and Weitling in Germany (before Marx), and of the numerous disciples and offspring of Saint-Simon and Fourier in France are among them. Here was a veritable chaos of socialistic ideas. Socialism before Marx reminds one of Protestantism before Calvin—in danger of perishing from its very profusion and popularity, in need of discipline and unity to save it. A rigorous logician of iron will would

Cabet

Other Pre-Marxists

come in both cases to impose that discipline, at the cost of variety. Karl Marx would have recourse to the resources of German philosophy in this task, so that it is logical at this point to turn to the thought of the last and perhaps greatest of the German classical philosophers, flourishing during these years.

HEGEL

French political and social thought, British economic theory, and German philosophy, these were the three outstanding areas of new ideas in the period 1815–1830, it was frequently said. In 1831 died G. W. F. Hegel, Kant's successor as the leading German philosopher and much more a system-builder· than the essentially critical Kant. Hegelianism so far triumphed in academic circles that by the end of the century even in Great Britain and the United States (where there was a certain resistance to this kind of thought), the leading philosophers were largely of this school, while in very unacademic circles it had also spread widely, especially through the theories of Karl Marx and other socialists who owed much to Hegel.

Hegel's was a vast, labyrinthine and, according to some, impenetrable system which despite its difficulties exercised this enormous influence. It may be well first to ask what message, stripped of all the technicalities, ordinary cultivated men got from Hegel. One of them, the Russian critic Belinski, who wrote that when he read Hegel he was overcome with emotion and the world took on a new meaning, got the message from Hegel's famous formula "What is real is reasonable and what is reasonable real." This meant that all of history is the unfolding of reality itself, the idea or mind of the universe; what happens in history is in effect the writing of a book of which God is the author. For those who believed Hegel, history and human affairs no longer were chaotic, jumbled, or meaningless; every great event had its place in an unfolding plot which when the book was finished would be seen to have no loose ends, nothing put in without purpose. As Belinski wrote, "For me there was no longer anything arbitrary or accidental in the course of history."

Undoubtedly Hegel's approach to human history *was* a revelation. He did not invent it; to go no farther back, an interest in history as rational process was taken up by Herder, pupil of Kant, who wrote an essay on the "Idea for a Universal History from the Cosmopolitan Point of View" in 1784, on which Kant commented, following which Fichte, Schelling, and others made it a leading topic in German philosophical circles.[4] But Hegel summed it all up, magnificently. Behind the ap-

History as
Rational
Process

---

[4] The famous formula of thesis-antithesis-synthesis, the dialectic of history, which Marx took from Hegel, was evidently first suggested by Fichte, not Hegel. (Nor did Hegel consider it the only kind of process.)

parently fortuitous jumble of events, the philosopher-historian can discern a great process at work, which is nothing else than thought, the Idea, working itself out in reality. History is a logical, rational process.

We have begun with the historicism[5] of Hegel, which undoubtedly (Belinski was right) constituted his greatest attraction. It was an exciting idea; we may ask what its implications were. For one thing, it stimulated great interest in history. Later historians, more positivistic by temperament and disillusioned with Hegel's overly rational history, have disparaged him, but all historians probably owe their basic professional debt to Hegel. (The conservative political theorists, too, encouraged the study of history.) It was in Germany that the great historical profession of the nineteenth century began, with such contemporaries of Hegel as Leopold von Ranke and B. G. Niebuhr developing the "scientific" historical method (use of archival source materials, careful criticism of the documents). We cannot seriously become interested in history so long as it has only an antiquarian or story-telling value, however amusing it may be; to be elevated to the dignity of a leading professional study history must be thought of as revealing significant truths about man and the universe. Bonald and Maistre saw in it the training school of politics; Hegel saw much more: nothing less than God's Will immanent in the world, the unrolling of a great purpose.

Hegel should be defended against certain criticisms of his history that are frequently encountered. He did not say that all events are logical, or that the pattern of history can be determined without reference to the events. The actions of history are the outward expression of thoughts, and these thoughts form a logical, necessary chain of reasoning. We should study the actions, the empirical events, but we should not stop there; we should "think them through" to discover their inner logic. This still seems sound enough method, whatever mistakes Hegel made in his actual historical reconstructions. The mind of the historian, it is clear, must supply *some* sort of structure for the facts, which by themselves are without meaning. Hegel of course felt that there was a single objective pattern into which all would fit, a faith few historians find relevant to their tasks today.

The three main phases of history, according to Hegel, have been the Asiatic, characterized by absolute monarchy, followed by the classical Graeco-Roman, marked by individual freedom, and finally by the Germanic-European which fused the two earlier civilizations in a synthesis of freedom in the context of the strong state. Hegel's disciple F. C. Baur applied the dialectic to New Testament studies by finding the thesis in Jewish nationalism, antithesis in Pauline universalism, and synthesis in

Phases of
History

[5] *Historicism:* defined here as the idea of history as a process above and beyond individual human actions; a will or destiny embodied in history which imposes itself on individuals.

the mature Church which emerged in the second century. An eagerness
to make the facts fit this framework led Baur into some serious mistakes.
One may judge from him both how stimulating and how dangerous the
Hegelian formula might be. Few historians outside the Marxist camp any
longer regard it as more than occasionally useful. There is clearly *something* to the thought that a reaction often occurs: Romanticism was a
reaction against the Enlightenment, for example, while some of the post-
Romantics tried to combine both in a synthesis. But the Hegelian formula
is much too pat and would have to be used with care; in any case, one
must see if the phenomena fit it (and often they do not) rather than insist
that they must.

It is interesting and typical that Hegel defined his historical epochs
in political terms. To Comte, as we shall see, the key lay in modes of
thought, while Marx found it in the technological-economic sphere.
Hegel's preoccupation with the political probably reflected the urgency
of that problem in the Germany of his day, disunited and seeking to find
its political unit. Hegel has been accused of an excessive nationalism,
especially German nationalism, but in his time this was considered liberal
and progressive. The key institution of the present age, Hegel felt with
some justification, is the nation-state. He bequeathed to most German
historians, and indeed to most nineteenth-century historians in all countries, a belief that the proper subject matter of history is politics; "history
is past politics," in the definition of E. A. Freeman, the British master.
While there was a subsequent rebellion against the narrowness of this
definition, it might be defended on the grounds that the political order
has usually given the distinctive stamp to epochs and peoples, from the
oriental despotisms of earliest times through the Greek city-states, the
Roman Empire, feudalism, and down to the age of the territorial state. If
tomorrow should bring a world-state or even a federated Europe, this
development would surely be so striking and significant that an epoch
would be named for it. The "primacy of politics" is often a sound position.

History was actually only a part of Hegel's system, though the most
celebrated part. He started with that idea of a single transcendental
spiritual reality, so attractive to the post-Kantian Romantic philosophers.
Hegel had a rather unromantic temperament and made fun of his friend
Schelling's "Absolute" as a sort of vague nothingness, or everything-ness.
He wished to clarify it. Hegel had a logical mind; was not this ideal
reality nothing but logic, the logic of the universe, dialectical reason itself?
Reality is at bottom thought in motion. What Hegel in common with the
other German Idealist philosophers called the Idea, or the Absolute,
underlies all other phenomena, nature and mind; it exists objectively.
(When we speak of Hegel as an Idealist, we should remember that his
was not a subjective idealism but an objective idealism: the Absolute Idea
is out there, independently existing—God, if one likes—not a creation of

*Hegel's
Vision of
the Absolute*

my mind and yours.) Nature, the phenomenal world, exists, too, but the Idea underlies it and determines it. Most Romantics, we recall, shared this belief that there is an unseen spiritual world of essences, of which the world known to our senses is only the external manifestation. Hegel simply defined it as logic. It is in motion, *a dialectical process,* like a conversation in which the first statement is made, then answered, a new statement made, and so on. Progress is made; things proceed towards fuller freedom and eventually to the Absolute's complete self-realization. In all things, the dialectic works. Hegel made some effort to show that it may be found in physical nature and the plant and animal world as well as in human affairs. Nature and History are the two great realms of the knowable, the two modes of the Absolute.

Process and organism are Hegelian keynotes. As opposed to the static formulations of Enlightenment thought, he has everything in motion, to be grasped only when its growth and development is understood; no one better reveals the nineteenth century's genetic, evolutionary outlook, or contributed more to implanting it. And, though somewhat obscurely, Hegel believed that the universe was not like a machine but like an organism, a view closer to both the older and the newer conceptions than to eighteenth-century mechanism. His logical methodology was based on the organic approach: nothing can be understood except by reference to the whole of which it is a part. With specific reference to the Kantian categories, Hegel held them to be bound together in a unity; not isolated and separate, but aspects of a single entity, the mind, which itself is a part of all the rest of reality. (That is why the real is rational and the rational real: our minds and the universe are parts of a single whole, hence obey the same laws.) We are almost back where we were before Descartes taught men to dissect, to break things down into simple components for purpose of analysis. Hegel was the philosopher of process, and of organism.

All this may seem rather difficult. Many found Hegel hopelessly difficult. But the spirit of his philosophy, when one gets hold of it, hangs together and communicates a special vision, an excitingly new one in its day. We asked what some of its implications were and may resume that discussion. Belinski, our Russian friend, drew from Hegelianism some highly conservative inferences: it seems to teach that whatever is is right, like all systems declaring the universe to be perfectly rational. With particular reference to history, it apparently requires us to believe that whatever has happened is for the best: in the Lisbon Earthquake controversy, Hegel would assuredly have been on the side of Rousseau and the churchmen against Voltaire's pessimistic protest. He has been accused of teaching that might makes right, and there is a certain truth in this, for "the hour strikes once for every nation" and whoever has the power at a particular moment of history is presumably in the right. Some

Practical Implications

nations are "world-historical" ones destined to contribute more than others to the pattern of history. And everything, including war, is a necessary part of the pattern. When Napoleon and Hitler were winning they were right, presumably, though when they were losing they were wrong; like all deterministic systems, Hegel's does not really tell us much, for we never know what the pattern is until after it has happened. Hegel in any case believed that individuals are the unconscious tools of the world-force, they have no wills of their own.[6]

**Hegel's
Definition
of Freedom**

Politically, Hegel might best be described as a conservative liberal. A writer of the Restoration era, he believed in constitutional government but preferred monarchy to democracy and opposed individualism. He shared some of the presuppositions of the upper bourgeoisie who greatly mistrusted the mob though in a certain sense they were liberal. Certainly Hegel claimed to believe in progress through orderly government—progress toward freedom. But his version of freedom was the so-called "positive" one. Freedom, that is, was not to him the negative practice of just letting people alone. The proper definition of freedom is realization of possibilities, Hegel believed. This may be made clearer by the example of the child, whom we compel to go to school, though if we gave him his will he would doubtless prefer the freedom of play. We are preparing him to be truly free by expanding his possibilities of growth. (Rousseau's "forced to be free" will be recalled.) Ignorance is slavery; the savage who is "free" is really far less free than the modern man who is bound by the rules of a state. No creature is absolutely free, but free only to realize its natural possibilities. A bird is free to fly, but not to swim. Man, as a creature of reason, realizes his freedom by developing his rational potential, and to do this requires making many sacrifices of his liberty of action. He must live in an organized state, obey its laws, and serve the interests of the community.

Hegel's stress on the state[7] as the highest unit led on to social-welfare protests against extreme individualism (see particularly T. H. Green in England, discussed later). It appealed to moderate, liberal men because

[6] In his study of an American politician, Henry A. Wallace, Dwight MacDonald notes the theme of an "American hour" in world history, prepared for by all previous happenings. God has brought forth the United States in due time to do His bidding in the cosmic drama of historic man. This sort of Hegelian "historicism" is obviously deeply laid within the popular modern mind.

[7] When Hegel glorifies the State we should understand that he uses the term in a rather special way. In his system it is the dialectical synthesis of family and civil society, or in his jargon the union of universal and particular in the "concrete universal." In more commonplace terminology, this means that the State (as an ideal) is the highest development of the community, the place where a perfect society would find its completest expression. Hegel, in brief, does not conceive of the state as a leviathan standing over against its subjects, ordering them about and intimidating them; it is more like Rousseau's General Will—the common rational spirit of the whole community—made manifest.

it claimed not to sacrifice the individual completely to the state, nor was it socialistic. According to Hegel, it is only as a citizen that the individual becomes wholly free and possessed of rights. This feeling for association against individualism, though with a conservative cast, made Hegel a significant founder of the more moderate movements of social reform. And if Hegel was a conservative, his disciples do not show it. While some went to the Right, and some to the moderate center, the "young Hegelians" including Karl Marx and Ludwig Feuerbach became material- ists and atheists. Belinski, too, was a socialist or anarchist.

Hegel was apparently a Christian, but Kierkegaard, the Danish pastor who is now considered the chief founder of modern Christian Existentialism, accused him of devitalizing Christianity, by rationalizing it and making it abstract. There is some truth in this. Hegel's new version of scholasticism made reason and religion coincide, but the highest syn- thesis is philosophy; Christianity is the symbolic or mythical mode of expression presumably meant for minds incapable of philosophy. Chris- tianity is done the honor of having its representations agree with Hegel's philosophy though in a slightly inferior manner. If many Christians had their faith confirmed by finding that it agreed with the most advanced philosophy, others like Kierkegaard resented the relegation. One could easily, with Feuerbach and Marx, forget about religion and take the philosophy alone. It could then readily be converted into a materialistic determinism. Hegel was closer to the atheism of Marx than he may have realized. One finds, for example, that in Italy Hegelianism was adopted by the anticlericals and laicists. The state represents the highest ethical ideal, and is above the church, they held. The Roman Catholic Church, when in 1864 it produced its great Syllabus of Errors or list of modern heresies, included Hegelianism as a form of anticlerical liberalism. Actu- ally, Hegel excluded religion from the historic sphere, regarding progress as social and political, not religious; in sharply separating private religion from public, political matters he was in a traditional Lutheran scheme.

Hegel and Christianity

Hegelianism exerted so strong an appeal in good part because it was a complete system, an organic whole, an exceptionally unified, "total" philosophy. It was the first of several such in the nineteenth century— Comte's was another, then Marx, Spencer. Of these at least one, Karl Marx's, owed its basic traits to Hegel. It was an evolutionary system, thus incorporating the nineteenth century's most characteristic point of view. By comparison with Kant, the evolutionary or historical element stands out; Kant had failed to see, Hegel thought, that reason is not static. What is true today was not true yesterday, and Hegel believed he had found here the answer to Kant's alleged proof (through the "antinomies") of the logical contradictions in any speculative metaphysics that goes beyond our experience, such as the nature of God or the origin of being.

Appeal of Hegelianism

Hegel's remarkable system of rational metaphysics based on historicism and dialectical evolution was hard to overlook; some have hated it, regarding it more as the scandal than the glory of the century, but like Marxism, its lineal descendant, it demanded attention and commanded allegiance because of the boldness of its stance as a complete reconstruction of human knowledge.

At the end of the century there was a decided reaction against the rigorous monism of Hegel's system. William James thought it a stuffy house with not enough air in it. In our time the "historicism" of Hegel, insofar as it meant a closed and deterministic system, has been assailed and convincingly refuted.[8] The enormous influence of Hegel is evident as much in his opponents as in his disciples. In protesting against Hegel, two giants of unorthodoxy in his time created movements of future significance: Schopenhauer and Kierkegaard, both of whom reacted against Hegel's cosmic rationalism and optimism to produce ideas of the irrational (Schopenhauer's "Will," a blind striving cosmic force) and of completely undetermined freedom (Kierkegaard's individual existent person). Today Kierkegaard's "existential" religion (see pages 228–229) is more popular than Hegel's rationalized religion. But Hegel's vision of an organic rather than a mechanistic universe was prophetic, and his stress on process, evolution, development, has been basic to the modern mind. His influence can hardly be overestimated. Moreover, there has recently been a significant revival of interest in Hegel.

Another novel and attractive implication of the many-sided Hegelian structure may be mentioned. In effect, very nearly, God is man, according to this philosophy—not the individual man, but humanity collectively in its historical evolution. The historic process is "the march of God through the world." The world spirit grows and develops through human history. From this one may derive a new explanation of the riddle of the human situation, with its lofty aspirations and its frustrations. Each of us has in him something of the universal man, whose nature is nothing less than potential perfection, the self-realization of the world. But each of us also is a particular person, bound to one time and place, destined to make only a tiny contribution to the splendid temple of reason that will someday be finished. Hence our soaring aspirations and our limited achievements. We can nevertheless do what our talents permit us to do in the confident knowledge that it does fit somewhere into the great plan. Nineteenth-century optimists who believed in progress found that Hegelianism fitted comfortably into their scheme of things.

[8] Karl Popper, in the important but argumentative book *The Open Society and Its Enemies*, Vol. 2, 4th ed., 1962—the work of a modern philosophical analyst with a bias toward liberalism—attributes practically all the sins of the modern world to Hegel's baleful influence (pages 25–80). L. T. Hobhouse blamed the First World War on him. This seems a little extreme!

More may briefly be said concerning the offspring of Hegel, a prog- Hegelian
eny of some importance to the modern world. Hegel influenced practically Offshoots
all schools of thought in Germany, also British Idealist philosophers of
the later nineteenth century such as F. H. Bradley and Bernard Bosanquet,
dominant in the British universities for some time, in Italy the philosophers Benedetto Croce and Giovanni Gentile, and many others. Socialists
made use of him, historians knelt at his shrine, both the religious and
the antireligious seized on pertinent aspects of his thought for their purposes. He lent authority to conservatives and radicals, reformers and foes
of reform. His ability to be all things to all men is perhaps an indictment
of Hegel as well as tribute to him.

A few notable descendants need to be pinpointed. Karl Marx, the The Young
most remarkable of these, will be dealt with subsequently. Marx in his Hegelians
youth belonged to a group known as the Young Hegelians, who were all
left-wing exponents of a modified Hegelianism. Among these, Bruno
Bauer and David Strauss showed a decided interest in Biblical and religious studies, Strauss' critical biography of Jesus being one of the
century's most sensational books, while Ludwig Feuerbach treated the
theme of religion in a more general way. All the Young Hegelians believed that Hegel's thought represented the most advanced creation of
the human mind thus far. But they thought it needed restatement, a very
sweeping sort of restatement, in a sense really the abandonment of
Hegelianism. For Hegel had been wrong in his Idealism. He should be
turned over, "set right side up." Reality is actually material, and ideas
are only a projection of physical being. The idea of God had been invented by men as a symbol for all their ideals and goals; as such it
served a useful purpose, but may now, at a higher stage of self-awareness,
be abandoned. Theology becomes anthropology, in Feuerbach's words.
We realize that only man exists, and "politics must become our religion":
the goal of man's perfection through his own social action is to be explicitly recognized.

Feuerbach was far from a great philosopher, but this somewhat
vulgar materialism, atheism, and (in the specifically modern sense)
humanism was extremely significant. Large numbers of moderns have
accepted it as their "philosophy." August Comte was even then pointing
out that the nineteenth century had witnessed the birth of the Positive
Age, replacing the ages of Theology and then Metaphysics. The new
God was materialistic science, the only goals practical, mundane ones.
The Absolute as well as God would have to be relegated to the realm of
fairy tales. It is remarkable that Hegel led in this direction, but in fact it
was possible to stand him on his feet in this way. (Hegel himself pointed
out that science was relegating art as well as religion to the sidelines in
the modern age.) Marx was the most celebrated of those who did so,
after Feuerbach.

The element of political ideology, then, in the seemingly meta-physical system of Hegel, becomes evident. The great object of knowledge is history, and especially political history; and at the end, by a slight alteration in Hegel, we decide with Feuerbach that "politics must become our religion." The sole aim and interest of man is to discover and create the good society on earth, with the aid of his scientific intelligence.

SOCIAL ROMANTICISM AND THE REVOLUTION OF 1848

Continuation of French Socialism

The ideas of Fourier, Saint-Simon, and Owen, formulated during the 1820s, enjoyed considerable popularity in the 1830s and 1840s and were joined by others. The disciples of Saint-Simon tended to split up, but the movement nevertheless went on. As their 1830 manifesto stated, they rejected the equal division of property and accepted the "natural *in*equality of man," thus favoring a hierarchical society; but "each is placed according to his abilities and rewarded according to his works" by planning and coordination, property being held by the state and not individuals. (The one-time secretary of Saint-Simon, August Comte, who will be dealt with separately, can probably not be classed as a socialist, though the influence of Saint-Simon remained on his thought in the form of a stress on authority and the subordination of individuals to the state.)

The most popular French political tract of the 1830s was probably the *Paroles d'un croyant* by La Mennais, or as he now called himself (the change is significant of a democratic shift) Lamennais. We may recall him as an enthusiastic disciple of the "reactionaries," a decade earlier. He now became an equally enthusiastic social democrat. The change is not so great as we might imagine, for most French socialists acknowledged some debt to Maistre and Bonald. The "words of a believer" came from one who was a Catholic priest, but was not long to be, for the Church would not tolerate his left-wing views. His Romantic eloquence made him the man of the hour and enthusiastic followers proclaimed Lamennais the new messiah, while Metternich, the statesman in charge of keeping down revolutionary discontent in Europe, grumbled about "this anarchist . . . fool . . . abject being." No work had more to do with the Revolution of 1848. In this and ensuing books, the Breton priest expressed a lyrical if vague awareness of a "tremendous revolution going on at the heart of human society," a revolution which was the march of "the peoples" and would produce a "new world." He denounced "wage slavery" and casti-gated the rulers of society for neglecting their responsibilities to society. "If you reject peaceful reform you will have reform by violence." The obvious British counterpart to Lamennais is Thomas Carlyle, whose electrifying prose called attention to the "social question" in an enduring classic, *Past and Present* (1843).

Lamennais and Carlyle represented a blending of Romanticism with social reform in what has been called "social Romanticism" (D. O. Evans) or "political Messianism" (J. L. Talmon). The late Romantic writers Victor Hugo, Lamartine, and George Sand were caught up in it. As David O. Evans observes in his little book on *Social Romanticism in France 1830–1848*, "*Les Misérables* was the culmination of a massive literature of social novels and dramas which flourished between 1830 and 1848," including those of Sand and Balzac, from whom Friedrich Engels said he had learned more than from all historical and economical treatises put together. The ground was thus prepared for that remarkable revolution of 1848 of which the leaders were a poet, Lamartine, and a social theorist, Blanc. As one might expect from Romantic poets and novelists, the spirit was rather more emotional than logical. The mood was messianic or apocalyptic; the "people" were on the march, tyrants trembled on their thrones or in their counting houses. A splendid new world would dawn after brave deeds by popular heroes had overthrown them. The French Revolution, heretofore unpopular, was rehabilitated by historians like Michelet and Quinet, not to speak of Louis Blanc. Had there not been something splendid, if terribly splendid, about that volcanic upsurge of the People? They had announced their arrival with an explosion which signalled the great revolution of modern times, the democratic revolution.

"Social Romanticism"

Lamartine and Hugo were not really socialists, 1848 was to make clear. Under the impact of that event, a split developed between the republicans or democrats and the working-class socialists which helped doom the revolution. Prior to 1848, these two strains mingled in a chorus of slogans about social justice, popular rights, and the march of the masses.

In England there was something similar, if more restrained befitting the national temper. There was nothing restrained about the Scotsman Carlyle, or such working-class spokesmen as the Irishman Feargus O'Connor. The novels of Dickens and Mrs. Gaskell contain their share of social protest. The Chartist movement was a more impressive organization of the actual working-class people than anything in France. But Britain already had her liberal reforms and she had a national Parliament with deep roots in the national tradition. The great debate of the 1840s turned on the relatively concrete issue of free trade versus protection. During this struggle to repeal the tariffs on grains, Richard Cobden and John Bright organized the Anti-Corn Law League and carried political debate down to the grassroots level. Great Britain avoided revolution in 1848 and proceeded toward social democracy at a more moderate pace.

Democracy might now be observed in relatively successful operation in the United States of America. In the mid-1830s Alexis de Tocqueville returned from his visit there to write *Democracy in America*, one of the political classics of the century. Countless others went to America and

Tocqueville and Democracy

wrote travel books, but Tocqueville's was a uniquely philosophical mind. He wrote against the background of a considerable discussion of democracy in France at this time. And he brought to the task the new ideas of a social-scientific methodology as proposed by Bonald, Saint-Simon, Comte. Consequently *Democracy in America* is a good deal more than a travel book; it is a work of systematic sociology. Highly praised at the time, it has kept a considerable repute ever since. It is a truly objective work, not a partisan one: Tocqueville was amused to find that some thought he had written against democracy and others that he had written for it. A liberal noble, Tocqueville reminds us a great deal of Montesquieu; he had learned from Burke, too, as well as many others. The integrity, moderation, and wisdom of a book that nevertheless sparkles with ideas has earned it its high standing in the literature of politics and society.

The question Tocqueville was really interested in was whether this new thing, democracy, which his historical sense told him was inevitably on the way, could be reconciled with liberty and with traditional European civilization. Was it a triumph of barbarism from within, a revolt of the blind masses certain to destroy culture? Would it lead to a new despotism? These things had been said. The social scientist in Tocqueville wished to test them by a method more fruitful than mere theorizing. So he went to the United States and observed.

Social scientist that he was, Tocqueville was not free from ideological influences. A moderate, a liberal, he wished, he said, both to "allay the terrors" of the reactionaries and "calm the ardor" of the radicals. Perhaps Tocqueville found in America what he wanted to find—as it has been alleged. The charge is only partly true. He did find a mixture of good and bad. For example, Tocqueville allayed the fears that democracy meant wild instability, dictatorship, destruction of property, and irreligion. Here in the democratic United States property was safe, religion flourished, and there was no fear of violent revolution. Give power to the people and they will become responsible, Tocqueville implied; democracy has its own safety valves. On the other hand, he found science and literature mediocre in the United States, the uncommon man intimidated by the mass, and he feared that this was a law of democracies; he was among the first to complain of democratic conformism and the "tyranny of the majority." To some of his contemporaries in Europe he apparently taught that democratic society destroys liberty. But in the main his temperate and sympathetic appraisal helped the republican cause in France. Tocqueville himself, though by no means an egalitarian, served in the short-lived Second Republic born of the revolution of 1848 and never learned to love the despot who ended its life, Louis Napoleon. Liberty was his passion. He loved England, as Montesquieu had, and John Stuart Mill was one of his friends; thus he seems close to British liberalism.

His moderate note was unusual in France in the 1830s and 1840s. Proudhon Among the new socialist voices of the 1840s there was Pierre-Joseph Proudhon, a man of the people himself, whose chief message was to abolish unearned increment and unproductive property: "What is the producer? Nothing. What should he be? Everything." An enemy of statism, Proudhon suggested "mutualism" or farmers' and workers' cooperatives as the answer to economic injustice; he was an ancestor of the anarchist-syndicalists, and perhaps also of the populists and Henry George agrarians. But his revolutionary spirit appeared in his advocacy of class war, his call to the working classes to rise up and throw off their chains, as the Communist Manifesto of 1848 put it. Marx later ridiculed Proudhon for the crudeness of his thought, but he influenced Marx, being in the 1840s and 1850s the best known of the radical socialist theoreticians. Proudhon had no faith in democratic processes as such; "social reform will never come out of political reform, political reform must emerge from social reform." "Universal suffrage is the materialism of the Republic." But Proudhon seldom stayed long in one position; he seemed "determined that none should share his views." Marx was right about the shoddiness of much of Proudhon's thought. But he possessed a style, an aptitude for phrase-making, along with a burning sense of social injustice.

Paris was discontented and bored with the prosaic "bourgeois monarchy" of Louis-Philippe, which had come into existence in 1830. Though liberal enough to permit free speech and encourage education, its constitution denied representation to all but a few and its social philosophy was largely laissez-faire liberalism—its motto, "enrich yourself." The dominant class was the "grande bourgeoisie." In the cafes of Paris lesser men listened to Proudhon's call to revolution. When the revolution came he disagreed with it; "they have made a revolution without ideas," he declared. He laughed at the panacea of the influential socialist Louis Blanc: state-owned factories. To Proudhon the root of the matter was demand, not production. Leave the working class without adequate purchasing power and the state factories would stagnate quite as much as privately owned ones, for want of a market. Proudhon's was the classical statement of the underconsumption theory of economic depression.

Background of 1848 Revolution

Proudhon's *What is Property?* (1841) had been preceded by Louis Blanc's *The Organization of Labor* (1840). At this time also, it may be recalled, Étienne Cabet's *Voyage to Icaria* appeared, with its message of utopian communism. Blanc, an indefatigable writer, produced a stream of works in these years including a laudatory history of the French Revolution and a *History of Ten Years,* in which he cataloged the sins of the capitalistic Orleanist regime. Blanc stood for a blend of Jacobin democracy and socialism that perhaps lacked logical consistency but was proclaimed with great eloquence; it rejected Saint-Simonian authoritarianism in favor of a more democratic political order, yet was socialist in its

Louis Blanc

attacks on private property in the means of production. Blanc did not, like Proudhon, call for violent revolution, or like the intrepid Blanqui, socialist working-class leader, seek to practice it. He evidently believed that the people would freely vote for socialism if given a chance. The results of the elections of 1848 severely disillusioned him, and he appears then to have discovered for the first time that France was a country of peasants and not of Parisian left-wing journalists. At that time he retreated somewhat from democracy. Later, however (he lived well into the Third Republic), he continued to support a moderate, democratic, and "gradualist" socialism against Marxists and Anarchists.

Mazzini   Among other rebels and prophets who led the way to 1848, there was the Italian Giuseppe Mazzini, a passionate Genoese who as a youth joined the *Carbonari* and vowed his life to the cause of national liberation for Italy under a popular government. He spent most of his life as an exile in London but returned during the revolutions of 1848 to take part in those tumultuous events, presiding over the short-lived Roman Republic of 1848–1849. His prolific and eloquent pen gained him a place as one of the chief writers of this time and a great leader of the Italian *risorgimento,* which in 1860–1861 became the most exciting movement in Europe. If the gallant soldier of liberty, Garibaldi, was the most popular figure of the Italian national political revival, Mazzini was its spiritual leader. Belonging as it does to the generation of "social romanticism," the eloquence that so bedazzled his contemporaries may seem bombastic and hollow today, though on the whole it wears better than most of that sort of thing. Mazzini, with Louis Blanc, belonged among the democratic socialists. Hostile to liberalism because it was too negative and selfish, he affirmed the value of both democracy and "association." He was equally against class war and individualism; all men should be brothers, there should be solidarity, and there should be religion, a religion of humanity. Mazzini quickly quarreled with Marx and Bakunin in the First International; he was too radical for Italian liberals, who fought him for control of the *risorgimento,* but too conservative for the left-wing proletarian rebels. Like Blanc, he called himself a republican and obviously derived from Rousseau and the French Revolutionary tradition; he was an Italian Jacobin. (Northern Italy had been as eager for the French Revolution as France; Mazzini's father had lived under the Ligurian Republic.) But his stress on national liberation and a social-democratic *mystique* put him in the center of nineteenth-century ideology.

Lamennais, Blanc, Proudhon, and Mazzini supplied a good part of the fuel for the engine of revolution that roared down the track only to crash in 1848. Broadly speaking they formed a brotherhood of social protest with generous ideals, but they failed to agree and their thought was often vague. These limitations must probably be held responsible in good part for the failures of 1848. Nevertheless the ferment of social thought in this generation must be recognized as a powerful force in modern Europe. It produced most of the ideas, in embryo, on which social reformers of all sorts have been living ever since.

But the experiences of 1848, a year which began with democratic revolutions all over Europe and ended with the confusion and dis- comfiture of these revolutions, caused a temporary reaction against all forms of "social romanticism." In general, the sad failure of the revolu- tions of 1848 was like a large bucket of very cold water poured on the slogan-intoxicated men who had begun them so hopefully. All over conti- nental Europe the sobering up was much in evidence; people felt that there had been too many daydreams and vague formulae, too little precise thinking. The reaction was toward realistic means and limited objectives. Like all reactions, it went far in the opposite direction. The feeling spread that power alone counts, and practical methods of politics. It was a Ger- man (evidently Ludwig von Rochau) who coined the word *Realpolitik;* but the same idea could be found from one end of Europe to the other. Thus 1848 was almost a repetition of 1789, in that the ideals and ideas which inspired it turned out to be too vague and were held to have caused more harm than good because of this flaw: zeal without knowledge. The counterparts of Rousseau and Voltaire were Proudhon and Mazzini; with more of Romantic fire, they had as little of concrete social engineering. If Bonald and Maistre had suggested a more realistic approach, this was swept aside because they were conservatives; if Saint-Simon demanded science, he had in reality supplied only ideology. Evidently much yet remained to do before that ideal human society could become more than a vision or dream. Again there was a reaction away from utopias.

Not until the 1880s did the socialist movement really revive; only in the 1860s did it show any spark of renewed life. "Social romanticism" and indeed Romanticism of all sorts went out of fashion among men of letters. The success of the Italian national liberation movement in 1861 might seem to be an exception to this; but in actuality this miracle was the work of realists and moderates, not of Garibaldi and Mazzini. During the French Second Empire, when another Bonaparte arose on the grave of the Republic, the reigning intellectual system was the austerely scien- tific credo of Positivism.

But it is also true that bourgeois liberalism and political economy became less harshly dogmatic. It too had had its heyday between 1830 and 1848; the uncompromising features of the *grande bourgeoisie's* political and social outlook had had not a little to do with bringing on that outburst of resentment, the revolutions of 1848. After 1848 the suffrage was less restricted, despite the apparent failure of that revolu- tion. Even Napoleon III was careful to have his mandate affirmed and reaffirmed from time to time by universal suffrage, which has never ceased to exist in France, whatever the regime, since its installation in

Disillusionment after 1848

1848. Dogmatic laissez-faire, too, received less emphasis. Napoleon ran something of a welfare state, the realistic conservative Bismarck installed sweeping welfare measures in Germany, and Great Britain began to move in that direction soon. *Realpolitik* turned away from romantic visions of utopia, but it also turned away in some measure from the absolute dogma of laissez-faire, equally visionary.

Whatever the final verdict, this generation of 1815–1848 must be granted primacy in the modern Western world, perhaps repaying close study more than any other one by those who wish to understand present-day problems, dreams, and outlooks. These ideologies—liberal, socialist, nationalist, conservative—are still the basic value structures for most people in Europe and its offshoots.

The history of the human race is the history
of growth.

FREDERIC HARRISON

If there is the mob, there is the people also. I
speak now of the middle classes—of those
hundreds of thousands of respectable persons
—the most numerous and by far the most
wealthy order in the community.

LORD BROUGHAM

Classical Ideologies
of the Mid-Nineteenth Century:
Mill, Comte, Darwin

3

THE MID-VICTORIAN ERA

After revolution and Romanticism receded in 1849, Europe entered
upon a period which could well be described as the classical age of the
nineteenth century. It was the mid-Victorian era, with all the phrase
conveys: middle-class domination, comfortable bourgeois virtues, industrialism and free trade, political stability with an undercurrent of working-
class distress. Victoria, the personification of the bourgeois virtues, reigned
only in Great Britain, but Great Britain led the way into the industrial
age, and in other places, notably Germany and the Low Countries, "Victorian" phenomena could be observed.

In Great Britain at mid-century, the classical school of economics
reigned, its laissez-faire injunctions slightly modified by the post-Ricardian
economists, but only slighty; by 1846 it had converted most statesmen.
Along with it flourished the popular ideology of self-help, making perennial best sellers of such books as Samuel Smiles' *Lives of the Engineers*,
the stories of poor boys who made their way to wealth and glory: Faraday
was a blacksmith's son, Stephenson a collier's, Telford a shepherd's.
George Orwell, the modern essayist and novelist, remarked that his father
had read only two books in his life, the Bible and Smiles' *Self-Help*—

The
Victorian
Frame of
Mind

probably a typical Victorian intellectual history. The powerful London *Economist* assumed dogmatically and without any question that the sum of private interests "is always the same as the public interest." Free trade conquered in the struggle concerning repeal of the corn laws (grain tariffs) in the 1840s. While the factory laws removed the worst abuses of child and woman labor, the country having been stirred by Parliamentary investigations into this cruel scandal, there still remained no protection for adult male workers against the law of the market in wages; the trades unions had barely begun their long march to respectability and power in 1850. (They did not receive legal recognition until 1870 and were not a strong factor before the 1880s.) With government as well as wages cheap, in this incredible paradise of private enterprise by modern standards (no taxes, no labor unions!), industry and invention flourished, the nation seemed to grow rich, and British power, influence, and prestige was never greater. Victoria came to excel even Queen Bess as a long-lived symbol of greatness.

This was the heyday of the middle classes, whose peculiar ethos permeated the era. Recently arrived through hard work and frugality, the middle classes radiated respectability. This was the "age of improvement," as historian Asa Briggs has named it. Some have spoken of a "mid-Victorian combination of Puritanism and Enlightenment." French morals were frowned upon (witness the reaction to Swinburne), also those practiced by English romantics and lords in the Regency era just prior to Victoria's accession. Such magisterial organs as the *Edinburgh Review* dispensed the dogmas of "free trade and tight morals," high intellectual seriousness, and a robust common sense ("masculine sanity," G. M. Young calls it) along with a deplorable lack of taste and imagination in the arts. Indeed, the arts were often declared to be a waste of time. The middle class doubtless shared some traits all over Europe, but Puritanism and individualism were not so prominent elsewhere. In regard to Puritanism, it may suffice to recall that over in Vienna, on the banks of the beautiful blue Danube, the bourgeoisie at this time built a culture marked by its music, gayety, and charm. Nor could the French bourgeoisie ever have displayed that egregious prudery found among the British middle classes, who (so we are told) segregated the male and female authors on library shelves.[1] Nevertheless, the high seriousness and

---

[1] Victorian prudery must not be misunderstood as an anemic rejection of the sexual impulse, however. As Walter E. Houghton points out, "The major reason why sex was so frightening to the Victorians was the glaring fact that . . . sexual license in England not only existed on a large scale but seemed to be increasing." The Romantic cult of free love (Shelley, Byron) survived, and French socialism and bohemianism threatened from across the channel. The Obscene Publications Bill of 1857 reacted to a large popular literature of pornography. The Victorians knew that sex was a potent force—so potent that, as Matthew Arnold observed, it needed restraining rather than encouraging.

earnest moralism of the Victorians was a bond that stretched broadly from Samuel Smiles to Matthew Arnold, whatever other differences the merchant and the poet-intellectual had. The wish to edify and to improve, to overcome evil and spread enlightenment, was at the bottom of it—no unworthy spirit, despite the prudery into which it might stray. For all their blind spots, the British middle classes, strong and energetic, led the way to prosperity and success, and wished to build a vigorous society in their own image.

On the other side of the picture, callousness, poverty, ugliness, and degradation caused Carlyle, Ruskin, and others to protest against the very foundations of this civilization, alleging it to lie in selfishness and materialism. Hazlitt had written that "the carriage that glitters like a meteor along the streets of the metropolis often deprives the wretched inmate of the distant cottage of the chair he sits on, the table he eats on, the bed he lies on." Shelley had burned with indignation at the factories of England and the suffering they imposed on the hapless creatures who labored incredibly long hours at work that was both body- and soul-destroying. Coleridge had declared that if society disclaimed all responsibility to the poor, as the economists and liberals preached, then the poor would feel no sense of belonging and would eventually rebel in a class war. Disraeli in 1844 wrote in his celebrated novel *Sybil* that there were indeed two nations in England, the rich and the poor, utter strangers to each other.

Victorian Social Protest

John Ruskin claimed that the ugliness of the factory towns, and the appalling lack of artistic sensitivity in the country generally, was a part of the social order, knit deeply into the outlook of the middle classes whose ideology was a blend of Puritanism and Utilitarianism, both absolutely hostile to all the arts. Certainly, until near the end of the century, the slums of London and other cities showed a subhuman degradation seldom if ever equalled in Europe, and until the 1880s very little concern about this was displayed by anyone; it was not society's business, but the individual's. In *Unto This Last*, Ruskin voiced an eloquent protest against the economics of irresponsibility and the social creed of selfish neglect.

Dickens in *Hard Times* (1854) flagellated a society that had just finished congratulating itself, upon the occasion of the great Crystal Palace Exhibition, for its infinite progressiveness. It is a world made up of Bounderbys, greedy capitalists unscrupulously pursuing success, and Gradgrinds, who, aided by Utilitarianism and Political Economy, have reduced life to statistics and forgotten its beauty. The city has become a place of loss of identity in the lonely crowd; the factory is a scene of ugliness and inhumanity; the bourse and market-place erase human connections. And this society does not even deliver its one specialty, more and more material goods, for hundreds of thousands are in want and "hard times" may throw the whole economic system into confusion.

The protest voice, thundering indignantly like Carlyle's and Ruskin's and Dickens', exposing the structure of exploitation as did, for example, Charles Kingsley's famous tract *Cheap Clothes and Nasty,* indicated a considerable Victorian social conscience. Not until after 1880 did it have much effect, but it undoubtedly prepared the way for the break-through against laissez-faire that then occurred. Carlyle became unbalanced in his hatred of the liberal orthodoxy and discredited himself by some of his later pronouncements, which have a Fascist ring to modern ears. (Such were the abjurations against parliamentary "talking shops" and in favor of strong, silent dictators; the contempt for democracy; the worship of heroes; the scorn for humanitarianism, seen as shabby sentimentalism. The Tory Socialist became more and more the Tory.) An incomparably vivid prose stylist, Carlyle was read by the Victorians but they discounted his views as chronically wrong-headed. (See John Morley's characteristic essay on Carlyle.) Matthew Arnold, perhaps the most civilized of all the Victorians, was a critic of the narrowness of the bourgeoisie, the "philistinism" of the middle classes as well as the crudities of the landed gentry; he scored their politics, their education, their manners. The fact is that almost all the greater Victorian writers were critics of their society. The charge of complacency will not stick against Tennyson and Browning, the great Victorian poets, though they have been accused of it.

The most celebrated and symbolic thinker of mid-Victorian England was John Stuart Mill. His early career may be familiar to many from the well-known account of it in his *Autobiography.* Brought up in the strictest Benthamite discipline, he rebelled and turned to Wordsworth and Coleridge for relief. His searching essays on Bentham and Coleridge reveal the patient catholicity of his fine mind, looking for the value in each figure while peeling off the dross. He became interested in Comte, finding in his discipline and social sense a corrective to British individualism though there was much in the Frenchman he could not stomach. Indeed Mill, who lies buried with his wife at Avignon, always owed much to Frenchmen, something to be remembered when one sees comments on his "typically British" philosophy. He read the novels of Dickens; he formed a firm friendship with Carlyle for a time. Tocqueville's great work on democracy attracted him; Kant and Hegel mostly repelled him, being too metaphysical for Mill's essentially positivist mind. In the long run the mark of Bentham prevailed: Mill was essentially the rationalist and liberal. But his thought has been summed up as a series of compromises, and no nineteenth-century thinker read more widely and sympathetically than Mill.

What compromises did Mill suggest? Empiricist and positivist in his philosophy, he refused to say with the Kantians (as he construed them) that the laws of thought are merely mental categories; he held them to exist objectively, and he prepared a systematic treatise of inductive logic. Classic defender of the liberty of the individual, he showed some sym-

Mill's
Compromises

pathy to Comte and French socialism, up to a point; fearing the element of compulsion that lurks in every socialist scheme, he approved voluntary cooperation. In his famous textbook on the *Principles of Political Economy,* his foundation was individualistic capitalism yet he was prepared to entertain exceptions to the rule wherever a sound case could be made —and the exceptions, it has been noted, grew with every edition of the *Principles,* so that Mill has been claimed as an ancestor of English socialism (Fabian). Sceptic in religion, near the end of his life he felt the bankruptcy of "scientism" and edged cautiously toward belief in a finite God; at any rate he recognized the human need for religious experience. He had always been willing to temper the narrower individualism of the Benthamites with some of Coleridge's feeling for the community. Doubting sometimes about democracy because of his love of liberty, he believed the strongest argument for it to be that it is a process of education; and Mill always remained the optimist, feeling perhaps that all men were potentially as rational as himself. British empiricism was deeply engrained in him, and a part of that tradition was an openness, including Locke's doctrine of a malleable human nature (Mill believed this strongly) and Hume's dislike of dogmas. Resolutely open-minded he remained all his life, and thus has seemed the classic "liberal."

His strongest hatreds were of censorship, intolerance, conformity— anything that interfered with individual liberty. His best-known work, the essay *On Liberty* (1859), to which his wife, Harriet, a remarkable woman, contributed much, is the classic argument for the maximum of individual liberty. "The only purpose for which power can be rightfully exercised over any member of a civilized community against his will is to prevent harm to others. His own good, either physical or moral, is not a sufficient warrant. He cannot rightfully be compelled to do or forbear . . . because in the opinion of others to do so would be wise or even right." (Mill stressed that this was in a *civilized* community; "barbarians" would do best with an enlightened despot.) The goal and purpose of mankind, the only end worth striving for, was to Mill the complete development of the individual's powers to the highest possible point; he quoted Humboldt and remarked that "few persons, out of Germany" comprehend this, suggesting a Kantian or Romantic source of his doctrine of freedom.

On Liberty

The argument of *On Liberty* then majestically unfolds for liberty of thought and discussion. The doctrine we suppress may be true, unless we assert infallibility for received opinion; or, if not true, it may contain *some* truth; or, even if it contains little or no truth, dissent is necessary to prevent intellectual stagnation; if we do not have to defend our creed, we will forget why we hold it.[2] Mill next makes it clear that under certain circumstances speech cannot be free, as when it is "a positive

Arguments for Freedom of Expression

[2] Mill's fellow Victorian, the great Roman Catholic John Henry Newman, adjusted his religion to liberalism by arguing, similarly, that heresy is necessary to faith. Unless error forces us to clear thinking, we do not perfectly know our creed.

instigation to some mischievous act." Justice Oliver Wendell Holmes later observed that there can be no freedom to cry "fire!" in a crowded theater, and this is about what Mill meant. One always wonders when reading Mill how far agreement could ever be reached on the exact or even approximate boundaries of the limits he mentions. Holmes used the above principle to ban free speech in war time by those who allegedly did not support the war, a ruling which others thought to be an outrageous violation of civil liberties. But Mill seemed to think that these boundaries can be made clear.

He believed at any rate that the liberty necessary to human dignity and growth was all too lacking in the modern world. He stressed the danger from the "tyranny of the majority," which had replaced regal despotism as a threat to liberty. "That so few now dare to be eccentric marks the chief danger of the time." Everything was becoming standardized, from shoes to ideas, and Mill complained, as so many have done since, of the mass culture that was stamping conformity and mediocrity on everyone. Reverting to his effort to defend the individual, Mill sought to meet the objection against his own criteria that, after all, everything we do *does* concern others. About all that Mill succeeded in doing was to reassert his position. When we have finished reading this extraordinary essay we are likely to feel that while Mill has presented an incomparable discussion of the issues and made an eloquent appeal for the free individual, he has not resolved the ancient dilemma of liberty versus authority, the individual against society. He has expressed a preference for the individual; but anyone who prefers to stress society's claims can easily turn most of Mill's formal arguments against him. (One such Victorian answer to Mill was written by James Fitzjames Stephen, *Liberty, Equality, Fraternity.*) But this tract with its magisterial style and high seriousness remains one of the great Victorian period pieces.

Mill and Liberalism

Mill's social-economic views, while also fundamentally "liberal," were not complacent. He questioned in a well-known passage whether all the machinery thus far invented had yet lightened the toil of a single person, and said that "the restraints of communism would be freedom in comparison with the present condition of a majority of the human race." In the *Political Economy* he defined property as what one has "produced by one's own exertions" (or received by legitimate gifts from one who did so earn it). But he held that the worker in the factory is not entitled to the whole of his produce, because machinery and materials are also involved.

Mill may be credited with almost single-handedly giving to liberalism the larger meaning it has since conveyed to the minds of Anglo-Americans, of "an attitude rather than a set of dogmas" (Theodore M. Greene)—the attitude of open-mindedness, dispassionate and sceptical consideration of all views, faith in a process, a method, a climate of opinion rather than in any particular creed. Liberalism had previously meant, much more nearly, the doctrines of atomistic individualism, hedonism, and also laissez-faire: the "economic man" of Adam Smith, the calculating pleasure-seeker of Jeremy Bentham. As such, it had been a somewhat narrow and barren ideology, if a potent one. Generous-minded men, filled with large visions of hope in human brotherhood, men such as Mazzini, for example, who despised what he knew as "liberalism," were repelled by it, declaring it to be selfish and materialistic. But Mill imparted to English liberalism his own catholicity and libertarianism, his steadfast faith in the free individual as something spiritually noble. "The saint of rationalism" has recently been seen (by Maurice Cowling) as really at heart a kind of narrow-minded fighter for his own particular set of preconceptions; but this view is unusual and the interpretation strained: Mill's typical spirit is quite the reverse. Under his influence even liberalism's deep-seated fear of the state could melt; for no dogma is sacred, only the individual is, and perhaps he may be defended and strengthened by some forms of state aid.

Mid-century liberalism was represented in France, where it was weaker than in Great Britain but far from nonexistent, by Prévost-Paradol, whose *France Nouvelle* (1868) is a kind of Gallic *On Liberty*. (Both Mill and Prévost-Paradol, as a matter of fact, were influenced by Alexis de Tocqueville, perhaps the greatest liberal of them all and another Frenchman.) Prévost-Paradol regards democracy perhaps a bit more favorably than Mill, seeing in the people a check on Parliament, though he would have the popular will checked by an upper legislative chamber not popularly elected, an independent judiciary, and strong institutions of local government. This decentralization and pluralism carried echoes of the Ancien Regime in a France strongly centralized since Napoleon; antistatist and antisocialist, but libertarian and to a degree democratic (universal suffrage), Paradol's "New France" would indeed have been a new blend of ingredients in the French tradition, and was not so far from what soon came into existence in the Third Republic. He wrote it in the last days of the Second Empire, when even Napoleon III was making his way toward the "liberal Empire." After his defeat in war and the subsequent shock to French pride, against all expectations a liberal-democratic republic arose from the ashes and gradually put down roots in France.

French Liberalism: Prévost-Paradol

This tribute to the spirit of the age was matched by Great Britain's step in liberalizing the suffrage in 1867, after intensive debate and much lamentation from those who feared the death of liberty as well as stability at the hands of a mobocracy.[3] A new era of politics came in the wake of the Second Reform Bill, with new leaders and new issues. It was, for

Second Reform Act in Britain

[3] These "Adullamites," as John Bright derisively christened them, led by Robert Lowe, contributed the most brilliant and enthusiastic speeches to the great debate.

Britain, the decisive turning point of the century politically, the first Reform Act of 1832 having really not brought any marked change in the aristocratic tone and tenor of British political life. Whether the delicately balanced British political mechanism could really survive democracy, commentators as wise as Walter Bagehot honestly doubted; it was as much a gamble here as in France. But in both countries the feeling was that there could be no turning back, and for the rest of the century the task was adjustment to this potent force, mass democracy. Nothing influenced thought nearly as much.

Many dynamic processes were at work transforming Europe and the world in this epoch. Italy and Germany attained their national unification (1860–1871) in the most exciting developments on the Continent. Russia freed her serfs (1861) and began slowly to advance toward a modern industrial civilization. Europe achieved her greatest power ascendancy of all time in the world, expanding after 1870 all over the globe in the era of "imperialism." Wealth, power, and success in the realm of politics and social structure (relatively, at least) brought a mighty surge of confidence; belief in progress approached the status of a religion. Technology inspired daily gasps of wonder and practical science almost monopolized public attention, for this was the age of Faraday and Edison, Gauss and Siemens, Pasteur and Hertz. The national cultures of each European state came of age as popular education and patriotic history held up to admiration the success story of each people: England from Alfred to Victoria, France from Capets to the Republic, accounts of slow but inevitable growth.

Nineteenth-Century Progress

Spiritually, Europe was far from at peace; the surge of material power and wealth carried in its wake grimmer phenomena, such as industrialism's bleak landscapes and exploited workers, or a bourgeois vulgarization of culture. It also brought the celebrated Victorian crisis of religious faith. But the classic age of the nineteenth century produced some classic ideologies. Among the most important figures were August Comte, Karl Marx, Herbert Spencer, and John Stuart Mill, all of whom might be described as synthesizers of social doctrine, creators of systems of secular ideology. Charles Darwin fathered a scientific ideology for the age of science. Socialism, liberalism, and democratic nationalism assumed the stature of popular creeds by which men lived, with traditional Christianity's hold generally declining. Romanticism received a check, or at least a dilution: literary realism and naturalism became prominent, bearing strong social themes—we are more likely to meet novels about working people or ordinary burghers than about exquisite souls or North American savages.

Increase in Literacy

Europe was becoming more populous and more complex; far more people were being drawn into the charmed circle of literacy and intellectual culture each year. National education systems grew up in these years, transforming the populace of western Europe from largely unlettered to almost completely literate—elementary education, not secondary, as yet, but still an advance of incalculable importance. For the intellectual historian, this increase in the percentage of people to be considered as part of "the European mind" is as significant as the absolute increase in population, so notable a feature of this era which was dramatically diminishing the death rate through epochal advances in medicine, public health, and food production and distribution. Together, they accomplished a numerical revolution of staggering dimensions. The age of the masses was beginning.

But there were large differences between the nations of Europe in this respect: while England, on one extreme, gave an elementary education to just about every child in the kingdom by 1895, Russia advanced much more slowly and Italy had only about half defeated illiteracy. The industrialized countries of western Europe opened a large gap between themselves and the more "backward" peoples of eastern Europe, not only in education but in wealth, social mobility, degree of popular participation in civil liberties, and in government.

No single theme exhausts the richness of the generations lying between the revolutions of 1848 and the end of the century; indeed, eclecticism was a notable feature of the epoch, a drawing on all past styles in architecture, for example. But on the whole, intellectually speaking the dominant motif continued to be that of social ideologies, now extended into massive synthetic systems. Pure philosophy and religious speculation went on, but do not stand out for us as characteristic. Comte, Marx, and Darwin will always hold their rank as the classic statements of the century, whatever ravages time may make in their once proud systems. Comte and Marx offered what we see today as systems of secular religion based on science (though Marx would have vehemently denied that he created a religion). Darwin, strictly a scientist, revolutionized many areas of thought and infused strength into ideologies stressing evolution. These are the three giants of the nineteenth century's noontime, as Nietzsche, Freud, and Bergson were the masters of its twilight period.

COMTE AND POSITIVISM

Comte's first writings go back to the early 1820s, when he was working under Saint-Simon; the crux of his Positive Philosophy appeared in six volumes between 1830 and 1842. Partly overlooked during the romantic revolutionary excitement of the 1830s and 1840s, Positivism emerged, somewhat transformed, to become the reigning intellectual orthodoxy of the Second Empire, 1851–1870. Through John Stuart Mill principally, Comte's influence spread into England. It is recognized now as one of the leading systematic philosophies of the century, though, in common with the similar great "social syntheses" made by Marx and Spencer, its rating may not be high. These vast edifices of thought which tried to subsume everything in one system seem incongruous today; they were the work of amateurs who assumed omniscience. But the intellectual energy that went into them cannot be denied, and for the nineteenth century they were the nearest thing there was to a new synthesis of knowledge. Basil Willey has commented that Comte was a nineteenth-century Schoolman, basing his *Summa* "not on dogmatic theology, but on dogmatic science."

Comte's Mission

He did feel acutely the need for a complete reconstruction of ideas to replace the "intellectual anarchy" that was an aftermath of the French Revolution, a feeling he shared with Maistre, Saint-Simon, Hegel. As Saint-Simon's secretary, he came to feel that the socialist Count was too much in a hurry. He was right in seeking to found a new science of society based on the positive facts and scientific method, wrong in leaping to his conclusion about the shape of the new society. But when Comte branched out on his own he showed himself quite as doctrinaire as Saint-Simon. Certainly the note of authority was strong in his plan for social reconstruction. Order must be reestablished in Europe, and having found the right foundation Comte proposed to make everybody accept it, by means of a suggested authoritarian social structure of which the high priests of Positivism were to be the directors. Comte was as anti-individualist as any socialist, though he preferred to keep private property and the family. He was, if anything, more so. John Stuart Mill, who was attracted to some features of Positivism, pronounced Comte's social plan "the completest system of spiritual and temporal despotism which ever yet emanated from a human brain, unless possibly that of Ignatius Loyola." Its hostility to representative government and approval of the Napoleonic dictatorship gave it its standing under the Second Empire.

The Three-Stage Theory

Comte thought he had laid the foundations for social reorganization in his philosophy. The method appropriate to modern times is the scientific or "positive." Comte put forward his famous Three Stages theory of human development, according to which society passes from the Theological to the Metaphysical to the Positive stage, based on the dominant mode of thought typical of each period. His history, like Hegel's, was highly speculative; it seems impossible to fit the actual facts into this scheme. For example, anthropologists no longer accept the progression within religion as postulated by Comte, from fetishism to polytheism to monotheism (see W. T. Albright, *From the Stone Age to Christianity*, p. 171). Historians would have to point out among other things that science appeared as early as the ancient Greeks and metaphysics as late as Comte's contemporary Hegel. If we reduce the Comtean formula to the statement that primitive peoples are not capable of modern thought, it becomes little more than a tautology.

In brief, the same objections to so staggeringly oversimplified a scheme may be raised against Comte's as against other examples of this sort of thing: Marx's five stages, Hegel's three political epochs, etc.[4] Nevertheless, these "philosophies of history" though now outmoded were exciting at this time and the nature of their appeal may readily be seen. We have already discussed this in connection with Hegel. Comte had at least this advantage over the German, that his historical system purported to rest on the facts and not on a speculative theory, thus was attuned to the scientific age. So discriminating a critic as John Stuart Mill thought the three stages an illuminating and reasonably accurate key to the natural evolution of civilization.

Europe was now in the positive stage, and needed to reconstruct its civilization on that basis. To Comte this meant, to repeat, a highly organized social order. The existing stage of liberty and laissez-faire he regarded as the interlude of anarchy between two eras, an anarchy he proposed to bring to an end as speedily as possible. The new scientific order would not be less organic and hierarchical than the older orders dominated by priests and metaphysicians.

Positivism

Positivism means the method of observed facts, handled with the use of hypothesis but refraining from any conclusions about the substantive nature of reality. Comte agreed with Kant that science studies only the phenomena. In his own words: "The human spirit, recognizing the impossibility of obtaining absolute ideas, renounces the search for origins and goals of the universe and the effort to know the innermost causes of things, in order to concentrate on discovery, by experiment combined with reason and observation, of the effective laws, i.e. their unchanging relations of succession and similarity." This was not exactly new, and Ernest Renan later reproached Comte with having said, "in bad French," what all scientific minds had known for two hundred years. This was not quite fair; it had really only been known widely and clearly since Kant, and Comte undoubtedly revealed some of its practical implications. He was perhaps philosophically more astute than Marx, though the latter held a Ph.D., for Marx assumed a dogmatic materialism which Comte knew was untenable: we are not justified in saying what the essence of reality is. (Marx held a low opinion of Comte, perhaps in part because he was a rival; "this is miserable compared to Hegel," he thought. Lenin would follow Marx in discarding positivism or phenomenalism for

---

[4] In Italy the "new science" of G. Vico, dating from the eighteenth century, came into its own at this time. Vico's phases of all civilizations were the religious (theocratic), heroic (aristocratic) and humane (democratic). Somewhat like Hegel, the Neapolitan philosopher posited an ascending spiral, history having cycles but with something new always being kept.

a direct-copy theory of sense perception which seems naive but permits a full-blooded materialism. The Marxists have seemingly felt there is something wishy-washy about Positivism, inappropriate to revolutionaries.) Comte felt that we are not justified, either, in atheism, only in accepting the impossibility of having certain knowledge about God. Science is descriptive only; we should not even speak of "causes," only of "observable sequences."

In his Course of Positive Philosophy Comte undertook to arrange the sciences in a logical order; his, obviously, was a mind delighting in tidiness. From the most abstract, mathematics, we proceed through astronomy, physics, chemistry, biology, and finally to the most concrete, sociology, a word of Comte's invention which has stuck in our vocabulary. Sociology, at last possible in the Positive stage, steps forward to become queen and capstone of all the sciences. Of this last and greatest science Comte, of course, regarded himself as the discoverer.[5] It included what we should now call social psychology, economics, politics, history, and originally ethics. Later, Comte put ethics and religion at the top, above even sociology, and gave the world the Religion of Humanity.

The Religion of Humanity

Comte seems hopelessly to have confused his multiple roles as social scientist, social reformer, and inventor of a new religion, though he believed he had unified them. As one of his British disciples, Frederic Harrison, observed, "Positivism is at once a scheme of Education, a form of Religion, a school of Philosophy, and a phase of Socialism." Could it be all these things at once, effectively? As a school of philosophy it has survived, though Englishmen would be more apt to think of Hume as its founder. Sociology has survived as a discipline, but many others than Comte have contributed to it, and its scope is much narrower than Comte conceived. The Religion of Humanity for a time showed a surprising vitality, Postivist societies being formed in England and France for the worship of great men; there were Comtean churches as far afield as Brazil. (Positivism had a considerable popularity in Latin America.) This was in George Eliot's mind (she was an enthusiastic Comtean) when she expressed her poetic wish,

> O may I join the choir invisible
> Of those immortal dead who live again
> In minds made better by their presence.

Hero-worship had a considerable Victorian vogue, in wider circles than Comte's disciples; quite evidently it "inherited the functions once fulfilled

[5] It is to Comte's credit that he recognized that each of the sciences has to have its own methods; you cannot "reduce" social science to biological, or biological to mathematical. Certain American sociologists who seem to wish to convert social phenomena into statistics are ignoring the warning of the founder of their science, that this sort of procedure often "disguises, under an imposing verbiage, an inanity of conceptions."

by a living Church" (Walter E. Houghton)—it was a substitute for religion. From Sam Smiles to Ruskin, many a Victorian author held up to admiration, for inspiration, the lives of Great Men. But as such, the Religion of Humanity fell far short of its author's expectations. Positivism served chiefly as a rallying point for the militantly antireligious.

In regard to Positivism as "a phase of socialism," if we may so define it, it never had much appeal. Comte's social utopia most closely resembled an iron dictatorship of social scientists, which is perhaps a fate to be avoided. In practice, he sanctioned the ill-fated "democratic despotism" of Napoleon III. But it may be conceded that Comte did something to advance the cause of socialism by his criticisms of laissez-faire and by his belief that the social instincts evolve with humanity. The path of development is from selfishness to altruism, he taught.

Louis Napoleon's regime, established in 1851 on the ruins of the Second Republic, was much influenced by Saint-Simonian and Comtist ideas and undertook some interesting if inconclusive experiments in state socialism. Its economic and social policies were not failures, the collapse coming from an ill-advised foreign policy and defeat in war at the hands of Prussia. But its denial of representative government and full liberty caused its demise to be unlamented. Comte and most of his followers rejected individualism and democracy as the equivalent of anarchy. (See the discussion of Charles Maurras, page 188.)

If many of the details of Comte seem absurd, his central conception may be a valid intuition of modern man's problem. It is easy to agree with Comte that modern European civilization is "positivist." (See, for example, Karl Jaspers, *Man in the Modern Age,* page 47, Anchor paperback edition.) Is it possible to have a civilization on this basis, that is, without faith in God, without a metaphysic, with only science and technology, which supply our wants very well but give us no values, except to go on supplying more and more wants? Is modern society condemned to be "fissiparous," with no unity—soulless, with no values?

Many of Comte's successors were absorbed in just such problems. Positivism became extremely fashionable in France between 1850 and 1870. Its disciples included Emil Littré the lexicographer, Claude Bernard the psychologist, Hippolyte Taine, critic and historian, and Ernest Renan, one of the most brilliant and versatile French men of letters of the century. This group tended to reject Comte's dabblings in religion as an eccentricity, and accepted only his scientific method. They distinguished themselves from atheists and materialists in the manner indicated: we cannot know ultimate things or essential qualities, only the observed phenomena. They evidently thought, however, that science does give certain knowledge, which a thoroughgoing phenomenalist (*vide* Hume) could hardly believe. They searched for a religion of science. Most of them finally became aware that science itself cannot give us values, ideals, goals. Insofar as we have these, they must come from outside science.

Renan, a passionate seeker, deeply troubled by his scepticism, looked long for a religion he could square with his scientific outlook. He rejected Christianity on the grounds of evidence (his *Life of Jesus*, his best-known work, shocked the orthodox all over Europe by its critical handling of the supernatural claims), and he rejected Hegelianism as too metaphysical. He occasionally came close to doing what some disreputable young poets were about to do, make a religion of art. Like Matthew Arnold, his British contemporary and perhaps kindred spirit, Renan felt the need for religious experience and suggested an esthetic equivalent. But a "religion of science" remained his lifelong quest and he failed to find it, ending in scepticism. He came closest to finding it in a positivistic version of Hegelianism, a theme of progress running through history which gives evidence of God.

In France after 1870 Positivism suffered a decline. True, there were some eccentric survivals, especially the leader of the reactionary, nationalistic *Action Française* movement of the twentieth century, Charles Maurras and also, so vigorous a literary personality as Julien Benda. But strong forces in French thought rejected "scientism" and returned to metaphysics and religion in flat defiance of the Positivists. (Compare Henri Bergson, or the Catholic revival, or more recently Existentialism; in literature, Symbolism and Surrealism.) Intellectual France has never since felt much attraction for Positivism, apparently having received a thorough immunization in the 1850–1870 period.

In Italy, Positivism reigned as the leading philosophical school in the later part of the century, its chief systematizer being Roberto Ardigo. Comte's influence in nineteenth-century England (and the United States) was far from negligible: in the former, to the well-known names of John S. Mill, George Eliot, and Frederic Harrison one must add a number of others. In Germany, Comte's direct influence was not great, but there was a parallel movement in the form of "back to Kant"—the positivist or phenomenalist Kant, in reaction against the Romantic and Hegelian metaphysics; one might also include the materialism of the Young Hegelians (see page 71). By and large, the 1850–1880 period was uniquely "positivist." [6] Anglo-Saxon philosophy since World War I has been invaded by other forms of positivism (logical positivism) which owe less to Comte than to other sources, though there are affinities. This more recent chapter in intellectual history will be handled later.

In the broadest sense, it might be said that modern Western civiliza-

---

[6] James H. Billington, "The Intelligentsia and the Religion of Humanity," *American Historical Review*, July, 1960, discusses the vogue for Comte among Russian intellectuals in the 1870s; the French Positivist tended to supplant Hegel and to precede Marx as the leading influence from the West on Russian socio-political thought.

tion is positivistic, in that metaphysical or religious modes are not congenial to it. This would be true of the average mind, the common man's, more so than of the intellectual's or artist's. Everyday life is so surrounded with the technological and the scientific, so extensively "rationalized," so conditioned to mechanical models and explanations, that conscious mental life runs naturally and normally in grooves that can be called "positivist," that is, scientific, rational, nonmetaphysical, averse to mysticism or any truths not immediately verifiable by experiment or demonstration. For better or worse, that is the kind of culture most people live in. "What grows upon the world is a certain matter-of-factness," Walter Bagehot wrote. He blamed it on business as well as science. So Comte, though far from inventing this feature or being the only thinker to express it, identified himself with a basic trait of modern civilization. And his belief in a tightly organized, hierarchical society ruled by the scientists may not miss by much the modern forms of totalitarianism.

The Positivism of Modern Life

A footnote on the Positivist generation is provided by imaginative literature in the mid-Victorian years. In various ways it reacted strongly against Romanticism, by retreating to a realistic, even humdrum description of the ordinary. Romanticism had begun to fade by the 1840s and was almost fully out after 1850, despite lingering vestiges. In France, the Art for Art's Sake movement accused the Romantics of sentimentality and sloppiness, demanded a greater sense of form and discipline, and also rejected Romantic subject matter ("Deliver us from the Middle Ages!" cried Theophile Gautier, the leading spirit of this school.) "Art pour l'art" insisted upon more careful craftsmanship as well as less moralizing and philosophizing in literature. These French writers were disgusted with bourgeois society, retreated to a private world, became rebels and "bohemians" and thus began a literary attitude destined to carry on into the later period. In the remarkable Baudelaire, one may see something of Romanticism, but it was at least Romanticism with a difference. Flaubert, the leading novelist of the 1850s and 1860s, practiced a severely objective, "scientific" approach to literature, and dealt realistically with far from heroic people. (See further, pages 177 ff.)

Positivism in Literature

The French writers shocked the English; but in Britain too there was an anti-Romantic reaction. The great Victorian novelists—Thackeray, Trollope, George Eliot—followed what might be called the cult of the commonplace; "the setting of tragedy moves to the abodes of the humble," observes Mario Praz, whose book on the Victorian novel is titled *The Hero in Eclipse*. A democratic art, celebrating the simple virtues of ordinary people, may be found here. The great poet Robert Browning examined man as he is. This Victorian literature differed as far as possible from the French in that it observed the Victorian reticences about sex and was highly edifying and morally earnest; the exceptions, like the Francophile Swinburne, were scandals. But the same theme of realism may be seen in both, and it is in good part a reaction to the excesses of Romanticism.

THE DARWINIAN REVOLUTION

Progress of Science

The progress of science had continued, at the end of the eighteenth century and into the nineteenth. More precise calculations on the moon, planets, and comets perfected the Newtonian system. The discovery of the planet Uranus and the satellites of Saturn owed most to the German-born English astronomer, Herschel. Having measured accurately the distance to sun and moon, and arrived at a notion of the fantastic distances of the stars, astronomers by the end of the century came upon the stunning fact of the existence of other *galaxies.* Herschel and Laplace formulated hypotheses concerning the origin of the stars and planets. The latter in 1796 summed up the *System of the World,* presenting it almost rhapsodically as a triumph of scientific method and a proof of the orderliness of nature.

There was also the break-through in chemistry. It is interesting that Coleridge, speculating about the influence of scientific ideas on other branches of knowledge, thought that the discoveries of Scheele, Priestley, and Lavoisier, "reducing the infinite variety of chemical phenomena to the actions, reactions, and interchanges of a few elementary substances," would affect philosophy and other fields of thought no less than Newtonianism had done in the eighteenth century. It did not quite prove so, but the influence was hardly negligible. It may be significant that Fredrich Engels, when illustrating the laws of dialectical materialism in the physical sciences, tended to use examples from chemistry.

The path of progress in electrical phenomena, from Volta and Galvani at the end of the eighteenth century to Michael Faraday's discovery of the generator in the 1830s, prepared for that mighty invasion of the life of man by electricity later in the century (electric lights, trolley cars, etc.). But with all due regard for these celebrated achievements, destined to alter the lives of millions and contribute to their welfare, the most significant developments in the sciences in the nineteenth century, at least from the standpoint of thought in general, lay in the realm of biology, of life, especially its evolution. The Frenchman Pasteur has been called "the Galileo of Biology" (Karl Popper) because of his contributions to bacteriology and medicine; but in the history of ideas by far the largest figure is Charles Darwin.

Geology

The road to Darwin's theory of biological evolution actually led through another science. The science of geology came into its own in the closing years of the eighteenth century. The Geneva geologist, de Saussure, seems to have been the first to use the term, in 1779. It may be said to have attained full status in 1788 when the Scotsman, James Hutton, presented his "uniformitarian" theory. All during the eighteenth century there had been speculation about the meaning of fossils and about the earth, but it was often fanciful. The German mineralogist, A. G. Werner, proposed a hypothesis in 1780 that the earth was originally engulfed in ocean, which subsided leaving behind the various formations, minerals, and fossils. This was the "catastrophist" or "neptunist" school, which had many followers, in part because it squared well with Biblical stories. Hutton then caused a sensation by proposing to account for the phe-nomena by the steady operation of the same natural forces over what then seemed immensely long periods of time. This was "uniformitarian-ism," and it stirred the wrath of some religious critics because it could hardly be adjusted to a literal reading of the Old Testament. Between the Catastrophists and the Uniformitarians a lively competition ensued— which is always good for the progress of a science. We would say today that both were partly right; but concerning the matter of the time element Hutton was right, and this revolution in time constitutes on any reckoning one of the great changes in man's conception of his world. Coming between 1788 and 1830, this revolution is comparable in some ways to the seven-teenth- and eighteenth-century revolution in astronomy: to the immensity of space, it has been well said, was added the immensity of time. "Oh, how great is the antiquity of the terrestrial globe," Lamarck, the French paleontologist, exclaimed. "And how little the ideas of those who at-tribute to the globe an existence of six thousand and a few hundred years duration from its origin to the present!"

The Revolution in Time

There were those, during the period of conservative domination in England from 1794 to 1820, who attacked Hutton and his followers as dangerous subversives; so also Lamarck in France. But as data were collected, especially in the area of paleontology, rigid conservatism had to give way. The Reverend William Buckland, an Anglican clergyman, became a leading geologist and fathered a sort of compromise between scriptural and geological views; he seemed to uphold the Deluge, yet the Bishop of Chichester noted his ambivalence in a witty paraphrase of Pope on Newton:

> Some doubts were once expressed about the Flood:
> Buckland arose, and all was clear as mud.

At this time geology, it has been said, became something like the favorite outdoor sport of the English upper classes; certainly it flourished there preeminently, though French scientists such as Cuvier and Lamarck made signal contributions.

It remained for Charles Lyell, in 1830–1833, to write the definitive geological synthesis. Lyell was a thoroughgoing uniformitarian, and he brushed aside religious objections as irrelevant. His geology formed an important part of the background for the biological discoveries of Darwin; "I feel as if my books came half out of Sir Charles Lyell's brain," Darwin once wrote. The time-revolution disposed of one obvious objection to an evolutionary theory, while increasing knowledge about fossils suggested its possiblity. But Lyell was not an evolutionist. He could not find in the fossils sufficient evidence for the transformation or progression of species, that is, one actually growing out of another. Indeed for many centuries this had been the invincible obstacle; it was a stumbling-block to evolution comparable to that which the problem of motion had presented to the Copernican theory. As in the case of the slow acceptance of the Copernican hypothesis, one finds here that Biblical prejudices played a smaller part in delaying the evolutionary theory than is often suggested. The real difficulty lay in overcoming the dogma of constancy of species, which the biological evidence seemed to support. No examples of such change of species seemed to be found in nature; on the contrary the evidence showed the opposite, such as the sterility of animal hybrids.

Earlier Hostility to Evolution

Since time immemorial, reaching back to Aristotle, European thought had speculated about a "great chain of being," a logically complete range of life forms arranged in a hierarchy from lowest to highest. The chain ascending upward may suggest evolutionism to us, but it was always then conceived as a *static* hierarchy, a plan emanating from God's mind which was pleasing in its order and which was given for all time. Forms stayed as they were and did not change. The chain of being might be conceived as organically related, like a single great body or like an electrical circuit; and it could evolve into an evolutionary theory. But the received doctrine did not entertain any notion of evolution through time, of the transformation of species by gradual and natural means. Aristotle held that the world was created from all eternity, and had no beginning —a most profoundly unevolutionary outlook. This is not to say that no one had ever proposed the idea of evolution. Among the ancient Greeks, who canvassed all ideas, Anaximander and Empedocles suggested it. As in the case of astronomy, Aristotle prevailed over their view.

The eighteenth century had shown an enormous interest in biology. Buffon was one of the most popular writers of the age, and other distinguished *philosophes* and scientists (Maupertuis, Diderot) speculated on the origins of life, the nature of species, etc., speculations quite natural in any curious age released from conventional explanations. Biology may be seen as a factor in Romanticism and German philosophy, suggesting organic to replace mechanistic images. Diderot and Maupertuis may readily be seen as anticipating Darwinism, but, again, there seemed no convincing evidence for transformation of species, and the great authority of Buffon was, on the whole, it would seem, thrown against it. These stimulating writings did serve to arouse great interest in the question. It can be said that this period between about 1750 and 1850 was like that century that elapsed between Copernicus and Newton: the question had been raised, there was much interest in it, and growing knowledge; eventually a master jigsaw-puzzle worker would fit all the pieces together.

The pieces to be fitted together came, in a fascinating manner, from many different areas of thought. Darwinism constitutes one of the most interesting of all studies in intellectual history because it shows how much science is a part of the "climate of opinion" of its day. The idea of "survival of the fittest" which Darwin was to turn to such good account as an explanation of biological evolution was suggested to him by Thomas Malthus and Herbert Spencer. Reading Malthus' *Essay on Population,* which expounded the tendency of population to increase faster than food supply, Darwin saw that this must lead to a struggle for survival in which the less durable human organisms would die and fail to reproduce themselves.[7] As for Herbert Spencer, this Victorian oracle preceded Darwin in setting forth a ruthlessly competitive natural order. The idea of natural selection through competition in a world where some must go under because there is not enough sustenance for all, came first from the economists. It was "in the air" by the 1830s and Darwin, a naturalist, picked up and applied it to his field of study. He had his hypothesis many years before he presented his proofs in 1858.

From 1800, Europe seemed to be grasping for the concept of evolution, though not until 1858 did Darwin (and, almost simultaneously, Alfred Wallace) cage the elusive idea. The Romantic approach to science known as *Naturphilosophie,* an interest of some German philosophers, thought in evolutionary terms, and sometimes believed in transmutation, but, not strictly scientific, its explanation was closer to what later became known as vitalism, that is, a life force immanent in nature which strives to fulfill itself. Schopenhauer, the interesting German philosophical pessimist, strongly believed that this life force appears in us as an instinct to live which nature uses to trick us into striving, so that the species may be reproduced, an outlook some of which may have worked its way into Darwinism. We need hardly remind the reader how historical-evolutionary the popular systems of Hegel and Comte were; this undoubtedly conditioned men to think in terms of the genetic, developmental explanation of things.[8] So it seems that the century conspired to bring about the theory of evolution.

Already, before Darwin, the French paleontologist Lamarck had

> [7] "It at once struck me that under these circumstances favorable variations would tend to be preserved, and unfavorable variations would be destroyed. The result of this would be the formation of new species."
>
> [8] But Hegel, an evolutionist in his philosophy of history, was not so in his philosophy of nature. There is no temporal, only a logical relationship between man and the lower organisms. "Nature and history are different things," and "Nature has no history" were Hegelian axioms. The cycle of nature is endless repetition from which nothing new evolves, contrary to the situation in human history.

Nineteenth-Century Evolutionary Gropings

Lamarck proposed a theory to account for the evolution of species. He believed that developed characteristics could be inherited. There are (to choose an example) Polynesian swimmers who have developed in the course of generations an unusual lung capacity, enabling them to stay under water (so we are told) as long as six or eight minutes. Lamarck would have explained this as, perhaps, many people today might do unthinkingly: each generation stretched its lungs by long practice and then handed on this lung power to the offspring. This is wrong, according to modern biologists, who follow Darwin; what happened was that people with unusually large lungs became divers, and the others did not, or perhaps drowned. Darwin usually disparaged and ridiculed Lamarck, whom he accused of intruding desire or purpose into the picture, as if the bird's *wish* to fly gradually succeeded in stretching an organ into a wing. Evolution is simply the mechanical result of survival value, on Darwin's more "scientific" explanation. Some birds happened to have more nearly winglike organs and these survived, the process being repeated for many generations. Lamarck's theory, of course, rested on the vulnerable hypothesis of the inheritability of acquired traits, though to be sure Darwin did not entirely avoid this, either.

In 1844, the Scottish encyclopedist Robert Chambers published, anonymously, *The Vestiges of the Natural History of Creation*, a work which substantially set forth the Darwinian hypothesis though without Darwin's careful accumulation of scientific evidence. It caused a considerable stir of controversy. Thus the state of the question when Darwin arrived was about as follows. The hypothesis of evolution, in the sense of the transformation of one species into another, all descending from one original form of life, was already familiar, but the evidence for it did not seem sufficient to overcome long-standing and apparently strong objections to it—chiefly, the seeming fixity of species, as attested by the sterility of hybrids, but also certain moral and theological prejudices. Geology and paleontology, however, had strongly suggested its possibility. The "climate of opinion" was favorable to the evolutionary outlook, and some economic writers had called attention to the struggle for existence. It was urgent, it seemed, to either prove or disprove the assertions of Chambers, which had aroused controversy. The Lamarckian theory was not convincing. Rapidly developing scientific knowledge in a number of fields, and far-ranging scientific expeditions over the whole face of the Voyage of globe had produced much new data about life on earth. Darwin himself the Beagle had sailed on the famous *Beagle* voyage, 1831–1836, studying and collecting zoological evidence. Thus aided, Darwin assembled all the pieces and gave an answer which convinced most independent minds of his day.

In so doing he wrote the most important book of the century, by rather general agreement, and took his place along with Galileo and

Newton among the greatest of scientists, those who have altered the entire mentality of man. A poll of distinguished people taken at the end of the century to determine the ten most influential books of the century showed that *The Origin of Species* was the only book on every list. Today, the story would hardly be different, though one or two others might also gain unanimous support.

Darwin's achievement has occasionally been disparaged, because so many other people *almost* hit upon his idea, but the soundest judgment remains in his favor. While scientific discovery like technological invention is always a social product, no credit may justly be taken away from the man who has the genius to make that discovery. Darwin was a very plain and straightforward professional scientist, without philosophical pretensions. His last work was on *The Formation of Vegetable Mould through the Action of Worms*! Subsequently he was drawn into some philosophical issues which were perhaps beyond him. But the combination of scientific research and clear thinking found in *The Origin of Species* is very nearly up to Newtonian standards.

Darwin, then, did *not* originate the theory of evolution. What he did do was (1) provide a wealth of evidence for it, that is, for the mutability of species and (2) propose the theory of natural selection to account for it. Darwin convinced most people that evolution had occurred, and today scarcely anybody doubts it. The painstaking nature of Darwin's work may be judged from the fact that it was more than twenty years between the time he got his clue from Malthus and the publication of his *Origin of Species* in 1859. Assembling data from paleontology, anatomy, experimental breeding, and other fields, the new view represented a triumph for thoroughness and collation of scientific research, a victory which rightly enhanced the prestige of science as a social institution. That is to say, it became clear with Darwin that scientific discovery is less the fitful inspiration of genius than the certain result of steady accumulation of data and the patient collation of it. Darwin had genius, but his warmest admirers confessed it was the genius of infinite pains rather than superhuman intelligence.

What Darwin Did

Darwin was persuasive not only because of the empirical evidence he drew together but because of the striking hypothesis he put forth to explain how evolution takes place. It is noteworthy that the two things were intimately connected: Darwin began his great twenty-year campaign of fact-collecting *after* he hit upon the hypothesis of natural selection, from which we may infer that a good hypothesis both stimulates and directs research. But it could be that the hypothesis was wrong as explanation, that evolution indeed has occurred but not in the way that Darwin imagined. The theory of natural selection has been modified since Darwin, principally by an understanding of the mechanism of heredity, which was not generally known until 1900.[9] Today few if any biologists deny natural selection's importance but the function of mutation, including macromutation or the accidental production of extreme variants, has brought in an additional factor. The majority of scientists think that variations in heredity *plus* natural selection account for evolution. There are a few who question whether natural selection is really a *major* cause of evolution. (No one can deny that it occurs, and plays *some* part.) It should be noted that Darwin was wrong insofar as he proposed slow and gradual evolutionary change, declaring that "nature makes no leaps." Modern mutation theory stresses the sudden leaps. The giraffe did not get his long neck inch by inch, as Darwin thought, but by monsters of long-neckedness that sporadically appeared and proved to have survival value —so runs the current view, roughly, as against original Darwinism. Darwin's view that offspring blend the characteristics of their parents rested on ignorance of the mechanism of heredity (as he knew) and entailed difficulties he could not solve.[10]

All this may be studied in textbooks of biology or zoology. Clearly Darwin was the founding father of large and important areas of modern biological science, whatever modifications of his original theory new knowledge has made necessary. Our interest is in his impact on wider areas of thought, and in the sharp moral and religious controversies that ensued.

Reactions to Darwinism

"With the one exception of Newton's *Principia,* no single book of empirical science has ever been of more importance to philosophy," Josiah Royce wrote. Equally important to social and religious thought, and soon brought into the hustings of popular debate, Darwinism eventually affected just about everything in the modern world. It was immediately controversial, as Darwin had foreseen. Many were dismayed, a feeling not confined to clergymen and little old ladies, shocked at the refutation of Genesis. Some of the keenest minds of the age, and some of the least orthodox, joined in the dismay. George Bernard Shaw wrote that "If it could be proved that the whole universe had been produced by such selection (Darwin's "survival of the fittest"), only fools and rascals could bear to live." Von Baer, the distinguished German scientist, refused to believe in a theory that made men "a product of matter" and debased them to the level of animals, while the Professor of Geology at Cambridge, Adam Sedgwick, declared that acceptance of Darwinism would "sink the

[9] The Austrian monk Gregor Mendel published his pioneer findings in 1866 but they were ignored by the men of science until 1900, an example of scientific arrogance.

[10] If a slightly longer necked giraffe did appear, by mating with an ordinary one the effect of the mutation would be partly lost, on Darwin's supposition. Modern genetics has established that heredity does not work by simply blending the parental traits; in the genes all traits are preserved and may appear unimpaired in some later individual.

human race into a lower grade of degradation than any into which it has fallen since its written records tell of its history." Was not Darwin another Schopenhauer, his science teaching that only accident and blind will rule the universe, or, if gods, "gods careless of our doom," as Matthew Arnold put it? Apart from the fate that might overtake orthodox Christianity, were *any* moral values possible in a Darwinian world? The implication that man is no unique child of God endowed with a soul, but rather an offspring of the amoeba by way of other animals, was disturbing; so was the view of all life as an amoral struggle, "nature red in tooth and claw," filled with pain and death, the sacrifice of countless individuals to the species. Still more so was the indication that the universe is nothing but chance and luck.

Though Darwin made some gesture of appeasement to the religious in his book, he was not a religious man, and steadily grew less so. In his *Autobiography*—the undeleted version—he explains how he first rejected Christianity about 1840 and later also dropped the "theism" that appears in the last two pages of the *Origin*. He undoubtedly shared the position popularized by his vigorous proponent Thomas Huxley as "agnosticism." The acrimony with which the war between science and religion soon began to be waged owed much to the belligerence and even arrogance of Huxley, as well as to the blindness of his most famous adversary, "Soapy Sam" Wilberforce. Huxley and Bishop Wilberforce met in a debate in 1860 on which occasion a famous exchange of insults took place, the clergyman observing that he would rather not claim a monkey for an ancestor and Huxley retorting that he would rather be descended from an honest ape than from one who though endowed with brains refused to use them! These two were hardly typical specimens. Huxley was driven by a rage against the clergy which led him to write privately of an urge to "get my heel into their mouths and sc-r-unch it around"; he made the wholly inaccurate statement that "Extinguished theologians lie about the cradle of every science as the strangled snakes beside that of Hercules"! By no means all clergymen rejected Darwinism—some soon began to find it agreeable to theism—while its foes included many nonclergymen, scientists among them. Roman Catholics were more inclined to accept, or at least to tolerate, Darwinism because they were freer from Biblical literalism.

But Darwin undeniably moved away from religion. His life story reveals one who early was quite pious but whom Lyell's geology led away from Biblical Christianity; then the hypothesis of natural selection destroyed in his mind the classical arguments for natural religion, drawn from the evidences of design and purpose in organisms. His concluding paragraphs in the *Origin* point to a theism which was in fact quite widely adopted: it is not less wonderful, but *more* so, that God chose to plant the seeds of all life in a few simple forms rather than create each species

Darwin's Agnosticism

separately. But Darwin abandoned this position, as a study of his letters and subsequent published writings reveals. There was too much chance and too much evil in the biological world he saw to permit him to believe in a benevolent plan. "I cannot persuade myself that a beneficent and omnipotent God would have designedly created the Ichneumonidae with the express intention of their feeding within the living bodies of caterpillars, or that cats should play with mice." It was the old Problem of Evil that destroyed Darwin's faith, along with the muddle and untidiness in the evolutionary picture which went far to discredit the notion of an orderly plan. Darwin was certainly not, like Huxley, a naturally irreligious man. He simply was driven by the evident facts to lose his faith in a "beneficent and omnipotent God." If reproached for destroying religion, he could only answer that he did not invent these harsh facts; they existed.

The thought also struck him, later, that the mind of man itself is a product of the evolutionary order, thus merely a tool of survival. This same idea was to jolt others. The result was evidently to dethrone intelligence or soul as a separate principle, making it merely a factor in evolutionary adaptation. Oddly enough, this would seem to destroy science along with theology, as having any higher validity; everything would have to become just a weapon in the struggle for survival. At any rate Darwin's somewhat confused speculations mirror those of many others; all had been thrown into disorder by this amazing new knowledge. Unwilling to be dogmatic, Darwin called himself an "agnostic," though a recent careful study of his religious views concludes that it would not be too unjust to equate them with atheism. Darwin found absolutely no evidence for a divine creation and providence; that he was not an atheist was owing only to his reluctance to be dogmatic about anything. Perhaps —who knows?—such evidence might appear in the future. Darwin did not find it.[11]

French positivists were already agnostics; in England, George Eliot did not find Darwinism terribly exciting, and it had its least influence in France. But in Great Britain and the United States, as well as in Germany, the impact was shattering. In some respects, then, Darwin was the English Comte. Actually, since the Cambridge scientist laid few if any claims to be a social philosopher, more nearly the English equivalent of the French positivist was Herbert Spencer, Darwin's contemporary and fellow

---

[11] The disciples of Darwin have continued to be militantly antitheist. Thus Julian Huxley, grandson of Thomas Huxley and distinguished twentieth-century biologist: "Newton's great generalization of gravitational attraction made it possible and indeed necessary to dispense with the idea of God guiding the stars in their courses; Darwin's equally great generalization of natural selection made it possible and necessary to dispense with the idea of God guiding the evolutionary courses of life" (*On Living in a Revolution*, 1944). Huxley's comment on Newton is inaccurate, in that eighteenth-century men did not so construe Newtonianism.

evolutionist, perhaps the most widely read and respected Victorian philosopher. The Darwinian revolution was bigger than Darwin.

THE AFTERMATH OF DARWIN: EVOLUTIONARY CONTROVERSIES AND PHILOSOPHIES

> I find no hint throughout the Universe
> Of good or ill, of blessing or of curse;
> I find alone Necessity Supreme;
> With infinite Mystery, abysmal, dark,
> Unlighted by the faintest spark
> For us the flitting shadows of a dream.

So wrote James Thomson in "The City of Dreadful Night." Thomson was by nature a pessimist, but he was not alone in drawing gloomy conclusions from Darwin and science. At a time when belief in the divine inspiration of every line of Scripture was still regarded as the sole foundation of Christianity (Gladstone, the great Oxford-educated Liberal statesman, so argued in 1865), and Christianity was regarded as the foundation of the social order, the discrediting of Genesis was no small matter, and the blows that came from Lyell and Darwin fell on a body already bruised by those of the Positivist historians and the schools of Biblical criticism. The theological-Biblical debate has today lost in importance, for most Christians no longer construe the Scriptures so literally, but as late as 1925 in the United States (the Scopes trial) it retained considerable power to arouse emotions. Wider than this was the moral debate, concerned with the question of whether Darwinism did not destroy all values by eliminating purpose and design from the universe; many who were not at all orthodox Christians joined in disapproving a creed apparently consistent with no sort of belief in rational order in the world.

Samuel Butler, the eminent Victorian novelist and essayist, is an example of the latter. By no means a yea-sayer, the author of the biting satire *Erewhon* and of that tale of youthful rebellion, *The Way of All Flesh*, had himself rejected Christianity and at first welcomed *The Origin of Species*. But he came to reject natural selection though accepting evolution. Evolution is consistent with a religious view of the universe, though hardly with an orthodox Christian one; natural selection is not, but Darwin and Huxley, Butler thought, had falsely persuaded a gullible public that the two things cannot be separated. Religion and science, properly understood, are not in conflict; it is only ignorant theologians and arrogant scientists who are. Butler, and likewise George Bernard Shaw, returned to Lamarckianism against the "ghastly and damnable blasphemy" (Shaw) of the Darwinian process. Needless to say, they did not carry the scientists with them. (St. George Mivart, a Catholic scientist, was an exception.)

Critics and Revisers of Darwin

There were harmonizers and accomodaters who sought to show that even Darwinian evolution is consistent with divine purpose. Was there not something sublime in the *ascent* of man through the eons from primeval slime to intelligent and spiritual being (Henry Drummond)? Admit the cruelty and suffering, one still had as an undeniable fact the grand result. Asa Gray, the American naturalist, complimented Darwin for having *restored* teleology to nature! There was design, if "on the installment plan": Darwin himself had once been reduced to awe at the greater wonder of God contriving to draw all life from a single simple beginning. In any event, as Mr. and Mrs. Carlyle had pointed out, whether we are or are not derived from the amoeba is irrelevant to our spiritual life. Josiah Royce, the distinguished American philosopher, held to an evolutionary idealism and pointed out that the human mind does seek values, is not animal-like: these are facts as incontrovertible as Darwin's, if puzzlingly different from them. Darwin had not and could not make man a brute. He had given him new and puzzling knowledge, but so long as human consciousness exists it will rise above matter to seek understanding and the good.

Vitalism

There were also vitalist approaches to evolution which pointed out that Darwin had not addressed himself at all to the important question of what really (in a final sense) causes the evolutionary process. Granted that natural selection does take place, and with an apparent blindness and cruelty (millions of individuals, whole species even, may perish because of some accidental change in their environment), it would seem that other factors are present, too, including an intelligence that runs through all life. The behavior of organisms is often so remarkably purposive that one has difficulty in attributing everything to a mechanistic process. At any rate can natural selection account for the emergence of life itself? There is also running through life a will to live, as Schopenhauer and Bergson noted. Can this inextinguishable vitality be the result of a mechanical process? It must have been there to begin with, though strengthened by natural selection. Perhaps this life force is really the "cause" of evolution, natural selection only the means it uses. If we see a large group of men running a long race, and notice that some of them fall or drop out, while a few run strongly and forge to the front, it would seem odd to say that the cause of the winning of the race (evolution) is the fact that some drop out from unfitness (natural selection), without raising the really interesting question, why are they running? Why do they bother with this rigorous competition at all? Why do they not all sit under a tree and rest? Darwin pointed out that there is competition in nature, and refrained from speculating about the reason. Good; but was he justified in implying that the question has no importance and need not be raised? If natural selection is made into a dogma, it may divert our eyes from other questions of great moment and distort our outlook on nature. So, at least, Henri Bergson was to argue.[12]

The outcome of all these efforts at accommodation with evolution was perhaps uncertain, but in general men learned to live with it, sometimes by making a separation between animal world and human world, nature and value. On this view a great change had taken place in "nature." "Nature" to the eighteenth century had suggested order, harmony, benevolence, indeed something to be imitated, an agreeable model for man. After Darwin nature might be thought of as fascinating but it was in part terrible and it was not a proper model for human beings. But on the other hand, there were those who embraced the new "naturalism" which placed man in the setting of the natural order and did not separate him so sharply from it as had, for example, the Cartesian or Kantian dualism. Darwinians were "monists" (their foes said materialists) who could not accept any mind-body dualism, any separation between the physical world and the mental. The human animal is an organism like any other, responding to his environment and in part shaping it as he responds. Man became a part of the biological natural order as he had not been before.

Concept of Nature

If some of the more thoughtful drew pessimistic or tragic conclusions from evolution, most people probably integrated it casually with the reigning belief in progress. Constant and inevitable progress does take place on Darwinian terms, progress of the species or race if often at the expense of individuals. Organisms adapt to their environment and grow steadily more efficient; if the unfit perish the fit live, and life evolves from lower organisms to higher. It was one version of the "idea of progress" for which Victorian stability and economic prosperity provided a favorable atmosphere. Is not the mighty spectacle of nature surging forward over the corpses of countless individuals an inspiring one, if awful?

Philosophically, Darwinism helped discredit idealism or intellectualism. Young philosophers like John Dewey abandoned Hegel for some more naturalistic outlook. Mind, it seemed, must be a product of evolution, ideas of natural selection. Mind could hardly be detached from the organism and erected into a separate principle. If we even believe that the universe makes sense, as Nietzsche was fond of saying, is this not just because those of our ancestors who could not make sense of it failed to survive, and natural selection bred those who did? An instinct, will, or life force may throb through the universe, but intellect is its tool; reason is a survival trait. A character in a Shaw play remarked that the modern view is not "I think therefore I am," but "I am therefore I think." A new reason for distrusting reason had appeared: reason is a product of the nature it purports to understand. If I believe in God, or say that the universe is orderly, I may be doing so because of traits bred into the in-

Philosophical Naturalism

[12] There were other French vitalists—Vandel, Mercier, Varagnac, and more recently the celebrated Jesuit father, Teilhard de Chardin.

tellect by the struggle for survival, and if I am tempted to assume the absolute truth of these beliefs I am caught up by remembering that my mind itself is an evolutionary product, hence essentially a survival tool, like the monkey's tail or the giraffe's neck! This "irrationalism" might take various forms: pessimistically, it could be presented as grounds for despair with blind will and instinct ruling the universe; optimistically, it might be said that human intelligence is no less a creative tool for being a part of the natural order. But there remained a fundamental difference between all the new thought and the old, in that for many it was no longer possible to set the human mind *outside* nature. Being a part of nature, the mind had to give up its proud claim to be able to understand it as one understands something from which one is detached. The mind is just that part of our organism that participates in a certain way in the great game of life. Man was no longer Pascal's "thinking reed," his intelligence set against the world.

The implications of Darwinism are too numerous to be recorded. A recent discussion of Darwinism has observed that "evolutionary views have deeply penetrated our present thinking in almost every conceivable field. . . . It has become regular procedure to study phenomena in terms of their development. . . . Interest in evolution has moved out of academic circles even into the field of commerce and industry."[13] Perhaps this judgment attributes too much to Darwinism as such, for the bent of the nineteenth century toward historical explanations and the idea of progress was rather more general; Darwinism may be seen as only a part of this larger pattern, which included such independent forces as Hegelian philosophy, Burkean political thought, aspects of Comteanism, and the maturing profession of historiography. But it is interesting to note that John Dewey, in his famous assessment of Darwin's impact on philosophy (*The Influence of Darwin on Philosophy,* 1909) attributed to him the enthronement of "the principle of transition" or seeing things as involved in processes of change, rather than as Platonic "eternals." Clearly Darwin did exert the greatest force in this direction. For unlike Hegel and Comte he seemed truly scientific. Dewey added that Darwin had shattered the closed metaphysical system of Hegel in favor of a pluralism and experimentalism. One did not simply postulate movement here, one *studied* it, looking closely at every natural object with the eye of the scientist, but looking at it in motion, in process. Thus to many living in the later nineteenth century a whole new vision of things opened up, and evolutionism seemed a refreshing breeze blowing over the somewhat desiccated landscape of Idealism.

The rise of science as the prevailing mode of thought, predicted by Comte, owed more to Darwin than to any other one figure. Many noted

[13] Walter J. Ong, in *Darwin's Vision and Christian Perspectives,* 1960, pp. 1–2.

this change at mid-century. Mark Pattison dated it between 1845 and 1850. Oliver Wendell Holmes, Jr., the great American jurist, reminiscing many years later, thought that of all the intellectual gaps between generations, that between his own and his father's (about 1865) was the greatest: "It was the influence of the scientific way of looking at the world." He mentioned, in addition to *The Origin of Species,* Herbert Spencer and Henry T. Buckle.[14] Buckle was an amateur historian, author of a multi-volume *History of Civilization in England* (1857–1861), the Toynbee of his day, whose volumes lined the shelves of many a Victorian library, and who sought to reduce history to an exact science. More famous yet was the apparently omniscient Herbert Spencer, who did not confine himself merely to human history but claimed to have reduced the whole of the cosmos to an exact, and evolutionary, science.

The Scientific Outlook

Spencer, the most celebrated of mid-Victorian philosophers, was a sort of combination of Comte and Darwin. Like the former, he was a tremendous synthesizer of every field of knowledge, under the general rubric of a scientific or positivistic method—a synthesis which greatly impressed his contemporaries, eager for an integration of thought, but which has since considerably depreciated in value. Someone has called him "the Marx of the middle class"; he could equally well be called the British Comte. A distinctive feature of his philosophy was its stress on evolution, a stress indeed not lacking in Comte, Hegel, and Marx, but which in Spencer is even more pronounced. Influenced by Lyell and von Baer, he popularized "survival of the fittest" before Darwin. Unlike the Cambridge scientist, Spencer proceeded to set about creating a full-scale philosophy of evolution. While Darwin was largely content to nail down the lid on evolution with a large supply of experimental facts, Spencer assumed the case closed and set off on cosmic speculative adventures with it.

Herbert Spencer

The entire universe obeys the same laws of evolution, Spencer affirmed. He wished to show that the evolution not only of life but of the physical cosmos and human society could be reduced to the same laws—an exciting idea, indeed. The laws Spencer found were as follows: things invariably evolve from (1) the homogeneous to the heterogeneous, (2) the undifferentiated to the differentiated, and (3) the unintegrated to the integrated. "From a relatively diffused, uniform, and indeterminate arrangement to a relatively concentrated, multiform, and determinate arrangement." The cosmos began with separate, simple atoms uniformly dispersed through space, and will end, presumably, with highly organized structures working together in a single complex system (rather the reverse of the "primeval atom" theory now popular). Human society began with

Universal Laws of Evolution

[14] Leonora C. Rosenfield, *Portrait of a Philosopher: Morris R. Cohen,* 1962, p. 321.

isolated individuals performing simple tasks without specialization and proceeded towards an order at once more diverse, specialized, and interdependent. Writing voluminously with an encyclopedic knowledge few could match, Spencer tended to bowl over opposition by the sheer weight of this formidable erudition; but in time many of his generalizations came to seem rash, founded on inadequate evidence, made by one who was determined that the facts prove his theory. A Victorian giant, Spencer's reputation has fallen perhaps faster than he deserved, for he seems at least the equal of Comte, Hegel, and Marx. But like those other ambitious "scholastics" he was certainly guilty of letting his speculations outrun the facts on which they were supposedly based. Little if anything now remains standing of his vast intellectual edifice.

Spencer's Positivism

Spencer combined with his evolutionary outlook a Comtean positivism (it came to him from more native sources) which insisted that scientific laws are descriptive statements only, telling us nothing about essential natures or origins. The latter doubtless exist but are "unknowable." Like Kant, Spencer invites us to a certain sense of awe before this realm, but we can have no real knowledge about it. Positivists have generally been divided between those who say that there is no point in even talking or thinking about what we cannot know, and those who would not rule out our speculations and intuitive insights into it provided we do not confuse these with knowledge of a scientific order. Spencer belonged to the latter group; he does not forbid us from speculating about the Unknowable. Still, faithful Christians classed him among the "agnostics" who did so much to undermine religious faith. At the same time, it is obvious that (like Marx) he really offered a sort of religion, in the trappings of science.

Natural Selection and Laissez-Faire

An editor of the *Economist* at one time, Spencer knew the tradition of laissez-faire liberalism before he turned to evolution and shows us the intimate connection between the two. John Maynard Keynes, the modern economist, wrote that "the principle of the Survival of the Fittest could be regarded as a vast generalization of the Ricardian economics." Typically British, the principle of individualism remained powerful in his evolutionary synthesis. While society grows more complex with progress, it also grows freer and more diverse. The evolution of the individual is toward greater freedom and less constraint. Competition is the key to progress. Spencer's complacent identification of the poor with the unfit who may safely be left to die out is in good part responsible for the later dislike of his whole philosophy. There seems a radical contradiction here in Spencer's individualism, for it overrides the individual in the name of the race. The oft-quoted passage in *Social Statics* (first published in 1851, revised in later editions but not changed in any significant way) argued that "to prevent present misery would entail a greater misery on future generations"; "when regarded not separately but in connection with the interests of universal humanity" individual suffering is seen to be for the best. Whatever may be said about this, it is a strange creed to be offered in the name of individualism.[15] However, Spencer was sure that "As civilization advances, government decays"; in this opinion, he was as far as possible at odds with Comte, whom in some other ways he resembles. He takes us back to the Godwinian anarchists at the beginning of the century. Radical antistatism of this sort was still very much alive in late Victorian England though it began to be criticized from 1880 on.

It may be noted that Spencer's extreme individualism was so extreme because it contained strong doses of *both* of two ingredients which have contributed to the laissez-faire position. It has been pointed out[16] that the roots of this position are on the one hand an extreme individualism, and on the other an extreme organicism or awareness of the complexity of society. There is that tradition which, beginning with Hobbes and especially Locke, put all the stress on individual rights and saw society as nothing, or no more than the sum of individuals. And then there is the tradition of Burke, which reached a negative attitude toward social reform by the almost opposite route of finding society to be too delicate and complicated an organism to be tampered with safely. Burke and Hegel (*Philosophy of Right*) feel very strongly about the claims of society, but cannot usually approve of any extensive reform of society because they see this as ignorant and utopian. Bentham and Mill feel very strongly about the rights of the individual, and see society, or any kind of community interference, as the foe of these rights. Spencer joined together these feelings. He was a strong libertarian and also an organicist. He damned use of the power of the state for social reform because he saw it both as an infraction of liberty and as an impugnment of intelligence. Well-meaning attempts to legislate improvements should be fought off for two basic reasons: because these hamper the individual's liberty and because, given society's complexity and interrelatedness, they cannot accomplish what they naively set out to do, anyway.

With Mill, Tocqueville, and other mid-century liberals, Spencer shared a mistrust of democracy: the divine right of popularly elected parliaments, he said, must be resisted as much as the divine right of kings if it should threaten liberty. Spencer's world view resting on science betrayed his own bias of time and place, middle-class Victorian England, just as Comte smuggled his Saint-Simonian predilections into a system supposedly scientific.

As an evolutionist, Spencer also took issue with Comte's intellectual-

<hr />

[15] Walter M. Simon has pointed to the contradiction between Spencer's individualism and his conception of society as an organism. "Spencer and 'Social Organism,'" *Journal of the History of Ideas*, April-June, 1960.

[16] See, for example, David Nicholls, "Positive Liberty, 1880–1914," *American Political Science Review*, March, 1962.

ism. He was a social determinist, like Marx, holding that ideas are largely a product of our emotions and of "surrounding conditions" including "the social state." "Ideas do not govern and overthrow the world; the world is governed by feelings, to which ideas serve only as guides. . . . Not intellectual anarchy, but moral antagonism, is the cause of political crises. . . . Though advanced ideas, when once established, act upon society and aid its further advance, yet the establishment of such ideas depends on the fitness of society for receiving them." He seemed to feel that Comte held that ideas determine the social state rather than, largely, vice versa. The comparison of Spencer, Comte, and Marx on this point makes an interesting study.

Spencer's brand of "social Darwinism," with its sanctioning of a ruthlessly competitive social order ("root, hog, or die" is the law of life, the American social Darwinist William Graham Sumner bluntly put it), created something of a dilemma for other Darwinians, less inclined to grant indulgent smiles to a capitalistic society. In 1893 Thomas Huxley, the aggressive champion of Darwinism, argued in a well-known series of lectures that in human affairs natural selection is *not* the rule to follow. Progress, he said, consists in working *against* nature and evolution, "checking the cosmic process at every step." He could agree with Matthew Arnold that

> Man must begin, know this, where Nature ends;
> Nature and man can never be fast friends.

"It is an error to imagine that evolution signifies a constant tendency to increased perfection," Huxley wrote. What survives, because it is the best adapted, is not necessarily or usually the best in an ethical sense. Unguided evolution may well lead to moral regression and social failure. Thus did Huxley in part withdraw his faith in evolution.

Clearly this must be so. Victorian social Darwinists usually wished to approve a fairly civilized process of competitive economics, against any sort of state socialism. But if one applied Darwinism to human society literally and thoroughly, one would evidently revert to the prehistoric jungle. The biographer of Adolf Hitler (Alan Bullock) tells us that the only idea the infamous Nazi dictator held to was "a crude Darwinism." To Hitler this meant that only power counts, individuals may be ruthlessly sacrificed, the ill and injured put to death, whole races wiped out because allegedly less biologically fit. Anyone stupid or evil enough to take this sort of social Darwinism at its full value would seem to find in it sanctions for the law of the jungle applied *á outrance*. Though nature might be "red in tooth and claw" in the animal world, no sane person could wish to reduce the society of man to such a condition.

There were those who pointed out that even in the subhuman biological realm conflict is not the only rule. Cooperation also exists as a means of biological survival, as numerous examples of symbiosis and social organization in the animal world testify. Moreover the will-to-power, the life force, the instinct to survive that pulses through all living things, can be "sublimated" so that it works for good rather than evil. Mankind, in particular, evolves by inventing new modes of social cooperation; it has passed to a higher phase of evolution, *rational* evolution, involving the use of brain power rather than brawn. Animals do this to some extent; man has made it supreme. Why should "natural selection" mean physical strife and bloodshed? There is more survival value in the intelligence that organizes peace and social welfare. It was possible in this way to turn the argument against Spencer's cult of dog-eat-dog competition. And, in fact, after 1880 western Europe turned rapidly toward social-welfare modifications of the competitive economic order.[17]

Mutual Aid as a Natural Process

At least one substantial common denominator in all these nineteenth-century ideologies was Progress, that Idea the nineteenth century so generally bowed to. "The history of the human race is the history of growth," the English Comtean historian Frederic Harrison proclaimed, as "the meaning of history." The Hegelian, holding that the spirit of God dwells within the historical process and guides it to ultimate completion, and the Positivist, refusing to acknowledge such a metaphysical hypothesis as God or Absolute, were equally sharers of the optimistic world view that found in history a steady advance from one beginning to one end, and that a glorious one. One thought that progress worked through the Absolute without man even being aware of it; the other believed that only in rejecting the Absolute and becoming conscious of his human powers did man learn to advance; neither doubted the existence of Progress. Marx, next to be considered, inherited the Hegelian spirit; Comte's lived on in many bourgeois versions, liberal or conservative, of the idea of progress. (J. B. Bury, in his classic study of this idea, wrote that Comte did more than any other thinker to establish it as a permanent fixture on the mental landscape.) Mill agreed with Comte on this, and Darwin taught most men that incessant advance is the law of life, though doubtless they mistook him if they thought he believed in a purposeful progress. A disillusioned post-1919 critic, Emil Brunner, called the idea of progress "an axiomatic belief which needed no proof nor could be disproved . . . a pseudo-religious creed, which to negate was a kind of blasphemy." One can round up some doubters, but there were not many at the high tide of Victorian optimism, and as late as 1908 the distinguished statesman-

The Idea of Progress

[17] In "Why Darwin Pleased the Socialists," G. B. Shaw made the half-serious point that it took capitalists down a peg to be told that they were rich neither because of their virtue nor by design of providence, but simply by accident. Darwinism's hostility to religion, along with its reenforcement of a "naturalism" that looked squarely at harsh social facts, also rendered it pleasing to the Left.

philosopher of Great Britain, Lord Balfour, proclaimed that "there are no symptoms either of pause or regression in the onward movement which for more than a millennium has been characteristic of Western civilization." What seems remarkable to us is that these beliefs in progress assumed not only a steady onward and upward movement, but a movement of the entire society. We would be inclined to say today that some things doubtless "progress," if we define the term in certain ways—technology becomes more efficient, scientific knowledge accumulates—but other phases of life remain much the same and some deteriorate. It would be a rash man who would claim that art, morality, even political wisdom have advanced. The nineteenth century optimists supposed that the society is a unit which progresses as a whole, so that every part of it is engaged in constant improvement.

This optimism, fed by a steady procession of technological gains, survived the Darwin-induced crisis of faith. And it is a tribute to it that even the greatest critic of Victorian society, Karl Marx, embraced it too, in his way.

If previously the gods dwelt above the earth,
now they have become the center of it.

KARL MARX

The fundamental problem of social science is
to find the law of motion according to which
any state of society produces the state which
succeeds it and takes its place.

KARL MARX

Nineteenth-Century Ideologies: Marxism

4

FOUNDATIONS OF MARXISM

Karl Marx first became acquainted with Friedrich Engels in Paris Marx's Life
and Career whither he had gone in 1843. Prior to this, attendance at the University of Berlin had exposed him to the school of Hegel, though the great philosopher had died a few years before, in 1831, and this was a lasting and significant influence, much though Marx might disparage certain aspects of Hegelianism. Marx obtained his Ph.D. at Jena with a dissertation on the ancient materialists, Democritus and Epicurus—an appropriate topic for him in view of his long commitment to philosophical materialism. A career in the German universities might have been in the offing for the brilliant young man, as it had been for Hegel and would be for Nietzsche; but Marx was always uncompromisingly radical. He had adopted the atheistic and naturalistic views of the young (left-wing) Hegelians of whom the foremost was Ludwig Feuerbach. Outspoken impiety doomed his chances for a professorial post.

Marx turned to journalism, then went to Paris to breathe the intoxicating air of that intellectual capital in the giddy forties, when the socialist ideas of Fourier, Saint-Simon, and especially Proudhon were being discussed. Here also came colorful Russian revolutionaries such as Michael Bakunin. The meeting with Engels resulted in a friendship for life, bringing to Marx support both financial and intellectual on which he was often to lean. Uncompromising, prickly, and self-righteous, Marx quarreled with everyone—except Engels. The two men evidently never disagreed, an unusual partnership, and one of considerable moment, for without Engels, a man of some means, Marx could surely never have spent his life writing books which few bought. For Marxists, it would seem to be an awkward fact that the proletarian theory owes its existence to the money of Engels, a capitalistic factory-owner. (Engels was the son of a German textile manufacturer, manager and part owner of a branch his father set up in Manchester, England, ultimately inheriting the business on his father's death.)

Marx eagerly imbibed socialist ideas in Paris. Then came the revolutions of 1848, and the *Communist Manifesto,* a brief work written by Marx and Engels for a left-wing organization, which had little influence on the events of 1848 but was destined to lasting fame as the most concise and eloquent statement of the Marx-Engels position. (The first draft of the *Manifesto* had been made in 1847, before the Revolution.) For by this time the main contours of Marx's thought were pretty well set. Like Darwin, he had his thesis and would spend the rest of his life supplying the documentation. The excitement of 1848 probably never left Marx; he spent the rest of his life preparing for other revolutions, which never came. Marx returned to Germany to edit a newspaper in Cologne for a time, but to his disgust the revolution failed and he was forced to leave the country. He came to London in 1849, home of all refugees, and lived there the rest of his life, happily married to a wonderful woman but perennially poverty-stricken until the last twelve years of his life (he died in 1883 at 65). He would not adopt the suggestion of his mother-in-law that he write less about capital and make more of it! He burrowed in the British Museum library, wrote, and organized communist associations. Mostly he wrote; as an organizer he left something to be desired, the famous First International of 1864 amounting to little at the time. His chief opus was *Das Kapital,* the first and only completed volume of which appeared in 1867, written in Marx's native tongue. A second and third volume were edited after Marx's death by Engels from his fragments, a fourth later by Karl Kautsky. Marx's failure to finish his *magnum opus* probably indicated problems in his theory he could not solve. There were other tracts, polemical, journalistic, or theoretical. He died and was buried in relative obscurity in London, though his fame was beginning to spread on the Continent in the last years of his life.

His intellectual background was an unusually rich one. He had experienced the best of German, French, and British thought. Having gotten philosophy virtually from the mouth of the great Hegel, he then drank up socialism in the cafes of Paris at a vital moment, and went on to study economic theory and economic history in London, where he laid the great library of the British Museum under heavy contribution.

He kept abreast of current thought in this age of ideas and proved to be one of the ablest of all synthesizers. He blended German philosophy, French social doctrine, and British political economy in a system that could well claim to have drawn on all the best minds of the nineteenth century and forged them into a harmonious unity. With considerable confidence, to say the least,[1] he believed that he had superseded all previous thinkers and ushered in a new age of man of which he was the pioneer theorist. On his death he left a movement, organized as the Social Democratic party, which soon was the most vigorous and successful socialist party in Europe and went on to play a vital role in modern history. Of this movement the Communist party was an offshoot. The success of these parties could be traced directly to the vigor and apparent clarity and profundity of Marx's thought.

At the same time, critics thought they detected major flaws in Marx's system early, and it never received much acceptance in the academic or professional worlds. Some of his own followers conceded by 1900 that since his main prophecies had turned out wrong, his theory would have to undergo fundamental revision. Accepted today in one part of the world at full value as the greatest thinker of modern times, he is widely regarded in the other as an intellectual mountebank who really founded a peculiarly narrow and intolerant religion. There are yet others who think that Marx was truly one of the seminal thinkers of the modern era but that he suffered at the hands of his own excessively enthusiastic disciples, who made him into a messiah and built a church around him in a way that he would not have approved. So there is a Marxist puzzle. What no one doubts is the enormous influence of the ideas produced by Marx and, lest we forget, Engels. A number of works once attributed to Marx were actually written wholly or in part by his self-effacing friend, who accepted the intellectual superiority of Marx but was himself a surprisingly industrious scholar for one who also earned a living.

Most people probably associate Marxism with either (1) the economic analysis of capitalism, purporting to show its inevitable destruction from its own "contradictions" and replacement by socialism or communism or (2) the broader materialist interpretation of history, which alleges that the fundamental causal factor in social change at any time is the technological or economic. But it is necessary to begin, as

Marx's Debt to Hegel

---

[1] He was in fact intolerably arrogant according to most accounts. Carl Schurz's comment is classic: "I have never seen a man whose bearing was so provoking and intolerable. To no opinion which differed from his own did he accord the honor of even a condescending contradiction. Everyone who contradicted him he treated with abject contempt. . . . I remember most distinctly the cutting disdain with which he pronounced the word 'bourgeois,' and as a bourgeois, that is as a destestable example of the deepest mental and moral degeneracy, he denounced everyone that dared to oppose his opinion."

Marx did, with the philosopnical framework of *dialectical materialism*. "Materialist in substance and dialectical in manner," this philosophy sought to combine the Hegelian dialectic with a materialist view of reality. It is important to grasp Marx's position here, to realize the curious way he attempted to combine a scientific with a metaphysical outlook. In many respects, Marx was hard-headedly empirical or positivistic, that is, he would not accept knowledge that was not evident to the senses. A true child of the age of Comte and Darwin, he ridiculed Hegel's "speculative idealism." Nevertheless he insisted strongly on retaining Hegel's dialectical *method*, the formula of dialectical movement. This, Marx claimed, is how things actually do behave. When we look at nature or history we find that everything exhibits in its activity and development a dialectical pattern of action and reaction. The dialectic is a characteristic of matter. It is important, but difficult, to know whether Marxists assert this as an empirical observation, which in that case might not always be true, or as a dogma beyond criticism.

Marx and Engels were quite insistent that dialectical materialism *is* Marxism. "Dialectics," Engels wrote, "is nothing more than the science of the general laws of motion and development of nature, human society, and thought." It unifies the sciences, which are found to be one, everything obeying the same dialectical laws. This element of Hegel lingered on in Marx; and indeed for the philosopher who was his master Marx had a high regard. Hegel had only got the terms reversed; reality is not thought and mind, as he thought, but brute matter; yet he had correctly divined the way reality *behaves*. Dogmatic Marxists have always equated the dialectical method with the scientific method, and assume dialectical behavior to be an inherent property of all things.

As stated by Marx the three laws of the dialectic are (1) the trans-

Laws of the
Dialectic formation of quantity into quality, (2) the interpenetration of opposites, and (3) the negation of the negation. These rather mystifying formulae may perhaps be clarified by the following examples. (1): Water suddenly becomes ice at a certain point of coldness, thus a qualitative change takes place as a result of a series of quantitative changes. Or, a revolution finally takes place after years of cumulative pressures. Pile one thing on another and at a certain point you cease to have just a pile of the same things, you have something entirely different. A humbler and possibly facetious example might be the inflating of a tire: keep putting in air, and finally at a critical juncture you get not a tire but an explosion. (2) and (3): Change is the rule of nature because everything contains within it its own opposite, which negates it and in turn will be negated. The seed contains within itself the plant that it will turn into; the plant will decay, giving rise however to new plants. A social order, such as capitalism, creates out of its own body the socialism destined to destroy it. Socialism thus interpenetrates capitalism, and negates it. Struggle and conflict punctuate this process: the old organism produces its violent destroyers.

As applied to the sciences, it has seemed to critics of Marx that the dialectical method does not mean much, or if insisted upon as a dogma, is harmful to science. Soviet Russian scientists work like western ones. Whenever (as happened on one or two occasions, notably in the Lysenko case) there has been an effort to force on them a Marxist scientific orthodoxy, the results have been unfortunate for science. Either dialectical materialism is so commonplace that even "bourgeois" scientists follow it without knowing that they are doing so (like Molière's M. Jourdain talking prose!) or else it is a failure. The attempt to distinguish a Marxist science from a bourgeois one, with the former being superior, clearly has failed. Nevertheless from Marx and Engels on down to such unlikely philosophers as Stalin, all Marxists have insisted that dialectical materialism is the distinctive foundation of their science, and the famous analysis of capitalism is meant to be but a special application of it. In our time scientists in the Soviet Union have suffered pains and penalties because they appeared to stray from the dialectical path. Not only human affairs, but the natural sciences are expected to conform to dialectical principles. To be a Marxist, one must be able to enter into the spirit of the dialectical universe and visualize things in motion and in contradiction, giving birth to their own opposites, negating and renegating, occasionally bursting through the barriers of quantity to create a new form. A vision not unlike this is to be found in the more recent school of Emergent Evolutionists, who in other ways do not resemble Marxists, however. They stress the freedom and unpredicability of life, ever proliferating in unexpected ways, whereas Marxism is deterministic. It is not a bad picture, if one does not become a prisoner of dogmas.

Many of the examples given by Marx and especially by Engels are from the natural sciences (the freezing of ice and the sprouting of the seed are theirs). But no one associates these German worthies with a revolution in chemistry or biology.[2] Many do associate them with a revolutionary new conception of the historical process, as well as with the first effective socialist economic analysis. They applied the dialectical method to these areas more consistently and successfully. It is well, though, to remember that this method was the tool of thought they always used, and that they held it to be of universal validity, *the* scientific method.

The dialectical method was after all Marx's distinctive contribution.

2 Marx and Engels knew about Darwin, of course, and regarded him as possibly congenial to their system. Engels claimed in his funeral address on Marx that Marx had done for the social sciences what Darwin did for the biological. But the attitude of Marx is indicated in his request to Engels to "study Darwin and see if there is anything there we can use"!

Predecessors
of Marxian
Social
Doctrine
Today because he is the most famous socialist or communist he is often thought of as the man who invented socialism, but this, as we know, is not so. The protest against the suffering of workers under capitalism antedated Marx, as did the idea of social ownership of industry as a remedy for the evils of "capitalism." The Chartists, Robert Owen, Saint-Simon and Fourier, Proudhon, Blanc, etc., all came before him. We have previously discussed these pioneer socialists (pages 59–64). In Rousseau's vision of an original state of primitive communism, when there was no wickedness and exploitation, followed by the "fall" due to eating the apple of private property, there is much of the basic vision of Marx, too, the latter more sophisticated, spelled out in greater detail, but in its archetypal essence quite similar.

Likewise, other concepts associated with Marxism such as the class struggle and the class conditioning of morality and thought were hardly original. "Of all maxims none is more uncontested than that power follows property," Joseph Addison remarked early in the eighteenth century, an idea which may have come to him from James Harrington. John Stuart Mill, in *On Liberty,* a contemporary work (1859) but one not influenced by Marx, whom Mill at that time had probably never heard of, observed (parenthetically) that "Wherever there is an ascendant class, a large portion of the morality of the country emanates from its class interests and its feelings of class superiority." Mill could have found this in the ancient historian Thucydides, among others. Also, the labor theory of value, on which Marx based his famous analysis of capitalism, came to him from Adam Smith and David Ricardo, while socialists such as Thomas Bray had already, before Marx, claimed that "by a fraudulent system of unequal exchange" the workman's just wage is taken away from him by the capitalist.

Of all these ideas Marx made a unique and powerful synthesis. The dialectic enabled him to tie them all together in a seamless system, much like Hegel's in that respect. There is a plan and a purpose to history, Marx claimed; and moreover there is a method, the understanding of which enables us to decipher the meaning of history and thus collaborate with it in its purposes. He claimed to have provided this key that unlocks the golden gates of social science and shows us how every event fits into its place. The key was dialectical materialism.

We might think that a dialectical philosophy would stress freedom
Determinism
and not determinism, for it is expressly opposed to a mechanistic outlook on nature, holding rather that the world is not static but like a developing and proliferating organism, or like a conversation. We can scarcely predict the results of a dialogue in which a statement is made, is contradicted, restated, again objected to, and so on. This may be a good way to knowledge, but it is hard to see how we could know the

outcome in advance.[3] We could argue that God does; but Marx, of course, did not believe in any God. He held that only matter exists—matter in motion, in evolution. Marx was a determinist, believing that the laws of matter's motion can be precisely determined and used to predict the future. This world made up only of dynamic matter knows where it is going, and sharpwitted men can know it too. Some critics of Marxism have wondered how Marx could exclude God or the Absolute yet insist on a rational, purposeful world, obeying regular laws. Or is Marx a pantheist, like his fellow apostate Jew, Spinoza?

All we can say is that Marx shared to the full the positivist bias, that is, he wished to be scientific, to believe only in "facts," to dismiss such nebulous abstractions as God or the Absolute. He got this from the materialists of the eighteenth century as well as from the scientific atmosphere of his own time. But he married it to the very different system of Hegel. The marriage may have been incongruous, but it produced some lusty children.

HISTORICAL MATERIALISM

Marx's theory or philosophy of history occupies the central place in his thought. He was strongly impressed by the "historicism" of Hegel, and often spoke of the processes of history as operating independently of men's will. The historical process is an "it" that sweeps men along without regard to their wishes; one thinks of Thomas Hardy's phrase, the "immanent unrecking." This conception of a world-historical force was strong in Marx as it has been in all its disciples; that is why Comrade Khrushchev is so sure capitalism is doomed and communism will triumph—this is not just a matter of probability or possibility but a certainty, decreed by the iron laws of history. Marx did not wish to think of the "laws" of society and history as merely descriptive of trends or tendencies, in the Positivist sense, but rather as decrees imposed for all time, existing objectively and requiring men to conform to them. Nor did he wish to think of many small areas for social investigation, but of one great pattern sweeping though all history.

On the other hand he also had a considerable feeling for the active participation by men in shaping the historical process. This activism appeared in Marx in his famous statement that philosophers must not merely describe the world but must help to change it, in his own career

Marx's Theory of History

[3] Neither inventions nor scientific theories can be entirely predicted, and these are what Marx regards as the basic factors; much less can future political and economic developments. Prediction in general is possible only for a very short time ahead, and for very general things. These points have been most fully established by present-day philosophers, especially Sir Isaiah Berlin (*Historical Inevitability*, 1954) and Karl Popper (*The Open Society and Its Enemies*, 4th ed., 1962 and *The Poverty of Historicism*, 1957).

as organizer of the First International and participant in other political movements, and in his statement that with the arrival of his philosophy men passed from the "kingdom of necessity" to the "kingdom of freedom." Marxists have of course made their great place in the modern world by this sort of dynamic revolutionary activism. Is this inconsistent with a deterministic outlook?

Whatever the possible discrepancies in logic, such a combination of activism with determinism produces a potent psychological stimulus; a similar combination was found in Calvinism. Adherents of Marxism feel that history is on their side and so they are bound to win, as well as serve nature's purposes; yet they can collaborate with nature, helping to make history by understanding its laws. Marx probably meant that (1) history is only determined within broad limits, leaving scope for variation in the particulars and in the pace; like a very large boulder bouncing around in a large and uneven chute, it will eventually reach the bottom but may pursue an uneven course and may be temporarily delayed. Present-day Communists assume that capitalism will eventually be destroyed but do not specify time or place; it might be now or in two hundred years; the process might move next in Vietnam or in England. In this way a general determinism can be reconciled with a practical voluntarism. (2) As in all social determinism, one must concede that men are a part of the social order and in acting and willing they play their part; fatalism is not the same thing as necessitarianism.

Here as elsewhere, Marx was somewhat impatient of fine-spun theoretical discussions, though theory was important to him. It has been pointed out that Marx uses terms like "condition" and "determine" (*bedingen* and *bestimmen*) much too loosely and indiscriminately. They do not mean the same thing, obviously. There is a significant difference between saying that human intelligence is conditioned (influenced) by society and saying that it is determined. No one would deny the former, almost everyone the latter. There is a characteristic flavor of rhetorical exaggeration about much of Marx's thought. In his materialistic explanation of history, that is, the theory that "material" factors (technological, economic) are "basic" in history while other factors may be relegated to a secondary role, such confusions of terminology and thought appear in profusion. Yet nowhere did Marx prove to be so stimulating and provocative as here.

Marx differed from Hegel, of course, in finding the motive forces of
Materialistic Interpretation of History history in material factors, in the "productive forces," by which he evidently meant tools and the economic relations derived from them. Strictly speaking, the motive force of history is the class struggle ("All history is the history of class struggle"), but the techniques and modes of production of any given period determine the class structure. The windmill, said Marx, gives us feudalism (he would have been nearer the mark,

according to modern economic historians, had he said the plough and the stirrup). He went on to claim that all the rest of civilization and culture depends on this economic foundation. In his speech at Marx's funeral, Engels put it this way: "The production of the immediate material means of subsistence and consequently the degree of economic development attained by a given people or during a given epoch form the foundation upon which the state institutions, the legal conceptions, the ideas on art and even on religion . . . have been evolved, and in the light of which they must, therefore, be explained. . . ." Marx, he claimed, had been the first to notice this "simple fact." This is the "materialist interpretation of history."

Here we encounter difficulties. If Marx and Engels are saying that men can not think, write, worship, etc., without first finding some means of sustenance, then they are asserting an obvious truth, surely not original, to which no one would object. If they mean that the mode of production and the economic relationships of society influence or condition modes of thought in significant ways, it is also difficult to disagree with them, and once again the idea is hardly original, though Marx surely gave it more striking expression than any other writer one can think of. If however it is claimed that (1) all ideas and institutions are determined by the economic "substructure" and (2) play no real part or independent part in life or history, the claim appears almost self-evidently false. The saints may have been deluded, but they gave up their possessions to follow a religious ideal; others, including philosophers, adventurers, soldiers, political reformers, scientists, have followed their gleam without significant reference to capitalism or any other economic order. Marx himself is a classic example of a man possessed by ideas to the exclusion of pecuniary motives, and the system he created is a prize instance of the power of an ideology. In this respect he is not a unique case, as he may have implied, for history is filled with prophets crying in the wilderness, philosophers teaching in the marketplace, angry young men (and some old ones) denouncing the existing "establishment." There are manifestly human drives of a very fundamental nature, other than the desire to rule and the desire for gain: drives sexual, esthetic, intellectual, spiritual. It strains our credulity to believe that Beethoven and Brahms wrote their music to serve the bourgeoisie and cover up their shameful exploitation of the workers, yet this is what Marxism requires us to believe. Engels and Marx conceded that this might be done unconsciously, without the individual being aware of it; but that is *really* what is motivating him, nonetheless.

What did Marx mean? He and Engels are not very clear. The "superstructure" consisting of all that is not economic is said to be only a "reflection" of the economic "substructure." Social change can only take place in the latter, the former following along in its wake. Also, "the

Difficulties in Historical Materialism

ruling ideas are those of the ruling class." It is clear, though, that Marx was no crude economic determinist (such as would, for example, explain Milton's poetry by his occupation) and also that he granted at least some ideas a powerful place in history. He undoubtedly knew too little of the history of human thought and action to support his bold generalizations and he tended to conceal by vague language some difficult problems. At the same time he was onto something in proposing an investigation of the origin and social relations of religions and philosophical systems. Nor can it well be denied that there are such things as ideological systems designed to support political regimes—that, indeed, institutions excrete ideologies as a normal function. The situation was much more complicated than Marx imagined when with typical dogmatism he proposed some outrageously exaggerated formulae, but he opened up fruitful fields of inquiry.

Marx's singular allegation, then, is approximately as follows: Ideas and ideologies of all sorts, legal and political institutions and processes, artistic and literary expression, all of religion, culture, and politics, all except the technological or economic is "superstructure" and ultimately dependent on the latter. Changes in the superstructure do not take place without prior changes in the economic foundation, to which they respond; or, if such changes take place, they are not significant. Marx evidently asks us to believe not only that Christianity is a tool of the ruling classes to divert and pacify the masses (not necessarily a deliberate tool, for remember that Marx holds that this process may be and indeed normally is unconscious), but that all other phenomena in some sense are the same. The class structure cannot be escaped. The bourgeois judge who thinks he is administering perfect justice is really doing so within the boundaries of the capitalist order and so engaged in defending it. Presumably Stravinsky wrote capitalistic music and Cézanne painted bourgeois pictures, much though these artists themselves despised "bourgeois" culture. Marxist literary criticism has applied much ingenuity to exactly this sort of demonstration. Freud was a capitalistic psychologist, according to present Soviet orthodoxy—a view which certainly would have surprised him. Though this is the evident import of Marxist theory, it should be pointed out that Marx himself did not conform to it: he was a great lover of classical Greek drama, which evidently had for him a value independent of its function in the class struggle.

Most people today are inclined to listen sympathetically to claims for the primacy of technological or economic change because they know what a dynamic agent it has been. The most common sort of "cultural lag" is perhaps the sort caused by a rapid advance in technology to which ideas and institutions have not adapted though such adaptation is required. One might instance national states in an age of nuclear weapons. But this is not the only possible kind of "lag," and the reverse might be true. We might come up with a new idea or theory that forced changes in our physical equipment. Freudian psychology has modified our teaching practices and resulted in a new profession with at least some physical equipment (couches!), for example. A new theory of military strategy causes our government to build different types of weapons, abandoning others. It is important to note that Marxists are committed to the proposition that the economic factor is the *only* independent variable, not just that it is one possible variable. Nobody doubts that technological and economic forces are important; the Marxists hold that nothing else is important.

Karl Popper presents an interesting example: Suppose, he says, that all the existing physical plant and scientific apparatus were destroyed, but the knowledge behind it, in books and human brains, were left in existence—the physical apparatus could be rebuilt, though no doubt with great expense and difficulty. But suppose the plant were to remain and the knowledge be lost—as might happen if primitive savages suddenly replaced modern man, and had no knowledge of modern technology. Then the machinery would fall into disuse and perish. In this sense, Popper concludes, knowledge, ideas, seem more "basic" than physical equipment, tools. What his example really indicates, however, is the impossibility of ever separating tools and brains; what he postulates could not happen. Since the beginning of mankind, tools and knowledge have evolved together in intimate association as aspects of the same process. We could not have brains without tools nor tools without brains. The skillful hand and the contriving brain (to borrow a phrase of James C. Malin's) go together. The experimental laboratory and the theorizing intellect must collaborate to make science and technology possible. Marx erred in attempting to separate the two things and make one of a different order than the other. As a matter of fact, he wavered in his view of scientific knowledge, sometimes putting it in the superstructure and sometimes in the foundation—a significant ambiguity.

It seems especially important to recognize the sense in which the strictly *political* element may be primary. The story of some of the new nations today underscores the fact that economic development can scarcely take place until stable government has been secured. Until a political unit is secure both internally and externally, investment, trade, and labor can hardly function in any successful way. Unwise political decisions may cause deterioration of the entire economy, as has apparently happened in some South American countries with great economic potential but a poor political foundation. The political process is often, it would seem, more "primary" than the economic. If man has to eat before he can live, he also has to cooperate in social units before he can eat, or at any rate live much above the level of the beast. Anyone with much experience of the world knows that political processes exist in their own right, independently of economic ones. The fact that we often divide history into epochs based on politics is an indication of this political primacy. The age of the Roman Empire, the age of feudalism, the age of the national state—and, if such evolution took place, the age of the world state—unquestionably suggest politics as the decisive factor. These political classifications have at least as much claim to primacy as the age of slavery, of manorialism, and of capitalism. Political processes are acted upon by economic ones, but then the reverse is also true.

One of Marxism's most startling failures is its inability to mark off any significant difference between the various *national* cultures. France, Germany, Great Britain, and the United States must all be substantially alike, except insofar as they are in slightly different stages of capitalist development, because they are all "bourgeois capitalist" states; but everyone except the Marxists knows that in important respects these nations differ because of the role of tradition, that is, because of their different historic experiences. The Marxists expected revolution to come first in Britain because capitalistic development had proceeded farthest here. They overlooked the potent reasons why revolution was *least* likely in the land where due to a complex variety of historical factors the political constitution was the most stable in Europe. With their eyes fixed on only one set of forces, they were blind to the central facts of British history. Marxists were disgusted with the failure of socialism to take root in the United States and could only declare that somehow, for unknown reasons, the American workers were hopelessly "petty bourgeois" in their outlook. Again, Marxists least expected revolution in Russia—a country for which, ironically, Marx entertained the deepest disdain—because it was economically backward. This is not to say that some investigators did not creatively pursue answers to the interesting question why these various peoples utterly failed to conform to the Marxian theory. Again, Marx may be given credit for stimulating much fruitful inquiry, but it was necessary to go beyond his system to find the answers.

Such argumentation can go on indefinitely. Clearly Marx started an interesting debate, but just as clearly he failed to finish it. More sophisticated modern discussions of this problem make Marx seem crude and dogmatic. But he did present the first approximation of a theory that subsequent historians and sociologists such as Max Weber, Karl Mannheim, Karl Popper, and others were to work on.

Like Comte and Hegel, Marx divided history up in a rather arbitrary manner into a few great epochs, his division based of course on economics: primitive communism, ancient slave society, feudalism, capitalism, and communism. In a rough way one might say that these describe the history of Western civilization in certain of its aspects, but they scarcely exhaust the subject and seem inherently no more valid than

Marx's
Stages of
History

Hegel's political classification or Comte's intellectual one. (For non-Western civilizations, they are less accurate.) The fact is that we can look at history in various ways, each equally valid. We can arrive at different periodizations, depending on our criteria; each one will be useful for its purpose, but not objectively truer than the others.

According to Marx the dynamics of history spring from the inner contradictions of the first four of these epochs, issuing in class conflict and revolution. The dialectical principle expresses itself in this process of clash and conflict, with one order emerging from the womb of another. The oppressed class or classes represent a negation or counterstatement destined in time to destroy the old society. Feudalism brought forth bourgeois capitalism from its own contradictions; capitalism in the same necessary way gives rise to the proletariat and to socialism. "The material powers of production, at a certain stage in their development, come into conflict with the existing relations of production. . . . Then comes the period of social revolution." To repeat, men are the unwitting instruments of historical destiny. The bourgeois does not want to create socialism, but he cannot help it, it arises from the very things he must do.

Marx's vision of the historical process made a powerful appeal to the imagination. History not only has a plan and a meaning, but it is tremendously dramatic. Something of his Jewishness surely emerges in this essentially apocalyptic account of man's journey through time to reach a mighty climax at the end. For at the end, we are given to understand, with the triumph of the proletariat over the capitalists, we reach the end of history.[4] There are now no more classes to create another negation and another turn in the great cycle of history; this last victory of the submerged ushers in the classless society, and we have come full circle from primitive communism to communism as the highest stage of human society.

MARX'S ANALYSIS OF CAPITALISM

In his *magnum opus, Capital,* Marx sought to apply his method in detail to the existing social situation. Here he drew on Ricardo and the classical economists as well as on socialism and the dialectic. Marx

---

[4] Condorcet had placed human history near the end of its days, and so apparently had Hegel; in 1841 so judicious an intellect as Matthew Arnold declared, in his Oxford inaugural address, that the modern age bears all the marks of being "the last step" in the story of man. This somewhat curious finalism can perhaps be traced to several sources, but chiefly would seem to have rested on observation of the tremendous growth of modern Europe, in political units, population, extension of power, increased popular participation, etc. Could one imagine anything larger than the nation-state, except the world state, an obvious finality? Or any further extension of democracy except to the lowest class, the proletariat?

stumbled upon difficulties, and failed to complete his book, but he left a deep impression upon the budding socialist movement with this major effort of economic theory.

Prior to Marx many less weighty socialist theoreticians had charged that the factory owners exploited, in other words, cheated, their employees. Indeed, this had emerged for all to see in the famous Parliamentary investigations into conditions in the textile factories and mines in England—on which Marx and Engels drew heavily for their ammunition, though their philosophy would seem to deny that these bourgeois bodies could be capable of such exposures.[5] The revelation of brutally long hours and pitifully low wages, frequently using child labor, while the owners drew large profits, had projected the "social question" (in Carlyle's phrase) onto the conscience of Europe when Marx was still a juvenile. In France, there had been the great insurrection of silk weavers at Lyons in 1831. The notion quickly grew that the wage system was a method of exploitation. A workers' jingle current before the *Communist Manifesto* was written (1848) made the point:

> Wages should form the price of goods
> Yes, wages should be all,
> Then we who work to make the goods,
> Should justly have them all.

This was a crude statement of the labor theory of value on which Marx erected his economic analysis.

Labor
Theory of
Value

The labor theory of value may be traced a long way back; it was forcefully stated by Adam Smith and adopted by Ricardo, where Marx found it. Later economic theory was to discard it as unscientific, but Marx seized upon it and attempted to work out all its implications. It was still partly economic orthodoxy in Marx's time though the "bourgeois" economists did not put it to the uses Marx did, needless to say. Value was "cost of production" which included materials and the natural reward of capital (the result of "abstinence" from present consumption) as well as labor. Senior had pointed out that some things have much value without any human labor at all: the pearl I chance to find in my oyster, for example! Yet remnants of the Ricardian labor theory of value existed in classical economics as represented most popularly by J. S. Mill at this time. The clean break with it was not to be made until Alfred Marshall and W. S. Jevons about 1870.

The labor theory of value, plus the subsistence theory of wages, suggested to socialists that labor does not get its full and just price because wages are determined in the market, by the principle of supply and

---

[5] Engels' *Condition of the Working Class,* 1844, made extensive use of the testimony before the Parliamentary committees.

demand, whereas the products are sold for their "true" price, based on the Labor Exchange Schemes amount of labor put into them. The difference was said to represent a surplus of value appropriated by the capitalist. Robert Owen had tried to change this pernicious system by using a currency reflecting units of labor, so that the price of a product would be exactly the amount of labor put into it. This naive idea proved entirely unworkable. Agreement could never be reached on just how many labor units commodities are worth, a major objection to the labor theory of value being that labor values submit to no accurate quantitative measurement. One carpenter might make a table in half the time another took; and how could you compare highly skilled labor to unskilled—how many hours of carpenter labor is one hour of an expert surgeon's time worth?[6] In practice, the market price based on supply and demand would prevail anyway. The only alternative would be an elaborate system of administrative pricing based on the arbitrary decrees of a state bureaucracy, a system with many disadvantages and few advantages.

Marx ridiculed the labor-exchange idea. He believed that only the abolition of capitalism—of private property in the means of production— would solve the problem, and he used the labor theory of value not to support labor-exchange or social-credit schemes, but rather to demonstrate, as he thought, the dynamics of capitalism as it worked towards its self-destruction.

Among the features of capitalism which seemed alarming in Marx's time were the periodic panics or depressions that afflicted it, tendencies toward monopoly, and of course the low wages and deplorable working conditions that frequently were the lot of the factory hands, to which one might add the demoralizing separation of workers from their tools and products, as they worked with machinery owned by others to produce goods that were not theirs to sell. For all these observable features of the nineteenth-century economic order in western Europe, Marx tried to supply explanations based on "laws." The whole of his argument was designed to show that capitalism is a doomed system because it is unavoidably digging its own grave. The labor theory of value is the foundation stone for Marx's concept of the *falling rate of profit*, which is chiefly how he explained crises, consolidation, and the increasing misery of the working class.

Profits must come out of labor. Therefore the increasing use of ma- Law of Capitalism's Decline chinery forces the capitalists to exploit their workers ever more mercilessly. They are forced to adopt machinery because of technological advances and competition; but as they increase the proportion of this "constant capital," as Marx called it, they have less and less of labor

---

[6] Marx attempted to meet this objection by postulating a "socially necessary" amount of labor for every commodity, but this hardly removed the problem.

power or "variable capital" from which to make profits. Today it seems odd that Marx should have supposed that mechanization destroys profits by displacing human labor. We should assume that it would be more likely to *increase* profits, by cutting down the wage bill or stepping up efficiency of production. But he had his eye fixed on the labor theory of value, from which his conclusion seems logically to follow. This is the chief of the "contradictions" of capitalism according to Marx: that as it progresses, measured by the use of advanced machinery, it must intensify the misery of the working class, for profits must be squeezed out of human labor power.. The more machinery used, the lower the wage of the worker has to be.

Strive as they will, the capitalists cannot however prevent their profits from declining. Of this unhappy fact another result is that some manufacturers are driven to the wall and fewer and fewer capitalists exist, holding bigger and bigger enterprises. This, too, unwittingly prepares for socialism; the huge industrial concern is already socialized, and at the last there are scarcely more than a handful of capitalists left to be taken over by society.

Having demonstrated to his own satisfaction that the workers were getting steadily more miserable and capitalists fewer, Marx went on to suggest an explanation for the depressions that periodically afflicted capitalism. His most original and characteristic explanation was that these depressions are a periodic annihilation of fixcd capital which delays the collapse of the system by temporarily increasing the proportion of variable capital, in other words, labor. Depressions are the result of a need to destroy the machinery that capitalism feeds on yet cannot digest, a sort of periodic regurgitation. It is sometimes inaccurately said that Marx explained depressions by underconsumption, that is, by the failure of the consuming classes to be given enough purchasing power; but this was the theory of Marx's scorned rival, Proudhon, and he does not assign it the main role as economic villain.

The labor theory of value on which Marx leaned so heavily was soon

Failure of
Marx's
Predictions

to be abandoned by economists, and today most of them think that it will bear little or none of the weight he put on it. His explanation of depressions, then, along with his theory of profits and wages, seem invalid. As for his predictions that small business would succumb entirely to big, and that with the advance of machinery people under capitalism would be worse off and not better—the doctrine of the declining rate of profit and the increasing misery of the working class—these things have not come about, though at times they may have looked plausible. By the end of the century many of Marx's own followers came to feel that a wholesale revision of his economic theories was needed. The main stream of economic analysis travelled away from Marx, and in recent times John Maynard Keynes unquestionably spoke for professional economists of virtually all schools in calling *Das Kapital* "an obsolete economic textbook." But Marx's doctrines have of course exerted an enormous influence on the Soviet Union since its revolutionary birth in 1917. Still, economic practice even in the USSR does not owe much directly to Marx, who failed to describe in detail the economics of socialism. He thought he had charted with scientific accuracy the last fatal illness of capitalism, and all Marxists continue to believe that "capitalism is doomed."

Perhaps it is, but apparently not for the reasons Marx gave. Sometimes it is suggested that Marx was a good prophet in a general sort of way though he missed many details; for has not our economic order, even in the West, travelled a long way from the unregulated individualism of the nineteenth century toward a "welfare state" system which is in the broadest sense socialistic? It has indeed, but we should note that Marx has not really proved a good prophet here. The welfare state or "interventionist" economy (the French have a word *dirigiste*—directed— which is useful) was not really what he had in mind. Marx believed the state would die; his vision of the future was essentially anarchist, or perhaps utopian. Social ownership of the means of production did not mean to him statism. About this he had little to say, to be sure. One cannot really give him much credit for anticipating the course of the future. Bear in mind that he expected the middle class to be ground to bits, the class struggle to become more acute, the factory workers to grow ever poorer until they rebelled, and the capitalist order to end in revolution, with private property in the sector of production disappearing. In all these respects he proved a poor prophet. It took a disastrous war to bring socialist revolution to Europe, and then it came to a backward, almost precapitalist society, quite contrary to the expectations of most Marxists.

Even as Marx was writing *Das Kapital* economists such as Stanley Jevons were criticizing the labor theory with devastating effect, doing away with the mystical idea of a true or inherent "value" of a commodity that is not the same as its market price. They substituted a sophisticated version of supply-and-demand, the marginal utility theory.[7] Others pointed out that Marx's surplus value would not do; why should not competition cause it to disappear? It was argued that capital is certainly

Criticisms of Das Kapital

[7] Developed almost simultaneously by Carl Menger in Austria and M. E. L. Walras in Switzerland along with Jevons in England, marginal utility analysis represented on charts the curve of diminishing utility as an individual—or, by extension, a nation—acquires successive units of a commodity. To a hungry man the first loaf of bread is extremely valuable, but each successive additional one decreases in its value to him. The final increment, the marginal one, determines exchange value. "Commodities exchange at ratios such that their marginal utilities are equal" (Edmund Whittaker). The student may consult textbooks of economics for full understanding of the principle. Employed by the influential economists Alfred Marshall in Britain and J. B. Clark in the United States, marginal theory tended to dominate academic economics in this "neoclassical" phase. Marshall's *Principles of Economics* supplanted Mill as the standard textbook.

productive, which Marx denied. But if in the eyes of experts not much was left of Marx's elaborate theorizing in his *magnum opus,* which he left unfinished, it remained a compelling document. In many portions of the book Marx abandoned the pretence of scientific objectivity to emit thunderous indictments of working conditions in the factories and the iniquity of capitalism. And the whole seemed an impressive vindication of the larger dialectical philosophy. Apparently Marx had shown in detail how capitalism destroys itself and in the process creates socialism, its "negation" which had always been included in itself. Socialism emerges out of the very womb of capitalism, as the dialectic predicts. Capitalism brought into existence the working class, forced it into the factories, and reduced the number of capitalists thus inadvertently "socializing" the economic order and the technological system; it created advanced machinery, broke down parochial social units to create the national and even international economy and also accustomed men to a rational, materialistic outlook. According to Marxists capitalism had an indispensable historical role to play, and until Lenin they practically all felt that every society must work its way through capitalism before it is ready for socialism. There was an ambiguity here, to be sure, revealed in the later history of the Marxist movement. One might choose to dwell on the horrors of capitalism, the misery it caused the workers, the need to destroy it; or one might point to its inevitability and the things it achieved to prepare the way for socialism. But it is the latter that is most characteristic of Marx as opposed to the mere moralists whose outlook he despised because it was not "scientific."

Perhaps the leading source of confusion in evaluating Marxism has been its enthusiastic believers' insistence upon the scientific, rational character of their creed, whereas in fact they have really committed themselves as an act of faith to a kind of religion. However fine and courageous a thinker Marx was, his overly ambitious system contains so many contradictions that, as Karl Popper (a sympathetic critic) observes, and as we know all too well today, those who remain dogmatic Marxists, like the Communists, "must become mystics—hostile to reasonable argument." They repeat the formula by rote and refuse to listen to objections; they ignore the real world and live in a dream world. It has become increasingly clear that theirs is a form of faith which has taken on the outer trappings of scientific positivism while preserving the inner structure of an emotional ideology. Many have pointed out the startling resemblance of Marxism to the psychological structure of religion, especially the Judaic-Christian framework transposed into secular terms. We have the original innocence of primitive communism, followed by the Fall (private property), the coming of the doctrine of salvation, the nature of evil and the struggle against it, finally the apocalypse and last state of blessed-

Marxism a Science?

ness. It is clear that this secular religion was in the making before Marx, for Rousseau and the Romantics contributed much to it; he gave it final form and further equipped it with enough intellectual content to satisfy a rational age. In a fine phrase of Professor J. Herman Randall, Jr.,[8] "Marxism is the last of the great Romantic faiths, lingering on in a scientific world."

The characteristic of such "ideologies" is that they are held with a quivering emotionality that erupts into antagonism when any article of the dogma is criticized, and that the holder of the ideology is dominated by it, constantly engaging in efforts to make other phenomena, and other people, conform to his vision. The person possessed by a religion or an ideology can doubtless be described as neurotic, yet this possession may be a source of great energy and dedication. History has been shaped mainly by the "true believers," from the prophets of Israel and the Christian martyrs down to the leaders of the French and Russian Revolutions. And it seems plain that Marxism has proved a potent faith.

Marx represents a blend of simple, emotional faith with a critical and rational intellect. Often he furiously condemned and ridiculed the simpler variety of socialist as "utopian" or soft-headed, wooly-minded. Yet he himself appears in some respects simplistic and utopian. Despite his protests he was essentially not scientist but prophet. Judged in this light, he has received praise from some in our time who have rejected his philosophy as meaningless and his economics as outdated. As a moral critic of capitalism, voicing a protest against its alienation of the worker from his work, its destruction of esthetic values and human dignity, Marx adds his powerful bass to a whole chorus of such nineteenth-century indictments. He would have indignantly rejected the classification of his thought as ethical, but his moral criticism seems to have survived his pseudoscientific theorizing, through most of the Western world. He was the founder not, as he thought, of the social sciences but of the greatest religious movement of modern times.

Marxism is for millions in some parts of the world today a faith to live by, and we may well ask why—wherein lay its peculiar potency as a religion? The answer would seem to be in its strong combination of emotional-ideological with rational-scientific factors, a combination, if you like, of the Enlightenment and Romanticism; or a new *Summa*, like St. Thomas's, blending faith with reason. If today we are inclined to "see through" the allegedly rational and scientific portions of Marx, this is not to deny that they were there and could carry great conviction for all but the most searchingly critical intellects. One way in which Marxism seems curiously old-fashioned today is in its absence of any sense of the irra-

[8] "The Impact of Darwin on Philosophy," *Journal of the History of Ideas*, October-December, 1961, p. 450.

tional or nonrational factors in man. Marx scarcely has a psychology, and modern Marxists have usually strongly resisted Freud, Jung, and the Existentialists, calling them bourgeois and decadent. Likewise Marxism contributed little to the study of politics as such, a rather strange neglect for a political creed. Politics is the mirror of economic-class interests, which are clear and calculable, without separate identity of its own, according to Marxism. All this testifies to an old-fashioned, Enlightenment rationalism in Marx.

The religious features gave expression to a powerful ethical imperative: one's duty was to advance the course of history by assailing the evil of capitalism and thus to prepare the way for the final kingdom of righteousness. Like Calvinism, socialist historicism made you feel that the fates were fighting on your side, and thus was a great energizing factor. So in many ways this was the "religion of science," or the scientific religion, for which Comte and Renan had searched. He who adopts Marxism may well feel that he understands the world, and from this he sees what he must do to serve the good cause.

It may be unnecessary to add that this Marxist religion, an intolerant one, could lead to ruthless behavior. Lenin's pronouncement is well known: "morality is what serves to destroy the old exploiting society." Hegelian historicism encourages the morality of being on the winning side, we know; to this, Marxism added a ferocious hatred for the old "exploiting society" and a keen desire to hasten the coming of the revolution. The Communist followers of Marx and Lenin were prepared to employ cruelty, force, treachery, and deceit so long as these weapons were used against the bourgeoisie in behalf of the socialist revolution. These features were more evident in the Russian followers of Marx than among the milder Social Democrats of the western countries, but they are easily drawn from his doctrines.

In many ways the social ideologies we have been considering, though they were tremendously influential, were out of touch with realities in their age. Of Comte, Marx, and Spencer alike, A. D. Ritchie has observed that "All three smell of the midnight oil and the ivory tower. They none of them have the proper smell of places where collective or public human action occurs, where discussions go on and decisions are made." It is difficult to object to this characterization. Few more pronounced "outsiders" ever existed than Comte and Marx, impoverished obscurities in their lifetimes, writing books nobody read until some years later. But not so unusual (Bentham is a good example, Rousseau another) is the phenomenon of the eccentric recluse-philosopher who proves to be a fountain of ideas destined to the utmost importance when taken up by others. These ideologies we have found emerging from the nineteenth century answered some great need. They all thought they were sciences; but clearly today we must see them as more nearly "miscellaneous prejudices dressed up to look like science." They did not serve any useful purpose in meeting practical problems of the day, such as statesmen and business-men faced in their daily affairs.

Yet they were, or became, very popular. Nobody now reads the works of Comte or Spencer, yet a century ago "Spencer's books were read all over the world in many languages by thousands of devoted disciples." Marx's still are. The reason for this is that these imposing systems of thought offered to restore to European man his lost vision of an inte-grated universe, the source of values. In brief, they substituted for re-ligion, and for the metaphysical systems of the past. Comte was right in divining that modern man had lost his capacity for traditional Chris-tianity and metaphysics. He had not and could not lose his need for religion in the broader sense—as a fairly simple, comprehensible, satis-fying picture of the world revealing its structure and purpose. Walter Marshall Horton has defined the human needs which faiths satisfy as three: "the need for an ultimate object of trust and devotion; the need for a final goal of hope and endeavor; the need for a concrete connection between trust and hope. . . ," in other words, a way of salvation. The increasingly numerous and somewhat disoriented masses of modern life, often uprooted by industrialism from traditional societies and cast into the maelstrom of an anomic civilization, have urgent needs of this sort. They may cling to traditional religion but increasingly they have adopted substitutes. No doubt this explains the significance of the nineteenth century's classical ideologies.

Nineteenth-Century Ideologies as Modern Religions

REVISIONISM, FABIANISM, AND OTHER FORMS OF SOCIALISM

Not well known in Europe until the 1880s, Karl Marx's formidable system thereafter tended to mold and dominate Continental socialism but never had that kind of success in Britain and never monopolized the field anywhere. Socialism was far broader than Marxism. It ranged, taking the term in its largest dimensions, from a fairly conservative bourgeois right wing, including Christian Socialism and moderate welfare-state reformism, to a revolutionary far left which by the 1880s had come to be designated "anarchism." In between lay many species in rich variety. Marx's contemporaries included Michael Bakunin, the Russian revolu-tionary, with whom he did many a battle; Louis Blanc, in exile in England after 1848 but tough enough to outlive the Bonapartist regime and return to France in 1871; Mazzini and Garibaldi, the Italians who became internationally famous in 1861; and the American, Henry George, whose book *Progress and Poverty* exerted a remarkable influence in Britain and parts of the Continent. Then there was William Morris, the great Vic-

Varieties of Socialism

torian artist, poet, and craftsman, who popularized "guild socialism," a return to the spirit of medieval artisans. Proudhon, the French "mutualist," long retained a strong following in France, and the First International of 1864 produced quarrels between the Marxists and Proudhonists. In Germany, Ferdinand Lassalle, a romantic figure who disagreed with Marx on some matters, was a more important leader in the 1870s than the latter.

Then, within a few years after the major reception of Marxism and its success in the 1890s in capturing the strongest socialist groups on the Continent, came a major effort to "revise" Marx in the light of new developments; while in Great Britain the important Fabian movement rejected Marxian theory to build a more eclectic but extremely effective brand of reformist socialism. All this and more is part of the rich history of socialism and social reform in these latter decades of the nineteenth century, when Europe moved rapidly toward an order both more urban, industrial, and democratic. A brief review of this long story follows.

Proudhonism; the Paris Commune

Revolutionary socialism, or working-class socialism of any sort, sank almost out of sight after 1848 for some time, suffering from repression and disunity. The Second Empire in France jailed Proudhon, exiled Blanc, and stifled press freedom while "buying off" the workers with its great public works projects. With the softening of Louis Napoleon's regime in 1860, socialism revived somewhat, only to be crushed again in the gripping episode of the Commune of Paris, 1871. Working-class socialists were accused of fomenting class war in Paris and the reaction again brought severe repression. This phase of French socialism was Proudhonist. Under the banner of "mutualism" these followers of the Besançon-born working man, who died in Paris in 1865, manifested a hatred of the state and centralized power that marked them off sharply from other socialists. They thought proletarian revolution should lead to a decentralized, "federal" political structure, for Proudhon could see no purpose to the existing state except militarism and the repressive defense of property, both of which would vanish with the bourgeoisie. The economic order would be one of cooperatives, the workers in each factory, farm, or store jointly managing it. Somewhat fuzzy and inane, Proudhon's utopia had the merit of upholding liberty; he accused Marx of fomenting a new tyranny while Marx sneered at the simplicity of the Frenchmen's economic ideas. In 1871 when the Parisians decided to secede from the rest of France after the abdication of the Emperor Louis Napoleon (defeated by the Germans in war), they were acting in large part on Proudhon's ideas. (Communes were proclaimed in several other French cities.) The defeat of this revolt, and the brutal reprisals, caused the death or banishment of some 20,000 "Communards" and crushed French working-class radicalism to earth for another generation. One of the casualties was the First International, organized in 1864; always a scene of contention, it split, with the "Federalists" or "Anarchists" (Proudhonists) taking over what was left of it for a while only to see it die in 1877.

From the shattering defeat and civil strife of 1870–1871, France headed slowly toward the Third Republic, under which freedom would revive and a new socialist movement gradually reappear. In Germany, laws against the Socialists were enforced in the seventies and eighties while at the same time Bismarck tried to alleviate the lot of the workers with Europe's first state-administered social welfare system, including old-age pensions and insurance against sickness. But the German Social Democratic Party, now firmly Marxist, survived the persecution, developed able leaders and a magnificent organization, and after being legalized in 1890 following Bismarck's removal from power, went on to become one of Germany's largest political parties (*the* largest by 1912) and the dominant force in the Second International. The latter world organization dates from 1889–1890 and enjoyed considerable success until 1914, its international congresses and its annual May Day demonstrations being impressive. It counted 12 million members by 1914; the war destroyed it. Second International

The 1880s and particularly the 1890s saw a widespread interest in social legislation on all fronts; it is the watershed for the change of direction from laissez-faire economic liberalism to a more socially conscious, state-interventionist order. There were many signs of this and many versions of it. Here are a few. In 1881 the philosopher T. H. Green began at Oxford University a school of social thought influenced by Hegel and stressing the social origin of rights, the social responsibilities of property. The rapidity of the change in outlook may be judged from a comment of Lord Milner: "When I went up to Oxford (in the early 1870s) the laissez-faire theory still held the field. . . . But within ten years the few men who held the old doctrines in their extreme rigidity had come to be regarded as curiosities." This was a respectable revolution. Green borrowed from Hegel a feeling for the claims of society and the positive role of the state, without any admixture of revolution or violence. At University College, London, economist Stanley Jevons undermined dogmatic laissez-faire by simply asking for scientific, empirical investigation in particular areas to determine "where we want greater freedom and where less," a solution of problems piecemeal, rather than in accordance with some general formula. This was the path taken by the Fabian Socialists. It was a reaction against the dogmatic individualism often proclaimed by Victorian liberals (for example, Auberon Herbert and the Non-Interference Union) as much as against dogmatic socialism. Welfare Statism T. H. Green's Social Philosophy

In 1887 the young Irish critic, essayist, orator, novelist, and playwright George Bernard Shaw introduced Marx (as he was soon to introduce Nietzsche) to the British public. But the sharp-witted young men Fabian Socialism with whom Shaw joined to form the Fabian Society at about this time soon rejected Marx's labor theory of value and with it the rest of his economics; they retained only his moral indignation at the alleged stupidities and wrongs of a capitalistic, acquisitive society, and this they got from others besides Marx—from Carlyle, Ruskin, Mill, Morris, Nietzsche. The Fabians emerged from the chrysalis of something called the Fellowship of the New Life, founded by a remarkable Scotsman, Thomas Davidson, in 1882. The Fabian Society broke away from Davidson's group in 1884. Shaw joined it in 1885. He had turned socialist after listening to Henry George. Fabianism was eclectic in its origins, not imprisoned by a dogma, and permeated with the spirit of British empiricism. Initially, after Jevons and Alfred Marshall had discredited the Marxian labor theory of value in favor of a marginal utility theory, the Fabians tried to elaborate a general theory of exploitation on this basis, using the Ricardian theory of rent. But before long they decided that "abstract economics" was not of much value. A mentor of Fabian founder Beatrice Webb was Charles Booth, author of an exhaustive pioneer social study of *Life and Labour of the People of London* (9 volumes, 1892–1897). "The *a priori* reasoning of political economy, orthodox and unorthodox alike, fails from want of reality," Booth wrote. Booth had been influenced by Comte and by the German historical school of economics (Schmoller). The result was an economics mainly historical and descriptive; the chief works of the Webbs were massive historical studies of local government, trade unions, and poor relief. Problems should be tackled piecemeal with the aid of thorough factual documentation, they believed. Fabian pamphleteering was often hard-hitting, and bitterly critical of bourgeois society. But the movement's enduring importance lay in the patient accumulation of facts and ideas directed at particular abuses, under the guidance of the industrious Sidney Webb and his wife, Beatrice.

Clearly a faith was at work here; the Fabians did not doubt that socialism was a higher form of human society, the next rung on the ladder of social evolution, and they worked for it with a missionary spirit. The following statement, by C. E. M. Joad, may suggest something of the mood, as he recalled it in later years:

> England before 1914 was a land of gross social and economic inequality, in which the poverty and misery of the many were outraged by the luxury and the ostentation of the few. Under Socialism we believed the poverty and misery would disappear and the inequality be rectified. This was the first, fresh springtime of the Fabian Socialism, and we saw ourselves marching in irresistible procession with Shaw, Webb and Wells— slightly out of step—in the vanguard, to the promised land of State ownership of the means of production, distribution and exchange which we believed lay just around the corner.[9]

[9] "What I Still Believe," *The New Statesman and Nation*, May 19, 1951.

In their early days at least, the Fabians were not too scholarly to take part in demonstrations and harangue working-class audiences. On November 13, 1887, Shaw, William Morris, Annie Besant, and other intellectual socialists were roughed up by the police at a demonstration in Trafalgar Square. After this they chose the path of gradual change by parliamentary means, their duty being to furnish the politicians with the facts of industrial life, so fully and plainly that even a politician could not do otherwise than recognize the necessity of social legislation. In this they were remarkably successful. If, prior to World War I, there was in Britain no very large Labour or Socialist Party (there was a small one, with less than 10 percent of the seats in the House of Commons), this was largely because the older parties, especially the Liberals, had been quietly infiltrated by a good deal of social-welfare doctrine.

If they rejected Marx's economic theory, the Fabians agreed with his faith in the future of socialism. It was, they thought, evident that socialism was the wave of the future. But it would come gradually, was coming everyday, rather than all at once in one great revolution. Parliamentary democracy and other institutions of self-government would ensure its peaceful adoption. The Fabians placed great stress on local government; contrary to a common opinion, they did not propose the nationalization of all industry, but at this time (pre-1914) hoped that the county and borough councils, recently established in Great Britain, would own and operate a great deal of it. They did believe in public ownership as a panacea that, by driving the landlord and capitalists out of business, would increase the workers' share and lead to an era of plenty for all. In this they were often quite naive.

But Fabian tactics helped ease the way to acceptance of social welfare principles by moderate men in Great Britain. Under conservative auspices, paternalistic perhaps and including such things as municipal ownership of utilities ("gas and water socialism") and state-run health insurance or old-age pension plans, it could attract broad support; in 1889 a British peer remarked that "we are all socialists now." The sheer facts of life in a complex, interdependent industrial society forced men to modify laissez-faire capitalism. Bismarck declared in his great speech to the German Reichstag on social insurance legislation that the modern state could not disclaim all responsibility for the welfare of its working-class citizens; if it did, it would invite revolution. More modestly, Birmingham industrialist Joseph Chamberlain found that the upper classes could not ignore sanitary conditions among the lower classes in a modern city, because cholera germs were no respecters of class lines. *"Gas and Water" Socialism*

Also, trade unions became accepted and respectable and gave the workers a modest voice in the affairs of industry and the state. They were at least a force to be reckoned with, backed by the weapon of the strike. In the 1900s British trade unions overcame the Taff Vale decision, making them responsible for damages in a strike. Bitter strikes swept France and *Trade Unionism*

Italy as well as Britain, in this decade. While in France "syndicalists" dreamed of accomplishing the revolution by a great general strike, trade union leaders were apt to scorn the socialist intellectuals who preferred theoretical argument to "practical work inside the labor movement" (Peter Gay). Orthodox Marxism deplored the "opportunism" of trade unionism which aimed at nothing more than getting some workers a bigger slice of the rewards without "changing the system." But in Germany the unions and the Marxist Social Democrats struck a close alliance. (The French unionists, by contrast, rejected such a relationship.) By 1906, it was the unionists who had the stronger position, but they accepted the SDs as their political arm. In all the countries of western Europe, the unions, growing rapidly in the 1890s, were strong in the 1900s.

"Socialism" in this sense, as a pragmatic modification of laissez-faire capitalism in trade-unionist and state-welfare directions, became an accepted part of the late Victorian political landscape, though not without its bitter controversies: as late as 1910 in Britain the Lloyd George budget, including an income tax for social insurance financing, inspired an opposition which ended only in the "swamping" of the House of Lords and the passing of a Parliament Act sharply reducing the power of the peers to block legislation. While Fabianism did its work, the small Labour Party held a swing position between the major parties and won concessions.

Quite different was the situation in Germany, where a strong Marxist party developed, by far the strongest and best-organized one in Europe. The German Social Democrats won great prestige by their success against Bismarck's efforts to destroy them. After 1891 save for one brief period the SDP thrived on legality, having shown it could survive illegality. It was a well-disciplined mass organization, publishing its own newspaper and led by educated Germans of the caliber of August Bebel, Wilhelm Liebknecht, Eduard Bernstein and Karl Kautsky. Entering into close association with the trade unions, in 1912 it was the largest single political party with one-third of the electorate. The Social Democratic leaders accepted the possibility of overthrowing capitalism by peaceful, democratic means. In the meetings of the Second International they opposed the radicalism of the Anarchists and preached the inevitability of socialism on the basis of Marx's theory of the self-destruction of capitalism, the dialectically necessary triumph of socialism. Unlike the Fabians they did not view socialism as a piecemeal program but awaited the day when the entire capitalistic system would crumble, meanwhile generally refusing to collaborate in government with the "bourgeoisie."

Bernstein went further in the direction of reformism. His efforts to "revise" Marx touched off a battle of words within the SDP in which revisionism was finally rejected. Bernstein believed that Marx's prophecies about the decline of capitalism and the increasing misery of the working-

The German Social Democrats

Revisionism

class had proved false. Small and medium property had not disappeared, but were even increasing; the working class was getting better off, not worse off; the class struggle had become less acute, not more so. Drawing conclusions from this, he suggested a reformism not far in spirit from British Fabianism. He held that political democracy, having arrived in western Europe, made it possible to establish socialism by parliamentary means. "In all advanced countries," he urged, "we see the privileges of the capitalist bourgeoisie yielding step by step to democratic organizations." The party refused to accept this gradualism in theory, remaining officially committed to the winning of the proletarian revolution by means of the class struggle. It would not participate in governments in collaboration with the "bourgeois" parties. It almost read Bernstein out of the party, though he was an old and dedicated servant. But it was not in practice revolutionary, or at least it was prepared to postpone thoughts of the revolution to the morrow, when its electoral power would have increased. This position was somewhat ambiguous.

Similar issues agitated the French Socialist party which, rent by schism, managed to achieve unity in the 1900s but not unanimity. In 1899, after the socialist Millerand had accepted a post in the government headed by the left republican Waldeck-Rousseau, the French socialists earnestly debated this policy, and it was the occasion for exchanges between their two outstanding leaders, Jules Guesde and Jean Jaurès. Jaurès argued that it was good to penetrate bourgeois positions in this way, for would not the capitalist regime fall little by little, and how could it fall if its outposts were never occupied? But Guesde carried the day, by a narrow margin, with an eloquent exposition of socialist orthodoxy: the doctrine of the class struggle, of the solidarity of the working classes, of the utter incompatibility of socialism and capitalism: there could be no "mixture" or in-betweens, it was a matter of either-or. In the 1914 elections the party won about a sixth of the seats; like its German counterpart it refused to take ministerial posts in any government in which it would share power. Right wing-left wing tension still existed, with unity maintained only at the cost of a rather imprecise program. *French Socialism: the Millerand Case*

Similarly in Italy there were reformist, revisionist spokesmen (for example, Filippo Turati) arguing that democracy had rendered revolution obsolete, but finding bitter opponents on the left to whom this was dangerous illusion. In Russia, the Marxist debate took a not dissimilar turn. Marxism entered Russia via the remarkable intellect of G. V. Plekhanov, a self-educated but exceedingly well-educated man who, exiled like so many other politically conscious Russians, lived and wrote for many years in Switzerland. In the 1870s the political faith of revolutionary Russians was populism, a courageous, self-sacrificing but intellectually not very clear movement, based on a belief in the uniqueness of Russia and especially of her communal peasant population. In reaction against the *Plekhanov and Russian Marxism* romantic excesses of populism, which resorted to assassination, climaxed in the killing of Tsar Alexander II in 1881, the cool, analytical approach of Marxism was welcome. A civilized, even fastidiously esthetic intellectual, Plekhanov believed in the Marxist laws of historical evolution and counselled waiting for a democratic revolution which would come about spontaneously after Russia went through a capitalist phase. Instilling Marxist precepts into a generation of Russian revolutionaries, Plekhanov found some of these disinclined to wait. In 1903, Lenin proposed the creation of an elite of professional revolutionaries, trained to seize power. To Plekhanov's orthodox Marxism this was little less than Bonapartism or Blanquism. The majority of the Russian Social Democratic Party followed him and a split occurred. Lenin's "Bolshevik" group was in fact in a small minority most of the time, the "Mensheviks" a more numerous and prestigious group. 1917 was to bring victory and fame to the stubbornly independent Lenin; prior to that, he was thought to have departed widely from Marxian orthodoxy, and was isolated at the far left of the socialist spectrum.

Mensheviks and Bolsheviks

To sum up the Marxist debate, on the Continent, though not in England, Marxism prevailed as the reigning orthodoxy in the Socialist or Social Democratic Parties which were well organized and gaining adherents, on the eve of 1914. But within the parties sharp debate took place centering on the issue of whether class struggle, revolution, and the complete destruction of capitalism at one stroke had not become an obsolete program in the era of democratic politics, trade unionism, and welfare capitalism. The usual answer was to refuse to abandon Marxism for Fabian gradualism (Bernstein) but also to reject stress on violent revolution through illegal or conspiratorial means (Lenin). The majority of Socialists held to their faith in an apocalyptic revolution that would change the entire system; but thought this could come peacefully as soon as their political party won a majority of the electorate, and they refused meanwhile to take any share of power. Their rate of growth between 1890 and 1914 held out some hope that this might happen. But this compromise was an uneasy one, and gave rise to a degree of internal tension. Between Albert Thomas and Jules Guesde in France, Eduard Bernstein and Karl Liebknecht in Germany, or Plekhanov and Lenin in Russia, one found a considerable ideological and psychological distance.

Socialist Tensions

Viewed more broadly, Marxism itself was a kind of center between a right and left wing of the entire "social" movement. To its left lay the Anarchists, who seldom could be contained in the same party with the Socialists though the congresses of the International provided a place for a less than friendly exchange of views. (The Socialists passed resolutions against the Anarchists at the International and told them they were not welcome, but, as trade union delegates, some Anarchists always got in.) Anarchism was weak in Germany (though sometimes spectacular),

Anarchism

stronger (as "anarcho-syndicalism" or direct action through the trade unions) in France, still stronger in Italy and Spain where the condition of the lower classes was more desperate and industrialism was less advanced. An "Anarchist" might be a peace-loving enemy of centralization, a Proudhonian friend of liberty and cooperation; but in the 1880s and 1890s a much more familiar type resorted to assassination and other violent actions. They all disbelieved in the value of political action through elections and parliaments. Some of them were Marxists, or partial Marxists: what they had learned from the master was that economics determines all, that representative legislatures are a sham to cover the dictatorship of the bourgeoisie (this from Proudhon, too), and that capitalism owns the state and always will until smashed in the proletarian social revolution. After the revolution, there would be no more parliaments or states anyway, Anarchists held; there would be the pure freedom of the classless society—no government at all.

Many varieties of anarchism existed and indeed by their very nature these individualistic radicals could not be regimented into any one creed. But significant numbers of them tried to foment revolution, preparing the workers for it by preaching or, better, by action. Ultra-anarchists engaged in a wave of assassinations in the 1890s that shocked not only the bourgeoisie but also the Social Democrats, who denounced them furiously. Others dreamed of the general strike as a revolutionary weapon, and meanwhile tried to stir up all the strikes they could to give the workers practice.

It is depressing to record so much hate, but the Anarchists were idealists who had many of them known the suffering of the most deprived classes in the community. Their intellectual antecedents were vague but plentiful: all the denouncers of injustice and leaders of revolt from Spartacus to Marx, all the haters of ruling-class sham from Lucretius to Baudelaire. If they were educated they knew these; most were not, except for scraps of second-hand learning. They were the extremists of a revolution, the Black Moslems of the nineteenth-century proletariat. Much of their spirit got into the Russian Revolution which, nominally Marxist, was led by men who shared a good deal of the anarchist *esprit*. Lenin was, really, a borderline case. One of the leading fountains of nineteenth-century anarchism had been the Russian Bakunin, followed by the "nihilistic" assassins of the 1870s.

If the Anarchists stood to the left of the Socialists or Social Democrats, there were many on the right, among whom we have named Fabians, simple trade unionists, and bourgeois upholders of the welfare state. British "Lib-Labs" or trade unionists often seemed highly out of place at International meetings taken up with debates between German Marxists and Italian Anarchists. Lord Harcourt, needless to say, who had said "we are all socialists," would hardly have been welcome there at all!

Right-Wing Socialism

Conservative upholders of the status quo, pillars of society, might show an interest in mild socialism. Bismarck, as well as England's Disraeli and Joseph Chamberlain, and Italy's Giolitti,[10] held that some concessions to the workers would keep them from following madmen into violent revolution; if to conserve is to preserve, preservation demanded an end to the irresponsibility of laissez-faire. In 1890, the Emperor of Germany, Kaiser Wilhelm II, having just fired Bismarck and repealed the anti-socialist laws, called an international conference to consider "international labor legislation." In France, following the turmoil of the famous Dreyfus Case, the bourgeois left wing (Radicals, and soon Radical Socialists) flirted with socialism: basically Jacobin-democratic, men like Aristide Briand and Georges Clemenceau were prepared to tax big property for the benefit of small, and the government budget of expenditures on welfare rose sharply. The *Solidarisme* of politician-intellectual Leon Bourgeois found nature as well as society filled with cooperation and interdependence, rather than dog-eat-dog competition. At the same time these Radicals showed no sympathy toward Anarchist violence, and used troops to break their strikes.

Christian
Socialism

Of these varieties of socialism, one more at least needs to be mentioned: Christian socialism. The great papal encyclical *Rerum Novarum*, 1891, was the most famous pronouncement here, though there were Protestant versions also. It was not difficult for the Church to approve a kind of socialism. Christian dislike of materialism and selfishness, the doctrine of stewardship by which the rich should aid the poor, the deeply implanted Christian concern for the meek and disinherited, all might be turned in this direction. Catholic social doctrine gained prominence earlier in the century from the writings of Lamennais, but the Breton firebrand had run afoul of orthodoxy. Albert de Mun and de la Tour du Pin subsequently brought to Catholic social doctrine an interest in the corporate economics of the Middle Ages; politically, they were conservatives. Pope Leo XIII was deeply interested in the cause of regaining the working class for Christianity. *Rerum Novarum* opposed modern capitalism and while rejecting "materialistic socialism" called for a fundamental reorganization of economic life to correspond with Christian principles. In France and Italy Catholic trade unions were organized, many priests devotedly dedicated service to working-class education, and there were individual examples of capitalists (like Leon Hormel) moved to experiment with "the Christian factory," but it is doubtful if the Catholic Social movement achieved very much. Christianity had lost most of the proletariat to the secular religion of socialism. Karl Marx was its new prophet.

[10] Who according to Denis Mack Smith "had studied *Das Kapital* with application and profit." Giolitti was the almost perennial Italian prime minister between 1900 and 1914.

By the 1900s, there were those who thought this secular socialism was dying of dogmatism and an obsolete, simplistic set of *idées fixés*. (See the remarks of Benedetto Croce, in *Cultura e vita morale*, 1911; or the view of Charles Péguy, leading French writer of the 1900s who broke with the Marxists to become a kind of Christian socialist.) In western Europe, considering the subsequent history of social democracy of all sorts, this was probably true. We need not be reminded that there were other parts of the world where it had quite a role to play. For western Europe, the later nineteenth century was the great age of this secular religion or ideology: the Age of Marx.

As a footnote to Marx's exciting if controversial historical scheme, we might add that history was becoming of serious interest to many in the nineteenth century. Despised in the seventeenth and developed only in rudimentary ways in the eighteenth, it received its philosophical certificate of legitimacy from Burke, Herder, and Hegel and became a respectable academic citizen in the mid-nineteenth century. For example, a chair of modern history was first established at Cambridge University only in the eighteenth century and for long after that amounted to little, but leaped to the front in the era of Lord Acton. The great historians— Voltaire, Gibbon, and on to Macaulay and Michelet in the earlier nineteenth century—had been amateur *literati,* more noted for their literary gifts than any professional competence, though often they did do capable research; now, beginning in Germany (especially at the University of Göttingen), history came of age as a specialized profession marked by the "scientific" use of materials, careful research in the primary sources, with thorough criticism and collation of knowledge. Making possible this advance was the collection and organization of historical materials in the great libraries, archives, and museums of Europe, something that was accomplished only toward the end of the eighteenth century.

Growth of Historical Studies

The Romantics stimulated imaginative interest in the past; German philosophers saw it as the unfolding of Truth, Burkeans as the school of political wisdom. It became possible to widen the range of historical studies to include social and economic history; this was partly a matter of having access to the sources of such knowledge, such as the records of medieval manors, but also partly the perspective of an age acutely aware of economic and social issues. In general, with the retreat of confidence in religion or metaphysics to answer the big questions about the meaning and conduct of life, people turned to history. There one found a repository of wisdom and experience, a treasure-house of knowledge throwing light on the present human situation. Darwin and other evolutionary thinkers popularized explanation of a genetic sort. With the arrival of professional methods and the organization of materials, history seemed to be passing from the realm of conjecture and opinion to the status of a genuine science. Quite a few others in addition to Karl Marx had the idea that a real science of history was now possible. Henry Buckle was dogmatic about it in England, Mill thought so more cautiously; the German scholars, doing their arduous detailed research, felt that some day, somehow, the fruits of painstakingly accurate spade work would be gathered in the form of a universal synthesis. French Positivists agreed.

The belief in a science of history in this sense—the sense indicated by historian J. B. Bury when he declared in his inaugural lecture as Regius Professor at Cambridge in 1902 (succeeding Acton) that "there will no longer be divers schools of history," only one, true history, since history is "simply a science, no less and no more"—has almost died since then. But the nineteenth was, beyond question, an historical century; Bury was not wrong in asserting that "In the story of the nineteenth century, which has witnessed such far-reaching changes in the geography of thought and in the apparatus of research, no small or isolated place belongs to the transformation and expansion of history." The leading ideologies, as we have noted, were historical—Hegel's, Comte's, and Spencer's as well as Marx's. Among the great intellectual figures of the century whose interest in history was much more than incidental one could list in addition Tocqueville, Renan, Mill, Arnold, Newman, and many others.[11]

And the reason for this "historical revolution" was that investigation of the past had become not just the indulgence of idle curiosity or trivial antiquarianism, but something charged with the deepest meaning because it could explain the fate and future of mankind. It could reveal the great laws of development, the cycles of growth of the human race from earliest times to today—and tomorrow. All the great nineteenth-century theories of history posited an ascent from lower to higher, in one way or another. Bitter critic of capitalist society that he was, Marx was as optimistic as any Victorian in the long run: one more turn of the wheel of history and the millennium would be reached.

---

[11] Acton, together with his German friend the Munich professor I. Döllinger, dedicated historians as they were, formulated an historical theology of Catholicism according to which the Christian truth gradually revealed itself in history through the medium of the Church. Unfortunately the Vatican could not accept this because of its implications that individual popes might have erred (did not have the full truth in the past), etc. It remains an interesting example of the impact of history on the age. "Metaphysics could not be relied upon to promote religion—that could be done only by history," as Acton reported the view of Döllinger.

[With] the development of intellectualism and the rationalization of life. . . . Art takes over the function of a this-worldly salvation. . . . It provides a salvation from the routines of everyday life, and especially from the increasing pressures of theoretical and practical rationalism.

MAX WEBER

It will no longer be a despot that oppresses the individual, but the masses. . . . I shall return to the Bedouins, who are free.

GUSTAVE FLAUBERT

The Crisis of European Thought: 1880-1914

5

It is common to mark off a new period of European history beginning in 1870 or 1871. One obvious landmark was the Franco-Prussian War, which brought to an end the Second Empire in France, led to the Third Republic there, and introduced Germany's Imperial Reich as the greatest state in Europe. The unification of Italy was also completed at this time with the annexation of Rome and the ending of the Pope's temporal power. There were other landmarks: In 1867, Great Britain made a further extension of the suffrage and followed it within a few years with other reforms, in education, the army, the civil service, which constituted a significant turn toward political democracy. After the victory of the unionists in her great Civil War in 1865, which had some influence on the turn toward democracy in England, the United States experienced a vast economic boom that contributed not a little to Europe's, while Germany also waxed prosperous on her new unity, beginning a classic period of international trade and development. Also, one can trace the beginnings of the "new imperialism" to the 1870s.

But periodization is often arbitrary, and it is just as easy to make the break a little later. Neither imperialism nor democracy really got into high gear until the 1880s: witness the Third Republic which was not firmly established until this decade, or British politics where Gladstone's Midlothian campaign of 1881 stands as the first really popular election. It is from the 1880s that we date the rise of trade unions and socialist movements, as the last chapter indicated; there is general agreement that this was the critical decade for the turn away from laissez-faire liberalism. Moreover it was the 1880s which introduced electricity, the automobile, and other miracles of technology, though no decade in the nineteenth century was without its contribution to this process.

For the intellectual historian, some time in the 1880s is preferable as a turning point. This decade produced not only Nietzsche, Freud, and Bergson, in addition to the important social thought just referred to, but also such things as the beginning of a new trend in science, dateable from the Michelson-Morley experiment of 1887, and a revolution in the arts— a revolution best placed here, it would seem, though it straddled the whole period 1870–1914. Involved are such writers and artists as Ibsen, Zola, Dostoyevsky, Tolstoy, the Symbolists, and the Impressionists. From the other end, one can hardly avoid seeing the 1870s as the evening of the mid-Victorian day, not yet quite done, its great figures still alive. One thinks of Mill, Marx, and Darwin in ideology, of the writers Tennyson, Browning, Carlyle, Ruskin, Arnold, and other "eminent Victorians."

One cannot be precise in such matters. The 1870s, the 1880s, the 1890s, the 1900s, each brought forth its novelties and its men of genius. What no one doubts is that 1914 was an epochal date, the huge war that settled its gloomy cloud over Europe in that year marking the end of an era in everyone's chronology. It is beyond doubt also that the years just before 1914 bore unmistakeable signs of being critically disturbed ones. An unusual number of old truths became uncertain, an unusual number of strange creeds and novel doctrines appeared. This was true in the sciences, where verities not challenged since Newton were overturned in a new scientific revolution. It was true in philosophy, in the arts, and in social studies. It was no less true in religion. It is possible that these years were the critical ones for the future destiny of Western man. Intellectually, they are the most exciting years of all, to one living in the twentieth century, for the ideas born here have largely shaped the mind of that century —something rather comparable to the way the 1688–1720 period set the directions of Enlightenment thought.

DEMOCRACY AND NATIONALISM

Imperialism

This was the time of Western civilization's spectacular conquest of the outer world, when the continents of Asia and Africa were forced to submit to the domination of the aggressive Europeans. This vast process was in the widest sense a tribute to the amazing success of Europe, its higher technical skills, and also its organizing genius. But it brought evil with it and to many thoughtful Europeans it was a dismaying moral lapse, perhaps a symbol of decline and fall. The man in the street certainly found it gratifying; but eventually it would produce revolutions against

Western domination on the part of Asiatic and African peoples. For the time being what it most notably produced was an inordinate pride and boastfulness, the jingoism that helped fan the flames of war in 1914.

The outbreak of the worst war in history lay ahead, constituting a terrific moral setback for a civilization that had believed itself on the high road to man's greatest success. In some ways the war reflected the conquest of nineteenth-century Europe by the sentiment of nationalism. Nationalism appeared in the wake of Napoleon's attempt to impose French domination on Europe; Fichte's "Addresses to the German Nation," written when Bonaparte invaded Prussia, might be called its manifesto. It went on after the Peace of Vienna, which tried to ignore it; and it played a prominent part in the revolutions of 1848. Thereafter it was to emerge truly into its own in the era of Italian and German unification, when Mazzini was Europe's leading prophet. It was still potent in the years before 1914 and was a basic cause of the war explosion of that fateful year.

Nationalism was not absolutely new, but its intensity and dominance in the nineteenth century made it a force as never before. "The outstanding feature of European history in the nineteenth century is the growth of nationalities," it has been aptly claimed. Nation-making in Europe goes back a long way, ultimately to the earlier Middle Ages. National consciousness, a different and later thing, may be found at least as early as Elizabethan England and Lutheran Germany. But other loyalties competed with that paid to the state or national group. Throughout the Middle Ages, a man was a Christian first, then a native of his home district, and only after that (if at all) a Frenchman, or German. The Church was universal; so, in theory, was the state, for a long time. Actually strongest were dynastic and feudal loyalties, based on a personal and not a territorial loyalty. Only gradually did the future nation-states become clearly defined; but for an accident or two, indeed, we might have Burgundians today instead of Frenchmen. And in Germany the territorial duchies (Bavaria, Saxony, Swabia, Franconia) remained the focus of patriotic sentiment until fairly recent times.

The decline of competing ideals and the consolidation in their permanent form of the nation-states paved the way for nationalism. But the Enlightenment was quite cosmopolitan. Though the work of knitting together the larger states of Europe administratively and economically went steadily on, the fashion in ideas did not then encourage the growth of nationalistic sentiments. The French Revolution and Romanticism did contribute to nationalism, as we know it, and yet there remained a substantial element of international feeling among men of letters and learning in the first half of the century. Writing to Thomas Carlyle in 1826, Goethe in his old age rejoiced that "for some time past the best poets and writers of all nations have aimed at what is common to all men," and hoped that

Origins of Nationalism

this might aid the cause of international peace.[1] There were many transnational European phenomena at this time. Not only were such secular creeds as liberalism and socialism much the same everywhere, but the arts, as well as the sciences, recognized no national boundaries. For example, in music Berlioz was an idol in Germany, Wagner in France—more so than either was in his own country!

But powerful forces were making for nationalism, and writers, poets, philosophers were to get involved. So were historians. The march of nationalism in the nineteenth century accompanied the advance of democracy. The German nationalist movement produced such popular figures as "Father" Jahn, who preached the fellowship and equality of all in the *Volk*—"Freies Reich! Alles gleich!" sang the *Turnerschaften*. The *Volksstaat* or people's state knew no privileged orders, only citizens under the nation, all equal.

Dangerous though it might be, nationalism in the nineteenth century offered a wider sense of community, along with material advantages, to the masses of people. In the exhortations of such prophets as Mazzini, nationalism took on the attributes of a religion, in the same way socialism did, equipped with regeneration, rebirth, and salvation symbols. Born of a spiritual revolution, the national people achieve a sacred brotherhood, which is their destiny and their salvation, and then they go forth to redeem the world. "Nationality is the role assigned by God to each people in the work of humanity; the mission and task which it ought to fulfill on earth so that the divine purpose may be attained in the world." Nationalists talked of universal brotherhood ("He who wants humanity wants a fatherland"); but typically they saw their own country as just a bit more privileged. Jahn pointed out that the Germans were the central people, the keystone of the West. In different accents but with a similar message, Mazzini reminded Italians of their ancient Roman heritage of ruling and civilizing Europe.

The Cult of Joan

The rise of popular nationalism in the nineteenth century can be illustrated by the creation of the Joan of Arc cult in France. The "virgin, heroine, and martyr to the State, chosen by Providence to re-establish the French monarchy" (to quote the subtitle of a 1753 book) had of course lived in the early fifteenth century; but her deeds excited little interest at that time and for several hundred years after. Bishop Bossuet's history of France granted her but a few lines, and Voltaire, singularly enough from a later point of view, treated her as rather a ridiculous figure in his play *La Pucelle*. (The *philosophes*, we know, were remarkably immune to the sentiment of nationalism.) A few always kept alive the story of the Maid's bravery and devotion, but until the nineteenth

[1] *Letters from Goethe*, translated by M. Herzfeld and C. M. Sym, introduction by W. H. Bruford, 1957.

century she remained fairly obscure. Napoleon, in 1803, referred to Joan as a symbol of French unity against English invaders. The Romantics of course were interested in the Middle Ages, unlike the Enlightenment, and we find the British poet Robert Southey as well as the German dramatist Schiller using Joan as a literary theme. Schiller's *Maid of Orleans* (also 1803) was indeed a key document: a German helped give the French their national heroine.

But it remained for the great nationalist historians of the nineteenth century to project the Maid as an image of French patriotism. Of these Jules Michelet was the foremost, and Michelet depicted Joan in eloquent prose as the mother of the French nation. The legend of Joan grew. Finally she was canonized in 1920 as a saint of the Church. Her canonization in French nationalist hagiography had occurred earlier. A notable worshipper at her shrine was the distinguished writer Charles Péguy (who died in 1914 at the Marne). Charles Maurras and the conservative *Action Française* made much of her; but so did socialists and liberals, anticlericals as well as clericals: Joan was the symbol of national unity. Conceivably it was because the French lacked a monarch that they settled their common loyalty on an almost mythical figure from the past. For the British public, of course, the figure of Queen Victoria functioned as a living mother-image and symbol of unity through much of her long reign (1837–1901).

The poet and the historian both participated in this shaping of national consciousness. "A nation," wrote Ernest Renan in a famous definition, "is the common memory of great things done jointly by our ancestors, along with the desire to remain united in order to do yet more of them." The nation, in brief, is a literary creation. The Italian nationalist movement began with Alfieri (1749–1803), who reminded Italians in romantic writings of their past glories. Koraïs performed a similar service to Greece, and an American named Smith is credited with beginning the "Arab Awakening"—so says the distinguished scholar George Antonius—when he revived the study of the Arabic language and literature midway in the nineteenth century. The Irish, who had almost lost their ancestral tongue, tried to revive it, or at least some literary men and Irish nationalists did; the Gaelic revival accompanied the Irish nationalist movement. A revival of Catalonian nationalism in Spain dates from the 1880s; so does Ukrainian separatism in Russia, while in southeastern Europe, an upthrust of nationalism threatened to blow up ancient multinational empires and destroy Europe's shaky balance of power.

In 1896 Theodor Herzl's book, *Der Judenstaat,* laid the foundations of the Jewish revival, focussed on the establishment of a modern Jewish state in the ancestral land of Palestine; the Zionist congresses began in 1897. The Dreyfus case in France and the ferocious persecution of the

Zionism

Jews in Russia, as well as anti-Semitic stirrings in Germany, had brought home to the Jews the fact that Europe was again in the grip of intolerance. Medieval anti-Semitism, the result in good part of religious emotions, had all but disappeared in the tolerant eighteenth century. Now toward the end of the nineteenth intolerance reappeared in the guise of nationalism. (It also had economic, anticapitalist overtones; the myth of the Jew as the sinister International Banker made its appearance. But the main charge against the Jews in the Dreyfus affair was that they lacked loyalty to France.)

Nationalism reached its apogee, or nadir, in the fateful epidemic of jingoism that accompanied the imperialist movement of the 1890s and preceded the great war of 1914–1918. A powerful social process involving all aspects of history, it cannot be left out of intellectual history, for many writers contributed to it. Of these, historians and novelists, thrusting into consciousness the past traditions of the people, were the most prominent. In addition to Michelet, the German historian Heinrich Treitschke, the American George Bancroft, the Englishman Thomas Macaulay come to mind, by modern critical standards rather lacking in strict accuracy, but eloquent and inspired in their evocation of the national story of their respective lands, in whatever guise they saw it. Never was history so popular as in this period when it dwelt on the rise of the nation and the destiny of its people.

Nationalism rose to an almost frenzied peak in the years just before 1914. Gabriele D'Annunzio, famed flamboyant Italian writer, a weathervane who had adopted almost all possible positions just for the fun of it, became a fierce nationalist about 1909, calling on Italians to sharpen their sword on Africa and then advance on the world, phrases which found an all too frenzied response. The *Alldeutscher Verband,* or Pan-German League, entertained fantasies of German domination of all Europe. In France, Charles Maurras' significant *Action Française* was anti-Semitic and anti-German, militantly patriotic and militaristic (see further page 188). In Russia, and throughout the east of Europe, there was Pan-Slavism, various versions of it. In the 1870s, Danilevski had argued that the next turn of the wheel of history would put the Slavs on top, the Latins and Germans having had their turn. Russia, the Pan-Slavist Fadeyev declared, must either advance to the Adriatic or retire behind the Urals; it was her destiny to unify all the Slavic peoples of Europe. The personification of nations as having "destinies" was common; no doubt this was what the British philosopher Hobhouse had in mind when he blamed the war on Hegel, this sort of thinking being obviously related to a vulgarized Hegelian historicism. Seeley told the British about their imperial destiny, and according to Esmé Wingfield-Stratford, "The Press reeked with blood and reverberated with thunder" (*The Victorian Tragedy*). "Every important nation had become acutely and aggressively race-conscious," the

Super Na-
tionalism on
the Eve of
World War I

English historian adds. It was the most apparent cause of the First World War.[2]

The accompaniment of nationalism was democracy. Here again the preliminaries reach far back, but no previous European age had felt the impact of the ideology and the practice of democracy as the one of 1880–1914. Most Liberals of the earlier nineteenth century stoutly opposed universal suffrage. "Because I am a Liberal," wrote a Member of Parliament and editorialist of the London Times in 1867, "I regard as one of the greatest dangers with which the country can be threatened a proposal to . . . transfer power from the hands of property and intelligence, and to place it in the hands of men whose whole life is necessarily occupied in daily struggles for existence." Tocqueville and Mill mistrusted democracy because they feared the degradation of intelligence and quality by the imposition of vulgar standards. Comte, as well as Bonald, equated democracy with anarchy, the absence of social order. Spencer wrote that the divine right of popularly elected parliaments would have to be resisted as firmly as the divine right of kings if it should threaten liberty. Marx and the socialists generally scorned political democracy as a fraud, designed to deceive the working classes, who could only win their freedom by a social revolution.

Yet throughout the century there was a democratic thrust, which the generation of Tocqueville and Chateaubriand had felt and which became irresistible after mid-century. It was associated with the economic revolution; it followed necessarily from the bourgeois revolution. Political rights could not be withheld from the masses once political authority became a matter of convenience, not sanctity, and when wealth became more widely diffused. Throughout the century illiteracy declined—thus, in France, from 39 percent to 18 percent by 1878 as measured by conscript soldiers— while the press became increasingly free, and increasingly cheap. In 1870 the Education Act established free primary schools in Great Britain, compulsory within a few years after that. The "penny daily" made its debut about the same time. These are landmarks without equal in popular intellectual history.

In 1867 and 1884, Great Britain took steps towards full manhood suffrage, and by 1910 the women were agitating for it. France never actually lost universal suffrage after 1848, but under the Second Empire it was managed and manipulated in a way that deprived it of much meaning; after 1874, however, the Republic came back. Imperial Germany had a Reichstag elected by universal suffrage though it lacked responsible powers. "An assembly of 350 members cannot in the last instance direct the policy of a great power today," Bismarck held. Perhaps it could not,

Progress of Democracy

[2] For other causes, related to this one, but more directly related to other pre-1914 intellectual movements, see pp. 191–193.

but in Britain, at least, the system of government by a cabinet drawn from and responsible to the House of Commons found success in these years. All governments had to pay more attention to public opinion—which might or might not be a good thing, critics noted, depending on how enlightened public opinion was. In the realm of foreign affairs, it was all too likely to be xenophobic, shrilly nationalistic, disdainful of the rights of foreigners. At home, those unconverted to democracy complained of unseemly and undignified electioneering methods, of political machines and bosses, of cheaper politicians driving out finer in a kind of political Gresham's Law. But very few discerning people thought that the rule of the few in politics and society was any longer possible. For better or for worse the rule of the many had come to stay.

Intellectuals were inclined to worry about this, perhaps, more than to hail it. In his essay on "Democracy," first published in 1861, and reissued in 1879, Matthew Arnold wrote, "Our society is probably destined to become much more democratic; who or what will give a high tone to the nation then? That is the grave question." A society is of real value not because large numbers of people are free and active, nor because of the creation of wealth; it is valuable insofar as it produces things that are noble and of good repute. When Arnold lectured in the United States of America on the need to "elevate" society, he seems utterly to have failed to make contact with the minds of Chicagoans. But America's sage, Walt Whitman, addressed similar warnings to his countrymen in his old age.

Opposition to Democracy

Democracy in itself, considered simply as the principle of mass or numbers, is no ideal, can easily become moral anarchy or mammonism; the old criticism made by Plato was repeated often in the later nineteenth century. Nineteenth-century European thought is filled with outcries against certain aspects or consequences of "democracy." "The crowd is the lie," wrote Kierkegaard. Democracy is "a form of decadence," declared the well-known French writer Émile Faguet, who had been influenced by Nietzsche. "If I am a democrat, it is without enthusiasm," observed the great French political leader Clemenceau, who had once led the popular party, in 1908. A notably hostile Victorian witness was Henry Maine (*Popular Government*, 1886). Treated later in this chapter are Nietzsche, Sorel, Pareto, and others who expressed hostility to democracy in aspects of their thought. Here we can note of the famous German that the rule of inferiors, the herd spirit, the debasement of culture to the mass level, were to him among the chief diseases of modern man, to be cured only by the most drastic elevation of supermen-heroes to the helm of state, men strong and ruthless enough to whip and drive the masses toward some worthy goals. Like Dr. Stockmann in Ibsen's play "An Enemy of the People," Nietzsche believed that "the minority is always right." The levelling of the human personality into the conforming mass-man appalled him, and he thought democracy was responsible for this.

There were, nevertheless, many efforts to come to terms with democracy, which in fact was in successful operation in Great Britain, France, and to some extent Germany and Italy by the end of the century. Until finally rebuked by the Pope in 1910, a group of French Catholics, led by Marc Sangnier and the journal *Le Sillon*, undertook the notable experiment of reconciling Christianity with democracy. The neo-Kantian Charles Renouvier presented a philosophical defense of moderate democracy during the period 1872–1890; his disciple, the famous political sociologist Robert Michels, declared that "we are proud to live in a democracy." Perhaps the most notable conversion was that of the Socialists. As we have seen, the Marxist Social Democrats as well as the Fabians accepted the possibility of achieving the social revolution by democratic means. It is also true that conservative and bourgeois circles previously sceptical about democracy grew to accept it, at least in a negative way, in these years.

So an undercurrent of controversy about this silent revolution that was occurring in society and politics runs through all thought in the *fin de siècle* period. Most of the serious thinkers and writers did not travel with the crowd. Indeed, their hallmark is very nearly a rejection of the crowd, of mass civilization, of the breakdown of values, the enthronement of mediocrity. They will use the word *bourgeois* as an epithet; likewise, often, the word *mass* or *popular*. By no means true of all, this is true of those who are the most striking and original: of Nietzsche, the Symbolists and Decadents, and the major political theorists. They did not find the nationalistic and democratic society of their time satisfactory, and they reacted against it as rebels, "outsiders," deniers and defiers of its conventions.

This is a remarkable feature of modern European thought, whatever we may think about it. The "alienation" of the artist and intellectual from society, these men retreating to a private world, inventing esoteric symbols, or even joining some nihilistic revolutionary movement in their hatred of the everyday world, mechanized, philistine, and commercial as it is, is a peculiarly modern theme. This is not to say that giants of thought were ever particularly popular with the majority. It is rather to say that the majority previously did not enter into intellectual society to any marked degree, while now they did. That which constituted the cultural community had been a restricted circle of the upper class, whether clergy, universities, or *salons*. Now this community was immeasurably broadened, and inevitably at first coarsened. At the same time the texture of thought and expression available to the educated or unusual person became more complex; individual sensitivity was sharpened and refined. So—we may hope temporarily—the gulf between writer and general public widened to a chasm, across which each looked at the other balefully and with bewilderment.

Adjustments to Democracy

The Intellectual in Modern Democratic Society

It should be repeated that this estrangement was a new phenomenon. Of the early Victorian writers Walter Allen remarks in his *The English Novel* that they "were at one with their public. . . . They accepted the society in which they lived. . . . The assumptions of their age they fully shared." They might and did criticize, but they did so as those who operate within the family, not as alienated outsiders; they strove to improve the common culture, not throw bricks at it from a distance. Granted that the Romantics in some measure began the myth of the alienated, lonely, superior artist, the Victorian age resembled the eighteenth-century society more than it differed from it in its integration, and the Victorian Sage was no bohemian. But when we get to Thomas Hardy near the end of the century, we enter another world; a threshold is crossed about the 1880s, whether we look at poetry, painting, drama, philosophy, or the novel. There is a real bitterness at the world's blind amorality, its utter lack of plan and purpose, its cruelty and its essential barbarity: Hardy's *Tess* does not live in the same moral world as the heroines of Trollope, Thackeray, Dickens, or even George Eliot. Something has happened. In part it was Darwinism, in part capitalism, in part mass culture, in part no doubt other things; the result is clear.

IRRATIONALISM: NIETZSCHE, FREUD, AND BERGSON

Will as Superior to Intellect

"Almost without exception, philosophers have placed the essence of mind in thought and consciousness; this ancient and universal radical error must be set aside. Consciousness is the mere surface of our minds, which, as of the surface of the earth, we do not know the inside but only the crust. Under the conscious intellect is the conscious or unconscious will, a striving, persistent, vital force, a spontaneous activity, a will of imperious desire." Thus wrote the eccentric essayist and philosopher Arthur Schopenhauer, an offshoot of the Romantic and Idealist German philosophers. Schopenhauer's distinction between Will and Reason, the former being fundamental, could be seen also in Darwin's scheme of nature in which the intellect is only a tool of survival, a part of the whole organism which struggles to adapt to its environment. Schopenhauer, the pessimist, thought the world spirit tricks us into making the struggle; the enlightened philosopher outwits the world spirit by suppressing desire, renouncing the game of life. He had been influenced not a little by the Hindu Upanishads, which became known to the West near the end of the eighteenth century and attracted some of the Romantic and Idealist philosophers.

The Oriental pessimism of Schopenhauer did not make much of an impression but the belief that the will is a deeper force than the conceptualizing reason left its stamp on the European mind. One whose mind was awakened on reading Schopenhauer was the brilliant German, Friedrich Nietzsche. Confronted with what seemed to him a decadent civilization, Nietzsche thought that he had found one cause of its enfeeblement in an excessive development of the rational faculty, at the cost of a creativeness that comes only with the spontaneity of instinct or will. The brilliant young philologist and classicist, whose first book was a study of Greek drama (*The Birth of Tragedy*), traced this disease far back into Western civilization. It had begun with Socrates and Plato, the triumph of logic over literature, reason over will. Another antirationalist of this era, the Frenchman Georges Sorel, independently made this same discovery that Socrates had been the root of all evil rather than of all good as conventionally taught. Excessive development of the rational faculty enfeebles; the habit of conceptual thought paralyzes the will. Europe had intellectualized too long; the result was the weary mediocrity Nietzsche thought he saw about him in this age of bourgeois materialism. In perhaps his greatest work Nietzsche has Zarathustra say, "I saw a great sadness come over men. The best were weary of their work. . . . All is empty, all is indifferent, all was." Western man had lost the capacity for believing in anything, his intellectualizing had led him to scepticism. The only solution lay in a new primitivism that would lead back to heroism.

The Birth of Tragedy (1871) revealed both his deep insights into Greek civilization and his almost frightening originality. Among other things it saw the genius of Hellas as stemming not primarily from joyous optimism (as so often suggested by the Romantics) but from tragic suffering, and consisting not in scientific and philosophical rationalism so much as in primitive emotionalism tempered by reason. Dionysus, whose cult engaged in ecstatic and orgiastic ritual dances, became for Nietzsche a symbol of this primitive force, without which men cannot be truly creative. The Greeks had been great because they had Dionysus, as well as Apollo. They had not been rationalists, but men infused with the will to live. Their greatest age was the time of the early philosophers and dramatists, of Heraclitus and Aeschylus. Plato and Euripides already mark their decadence, which Western civilization unfortunately inherited more than their grandeur.

This electrifying reversal of previous perspectives was typical of Nietzsche's sharply iconoclastic thought, his "transvaluation" of values. A lyrical poet as well as a philosopher and deeply learned man, Nietzsche's challenging, radical books were to wake up intellectual Europe in the 1890s. He wrote most of these books in a frenzy of creativity in the 1880s, against the threat of oncoming madness which was the result of a syphilitic infection contracted in youth. Widely rejected as a brilliant madman in the complacent atmosphere of pre-1914, a destructive and perverse

Nietzsche's Analysis of European Decadence

Dionysus

genius who could not be taken really seriously, he stands today as the major prophet of the tortured twentieth century, with its wars and its Caesarism which he predicted.

Among his rejections were Christianity (a religion for slaves, denying **Attack on** life), and traditional morality ("morality is the most pernicious species **Christianity** of ignorance"). The supermen needed to rescue a decadent civilization must be beyond morality, for they must be "without pity for the degenerate." Democracy and nationalism, the vulgar superstitions of modern dwarf-men, also were targets for his sneers. More remarkable, and celebrated, was his atheism: "God is dead"; European man had killed him; one could no longer believe in any principle of cosmic order. Nietzsche did find something to believe in, escaping from his terrible scepticism to a "joyful wisdom" which to most others must seem scarcely less pessimistic: the love of life, as it is, in all its disorder, ugliness, cruelty, just because it is life (*amor fati*: love of fate). We are part of the cosmos, which is a blind incessant striving (it goes around in huge circles, coming back eventually to repeat itself), and we can affirm our own life force by living and striving. We can accept Dionysus, and reject Christ. "You have understood me? Dionysus versus the Crucified"—these were the last words.

The universe is irrational, it simply *is*. We can reject it, choosing with Schopenhauer to renounce life by suppressing all desire like the Indian *fakir*; or we can accept it, fully realizing its irrationality, pain, and horror. Not easy to understand, and perhaps tending in his later works toward the madness that approached him, Nietzsche at his worst suggests a shocking hatred of civilization and a desire for barbarism; at his best, he reminds us that man can create values by his own nobility though the universe be hostile. The supermen he called for to reshape the human race should not be thought of as brutalized Hitlers, rather as enlightened poet-philosopher statesmen. It must be said in his defense, and has been said by recent students concerned to rescue him from wild misinterpretation, that he despised all nationalism and militarism, including German, and also was no racist or anti-Semite. His wilder ejaculations of rage against the human race can charitably be excused as products of the sufferings of a morbidly sensitive and physically sick man; of enduring value in Nietzsche is the hatred of falsehood and sham, of mediocrity and vulgarity, along with deep insights into human creativity, and a fierce sincerity: one should live one's philosophy. His fantastic sensitivity to ideas makes Nietzsche a barometer registering virtually every variation of the modern mind.

Chief among these insights was an awareness of the role of the **The** darker, submerged, unconscious, "Dionysian" elements in human nature, **Unconscious** which by being "sublimated" enter into creativity. For Nietzsche anticipated Freud in many respects. This force is partly sexual, and Nietzsche suggests that Christianity and conventional morality have grievously damaged Western mankind by surrounding sex with taboos. It is, more basically, just the joyous spontaneity of the animal. It is the dithyrambic dance of primitive man. Civilize it, smother it with morality and reason, and you destroy something necessary to man and to culture. The highest culture requires something of the intellectual element but too much of it means decadence.

Nietzsche combined and held in suspension an amazing number of modern attitudes. There is something in him of the alienated artist, saying with Baudelaire, "The world has taken on a thickness of vulgarity that raises a spiritual man's contempt to a violent passion." He is an important precursor of twentieth-century Existentialism, in question here being his call for man to create his own values by sheer will-power as well as his rejection of all merely theoretical philosophy. "I have written my works with my whole body and life," Nietzsche could say proudly. He is the gloomy prophet of the totalitarian state and modern mass-man. But most of all he is the philosopher of the will-to-power or life force—the irrationalist, prober of drives deeper than reason, anticipator of Freud and Jung, psychologist of the unconscious.

In all his moods and guises, Nietzsche is clearly something quite new and different, compared to Victorian orthodoxy. He has the flavor of the *fin de siècle*, over which indeed his influence was spread widely. André Gide, the French novelist, remarked that "the influence of Nietzsche preceded with us the appearance of his work; it fell on soil already prepared . . . ; it did not surprise but confirm."[3] As so often happens, an idea's hour seemed to have arrived and a number of people felt it independently at about the same time. One of the ideas this period seemed destined to discover and probe was the unconscious irrational within the human psyche. Almost contemporary with the great writings of Nietzsche in the 1880s came the first work of the Viennese physician, Sigmund Freud.

It would be difficult to overstate the influence of Nietzsche. It is an influence that has been felt much more on the Continent than in England, and may indeed be the most important single cause of that divergence between Continental and Anglo-Saxon modes so often noted today in philosophical circles (see pages 245 ff.). Whereas until recent times most British and American reactions to Nietzsche were hostile or uncomprehending, finding no sort of sense in this mad German (see the studies by Halèvy and Brinton), one must grasp Nietzsche, unquestionably, before one can understand the great European moderns (Thomas Mann,

---

[3] In his article on "Nietzsche and John Davidson," *Journal of the History of Ideas*, June, 1957, John A. Lester, Jr., notes another case of one who "may have been a Nietzschean before he ever heard the name of Nietzsche," but whose native inclinations were stimulated by contact with the German. There were doubtless many such instances.

André Gide, the German and French Existentialists, all sorts of others). As a recent writer (Werner Pelz) has commented, "It is not a matter of agreeing or disagreeing with his philosophical conclusions, but of having passed through his corrosives of metaphysical, moral, and psychological doubts. They leave a man scarred or purified; certainly changed."[4] Through this fire the mind of modern Europe has passed.

Freud, by contrast, quickly became acclimated in the Anglo-Saxon world, has perhaps even flourished there more than on the Continent, for the Austrian doctor was no sort of poet or mystic but (apparently) a hard-headed empirical scientist. He brought strange knowledge from the underworld of the human psyche but summed it up in perfectly rational concepts and offered a systematic clinical approach to it.

Significance of Freud

Freud is one of the seminal minds of the modern age, by almost universal consent; he ranks with Newton and Darwin as one of those scientists who altered the fundamental conditions of thought and changed Western man's view of himself in basic ways. He ranks also with Marx and Darwin, it is frequently said, among the big three of the nineteenth century. This despite the fact that, like those other two giants, his theories may prove to have been wrong in many details. Freud himself was convinced he had made epochal discoveries: "I have the distinct feeling that I have touched on one of the great secrets of nature," he wrote, and on occasion compared himself to Copernicus and Darwin. Freud was hardly an arrogant man, though inclined to be somewhat dogmatic, and in pointing to the importance of his ideas he was stating only a generally acknowledged truth. The greatest impact of Freudianism came in the 1920s and 1930s; today his place in modern thought is secure. His name has become a household word, and his influence extends to education, literature, the arts, religion and philosophy, morals, popular culture.

It may be that like other household words Freud is really not accurately understood by most people. But the story of the path to his theory of the role of repression in neurosis is fairly familiar. A physician engaged in treating mental illness, Freud found in 1885 that patients under hypnosis related events in their lives and that this narration had a therapeutic effect. It was not hypnosis but the narration, it seemed, that was effective. Freud developed the free-association technique and confirmed beyond much doubt the often startling relief from various neurotic disorders that comes from talking things out. (It was a truth, perhaps, that confessors in the priesthood had always known in less precise ways, possibly bartenders too!) On this rather slender underpinning Freud erected some ingenious, exciting, controversial theories.

The "unconscious" was already a familiar idea, having been suggested

---

[4] "Jesus and Nietzsche," *Listener*, May 3, 1962.

by Schopenhauer and the philosopher Eduard von Hartmann, among others; Freud did not invent this term or discover the existence of the unconscious mind. But he thrust it into great prominence by making it a central part of his theory. Some things, particularly shameful things, get pushed down into the unconscious part of the mind, and festering there cause mental trouble; bringing them up into the light of consciousness cures the illness. Freud drew a dramatic picture of the conflict in the mind between the *id*, the primitive unconscious where dwell all kinds of lustful, shameful drives and desires, and the *superego* at the other extreme, representing the inhibitions which society and conscience impose. The ego, in between, is a battle ground between these conflicting forces, a place of uneasy compromise between the id and the superego, the anti-social and the social.

Some of the implications of Freud were as shocking, if anything, more so, than Darwin. The role of sex, that subject allegedly under a Victorian taboo, was of course prominent in his work. The natural impulses of sex are suppressed because society brands them as shameful; the sexual drive, or *libido*, Freud thought to be the strongest human impulse and the key to life. Man has learned to be civilized at the cost of making neurotics and perhaps emotional cripples. Freud saw a tragic conflict between the demands of the individual and of society (especially in a later work, *Civilization and Its Discontents*, 1930). Sexual drives may be "sublimated" into great achievements. But suppression of antisocial wishes usually leads to varying degrees of unhappiness and neurosis. Freud more than anyone else has been responsible for a tendency in recent times to remove from sex some of the inhibitions and taboos. But it may be worth noting that on his own mature view, this will hardly solve the problem. The id, he believed, holds violent and antisocial impulses which society, and ultimately the ego itself, cannot tolerate. Freud appeared to think that rape, murder, sadism, all kinds of foul and nasty desires, lurk in the unconscious mind; and so any ordered society must in part sit on the lid of this disorderly basement of the human psyche. The superego is also a part of the mind, and its function is to discipline its uncouth relative downstairs.[5]

Nevertheless, the most sensational consequence of Freud was the new frankness about sex. He was not the only one working in this direction; the pioneer Australian sexologist, Havelock Ellis, may be mentioned. In the 1900s (Edwardian England) and especially in the 1920s, a glorious goodbye was said to Victorian "prudery." A typical piece of Edwardian fiction, Elinor Glyn's *Three Weeks*, delights in sophisticated adultery in a

Role of the "Unconscious"

Conflict and Repression

[5] Like Darwinism, Freudianism has its long prehistory in which elements of it were hinted at. Thus in the eighteenth century Diderot and Rousseau spoke of the war which rages in the human breast between the natural man and the artificial man. See especially Diderot's *Rameau's Nephew*.

manner that most Victorians could simply not have understood. Freud was a serious thinker and a great scientist, not a salacious publicity seeker, and much of what has been done in his name cannot be blamed on him. Yet he did dare, above all others, to bring out into the open what had long lain under a severe restraint.

Additionally, Freud stressed the importance of the child's earliest experiences, of infant impulses of love and hate and erotic play. To some, he had gone Darwin one better, removing from man his last scrap of dignity by exposing him as a creature driven by animal desires, even his finest ideals and creations really a product of secret lusts.

The reply, as usual, was that new knowledge of this sort cannot be swept aside, however dismaying it may seem at first. To increase our knowledge of man is to make it possible to enrich his life and civilization. To understand the darker side of human nature, which exists and must be dealt with, is a step toward controlling and directing it. Freud himself was no mystic. Hard-bitten and a little cynical, he was a scientist through and through, like Darwin, though in his later years he permitted himself some philosophical speculations. His task was to make it possible for men to live happier lives by removing their mental ills. Freud did not invent the irrational and libidinous side of human nature, but only dared to point to its importance.

Jung

In the 1900s Freud was only just getting to be well known. *The Interpretation of Dreams,* 1900, took eight years to sell its initial printing of six hundred copies. But the movement was well on its way to maturity, though Freud continued to work and grow, reshaping his thought in the 1920s. The Freudian school like all vigorous ones produced its debates and schisms. About 1912 Freud came to a rather painful break with the greatest of those who had followed, or accompanied, him in the pioneer explorations of the unconscious, the Swiss psychologist C. G. Jung. Jung, who lived until 1961 (Freud died in 1939), broke with Freud partly because of his belief that psychic energy is not exclusively sexual; Freud would tolerate no questioning of his gospel of the primacy of sex.

There were more basic reasons. Jung was less a scientific rationalist than Freud. Some have wished to deny to Freudianism the title of "science," on the grounds that it makes use of metaphorical and perhaps unverifiable concepts (repression, sublimation, dream analysis, id, not to speak of Oedipus complex and death-wish); but there can be no doubt that Freud approached his task of analyzing the human mind in a brisk, rationalistic spirit. Freud had no use for religion which he believed to be a neurotic manifestation derived from the Oedipus complex. His tendency to "explain away" religious and other ideologies, or modes of expression, as the product of a more "basic" and quite naturalistic condition, links Freud with Marx, Feuerbach, Durkheim, and others of this sort. If to Marx religion is a means of enslaving the proletariat, to Freud it is a means of compensating for a neurotic mind—to the former an excrescence of an unsound social order, to the latter an excrescence of an unsound psyche. This puts Freud in the camp of those who are "rationalists" in the sense of being foes of "religion," who believe that the healthy intellect should rest content with a wholly naturalistic view of the universe. This position is itself, however, an ideology or unprovable assertion of certain values—evidence of a type of mind or temperament, perhaps the type that William James called "tough-minded." (It is also an argument *ad hominem* which can be turned upon its user. If Freud tells me I am religious because of my mental history, I can retort that he is irreligious because of his.)

Jung, on the other hand, incurred the contempt of the scientific psychologists but the admiration of others by wandering into the fields of religion, art, literature, and history. He postulated a "collective unconscious," which he thought he observed to exist in remarkable ways, and he sought clues to the "archetypes," or patterns of imagery, which are basic to it. These appear in mythological motifs, in fairy tales, in art and poetry, as well as in dreams and in conscious behavior. They are found in all the great religions of mankind and in its literature. A fabulous scholar and polyhistor himself, Jung cast his net widely over civilizations past and present in his search for the archetypes of the collective unconscious. His disciples have tended more toward comparative mythology and toward the analysis of art and poetry than perhaps anything else. He manifested some deeply mystical and religious tendencies.

The Collective Unconscious

To Jung, religion and art were essential to the healthy human psyche. The great "myths," expressing as they do the language of the mind at its deepest level, with roots in the collective life of humanity, satisfy our fundamental instincts. Without them, human nature shrivels. Here Jung touches Nietzsche's conviction that modern man is overly rationalized and needs to regain contact with some healthy primitivisms. While Jung, too, always claimed to be an empirical investigator, his critics think that he often lost himself in fanciful speculations. But no other pioneer of what Jung called "the undiscovered self" except Freud himself has so drawn our attention to this strange, fascinating realm that lies within each of us, or so contributed to its elucidation.

Probably Jung's best-known contribution to psychology was his classification of personality types, into "extraverts" and "introverts" with subdivisions. He invented other striking concepts, such as "persona" and "shadow," which roughly correspond to Freud's superego and id.[6] "The

Jung's Psychological Types and Concepts

[6] The *shadow* is a figure of the unconscious containing evil, antisocial impulses but also other nonconscious elements. The *persona* is our social role, the part society expects us to play, a mask of artificial personality. (This seems to bear some relationship to what the Existentialists later called the "unauthentic" or "other-directed" self.) The fully mature or integrated personality must dissolve the persona and inte-

dynamism and imagery of the instincts together form an a priori which no man can overlook without the gravest risk to himself," he wrote in *The Undiscovered Self*. Overlooking them, he believed, could be held responsible not only for individual mental illness but also for such social horrors as German Nazism; for the forces latent in the Unconscious will break forth in wildly irrational ways if they are not understood and administered to properly. Modern man still lives, he thought, in a make-believe world made up of rational concepts, ignoring the underlying emotional determinants. "The psychiatrist is one of those who know most about the conditions of the soul's welfare, upon which so infinitely much depends in the social sum." The popularity of psychiatry today, growing from nothing to the status of a great profession in this century, offers some evidence that what Jung wrote is true, though we still stand at the mere threshold of real understanding of the Self.

Henri
Bergson

Better known in the 1890s and 1900s than Freud and Jung and more respectable than Nietzsche, was the French philosopher Henri Bergson, who may also be classed among the irrationalists or arationalists in this "Age of Unreason." Bergson, whose first notable work appeared in 1889 when he was thirty, exerted so strong an influence that by the 1900s he was easily the most important force in French thought, being frequently compared to Descartes, Rousseau, and Comte among earlier masters of an epoch. His lectures at the University of Paris were likened to those of Abelard in the Middle Ages for the sensation they created, and his repute spread widely abroad too. His considerable role in twentieth-century thought is generally conceded. Bergson's gifts of style assured him an audience. Like Nietzsche, he used metaphor and poetic imagery because he believed that conceptual thought does not best communicate the nature of reality. Also like the German, he appeared to his contemporaries as a liberator, opening up fresh horizons, calling for creativity and expressing it in his richly gifted prose.

In a Romantic manner, Bergson sharply distinguished between the rational, conceptualizing intellect and the intuitive understanding. The former, the scientific, analyzing function, is a practical tool, concerned with useful knowledge, but not truth-giving because reality may not be so divided up and conceptualized. (The student may here be reminded of Kant.) Reality is a continuum, to be grasped by the intuition. It flows through immediate experience, as the "life force" that is in all things. Intuition (meaning instinct become self-conscious and reflective) takes us to "the very inwardness of life," while the intellect is not in this sense in touch with reality. Bergson said that he began his philosophical specu-

---

grate the unconscious into the self. This is close to Freud's "sublimation" or to Nietzsche's fusion of "Dionysian" and "Apollonian" elements. This basic idea is that elements of the unconscious emotion must be used in the interest of a higher creativity.

lations by considering what is meant by *time*, and found himself led to conclude that the clock-time of everyday life or of the physicist is a convention very different from the real time of experience. The intelligence which analyzes and divides things has given us the former conception which is useful, but not true to experience. When we grasp immediate experience by intuitive means, what we find there is an indivisible continuum, a "duration" that we can scarcely describe save in poetic imagery; this represents a fundamental reality. So it is in other things. Science tells us that the sound of a bell is a series of vibrations, but we experience it as a whole. A melody is not a series of notes; it cannot be described; we intuit it. Science, as Wordsworth had written, "murders to dissect." Reality is indivisible and hence unanalyzable; insofar as we do analyze it, as for convenience's sake we must do, we falsify it.

This is no attack on science within its limits, but it *is* a rather sharp deflation of the pretensions of science to provide complete knowledge, pretensions which at that time existed. "Science consists only of conventions, and to this circumstance solely does it owe its apparent certitude; the facts of science and, *a fortiori*, its laws are the artificial work of the scientist; science therefore can teach us nothing of the truth; it can serve only as a rule of action."[7] Critics of Pragmatist and Bergsonian indictments of the "conceptualizing" process as conventional only were not lacking, as might be expected, and often pointed out that these philosophers themselves could not escape the use of conceptual or intellectual language. To do without it would be to abolish thought. To follow Bergson all the way in his intuitionism would be to destroy all analysis and lapse into chaos. It was generally agreed that concepts and reality are not the same thing, also that conceptual knowledge does not exhaust reality or constitute the only mode of dealing with it; but the implication that the two realms are completely divorced, that science tells us nothing at all about reality but only about its own arbitrary signs and symbols, was frequently rejected. Still, the persuasively conducted Bergsonian offensive against science made its impact felt; the chief result was to vindicate and rehabilitate forms of "immediate experience" such as literature, religion, and various mystic or nonrational experiences.

Bergson proposed a vitalistic evolutionary theory, arguing against Darwinian mechanism that life has within it some purposive forces, without which evolution cannot be explained (*Creative Evolution*, 1908). Doctrines of "emergent evolution" received the support of a number of philosophers at this time, the most prominent advocate after Bergson being the British philosopher Samuel Alexander. Reality creates itself gradually, rather than existing from all eternity; life evolves ever new and unpredictable forms. We participate in a universe that is not finished and

Vitalism

[7] R. B. Perry, *Present Philosophical Tendencies*, 1912, pp. 230–231.

help in the making of it. A striking idea, and as Bergson noted, a radically new one in the Western tradition, "creative evolution" turned the rather somber mechanistic atheism of the Darwinists into a feeling for the wondrous freedom of a world in growth.

In general, Bergson's persuasively presented philosophy urged the importance of spontaneity, of intuition, and of immediate experience, as over against those "tentacles of cold, prying thought" (Nietzsche) which give us useful knowledge at the cost of cutting us off from reality. Getting away from cold science and bathing in the refreshing waters of intuition clearly seems to have value, for Bergson. To him as to the American Pragmatists, the world properly seen is rich, inexhaustible, vital. Though his stress on spontaneity and immediate experience influenced the Existentialists, Bergson was on the whole not a tragic philosopher but a joyous one. The anti-intellectualism or antirationalism of which he may be accused was rather gentle, and to tie this deeply religious man to the subsequent movements of Fascism or Nazism appears perverse. Few philosophers have attached such basic importance to liberty. Among his leading disciples in prewar France was the editor and writer Charles Péguy, who so far as he can be classified might best be described as a Christian democrat and socialist. He was, in fact, quite an individualist. Bergson, like the pragmatists, encouraged freedom unbounded by dogma and tended not to set up any "school."

The Pragmatists[8] and Bergson broadly agreed in their attack on intellectual or conceptual knowledge. Immediate experience is deeper and forms the matrix within which intellectual knowledge takes place. As John Dewey put it, there is an "experience in which knowledge-and-its-object is sustained, and whose schematized, or structural, portion it is." We encounter "reality" only in immediate, intuitive experience, as distinct from intellectual ratiocination. We must reject, as Nietzsche cleverly put it, the dogma of immaculate *perception*. If we want to know the music, we do not analyze it into notes or vibrations, we simply hear it. We can perform, and usefully perform, the latter function, but we should recognize it for what it is, a secondary and derivative one.

The Bergsonian message, like that of Nietzsche and William James,

---

[8] The Englishman F. C. S. Schiller and the Italians Papini and Prezzolini represented Pragmatism in Europe, where it was much less important than in the United States. The vigorous American William James was a man of international reputation who knew Bergson as well as Schiller and Papini. Pragmatism had affinities with the message of revolt and liberation; it denied the existence of final, abstract truth, asserting that man makes the truth as he acts. Life is an open experiment in which we constantly test our hypotheses against reality and use our intellects as tools. Pragmatism was popular for a time in Italy around 1900 but dissolved because of a certain vagueness; it stood for "freedom, creativeness, and originality" and appealed mostly to poetic writers. Papini subsequently became a Fascist, indicative perhaps of Pragmatism's tendency to take on the color of its surroundings and embrace any active creed that seemed to have vitality.

must be set against the background of science's virtual monopoly of knowledge; he broke through the ban on religious or metaphysical speculations decreed by the Positivist regimen. "For the first time since Comte and Kant metaphysics had waged war against scientific determinism on its own ground and won it," Étienne Gilson has written in his recollections of what Bergson meant to his generation. (Gilson also recalls that a reigning school at the Sorbonne in the 1900s when Bergsonism arrived was the sociology of Émile Durkheim, a strictly "scientific" dogma to which anything religious or metaphysical was abhorrent.[9]) Charles de Gaulle has spoken of Bergson as one who "renewed French spirituality." Later events revealed some of the limitations of this cheerfully affirmative philosophy; it could lead to approval of almost anything that was active and dynamic, like war and fascism.

But Bergson lived on to add to his reputation with the book some think is his greatest, *The Two Sources of Morality and Religion,* published in 1932, a work of rich texture, interwoven with insights, whose general theme conforms to his guiding vision of man as needing to surmount his practical scientific reason with the creative insights of religion and poetry. Standing somewhere between Freud and Nietzsche, Bergson like them was essentially a gifted student of the human interior mind, the subjective dimension, the undiscovered self.

THE CRISIS IN SCIENCE

The popular prestige of science stood of course very high, in this period when almost every year brought some fresh technical miracle, whether electric light, phonograph, or automobile. For the more thoughtful, science offered its exciting theories, of which Darwin's natural selection was but the most sensational. The periodic table of the elements, worked out by the Russian Mendeleyeff; the atomic structure of matter, developed by Dalton and others; the law of the conservation of energy, associated with Helmholtz and Kelvin, a striking tribute to the regularity and constancy of natural phenomena; and other great discoveries aroused awe, but not dismay, since they testified to the orderliness of nature and the ability of science to disclose cosmic principles. "The men of science had become the prophets of progressive minds," to an extent that may be measured by a statement in the British *Annual Register* for 1884 that few other subjects except scientific ones received any attention from the intellectual world. Lonely prophets and off-beat poets, despite the attention we have properly given them, did not at this time seriously compete

Prestige of Science

[9] Gilson, *The Philosopher and Theology,* 1962. Durkheim held that religion was the collective soul of society, a necessary condition of social existence; but in the Positivist manner, science replaces magic or metaphysics as the basis of solidarity.

with the scientists either in the popular or the intellectual world. Durkheim reigned at Paris before Bergson arose to challenge him.

The widespread confidence in science rested on the belief that it was unfolding an accurate picture of reality, that it was solidly based and could not err, that other modes of knowledge such as metaphysics and religion were obsolete. This popular and slightly vulgar scientific materialism was purveyed in the works of such pundits as T. H. Huxley, John Tyndall, the Germans, Du Bois-Reymond and also Ernst Haeckel (*The Riddle of the Universe*). But at the turn of the century science was about to lose its confident common-sense air and to confront shattering paradoxes at the frontiers of physics.

The New Revolution in Physics

The popular, common-sense view of science included such opinions as that reality consists of material bodies, the atoms being thought of as little billiard-balls; that these material objects act in a spatial field and temporal world of the sort familiar to human experience, with an objectively existing space and time; that all bodies obey the same scientific "laws," like Newton's laws of motion and the law of the conservation of energy. The universe was pictured as a large machine, consisting of physical bodies in dynamic relationships. Before long, an astounded public was forced to hear from the mouths of the scientists themselves the refutation of all this. Matter, it seemed, consisted of invisible and perhaps merely hypothetical units called "electrons," which within the atom refused to obey Newton's laws, it seemed—an example of insubordination without precedent.

Even more surprisingly, time and space as they appear to human experience had to be abandoned, since these are relative to some arbitrary standard and no objective standard exists for the universe as a whole. Newton's law of gravitation, foundation of physical science for 200 years, was evidently not accurate. It became impossible to picture the behavior of "matter" as corresponding to anything within the realm of human sensory experience, either at the subatomic or the cosmic level. The universe was not like a machine, nor was there anything in it that one could readily call "matter"; it was even possible for scientists to hold that reality fades into an idea when we trace it as far as we can. "Matter," remarked Bertrand Russell, became a formula for describing what happens where it is not! Space, time, and matter all turned out to be fictions of the human mind, perhaps not so far from the convenient but unreal abstractions of scientific knowledge according to Bergson.

Relativity of Space and Time

A starting point for these complex developments was the Michelson-Morley experiment, performed in 1887 by two Americans wholly unaware that they were about to stumble onto a new era in science. They were trying to measure the speed of the earth by measuring the time it takes light to travel with, as compared to against, the direction of the earth's motion. The extraordinary result, after repeated experiments, was that there is no difference. It was as if two automobiles, each going exactly thirty miles per hour, started at exactly the same moment at an identical distance from me, and I walked toward one; presumably it would take that one less time to reach me, from which one could calculate my speed. But in fact, no matter how I walked, the two automobiles always took exactly the same amount of time to reach me! The result might also be compared to a man on a moving train, whose net speed was found to be the same whether he was walking or standing still. Put this way, some of the paradox may disappear. For the lesson is that all speed is relative to something else;[10] and if there is nothing in the universe that constitutes an ultimate yardstick of measurement, there can be no absolute speed. It had previously been assumed that there was an "ether" of some sort, a kind of space-stuff which formed the background for all objects in the universe, but this was now seen to be false. Space is a nothingness, not a something, and no such substance as the "ether" exists. The same thing is true for distance as for speed. Space and time viewed from a universal and not an earth-bound angle must disappear as absolutes. From this many odd conclusions emerged, for instance, that at the same moment it is a different time to observers in motion in different parts of the cosmos. If right now you are on one star and I on another, it is not the same time for us. If I journeyed to visit you on your planet and then returned to mine in a space-ship, I would find that a different interval of time had elapsed than that shown by my perfectly accurate clock. And so on.

Euclid's solid axioms of geometry were seen to be true only so long as we keep to the boundaries of the earth; for outer space, there are other geometries, based on different physical postulates, which turn out to be equally rigorous logical systems. Thus, it seemed, the quality of objective certainty that had always attached to pure mathematics vanished in relativity, too.

In regard to Newtonian gravity, the difficulty of conceiving a "force" of some sort acting at a distance had bothered Newton himself a little, and had bothered others since. We may recall that Berkeley and Leibniz had explored this weakness in a speculative manner. According to the great scientist Albert Einstein, whose first or special theory of relativity was presented in 1905, gravity is not a "force." We should not think of a pull exerted by objects on each other. Space having vanished in the sense of anything positive like "ether," this adjustment became necessary. Einstein's first theory asked a stunned public to believe that bodies move

Einstein's First Theory

10 We measure speed on the earth by reference to the earth itself, postulating that it is stable; but of course the earth is in motion around the sun, the planetary system is in motion, too, relative to other systems and galaxies, and so on until we reach the limits of the universe. Then what can we find to measure by? The speed of light, as the Michelson experiment revealed, being the ultimate speed of things in the universe, is a constant that does not vary relative to other motion and cannot be used to measure them by.

through the curvatures of space-time which, not being independent of each other, become merged in a single continuum. Others held that the physical principles of the universe cannot be visualized in terms of human imagery at all, they can only be indicated in mathematical formulae.

Whatever else this was, it was not common sense; the scientists were becoming more wildly paradoxical than the artists and poets. At the subatomic level, where in 1897 J. J. Thomson arrived at the concept of the electron or unit of negative electricity as the least unit of "matter," the belief that the atoms could be thought of as miniature planetary systems, with the nucleus as the sun and the electrons circling around it, soon had to be abandoned. Niels Bohr, the Danish physicist who lived until 1962 and became one of the leading theoretical pioneers of the age of nuclear energy, explained that the laws of motion holding for the solar systems do not apply at all within atoms. Thus the laws of Newton, always heretofore assumed to be universal, broke down on both the smallest and the largest fields and remained valid only within a zone of fairly gross sense experience. They were crude approximations which worked well enough only when the demand for precision was not too great.

Planck's
Quantum
Theory

The world within the atom soon became most puzzling, the behavior of electrons breaking all sorts of laws heretofore regarded as sacrosanct. At the turn of the century, Max Planck's quantum theory asserted that energy is emitted discretely and not continuously, in little packages, as it were, and not in a continuous stream. The electrons did not, then, behave as particles of matter would be expected to behave; they did not bounce or eject the way "ordinary" objects do in the everyday world. Further research by Einstein, Heisenberg, and Broglie disclosed that electrons have properties of *both* particles and waves, being sometimes one and sometimes the other, or being something capable of behaving on occasion like both.

Since electrons must be used to observe electrons, and exert a disturbing influence, we can never directly observe electrons, but can only infer their nature. This, to some, was a disturbing reminder that science has limits beyond which human knowledge can never penetrate. Likewise, the behavior of the subatomic particles can be predicted only within limits of probability, thus striking at that certainty and complete determinancy heretofore claimed and thought necessary for physical science. For example, we cannot know both the position and the velocity of a subatomic particle, in the way that we can know them of larger objects. If an airplane is bound for Boston from Chicago, naturally we can find both its exact position and its speed at any given moment. This cannot be done for an electron bound from one place to another. We *can* get general statistical trends, adequate for most predictive purposes, but the individual electron eludes determinacy and predictability. Heisenberg's "indeterminancy" principle, subsequently announced, summed up the unsatisfactory situation at the frontiers of physics.[11]

All this represented brilliant advances in the field of physics. Having for two centuries surveyed the land that Newton discovered, scientists now pressed on to a new world, and if at first this world seemed strange that was only to be expected. Nevertheless, this experience forced basic changes in thinking almost as sweepingly as had the seventeenth-century scientific revolution, though the exact directions of change were not clear. Possibly Einstein was playing the role of Copernicus, with the Newton of the new age yet to appear. Breakdown seemed evident in the lack of any one set of rules or laws that applied to all matter, and in the "uncertainty" invading such scientific bulwarks as continuity and causality, not to speak of time and space. The ultimate limits of investigation seemed to have been reached in the effort to track down reality to its smallest ultimate unit, and some philosopher-scientists were prepared to say that this vindicated the idealist position, overthrowing materialism. In the last analysis not even the scientist can get rid of the subjective factor, because as investigator he in part creates the truth; and such concepts, moreover, as atom and electron, space and time, turn out to be mental constructs not necessarily corresponding to objective reality. The interference factor, which makes it impossible to observe the tiniest units directly, cannot presumably be overcome; indeterminancy of electronic behavior also apparently is an ultimate fact, not a deficiency in knowledge that further investigation may remedy.

So far from making science useless, the new areas yielded knowledge that led to such things as television, nuclear energy, radioactivity, X-rays, space satellites. The Einsteinian formula was brilliantly vindicated by a spectacular observation in May, 1919, the most famous of all those that offered support of Einstein's gravitational theory, correcting Newton's. In the 1920s the new frontiers of science excited great interest; it was, in a phrase of Rutherford's, "the heroic age of physics." We will refer to this again later. For the time being, it may be enough to remark that a sharp adjustment in thinking was required for anybody who wanted to keep abreast of science; science ceased to be simple, perhaps ceased to lean on materialism and mechanism, revealed a "mysterious universe" destined always to remain, in part, mysterious and bumped up against puzzles it could not solve at the very heart of reality. Scientists themselves became a little more humble and talked of the mysterious universe

[11] In his book *Physics and Philosophy* (1942), Sir James Jeans summed up the consequences of quanta theory in six propositions (page 145): (a) the uniformity of nature disappears, (b) precise knowledge of the outer world becomes impossible, (c) the processes of nature cannot be adequately represented within a framework of space and time, (d) sharp division between subject and object has ceased to be possible, (e) causality has lost its meaning, (f) if there is a fundamental causal law, this lies beyond the phenomenal world, and so beyond our access.

rather than the march toward perfect knowledge. Laymen might still bow before the might of science but they lost their ability to comprehend it. The "world view" of European man since Newton had been dominated by a certain picture of the cosmos as a mechanical model, familiar to human experience. It now became difficult to use any such model.

No one with a knowledge of Western philosophy, from Hume and Kant to Nietzsche and Bergson, could be much surprised by the conclusion that scientific knowledge must be in part subjective, and also incomplete because phenomenal only. The limitation lies within the human sensory apparatus, which can hardly be adequate to full comprehension of the whole of cosmic reality. Why should we suppose that our senses or even our brains, fitted for living in a particular environment, should be capable of grasping and visualizing all this? Reason, employing mathematical abstractions and other tools, can take soundings of nature sufficient for practical advantages; but if by "understanding" we mean an adequate model or picture of everything, this must probably always elude us. In Kantian terms the "thing in itself" is not accessible to the categories of the understanding, while the intuition or imagination can only contact it fleetingly and imperfectly. This is the fate of man, who though marvelously endowed is not God. Ultimately, perhaps, this conclusion was the greatest consequence of the new science. It left man even at the peak of his grandeur, amid the greatest of his triumphs, shorn of his overconfident "titanism" and aware that after the best that science can do, vast mystery must always remain and there is abundant place for a religious attitude toward the universe.

THE CRISIS IN RELIGION

The Higher
Criticism

Religion too was in crisis. Nietzsche had announced that "God is dead"; Freud was an atheist; Darwinism had dealt blows to orthodoxy. The most severe blow to traditional Christianity probably came, however, not from any of these but from the "higher criticism." J. Wellhausen's *History of Israel*, first published in 1878, was a landmark of scholarship. For a number of years before this there had been uneasiness. In 1860 a turmoil in the Anglican Church over the book *Essays and Reviews*, in which some liberal churchmen expressed the view that the Scriptures should be examined like any other book, led to a trial for heresy. Ernest Renan's *Life of Jesus*, and David Strauss' somewhat similar book in Germany, raised eyebrows all over Europe in the 1860s. They were followed by J. R. Seeley's *Ecce Homo* in 1865, not an irreverent book but one which did seek the human, historical Christ. The trend of Romantic and Hegelian theology had been to play down literal Biblicalism.

Wellhausen offered persuasive support to a theory already advanced,

that a substantial portion of the earlier books of the Bible (the Penta-
teuch) was not written until much later than the events they describe,
and indeed not put in its final form until about 400 B.C. (the time of
Ezra), nearly a millennium after Moses. Wellhausen carried the day among
the scholars, especially the younger ones. The second edition of his
History appeared in 1883 and was translated into English in 1885, giving
rise to a considerable controversy. A French scholar wrote in 1894 that
"whoever is not totally prejudiced, whoever has not decided in advance
that any kind of criticism is false, must accept the idea that the Priestly
Code was not formed until after the Babylonian exile."

To some of the pious, this was a shocking conclusion, for it seemed
to cast doubt on the Bible as revealed truth, infallible because divinely
inspired. The arguments of liberal theologians, that the history of Israel
and Judea in the broader sense justified the claim of a unique religious.
mission vouchsafed to the Jewish nation, carried little conviction to men
brought up to believe (as did, for example, William E. Gladstone, the
famous British statesman) that the literal truth of every line of Scripture
was the impregnable rock upon which Christianity stood.

In 1872, George Smith called attention to a Babylonian version of
the story of the Flood—a significant and shattering discovery. The leading feature of the "higher" as distinct from the "lower" criticism was its
awareness of an immense literary tradition among the other peoples of
the Ancient World, which bore on the Bible at many points. No longer
was the Bible seen in isolation, as a totally unique and marvelous book.
The Old Testament fitted into an historical context that began to be
recovered and understood; thus seen, it perhaps lost none of its wonder
nor even its veracity, but it did inevitably become different—a part of
human history, not simply the record of a continuous divine miracle. A
good deal of the Old Testament has close parallels in the sacred and
wisdom literature of the Babylonians and other ancient peoples with
whom the Jewish people were in close contact. The uniqueness of the
Hebraic outlook—monotheistic, ethical, messianic—remained, but in innumerable details the Biblical story lost its ability to pass as something
quite outside the experience of the rest of the ancient world. The Jews
could never again be quite the "peculiar people" in the old sense. (This
was not displeasing to Hegelian philosophers, who declared the entire
"world spirit" of an age to be more significant than single nations or
individuals.)

By the end of the nineteenth century, also, critical research into the
New Testament had arrived at conclusions concerning the Gospels, which
included the view that the authors of Matthew and Luke leaned chiefly
on the Gospel of Mark as a source, and even the latter contains theological
interpolations not taken from Jesus himself. Again, the net result of
intensive historical analysis was, roughly, to cast some doubt on the

accuracy of the Gospels as accounts of the life of Jesus, and on certain sayings and ideas attributed by them to Jesus. Opening up the problem of the historical Jesus by no means meant destroying Christianity, but simple folk among the pious might understandably think so. A quarrel between "modernists" and "fundamentalists" soon divided most Christian churches. Popularizers of the higher criticism, with an antitheological axe to grind, sometimes exaggerated it and declared that, for example, Jesus never existed and the Bible was a tissue of fables.[12] Scandalized Christians reacted by denouncing the whole critical movement, and it took some time before balanced judgment was restored. In the Roman Catholic Church, "modernism" received a cautious green light from Pope Leo XIII but Pius X, his successor in 1903, checked this move toward liberalism as he did others, as for example, the Catholic democratic movement.

In 1864 Pius IX, embittered by the Italian liberal-nationalist movement which assailed the papacy's temporal power, had issued his celebrated Syllabus of Errors and in so doing placed the Roman Church in a state of war with much of the nineteenth century. Liberalism and democracy, as well as modern science, were declared to be irreconcilable with Christianity and the Church. In 1870, Pius IX had summoned the great Ecumenical Council, first since the Council of Trent in 1563, chiefly to solemnize the doctrine of papal infallibility. The goal was not achieved without a severe struggle, in which many of the German, French, and English bishops opposed the papal party, and after the decrees some liberal Catholics left the Church. Leo XIII, the great Pope who succeeded Pius IX, did not really retreat much from Pio Nono's position. Though anxious to encourage learning, and a friend of the Catholic social movement (see page 142) he continued to assert that the modern state, based on secular individualism, is fundamentally anti-Christian. In Italy Catholics continued to boycott national politics on papal orders, though in France there was finally an adjustment to the Republic. In the 1900s, Catholics who embraced liberal and democratic principles were rebuked. They were reminded that political society must be based on Christian principles, not on liberal scepticism and indifference; in regard to democracy, they were told that the Church cannot attach primary importance to the form of government; it can get along with democracy, but also with other forms, and what matters is that society be Christian, not that it adopt any particular political ideology. Marc Sangnier and the great Charles Péguy were perhaps the leading French Catholic Democrats who finally (1910) received this rebuke.

By that time, the Dreyfus affair had caused a sharp conflict between

---

[12] Bertrand Russell, the eminent philosopher, held that "historically, it is quite doubtful whether Christ ever existed at all, or, if he did, we do not know anything about him." Russell's *A Free Man's Worship*, 1910, was a sceptic's manifesto.

conservative and liberal France with the clergy ranged for the most part on the former side. The victorious partisans of Captain Dreyfus took their revenge by passing legislation to separate church from state in 1901, the occasion of further bitter exchanges between anticlericals and church-men. All in all, the Church found itself at war with basic trends in the modern world at this time, and subject to some divisive conflicts. We have discussed the Roman Catholic Church, but the same thing might be said in lesser degree of major Protestant denominations. There were liberals who sought to turn the church's major interest to social reform, abandoning traditional theology and accepting the higher criticism; there were conservatives who feared the extinction of Christianity if it thus merged itself into secular liberalism.

Strong winds blew in the direction of religion in this era. The trouble was that they tended to be diverted to nonorthodox, even non-Christian varieties of faith. The reaction against scientism, especially powerful in France, led to that interest in moral and interior experience we have already seen in the philosophies of Nietzsche, Bergson, and William James. There was indeed something of a Catholic revival, aided by the conversion of important men of literature. But this religion-seeking spirit more often ignored dogmatic orthodoxy. William James developed the viewpoint in his famous Gifford lectures on "The Varieties of Religious Experience" that the various myths or conceptualizations in which re-ligions are objectively embodied are not fundamental; they are the mere husks of religion. What is basic is the instinct to believe, the need for the human spirit to express itself. One could, presumably, just as well believe in any myth. One might, like the great Irish poet W. B. Yeats, invent a private mythology; one might, like Annie Besant or Mme. Blavatsky, embrace esoteric Oriental religions. The former's "theosophy" became a fashionable creed. The "truth" of a religion became somewhat irrelevant; one could never know that anyway. What mattered was the fact of belief itself.

The point was driven home by a later remark of Emmanuel Mounier, who declared that a century ago almost everyone was either a Christian or else a rationalist opposed to all religion, whereas today there are not too many of either sort. One had faith, but not necessarily a Christian faith, or if so only very loosely.

The greatest prophet of the pre-World War I era was doubtless Leo Tolstoy. The Russian novelist was a personality of such gigantic propor-tions that he captured the world's imagination, and became a living legend to whose estate at Yassnaya Polyana men came from all over the Western world to do homage. The brilliant novels *War and Peace* and *Anna Karenina* made him famous; but more striking was the spiritual odyssey of the later Tolstoy. Experiencing a deep crisis in which he saw life as absurd and meaningless, this man of passionate "commitment" (to

Tolstoy

use a modern phrase) was driven to reconsider the most fundamental questions of existence, and after finding neither the abstractions of the philosophers nor the facts and theories of the scientists to be of any help, he ended in a sort of primitive Christianity. There is much in the Russian's agony and redemption to suggest the later movements of Existentialism and Crisis Theology. He found that Christ's true meaning had been falsified by formal religion and by rationalistic conceptualizing. Tolstoy found in the simple message of Christ deep truths which no mere formula could express. His religious writings (for example, *The Kingdom of God Is Within You*) have tremendous force. He felt, also, the influence of the Oriental religions and tried to find the elemental truths that underlie all the great religions.

Tolstoy advocated and in some measure practiced a return to primitive Christian communism. Powerful denunciations of war and of all forms of coercion made him a hero of the pacifist movement, and in political principles an anarchist. The principle of nonresistance to evil, which Tolstoy could not always obey himself, was the cornerstone of his religious belief. In suggesting a return to a simple life pared of all artificialities he was reminiscent of Rousseau, or of the American sage Henry Thoreau. Tolstoy, a member of the Russian upper class, ferociously denounced the corruption of this class and its European counterpart. Believing passionately in art and literature, he condemned the decadence of European literature and insisted that only the peasant masses were culturally sound, however ignorant of books. In later years he wrote the simplest of parables for the people, though it is unfortunately doubtful that the Russian peasant responded. But a variety of others all over the world did respond, and Tolstoy became a figure almost unique in Western intellectual history. The Russian government, most despotic in the world, dared not touch him though he advocated anarchism, pacifism, and noncooperation with government. The affair of the Dukhobors was perhaps the most astonishing example of Tolstoy's power. He set out to save this sect of Christian communalists from brutal persecution by the Czarist government, and succeeded in gaining his end and in raising a worldwide fund for the transportation of the Dukhobors *en masse* to Canada.

Tolstoy gave away the money from his literary works and eventually before his death renounced all his wealth. A modern saint, he was formally excommunicated from the Orthodox Church in 1891, which only added to his popularity within and without Russia. The influence of Tolstoy was enormous, though difficult to evaluate. It would be impossible to say how much he contributed to that undermining of the Russian political system which prepared the way for the Revolution of 1917—certainly something, though this process was far bigger than even his outsize figure. He was a hero of the vigorous antiwar movement of this period; for example, we see William Jennings Bryan from the American prairies making his pilgrimage to Yassnaya Polyana. His most prominent disciple in the realm of practical affairs was to be the great Mahatma Gandhi, leader of the Indian independence movement, legendary saint and father of the modern Indian nation. Tolstoy cried out against materialism, capitalism, the corruptions of bourgeois society, and demanded a spiritual rebirth. He did not explicitly become an antirationalist, was certainly no mystic, yet his whole-hearted feeling of a need to find positive meaning in life through religious commitment was a more potent blast against merely cerebral philosophy or religion than anything else in his era, probably.

How unorthodox Tolstoy was may be judged from his reply to the edict of excommunication. He denied the trinity, original sin, the divinity of Christ, and all the church sacraments, which he called "coarse, degrading sorcery." He accused the clergy of ignorance and deceptiveness.

Tolstoy's equally great countryman, Fyodor Dostoyevsky, shared with Nietzsche a preoccupation with the idea of God's extinction and what follows from this. In his striking parable of the Grand Inquisitor (in *The Brothers Karamazov*), Christ returns to earth to be arrested and condemned by the wise old Inquisitor, who sees that Christian freedom is impossible for man, enslaved as he is and must be by superstitions. Existing organized religion is a fraud, but perhaps a necessary fraud. Men could not endure pure spiritual Christianity; it is possible for only a few, now. Into this parable, so often reprinted, is packed much of modern religious man's agony and tension. Modern man is depraved, he needs God but cannot find him, orthodox old-fashioned Christianity is bankrupt, the truly religious man today may be the atheist or anti-Christ. Dostoyevsky adopted a belief in the potential mission of the Slavic peoples to redeem decadent Europe because still capable of religion—a kind of spiritual Pan-Slavism. Nietzsche himself learned from this Russian genius, who spent some terrible years in Siberian prison camps for the crime of talking against the Tsar's government, then came to reject the revolutionary movement as spiritually shallow. No more significant figure exists for contemporary civilization.

(margin note: Dostoyevsky)

Nicolas Berdyaev has mentioned Tolstoy and Dostoyevsky among those he called the "forerunners of the era of the spirit," the predecessors of the post-1914 Christian revival. Others in this generation referred to by the Russian Existentialist were Solovyëv and Cieszkowski (a Pole) from the Slavic world, and two Frenchmen, Leon Bloy and Charles Péguy. The latter, a Dreyfusard and a democrat, a liberal Catholic, a moderate socialist, and a fine literary craftsman, edited prewar France's most important intellectual journal, the *Cahiers de la Quinzaine,* opening its pages to all kinds of expression. Though a Catholic, Péguy was essentially a free spirit, on whom the influence of Bergson could be seen prominently. Like Tolstoy, Péguy was in revolt against all that was false in a timid and

(margin note: Seeds of Christian Revival)

shoddy civilization, and sought to affirm the value of the human soul by preaching integrity, devotion to the spiritual and intellectual life, social justice, dedication to art.

So religion was abroad, but the winds of doctrine were various and confusing. The British scholar J. N. Figgis, writing just before 1914 of *Civilization at the Crossroads,* expressed his dismay at the babel of voices: Nietzsche, Bergson, James, Tolstoy, and Bertrand Russell—atheism, scepticism, intuitionism, the life force, the will to believe, the will to power, etc. Had the European tradition dissolved into a thousand fragments? Did civilization evolve from unity to multiplicity, from the Virgin to the Dynamo, as the American writer Henry Adams suggested? Some of the manifestations of diversity in the 1900s were wild indeed. In Russia, where the composer Scriabin upheld the artist's role as messiah and announced himself the chosen one, while the poet Ivanov preached the mystical union of Christ and Dionysius in "ecstasy for ecstasy's sake," there was a mood in which "every kind of new religion and superstition proliferated" (Martin Cooper). At the other end of Europe, James Joyce in Dublin encountered the Hermetic Society and the Theosophical Society, where Madame Blavatsky, Annie Besant (who had passed through Fabianism en route to Theosophy) and other modern mystics and would-be prophets were read. Another magician was the Greek Gurdiyev, who offered occult spiritual forces taken from prerational cultures and associated with artistic creation. In Italy, D'Annunzio preached the religion of art and of sexual love before settling, deplorably, on the religion of imperialism; spiritually perhaps a fraud, like the dictator Mussolini who so much resembled him, D'Annunzio was a fabulous personality, tremendously popular, expressing much of the *malaise* of the times.

The serious interest in abnormal psychical phenomena (spirit messages, telepathy, clairvoyance, poltergeists, etc.) might be added. As during the fourteenth century when papal control weakened Europe was swept by witchcraft and magic, so now in the aftermath of Christianity's decline something similar happened. The comparison, at least, may be suggested.

Spiritual
Adventurers

ESTHETES AND LITERARY REBELS

One of the great adventures of the last half of the nineteenth century lay in the realm of pure literature. It is impossible to avoid the conclusion that, with the decline of the traditional Church and of any agreed-upon orthodoxy in either religion or philosophy, the great imaginative writers have supplied many of the values of the modern world. Further, it is equally true that art became something of a religion for many in this generation. While criticism from Voltaire to Darwin had eroded Christianity's power to compel unquestioned adherence, there was

Significance
of the
Imaginative
Writers

also disillusionment in this period with scientific rationalism, as we have seen. The philosophers of the era, among whom Nietzsche, Bergson, and William James stand out, tended toward intuitionism or naturalism, rather than rationalism in the sense of formal, conceptual thought, and expressed their views more in poetic metaphor than logical analysis. Perhaps the greatest single advance in knowledge of the era was being made by Freud, who charted the mysterious, nonrational side of the human psyche. Nietzsche's insights, too, haunted all the writers of this era. Thus most of the major currents of the age combined to focus attention on the poetic, myth-making capacities of man.

This was a time when Europe discovered, for better or worse, the depths of the mind that lie beneath rational thought, where myth and symbol reign and strange, formidable powers lurk in hiding. Neither philosopher nor scientist can guide us here, but the poet or novelist perhaps can. In addition to probing the unconscious, these writers gave voice to much of the social criticism that filled the age, criticism of one or another feature of a bourgeois, industrial, democratic society repellent to sensitive souls. But their alienation pushed them toward pure art and toward purely subjective "private worlds" of imagination, for they were disgusted with the public world. Estheticism, art for art's sake, the poet's elevation to preeminence, these attitudes naturally accompanied rejection of the social and moral order by which a hated civilization lived.

The beginnings of this literature of revolt may be found at mid-century or even earlier, when reaction against the older Romanticism and disillusionment with a commercial and bourgeois civilization appeared together, a rock flung at Victorian orthodoxy, the esthetic counterpart of revolutionary socialism. The Art for Art's sake writers, offspring of Gautier and Baudelaire, were from the beginning a rebellious, less respectable lot, whose works sometimes had a *succès de scandale* as well as a genuine success of art. In 1857 both Baudelaire and Flaubert faced criminal prosecution, the former for his *Flowers of Evil* and the latter for the celebrated novel *Madame Bovary*. In England, the Pre-Raphaelites were criticized as immoral, but this was nothing compared to the storm stirred up by the deliberately provocative poet Algernon Swinburne in the 1860s. These writers, as their slogan implied, tended to make of Art and Beauty a religion, often with results that shocked the moralists. They were aggressively hostile to Christianity and conventional morality. In Swinburne's unpublished novel *Lesbia Brandon* we have the theme of homosexual love (handled also by Gautier in his seminal novel *Mademoiselle de Maupin*) accompanying an estheticism in which people cultivate their senses and live saturated in beauty. Baudelaire's "satanism," which seemed to ask the poet to seek out morbid and abnormal themes, was as famous as his theory that poetry should strive for a purity corresponding to color and music. Swinburne, John Morley wrote indignantly in 1866, was "the

Shocking the Bourgeoisie

libidinous laureate of a pack of satyrs." It is at this time that we begin to hear of Bohemia, where impoverished young painters and writers, the beatniks of their day, lived highly unconventional lives.

Whatever the case with Mimi and Rodolphe, Baudelaire, Flaubert, and Swinburne were great writers, and a shocked orthodoxy could not so easily cast them aside. The movement they began swept on, but took somewhat different forms: Decadence, Symbolism, Realism, or Naturalism. In all cases the desire to *epater le bourgeoisie*—shock the conventional—went along with an often exaggerated cult of beauty and artistic integrity. The Realists, like Flaubert and the Goncourt brothers, in England George Moore, and later the celebrated Emile Zola, dealt realistically with the sordid. Flaubert's famous portrait of the bored and adulterous wife of a provincial doctor in *Madame Bovary* led on to the low-life characters of the Goncourts and Zola: servant-girls, prostitutes, drunkards, criminals. "Naturalism" was a term also applied to this literature which presented "slices of life" without commentary. Zola claimed literature could be written "scientifically," and held that men were determined by their heredity and environment. But it is clear that Zola's novels do not really exemplify an objective scientific method. The method was, rather, the excuse for a special vision of mankind, a tragic one. Grim pessimism, man the helpless victim of blind chance, may be found also in Zola's English contemporary and fellow novelist, Thomas Hardy.

The 1880s brought Symbolism and the Decadents. The latter attained notoriety chiefly through the famous novel by J. K. Huysmans, *À Rebours* (*Against the Grain*), whose hero, Des Esseintes, was the prototype of all Dandies, those "super-esthetical young men" whom Oscar Wilde and the *Yellow Book* were soon to introduce to an amazed Victorian public. Emaciated, depraved, and sophisticated, the decadent or dandy felt himself to be the last pale but exquisite flower of a fading civilization, and amused himself with art, vice, and crime. A carefully cultivated exoticism, an extreme artificiality marked this mode of writing. Picking up a copy of the notorious *À Rebours*, Oscar Wilde's hero in *The Portrait of Dorian Gray* felt that "the heavy odor of incense seemed to cling about its pages and to trouble the brain." "The first duty of life is to be as artificial as possible," Wilde wrote, adding that "what the second duty is no one has yet discovered." Cold, cruel, green-eyed *femmes fatales* filled Decadent poetry and novels. Homosexual perhaps like Wilde, the Dandy might shade into more sinister types representing what Mario Praz has written about as "the Romantic agony." An exciting suspicion of nameless sins hung over this literary assault on respectability, around which grouped those who were weary of Victorian primness.

Less obviously designed to shock the bourgeoisie, Symbolism, born about 1886, represented the ultimate in Baudelairean estheticism, and produced some great poetry; its goal was to express the inexpressible

Literary
Naturalism

Decadence

Symbolism

by an experimental verse which followed the logic of the interior mind, revealing the reality behind the appearances of things by the use of archetypal images or symbols. Much of modern poetry lies under its influence. Verlaine and Mallarmé, later the brilliant young poets La Forgue and Valéry, were its prophets.

This sounds like a more sophisticated version of Romanticism, and this is not far from the truth, insofar as the idealist and poet-as-seer elements are concerned. For the poet was indeed a seer, a *voyant*, to the Symbolists. But the mood of Symbolism was deeply tinged with the related currents of estheticism and decadence. Turning their backs on a disgusting social and material world, many of the Symbolists were distinctly other-worldly. Their most celebrated literary character, the hero of Villiers de l'Isle Adam's *Axel's Castle* (which is the title Edmund Wilson gave to his now classical study of this movement), lived alone in a Wagnerian castle studying occult philosophy; when he and a girl who had come to murder him fell immediately and sublimely in love, they decided on suicide because reality could not possibly measure up to the perfection of their love as they felt and experienced it at that moment. Living, Count Axel and Sara thought, is too vulgar; "our servants can do that for us"! In the same spirit, Oscar Wilde once said that "any fool can make history, but it takes a genius to write it"! Art is superior to life. The earlier, "classic" Romanticists had not so distinguished and separated art from life.

Around the turn of the century, the more alert young writers of Europe were all smitten with the Symbolist message. The young James Joyce, his brother tells us, liked poems that "sought to capture moods and impressions, often tenuous moods and elusive impressions, by means of a verbal witchery that magnetizes the mind like a spell, and imparts a wonder and grace. . . ." Poetry must not be rhymed prose; if it is, there is little point in writing it as verse. Poetry is *sui generis*, its purpose being to convey, not ideas, not conceptual knowledge, but "moods and impressions," the subtle inner world of the mind with its emotional states. This is an appeal to immediate experience—the *données* of consciousness, as the philosopher Bergson called it—which lay very close to the heart of the matter in this period. The French poet Rimbaud, who believed that the poet's vision has power to penetrate a deeper reality and show men how to live (a Romantic idea), also believed that the poet can bypass conceptual thought to express reality, somehow, in an immediate, symbolic sense—a conception that may bear comparison to traditional religious mysticism, but was here presented by a man whose life was that of an alienated rebel. This strange and degraded genius has been made the object of a veritable religious cult by some moderns.

The French Symbolists' antisocial extremisms may perhaps be excused on the grounds of their intense indignation against a social order that was destructive of all beauty and integrity—the rule of plutocracy, of capitalism, of the bourgeoisie, "a hideous society," as Des Esseintes exclaims. The achievements of the Symbolist school are beyond question; they set the tone for modern poetry, especially in France but with a heavy influence abroad, too. T. S. Eliot brought Symbolism's manner and mood into English poetry a few years later. Just prior to 1914 the American Ezra Pound, along with T. E. Hulme and others, founded the "Imagist" movement in England, influenced by Bergson and related to French Symbolism, with some debts also to Japanese poetry.[13] The object was to get at reality in a moment of flashing insight embodied in a single image:

> The apparition of these faces in the crowd;
> Petals on a wet, black bough.

The impulse to create a "pure" poetry, purged of the traditional narrative or argument, was found earlier in Baudelaire and Verlaine and the French school known as "Parnassian" in the 1860s; it is one important ingredient in the modern movement. Its goal was to distinguish poetry from prose by its content as well as its form, a revolt against all previous literary doctrine and against the highly popular Victorian narrative or descriptive poem, such as Tennyson and Browning wrote. Poetry should not be an alternate mode of discourse. In the making of modern poetry the Parnassian strain joins the irrationalist (the mysticism of the Word, Rimbaud's "reasoned disordering of the senses") and the Symbolist (allusion, indirect statement, subtle symbolisms) as the leading operative features.

Nietzsche, as well as Richard Wagner, exerted great influence on French thought toward the end of the century. In 1861, when Wagner's music first caused furious controversy in Paris, Baudelaire brilliantly defended it; it had bowled him over much as had the writings of Edgar Allen Poe earlier (the latter a rare example of a decisive American influence on Europe at this time). "The *Revue Wagnérienne* was founded in 1885, not merely to study his music but also his esthetic doctrine —his theory of total art. Wagnerism came to be considered as a complete philosophy of life . . ." (Enid Starkie). As for Nietzsche, his message found some eager ears in *fin de siècle* France. That the great German had so much admired the giants of French literature did not impede this reception, of course. Émile Faguet, in his book *On Reading Nietzsche* (1st edition, 1904), wrote that "the gist of Nietzsche is that there is no good truth but that which we have discovered ourselves, nor any good rule of life but that which honestly and with effort we have created for ourselves." Wagner and Nietzsche represented the esthetic

---

[13] A minor chapter in intellectual history in this period relates to the discovery of Japan, so recently and dramatically drawn into communication with the West, by European writers and Americans ones (Lafcadio Hearn) too—discovery especially of the estheticism that runs through Japanese life.

view of life stressing absolute integrity, loyalty to one's personal vision. To the French tradition that ran from Baudelaire and Gautier to Verlaine and Mallarmé, this was a congenial note.

Also influenced by Nietzsche were the Scandinavians Ibsen and Strindberg, the former possibly the most stimulating and controversial writer of the epoch. Upon the performance of Ibsen's "Ghosts" in London in 1891, a shocked respectability called it filthy, disgusting, and immoral, demanding its prohibition. George Bernard Shaw was impelled to write a book, *The Quintessence of Ibsenism,* in defence of the Norwegian, a book which stands as one of the major critical works of the era as well as a tribute to the vitality of Shaw and of his age. For once, England vibrated to a theatrical controversy as France had often done; *Ghosts* was the modern *Hernani.* In his book on Ibsen, Shaw asked how it was that some hailed the Norwegian as the greatest living dramatist, the modern Shakespeare, a genius beyond compare, while others requested his suppression in the name of common decency and public order. (This occurred all over Europe, not just in England, the alleged home of Victorian prudery.) The answer to the latter question lay in Ibsen's shattering attacks on conventional morality. By later standards Ibsen was hardly daring, but in the 1880s and 1890s his brilliant, successful, interesting plays (as they certainly were then, and on the whole Ibsen's reputation has stood up) were a brand of defiance hurled in the face of the dominant European bourgeoisie. In *Ghosts* (written 1881), an apparently model wife and mother is shown to be living amid lies, unfaithfulness, and corruption, much as Nora Helmer is in the famous *Doll's House* (1879). In *The Enemy of the People* (1882), respectable society persecutes the honest man who would interfere with its material prosperity by telling the truth about the evil source of that prosperity. Hating "Pillars of Society" (the name of one of his plays), Ibsen had no use either for romantic, idealistic reformers. His *Peer Gynt* is a modern Don Quixote who makes himself ridiculous by blindly living as if dreams were reality. With all his symbols, Ibsen was a realist too, exploring with Zola the seamier side of modern life, if a little more subtle in his definitions of the sordid.

Shaw's own plays reflect a considerable Ibsenian influence, with a special flair for the drama of ideas and a flashing, Voltairean wit lacking in the Norwegian. A peculiar sensitivity to ideas marked this versatile Irishman, along with the ability to present these ideas in dramatic form. Some of his plays expose social evil or hypocrisy in the Fabian spirit; others reflect his fascination with Nietzschean and vitalist ideas then so much in the air. Most of them slightly shocked the public, but amused them so much that they tolerated the unconventional element. Shaw like Voltaire became a licensed iconoclast, privileged to criticize the idols of respectability because he did it in such a scintillating manner. The posi-

Henrik Ibsen

G. B. Shaw

tive message was socialist but more often after 1900 Nietzschean. Bold, free spirits stride through Shaw's plays, knocking down the proprieties and teaching people to assert their individuality. Following a suggestion of Nietzsche's, Shaw had his Don Juan find that the really best people are in Hell, not Heaven. The common rules are always reversed: girls drink brandy and smoke cigars, while men are cringing and cowardly; honorable professions are dishonorable, and *vice versa*, Mrs. Warren's Profession (the oldest) is really no worse than any other. Shaw's Caesar is a Nietzschean superman, action controlled by reason, beyond good and evil. *Back to Methuselah* popularized the theory of creative or emergent evolution, and indeed the "life force" became a persistent Shavian theme. Shaw lived on to a ripe and creative old age in the postwar years, another trait he shared with Voltaire being an amazingly long literary career. His noonday was between 1900 and 1917, his mission to force novel ideas on bourgeois England.

The new writers, who often themselves thumbed their noses at the

Nordau's Attack on "Degenerate" Art

crowd, were not always popular. One of the more notable denunciations of the new literature appeared in Max Nordau's book *Degeneration* (1895). Nordau, a rationalistic socialist, saw nothing but "degeneration" in the new literature and philosophy. Nietzsche, Walt Whitman, Wagner, Tolstoy, Ibsen, as well as the French Decadents, Symbolists, and Realists, all he declared to be so many morbid diseases. They were mad, they were antisocial, they were sex-obsessed (sexual over-stimulation ruins civilization, Nordau believed). Nordau, one suspects, was almost prepared with Plato to banish the artist from society altogether in the interest of social stability, though he did declare his respect for the "healthy art" of Dante, Shakespeare, and Goethe. Few of the moderns—Hauptmann's *Weavers* was an exception—passed his critical inspection. He rejoiced that the average man remained immune to these siren calls, continuing to prefer music-hall melodies to Wagner, farces to Ibsen.

Nordau's outburst was characteristic more of popular reaction than of avant garde thought, though he himself was a highly literate person. Nevertheless quite a few scholars and critics reared in the older literature bridled at the new mode of expression, and the mob persecuted it. Oscar Wilde, the chief prophet of the new literature in England in the 1890s, brilliant playwright and epigrammist, ended a broken man after being arrested and jailed for homosexuality. His illness neglected by the prison authorities, Wilde died at forty-six a martyr to the popular dislike of the estheticism he flaunted. The concurrent revolution in the arts and music excited even greater hostility. The riot that greeted Stravinsky's "Rites of Spring" in Paris in 1913, and the similar reception given to Post-Impressionist, abstract art in 1911, are famous examples.

The Russian writers, Tolstoy and Gorki, rejected modernist literature and art as unwholesome; see especially the former's *What is Art?*, which assigned to literature a moral function of communicating values to the masses and indignantly accused the European esthetes of having lost faith in man and civilization. (The latter would scarcely have denied this.) In Italy, on the other hand, the new literature gained some enthusiastic converts. Clearly Symbolism and Decadence were extremely sophisticated forms, possibly most at home in the older cultures. But Andreyev was one great Russian writer who was influenced by the Symbolists.

What seems clear is that there had been a literary revolution. Touched off by Baudelaire and Gautier, it gathered momentum as the century wore on and as the bourgeoisie tightened its grip on western Europe. The writers flung a challenge in the respectable face of late nineteenth-century society, while at the same time they created fresh styles and announced a new religion, the religion of Art. The alienated artist, or the writer as rebel, the frustrated intellectual as he appears, for example, in Thomas Mann's novel *Tonio Kröger,* is a modern phenomenon. No such gulf between the artist and thinker on the one hand and organized society on the other had been *typical* of any previous age, and in mid-Victorian times Tennyson and Browning, for example, had a socially accepted status not accorded to the defiant Decadents or Naturalists or Symbolists. Perhaps it is not too fanciful to ascribe the catastrophe of 1914 to this tragic estrangement between intellect and action.

IRRATIONALISM IN POLITICAL THOUGHT

"Most of the political opinions of most men are the result, not of reasoning tested by experience, but of unconscious or half-conscious inference tested by habit." This now not-so startling judgment is quoted from Graham Wallas' *Human Nature in Politics,* commonly considered a landmark in the history of British political thought. In this little book, first published in 1908, Wallas, one of the original Fabians, noted that since 1867 "representative democracy" had largely triumphed all over Europe; even the Austrian and Russian empires as of that year seemed to have followed the others in taking steps towards constitutional democracy. But amid these triumphs, students of democracy in the western nations seemed "puzzled and disappointed by their experience of it." It was far from the ideal system its advocates had expected. There were political "machines" (a keen student of them was M. Ostrogorski), and other political phenomena unknown to and unstudied by traditional political theory.

Wallas felt that political science had not learned to study real men in the real world, but dealt with abstractions often irrelevant to it. The largest fallacy was the assumption of rational man, whether in economics

Graham
Wallas

or politics, knowing his own interest and serving it. To some extent, Wallas suggested, there had been a decline of rationalism owing to the "de-localizing" of people, who, uprooted from the village where they had a secure place in society, were thrust into the mass anonymity of the city.[14] Also, the intrusions of vast numbers into politics made for the use of symbols and stereotypes—"ballyhoo," the Americans were soon to name it. But above all, the science of psychology had now begun the study of the semirational and nonrational mental processes which most men exhibit most of the time. Wallas opened up a subject other Anglo-Saxon students were to pursue before long. (See, for example, Trotter's *Instinct of the Herd* published during the war, or Walter Lippmann's *Public Opinion* published soon after it.)

Wallas obviously was one who hoped to extend the sway of reason by recognizing, studying, and thus controlling the irrational elements in human behavior. In France, one of the leading political writers of the prewar generation preferred to accept man's political irrationalism and exploit it to create a revolution.

Georges Sorel ranks with Charles Maurras among the outstanding French political theorists in the years before 1914. The influence he exerted on both Mussolini and Lenin, especially the former, entitles him to a place of renown if not, given the nature of those two gentlemen, glory. A Marxian socialist originally, Sorel adopted the irrationalism of the hour and married a Nietzschean and Bergsonian spirit to his revolutionary radicalism. He was a close friend of Robert Michels and joined him in charging the orthodox Socialists with having become bureaucratized and respectable. Their rationalism and materialism, Sorel felt, were quite inappropriate for revolutionaries. Doubtless he was right in recognizing that Marxism is really an apocalyptical religion. He was quite willing to accept it frankly as such. Do not all men live by "myths"? Socialism he compared to the church, the modern strikers being the equivalent of Christian saints and martyrs. He spoke of the social "myth of the revolution," or of the general strike. Sorel, a brilliant political theorist, had lost faith in reason and in society; in combining the twin spirits of Nietzsche and Marx, he suggested something like what later appeared in Mussolini's Fascism or Lenin's Bolshevism. Essentially an anarchist, a hater of the state and coercion, Sorel disapproved of the element of statism and nationalism in Italian Fascism, as he would have rejected Lenin's ruthless state dictatorship. But he did father the idea of a revolutionary elite violently sweeping aside bourgeois civilization in the name of a new myth or religion, that of proletarian socialism. In this "myth" the working class appears as clean, unspoiled, heroic, but brutal enough to dash to pieces

Georges
Sorel

[14] An idea to be found in German sociology, especially the well-known distinction of F. Tönnies between *Gemeinschaft* and *Gesellschaft,* community and society— the latter artificial, the former organic.

the old corrupt order. Without difficulty we can recognize Nietzsche's "blond beasts" clothed in overalls. A civilization must believe in something; modern European civilization under bourgeois leadership had lost the life-giving capacity for such belief. Only the unspoiled proletarians had it: they at least believed in revolution.

Scholars more learned and perhaps more serious than the unorthodox Sorel also displayed keen interest in the nonrational side of human political nature. The Italian Pareto (see further below) sought to distinguish the "residues" of nonlogical motivational patterns from the "derivations" or rationalizations of conduct. German sociology showed similar interests.

Max Weber was one of the founders of modern Sociology. A scholar whose tremendous range and productivity reminds us somewhat of Carl Jung, Weber, a professor at Heidelberg, suffered intermittently from illness and died in 1920 at the age of fifty-six. A good part of Weber's inspiration stemmed from Marx, whose crudities he wished to refine but whose central conception of a scientific approach to social, economic, and political phenomena he shared. Perhaps best described as a liberal, Weber longed to play an active part in public affairs but in Imperial Germany, of which he was a keen critic, found this path largely blocked. (He did perform some public functions in World War I, which he supported as a patriotic German at least at the beginning but later sharply criticized German policies.) He was a friend of the Social Democrat, Robert Michels, and when the latter was refused a university post because of his left-wing politics Weber bitterly denounced the vaunted German academic freedom as a fraud. All in all, Weber's combination of brilliance, erudition, and courageous political activism stamped him as an intellectual and moral leader of his generation in Germany; and his fame has endured through such of his writings as the stimulating *The Protestant Ethic and the Spirit of Capitalism*, or his lectures in *General Economic History*.

As a social scientist, Weber was aware of the irrational side of politics and made this one of his chief fields. He was fascinated by the forms of political leadership and by the path of historical development in society and state. One of Weber's leading interests was the principle of rationalization. He meant by this in general the tendency of things to get organized and subjected to rules and orderly processes. What Michels saw happening to the German Social Democrats, in their path towards bureaucracy, Weber saw as a universal principle in human history. Beginning in romance or magic, institutions or forms settle down into a stable routine. Music, for example, becomes a science. Government becomes bureaucracy. In this process spontaneity is lost, there is "disenchantment," the pedantic expert takes over from the free spirit; Weber sometimes with Nietzsche accuses the modern world of having lost its

Max
Weber

greatness of soul, producing petty time-servers rather than heroes. At the same time efficiency gains. There is, however, Weber adds, a limitation to the institutionalized or bureaucratic form of authority; it cannot cope with emergencies, being attuned only to times of stability. In times of crisis we still get a reversion to the type of leadership Weber called "charismatic." The great man arises, commanding allegiance by the peculiar force of his personality or genius. Napoleon in the nineteenth century revealed the charisma as much as Caesar two thousand years earlier, while on a lesser scale religious leaders, and leaders of other sorts, continued to appear. (Certainly there was no lack of prophetic figures in the late nineteenth century, from Tolstoy and Stefan George to Mary Baker Eddy and Mme. Blavatsky, exercising leadership in mysterious ways.) Charismatic creations are then institutionalized and reduced to routine, in tradition or bureaucracy. What we do or believe today from custom or because it is enshrined in the routine of law was yesterday the inspiration of some charismatic personality.

We have referred to only a portion of Weber's thought, though a significant and representative portion. His effort to employ the methods of science to understand the processes of human society represents one large theme of this era in European ideas. German sociology joined Viennese and Swiss psychology in this major advance on the frontiers of human existence with the tools of social science. There were other great sociologists, such as the Frenchman Émile Durkheim, the German Friedrich Tönnies, and the American Thorstein Veblen. It was a stimulating period for social theory. Social scientists were challenged by a complex, rapidly changing social and economic order, in a Europe being revolutionized by industrialism and urbanism. Perhaps the intrusion of the "irrational" was only a consequence of such rapid, disorienting change. Millions were being uprooted from a stable, centuries-old environment and thrown into a new one. The political theorists responded to this fact in one way or another. Just ahead of them, making most pertinent their comments on political irrationalism, the use of myth, and charismatic leadership, lay Lenin, Mussolini, and Hitler.

Pareto

One final example of the brilliant, yet oddly sterile advance of political and social theory in the first two decades of the twentieth century, stimulated by rapid social and political change as well as by the intellectual heritage of ideas, is Vilfredo Pareto's *Trattato di Sociologica Generale*, first published in 1916, translated into English as *The Mind and Society*. The Italian was a great economist as well as a deeply read humanist; he undertook to combine social theory with concrete historical data. His work was a massive attack on the problem of analyzing the basic motivational patterns of human behavior, which of course are nonlogical though they may take a logical or rationalized form. It is a kind of sociology of knowledge, reminiscent of Marx in its attempt to see beneath the surface of ideological "rationalizations" to some underlying grammar of intentions. But Marx's own mythical features are seen through. Pareto with Weber, Veblen, and others belongs to the second generation of sociologists, the one that followed up and refined the initial generalizations of Marx, Comte, and Spencer. His vast learning and flair for generalization is similar to theirs; the larger sort of sociological theorizing has not yet broken down, as it later would, into just a wilderness of *ad hoc* special studies, a "micro-sociology" instead of a "macro-sociology." One came close, in Pareto, to the sort of systematic and apparently objective science of society that men had dreamed of since the Enlightenment. But it turned out to be an arid achievement, disappointingly barren of practical results. Pareto became the dupe of Mussolini and Fascism in the 1920s, which did not detract from this impression of the sterility of his system.

Pareto together with another Italian social theorist, Gaetano Mosca, was notable for a stress on the ruling *elite*, which they sought to analyze rigorously. Some had expected that with the arrival of democracy "the people" would rule. But an elected elite might be just as much an elite as an hereditary one. Government must necessarily be the work of a small number, and there is always a tendency toward oligarchy. One can hope for a fluid elite, replenished from below by cooption; or one can hope for dissension among the ruling classes, the only practical source of liberty. These Italians reflected disillusionment with the democratic, parliamentary system in their country, where beginning with great expectations it had scarcely worked successfully. They were disabused of "ideologies" and tried to be severely scientific in their examination of social and political phenomena. Thus in some ways they carried on the tradition of positivism (Mosca was much influenced by Taine). But they were hardly as detached as they claimed to be, and their severely objective style cloaked an angry disenchantment.

Elites

Disenchantment with democracy spawned a whole school of elitists. The Nietzscheans, of course, spoke contemptuously of the dominion of inferior men, the reign of mediocrity, the need for aristocratic leadership. "I teach that there are higher and lower men." Nietzsche's friend, the Swiss historian Jacob Burckhardt (famed for his study of the Italian Renaissance), thought that Europe would not be healthy until its "natural order of inequality" was restored. Many succumbed to "cultural despair" in contemplating the invasion from below by the new barbarism of mass. Maurice Barrès, one of France's leading writers, associated democracy with the "uprootedness" of modern man who has been torn loose from the soil and deposited in the impersonal neighborhoods of great cities, there to become a faceless cipher. Barrès' program included socialism under a strong authoritarian leader, agrarianism, and anti-Semitism.

Cultural Despair

A more formidable French political theorist and leader was Barrès' friend, the intrepid monarchist Charles Maurras, founder of the *Action Française*. Maurras was in the tradition of French classicism and rationalism, of Voltaire and Comte. He admired order and stressed the French national tradition, which he saw as classical and rational. He inherited Comte's dislike of modern society as too anarchic and scorned democracy as lacking a principle of order. A prominent theme of Maurras' thought was the need for leadership by an intelligent minority. "The mob always follows determined minorities." The *Action Française* organized the *Camelots du Roi* to engage in agitation and street fighting, an idea subsequently adopted by Fascists and Nazis. Among other ideas it bequeathed to the postwar Fascist movement was that of the "corporate state," a favorite idea of Maurras' that came to him from the Catholic Social Movement in France, especially from Tour du Pin. Though hardly any threat to the state, the *Action* exercised a considerable influence on French university students just before the war. Violently hostile to the Republic in the 1900s, it tended to rally to its support after 1912 with war clouds on the horizon, for it was militantly patriotic and fiercely anti-German. It put out a well-known newspaper, and from Maurras' tireless pen flowed a stream of books and pamphlets. Nationalist, traditionalist, antidemocrat and anti-Semite, Maurras carried on a war against the liberal, parliamentary state and he looms ominously as perhaps the chief forerunner of the "revolutionary conservatism" of the postwar period. It is difficult to feel much sympathy for a movement so filled with violence and hate; but some of the things Maurras hated so fiercely were conceivably worth opposing: the lack of principle and purpose in modern society, the absence of strong leadership to shape the new masses into a civilization, the disregard of national tradition.

On the far left as well as the far right the theory of leadership by an elite appeared. Lenin, destined during the war of 1914–1918 to become a successful revolutionary leader, married a Nietzschean elitism to Marxian social determinism. "Lenin conceived of proletarian revolution as the product of great minds, who, conscious of inexorable trends, would create order and progress out of chaotic elements by organizing the raw material of history in a rational fashion" (Adolf G. Meyer). In this he differed from Marx, who had favored widening the franchise and other democratic political reforms believing that these would facilitate the triumph of the proletariat. Engels, living on into the 1890s, definitely stated that the time of "revolutions carried through by small conscious minorities at the head of unconscious masses" had past. The Socialists of western Europe placed their faith in democratic processes which made it possible to gain power by legal means. If Marx was right, the laws of social development were working relentlessly to destroy capitalism; the number of proletarians along with their class consciousness was supposedly growing so that soon they would be in the great majority. Revolutionary conspiracies were out of date in western Europe, precisely because Marx had revealed the inevitability of the transformation to socialism. But in Russia, where revolutionary conspiracy seemed the only possible recourse against a reactionary absolutism, Lenin sought to reconcile it with Marxism.

To Lenin the proletariat represented the will of history, but only potentially so; it must be organized and shaped by the "vanguard" of trained Marxians. The laws of social development exist, but they must be understood and exploited by this alert leadership. History does not make itself; it is made by men. When the decisive moment has arrived one must strike in a sudden act of revolution. The organized vanguard of the proletariat, disciplined, ruthless, and intelligent, must lead this revolution and install the socialist epoch. A Marxist, Lenin dissociated himself from mere revolutionary adventurism or terrorism, but was equally scornful of the passive, legalistic Social Democrats of western Europe. They had been corrupted by bourgeois democracy, on his view. Not by parliamentary means but by well-planned and prepared-for revolution would the proletariat succeed in its great mission, and this task called for the leadership of the vanguard elite. Here was one theorist who became the leader of a real, and mighty, revolution.

A German Social Democrat, Robert Michels, a friend of Max Weber and of Pareto, discovered what he called the iron law of oligarchy. Drawing much of his evidence from the German Social Democratic party, Michels thought the life history of political parties, as well as of other institutions, ran a course from democratic spontaneity to bureaucracy and oligarchy. By 1910 the socialists and the trade unions had grown mature and respectable. They were governed by an elite which made all the decisions and managed the party congresses, the rank and file being content to follow their leadership. The tendency toward oligarchy had afflicted even these groups which might be expected to be the most democratic. The apathy of the masses, the need for leadership, and also the tendency in modern times toward bureaucratic organization—Weber's "rationalization"—are themes that appear in Michels' celebrated study of *Political Parties,* which by 1915 had been translated and published in Italian, French, and English as well as German editions. Political parties are a part of the democratic political order, but they themselves are subject to nondemocratic forces. The right to vote may mean little if the machinery of politics is in the hands of a tightly controlled organization which names the candidates and introduces the issues.

Michels' Law of Oligarchy

Oligarchies, elites, vanguards, and creative minorities, then, were much in evidence in the political analyses of pre-1914 Europe. This is a bit odd in view of the fact that democracy was in fairly effective operation through most of western Europe. It had produced its disillusionments, however, and the intellectuals reacted against it. Some of them lived to regret this when after the war movements of political reaction or revolution destroyed democracy and replaced it with systems far more sinister.

These examples of political thought—Wallas, Sorel, Weber, Pareto, Maurras, Mosca, Lenin, Michels—seem to justify the generalization that the years from 1885 to 1914 exhibit uneasiness and point to a crisis. They are brilliant and stimulating, as well as seminal: in one way or another they are the headwaters of most contemporary streams of political theory. But they reflect a basic dissatisfaction with the existing order and they point ahead to the postwar collapse of that order in several parts of Europe; for if Lenin became leader and oracle of the Russian Communist Revolution, Sorel and Maurras rank as prophets of Fascism and Pareto lived to serve Mussolini. It would be wrong to put Wallas, Weber, Mosca, and Michels in such company, but their interest in the irrational side of politics and in elites at least suggests these postwar phenomena.[15] Of course, the war changed the whole situation.

[15] Weber, it may be noted, was in some respects far from a "liberal": an ardent German patriot and expansionist, and an archrealist in politics, he criticized the Kaiser for not being warlike enough, or rather not cool-headed and courageous enough to begin the inevitable war earlier on more favorable terms than Germany faced in 1914.

The best lack all conviction, while the worst
Are full of passionate intensity.

   WILLIAM BUTLER YEATS

Men will wish Nothing rather than not wish
at all.

   FRIEDRICH NIETZSCHE

The West in Trouble:
From World War I
to World War II

6

THE WAR AND ITS AFTERMATH

In 1914 Europe entered upon a catastrophe from which by mid-century she had not recovered. A good part of the twentieth century was to be dominated by the breakdown of international order in that year, leading to four horrible years of mass slaughter, out of which came red revolution in Russia, black revolution in Italy, and subsequently Nazism in Germany—the forms of modern "totalitarian" dictatorship. The war proved scarcely less demoralizing to the victor states than to the defeated. It hurled much of Europe toward bankruptcy and internal collapse. During the war, propaganda took over and truth suffered as never before, and out of the war there emerged a new kind of cynicism, a loss of faith in men and values, such as Europe had perhaps never before experienced in modern history.

It is tempting to find some parallels between this crisis of the political order and the crisis of thought and culture that seemed to exist as of 1914. Historians customarily describe the origins of the World War in terms of diplomatic and political history, and quite properly so: the clash of national interests, the alliances, the military plans, the conferences and confrontations. The rise of nationalism was an obvious cause of the war. Now and again statesmen could be heard observing, in a Darwinian spirit, that struggle, competition, and force are the laws of life. Democracy forced statesmen to take account of a public opinion that was often belligerent and narrow-minded, as well as fiercely nationalist. Diplomacy does not function in a vacuum; politicians are men of their age sharing its prevalent ideas. Cultural factors conditioning the political breakdown of 1914 apparently existed, but this relationship has not been sufficiently explored and remains something of an uncharted zone. We can, however, simply note that there *was* a "crisis of culture" in 1914 Europe.

We have said enough of the pre-1914 era of thought and expression to know something of what that crisis was. There was the breakdown of traditional Christianity and the emergence of many new faiths. There was the revolution that dethroned reason and made will or life force pre-eminent, a revolution that has been called the most basic in European intellectual history. There was the discovery of the unconscious mind, and of the irrational in politics. There was the separation between artist and society. There was the class conflict between proletarian socialism and middle-class liberalism. There was the impact of democracy on culture, with the resulting cleavage between the cultured minority and the now politically powerful mass. There was the sense of "decadence" or "cultural despair" that one found in leading men of letters, the sense of a civilization too old and ripe, or perhaps too rapidly being revolutionized by machine technology. There was the loss of anchorage in the sciences, the Nietzschean and Ibsenian and Dostoyevskian transvaluation of values, the revolution in the arts.

Some, as we have noted, had the impression of a babel, a confusion and profusion of voices, on the eve of 1914. This turbulence in philosophy, science, and art need not have meant destruction, and few in Europe before 1914 thought it did. On any showing, an intellectual revolution was in progress, but intellectual revolutions had happened before without destroying society. True, in the seventeenth century the Thirty Years' War and the English Revolution possibly showed some connections with the great alterations in basic outlook that accompanied the Scientific Revolution. But the Enlightenment presided over a century of stability and social progress. Nor had the mighty French Revolution and Napoleonic Wars, paralleled by the Romantic Revolt, halted Europe's surge forward. One can hardly prove, nor is it at all plausible, that the intellectual revolution *necessitated* some such calamity as the war of 1914–1918 and its sequels. Probably, though, it contributed to it. The recklessness with which peoples plunged into war and the fury with which they fought it could have been less had the framework of thought, the system of values, been more secure in 1914. It is very difficult to pronounce with assurance on such matters of historical causation. But it is relevant to quote the words of a German historian writing about the coming of Nazism: "Such a relapse into barbarism would have been impossible if moral and spiritual values had not already been undermined over a period not of years but of decades. National Socialism was only the final link in a chain of disastrous events, which originated in the sphere of ideas and theories."[1] The same thing may be said about the World War itself, which was itself one of the most important links in that "chain of disastrous events" that has afflicted the twentieth century.

More obviously to blame was popular nationalism, and most of the great pre-1914 thinkers—not all—were free from that. The best examples are Nietzsche and Sorel, often loosely charged with encouraging violence but in actuality haters of nationalism and militarism. The leading case on the other side is the perverse Maurras; Barrès too was a nationalist and so, as we have noted, was Max Weber. Just before the war, the *Action Française* was popular with French youth, especially intellectual youth, at the universities; and the German "Youth Movement," preaching a return to nature, may have been as innocent as the Boy Scouts but sometimes resembled a cult of primitive virility.

The young Bosnians who killed the Archduke Franz Ferdinand and thus provided the spark that set off the flames were themselves aflame with the restless ideas of pre-1914 Europe. Their idols included Gorki, Andreyev, Whitman, Wilde, and Ibsen. They had learned tyrannicide from 1848 Romanticism (Mazzini, "William Tell") and revolution from Ibsen; they lived in an atmosphere of youthful literary romanticism, fed by the exciting writers of the hour, with considerable Symbolist and Decadent influences. They were in touch with the international Anarchist movement.[2]

When the war began, it was wildly popular and not merely among the masses: Bergson and Weber were among the numerous leaders of thought who hailed and blessed the crusade. Indeed, at first few held out against the martial spirit. In Great Britain, these included Bernard Shaw (an Irishman) and Bertrand Russell, but their contumacy bore great risk to their reputations and even their persons. Russell was imprisoned, Shaw snubbed and boycotted. War fever infected most of the Socialists, though they had pledged themselves against it. Péguy went forth to a hero's death on the Marne and became virtually a canonized saint, like his beloved Saint Joan. "There is not one amongst the leaders of thought in each country who does not proclaim with conviction that the cause of his people is the cause of God, the cause of liberty and the cause of human progress," one commentator noted. Rudolf Eucken, the German philos-

The War and the Intellectuals

---

[1] Wilhelm Grenzmann, in *The Third Reich*, 1955, p. 203.
[2] See among other sources Vladimir Dedijer's article, "Sarajevo Fifty Years After," *Foreign Affairs*, July, 1964.

opher, hailed "the mighty spiritual movement which the war has called forth," while Romain Rolland, the French novelist, apostrophized, "O young men that shed your blood with so generous a joy for the striving earth! O heroism of the world!" There is a long, rather saddening chapter of such reactions; in part, they can be blamed on the fashionable creeds of vitalism, and the literature of what Mario Praz called "the Romantic agony." Tennyson, sixty years before, had given voice to a similar reaction at the time of the Crimean War, calling for "war, loud war on land and sea" as an antidote to bourgeois selfishness and materialism. This time, there was even less dissent.

Peace
Plans

It must be said, however, that many who supported the war because there seemed no other choice did so reluctantly and then channeled their frustrated idealism into the "war to end wars" crusade so strong in 1914–1919. (It was H. G. Wells who first coined this phrase.) They gave birth to a profusion of plans for the happier international organization of the postwar world, plans which issued in the League of Nations created in 1919. This was true in all countries. There were League of Nations Societies and Associations, Committees for a Durable Peace, Unions for Democratic Control of foreign policy. These plans were not only at variance with each other but wore an odd air of unreality in most cases; intellectuals struggled in an element alien to them and tended toward utopianism. Most of them were disillusioned with the real League of Nations that struggled to an imperfect birth in the atmosphere of power and hate at the Paris Peace Conference of 1919. The hundreds of tracts and pamphlets written during the war ended as less a contribution to human progress than a curiosity for the historian, a fact which contributed no little to the postwar despair.

Meanwhile the intellectuals shared the public's gullibility in swallowing tales of horrible atrocities committed by the enemy, and even helped in the manufacture of such tales. Afterwards there were contrite confessions and a chorus of *mea culpa* by those who had been taken in. Governments had rather deliberately lied to their peoples, in order to keep up the war spirit.

Revision of
War Guilt

If the war was initially popular, and blessed by the writers, it eventually gave rise to bitter disillusionment. "War is hell, and those who institute it are criminals," Siegfried Sassoon wrote from the trenches. In France, Great Britain, and the United States, nearly everyone assumed it was the Germans who were the criminal unleashers of war; but some combatted this notion even during the war, and immediately afterward a momentous investigation into the causes of the war began—indeed, it began not long after the first guns sounded—with results that were likely to be "revisionist." If scholars did not seek to show that Russia and France were more guilty of the war than Austria and Germany, they at least concluded, typically, that all had been trapped in a circle of fear where one could not well speak of "war guilt." No nation had been entirely innocent, none criminally guilty; the guilt might be said to lie with a system, or a civilization, or in the nature of humanity itself. This historical controversy gave rise to a vast and interesting literature, which proved only that no historical event is simple enough to grasp scientifically, but which suggested to millions that their leaders had deceived them in charging all blame on the enemy.

The war violently interrupted everything, and turned all channels of life into new directions. Old intellectual leaders lost prestige, and old circles were broken up; many writers died in the war along with the millions of others. The world after the war was another world, and a new breed of men arose to lead its thought. The Russian Revolution was a bomb thrown squarely in the middle of Western civilization. The collapse of prewar Socialism was not the least of the many interrupted and shattered traditions; discredited by their acceptance of the war, the great majority of its leadership lost control of their own movement in 1917–1919. Lenin's Bolshevik faction seized power in Russia and proscribed the Mensheviks along with all other political parties as enemies of the Revolution. In Italy, the ambivalence of Social Democracy helped pave the way for Mussolini's Fascist dictatorship. The Italian Socialists could not decide whether to be revolutionaries or to defend the democratic constitutional order, and ended by doing neither. In Germany, Social Democrats established the new Republic but had to employ armed force against Communist uprisings and thus threw themselves into the arms of the Right. When the smoke had cleared, Communists looking to Lenin's Russia had greatly increased their following at the expense of the moderate Socialists almost everywhere in Europe, though nowhere except in Russia had they been able to seize the state. Their embittered violence frightened the conservative classes into backing extremist regimes in Italy and, within a few years, Germany. In Great Britain, the war wrecked the old Liberal Party forever and caused a great increase in the Labour Party, which though not Communist had a hyperradical wing and pacifist leadership.

Sickened by not only the physical slaughter of millions of Europe's youth but by the moral carnage of a world convulsed by hatred and lies, the postwar generation was the "lost generation." Lost were faith and hope, belief in progress, confidence in the civilization of the West. By way of introducing what was after all a marvelously creative generation too, we may catalog some of these cries of despair that filled the two decades destined to follow one Armageddon and precede another. Some of these will be discussed more fully later.

Gestures of Disgust and Despair

Dadaism, a violent nose-thumbing at civilization, was the leading example of such gestures immediately after the war; its successor, Surrealism, ranged the artists against respectable "bourgeois" society as never before, though it was a logical outgrowth of prewar estheticism. It is difficult to think of any of the great writers of this era—D. H. Lawrence, André Gide, Ernest Hemingway, James Joyce, T. S. Eliot—who did not reject the civilization in which they lived, though it is no less true that this rejection usually antedated the war. They were marked wanderers; the American "expatriates," who joined Gertrude Stein in Paris or Spain, had a counterpart in such as Lawrence, who hated his native England and lived at various times in New Mexico, Mexico, and Italy; or Joyce, a refugee from Ireland who lived in Trieste, Paris, and Zurich. There were, of course, Russian refugees from Communism, Italian from Fascism, and subsequently German from Nazism. Physical flight from the homeland went along with imaginative flight from Western civilization, expressed in Lawrence's admiration for the Etruscans or the Aztecs, in Ezra Pound's importing of Chinese, or what he imagined to be Chinese, literature.

This straying "after strange gods" included a desertion of intellectuals to Communism or, less commonly, to Fascism. Pound and Wyndham Lewis might be placed in the latter camp, but the major movement was toward faith in Soviet Russia as a place where a brand-new and hopeful civilization was being shaped, however roughly. This attitude on the part of Western writers and intellectuals was quite obviously a projection of their own cultural despair onto Russia as wishful thinking, and after a few years as Communists or fellow-travellers the harsh realities of Soviet tyranny freshly disillusioned all but the blindest. This was "the God that failed" for a significant segment of serious people, especially in the 1930s, and this "pink decade" will need to be discussed again. Those who briefly believed in the charisma of Mussolini or Hitler as creative forces were also speedily disillusioned, of course. In the 1920s one mostly believed in art or in sex, if one believed in anything; in the 1930s, poets tried to be proletarians and novelists went off to fight in the Spanish Civil War. But the latter gesture turned out to be almost as despairing and futile for most as the former.

If there was whoring after strange gods, there was also an effort **The Return** to return to ancestral ones. The neo-Anglicanism of T. S. Eliot, American- **to Religion** born mogul of English letters (another odd case of literary expatriation), had counterparts in the neo-Thomism of a significant group led by Jacques Maritain in France, and the neo-Calvinism and neo-Lutheranism of Karl Barth and Emil Brunner. The return to religion resulted from the collapse of liberal beliefs in secular progress. These theologies in some ways were not orthodox, for they usually "de-mythologized" the Bible, perhaps drew on Jungian conceptions, and regarded Christianity as symbolically rather than literally true. But they found in original sin and Christian humility an antidote to the shallow complacency of those prewar liberals and socialists who had believed in rationality and progress. Perhaps old-fashioned Christianity could be a cure for the diseases of a civilization whose sin had been denying its own birthright, succumbing to pride, forgetting the meaning of Christ. Christ was seen less as a preacher of humane ethical precepts than as the apocalyptic or "eschatological" prophet who announced the end of the world and asked men to choose between God and the world. This was especially the bent of Continental neo-orthodoxy, which in the form of the "crisis" theology of Barth came near to Christian existentialism. "It is essential not to have faith in human nature," historian Herbert Butterfield has written. "Such faith is a recent heresy and a very disastrous one." At bottom, the tragic view of life is the true one, asserted many a chastened optimist of the postwar years.

Prophets of doom arose. Oswald Spengler's *Decline of the West* came out of a Germany shattered by defeat, but its message of Western civilization's senility went all over the world and was repeated in varying accents by many others. It was at this time that Arnold J. Toynbee began his even vaster historical study of the rise and fall of civilizations, the first three volumes of which came from the press in 1934. The Spaniard Ortega y Gasset's brilliant essay, *The Revolt of the Masses,* conveyed a somewhat similar theme of European decadence from lack of creative leadership. Paul Valéry's famous essay on the European crisis and T. S. Eliot's even more famous poem, *The Waste Land,* might be mentioned in this context. Proust's mammoth novel chronicled the decay of French society. Of course Communists, Fascists, and Nazis all proclaimed the decadence and imminent death of the old society; that they did so helped eventually to rally some support for traditional European civilization, since these rebels against it so obviously purveyed something far worse. But the 1920s echoed with dirges for the passing of the European age.

[margin: Decline of the West]

War novels, like Erich Remarque's *All Quiet on the Western Front* or Henri Barbusse's *Le Feu,* recalled the horror and misery of the trenches and kept alive a fierce pacifism. If there was anything men would have fought for between the wars, it was the right not to fight. In the 1930s anti-Nazism became a rallying point, reviving morale considerably, but the issue was confused by pacifism; the desire to fight against Hitler's tyranny conflicted with the hatred of war. With the disillusionment of many who had been attracted to Communism, morale was still not high on the eve of the second world war. In 1938 Jean-Paul Sartre wrote his first novel, titled *Nausea.* Nausea, a horrible sense of the emptiness and hopelessness of life, would seem to have been a recurring image of the 1919–1939 years.

[margin: Hatred of War]

With Mussolini proclaiming the "lie of universal suffrage" and Lenin the decadence of bourgeois democracy, democracy was under attack and found few defenders in the 1920s. Cabinets shuffled back and forth in France while parties degenerated into factions and only the Communists seemed to stand for principle; in the 1930s French fascism, descended

[margin: Reaction against Democracy]

from the *Action Française* and its *Camelots du Roi,* was also active for a time. M. Tardieu, French premier, retired from politics to write a treatise expressing disillusionment with the parliamentary system. The German Republic established in 1919 had to humiliate itself before the arrogant victor powers as its first act and thereafter lived a precarious life, though it had a few hopeful years between 1924 and 1930 before collapsing under the weight of the great economic depression that struck in the latter year.

Popular "Culture"

During the 1920s the "people" seemed more interested in channel swims, airplane flights, murder trials, mah-jong, crossword puzzles, movie stars, and Mickey Mouse. The Common Man seemed a sad joke, cultural democracy the last absurdity of an expiring civilization—ending, as Eliot put it, not with a bang but a whimper. To Ortega, the Revolt of the Masses meant the end of historic Europe; to Spengler, the Decline of the West began with liberalism and democracy. The war had indeed hastened a trend in Europe to raise up the common man and democratize culture. In the long run this was surely a gain, but in the short run democratization meant cheapening and standardizing. The mass newspaper and journal with their low intellectual content pervaded society, it seemed. The "shopgirl mentality" and the common man as "boob" (H. L. Mencken) were familiar sneers.

In the 1930s this mood changed, the intellectuals became socialists and created a new image of the people, probably equally an illusion. The People were now supposed to be proletarian revolutionaries ready to rise and destroy false idols in the name of comradeship and brotherhood. Julian Symons has suggested in his book on the Thirties that these illusions came to an end in Spain, when the Left writers, hurled into a real war, were forced painfully to realize that real wars are nothing like dreams of universal comradeship, the real "people" nothing like the ideal. Something similar, this, to what had happened in 1848.

Freud, Jung, and the new depth psychology made a great impression on the postwar decades. Even the shopgirl had now heard of repressions, sublimations, and dreams analysis. Freudianism suited the iconoclastic postwar mood because it licensed, or might be claimed as license for, unconventional moral behavior. In its own way the new psychology lambasted the bourgeoisie, too, the sin being prudery. Freud himself continued to write; his most pessimistic work, *Civilization and Its Discontents,* appeared in 1930. Art and the novel eagerly seized on Freudian themes, the return to religion on Jung. Little in the 1920s was untouched by the two pioneers, though academic psychology treated them with considerable reserve and preferred other systems, if any at all.

The problem of a democratic, "mass" culture marked by silliness, anti-intellectualism, shallowness, and stupidity was raised first and foremost in the United States of America, whence fled in the 1920s dozens of "expatriate" intellectuals and writers in flight from a world dominated by Henry Ford, Calvin Coolidge, and Mr. Sinclair Lewis's "Babbitt"— H. L. Mencken's bourgeois boob. Hemingway, Fitzgerald, and other American writers left some mark on Europe, for the same phenomena of popular culture were creeping into the Old World too, being products not of something uniquely American but of a process at work throughout the Western world. What was it? The Americans, vaguely, were in revolt against a host of evils—materialism, provincialism, prudery, democracy, public establishments, political mediocrity, conformism, cultural anarchy —some of them mutually contradictory. They were prepared to "debunk" everything from George Washington to Warren Harding, from ministers of the gospel to corporation directors, from ladies' magazines to war. They themselves drew on the earlier European esthetic movement, on Nietzsche and Bergson as well as Freud and Baudelaire, etc.; but they drew fresh inspiration from what they regarded as the frightful state of American civilization in the era of mass newspapers and movies, radio, urban mindlessness, and a narrow-minded nativism that developed in the United States as a reaction against contact with Europe in the "great crusade" of World War I. They helped persuade European intellectuals that the world was awry and only an esthetic revolution could set it right. Dominated by capitalism, technology, and mass democracy, it was becoming both mindless and soulless. Even had the great war not intensified the process, these destructive evils would have had to be met.

Europeans agreed with their American friends that American civilization was deplorable; André Siegfried's book, *America Comes of Age,* and C. E. M. Joad's *The Babbitt Warren,* both published in 1927, may be taken as samples of this genre. *Homo Americanus* was man without art or culture, a savage in possession of modern technology, a product of the destruction of civilization by the machine. The same phenomena could be seen rising in Europe, though perhaps not yet so frightening. In blaming democracy for war, a botched peace, and a world without order, the European intellectuals of the 1920s sometimes seemed to be repeating almost exactly the gestures of their counterparts of exactly a century earlier. But this time they had even fewer defenses, for no Conservative ideology really appealed to them. They were left in much greater despair and disillusionment.

The disillusionment of the 1920s appeared fashionably and brilliantly in the novels of Aldous Huxley, which were really fictionalized tracts or sermons. We see, in *Antic Hay* (1923), a succession of object lessons in the failure of values. Gumbril, the hero, listens to the clergyman, and then the schoolmaster, and finds both of them useless; the artist fails him, and so does the scientist. Romantic love is a sham, but the amoralist who tries to find satisfaction in perverse or diabolical behavior is equally absurd. The mordant criticism of all attitudes that try to give life meaning

Aldous Huxley

continued in *Those Barren Leaves* (1925) and *Point Counter Point* (1928); these clever, sophisticated studies in pale melancholy hit the decade just right and made Huxley a household word. That he was the grandson of the famous Victorian scientist and believer in progress made his gloom about the human race the more piquant. A search for values always goes on in the astringent Huxleyan way, and in *Point Counter Point* the memorable character-gallery of failures—scientists, artists, politicians—turned up one slightly hopeful face in a somewhat Lorenzian philosopher (Huxley was a good friend of D. H. Lawrence). Perhaps by a return to healthy instincts one might make one's way out of the desert. *Brave New World* (1932) carried on Huxley's war with modern civilization. In the 1930s he began to find consolation in withdrawal and mysticism. Not a great novelist, Huxley was a subtle prober of values and a sensitive barometer of the moods of his day among sophisticated Europeans who felt themselves in a dying culture and searched almost in vain for a firm intellectual anchorage for their lives. The same spirit may be found in many another novel, poem, or play of the twenties and thirties.

It might be noted that the mood was not, really, tragic in the deepest sense. There is a sunset charm about the dying culture; talk is brilliant, personality and ideas both richly abundant, there are always marvelous books to read. What literate man could really be unhappy in a decade that produced Joyce, Lawrence, Proust, Kafka, and a whole parade of other stunning commentators on the sickness of civilization? A funeral that attracted so many notable pall-bearers had at least its compensations. It remained for World War II to confront Europe with stark tragedy; for the time being, ruminating among the ruins was far from unpleasant. The civilized upper class to which Huxley belonged still existed if it had gone slightly to seed. If this was not "la belle époque" of pre-1914, neither was it yet the nightmare world of Nazism, Communism, depression, and war. The thirties and forties brought these things.

Nevertheless the disgust which their civilization inspired in many European writers was both real and ominous. It could lead them to disaster. One example from many: Louis-Ferdinand Céline, in 1932, wrote *Le Voyage au Bout de la Nuit*, a shocking book, both in style and content, misanthropic much beyond Huxley, scatological beyond Lawrence, a terrible satire on the human race—a book which had a considerable vogue. This talented writer ended an anti-Semite, a pro-Nazi, a collaborator with the German conquerors of France during the war—out of sheer hatred of his native culture, we surmise. He was truly one of those of whom Lawrence wrote in *Kangaroo*, a person driven to defiant estrangement from his fellows. The trend toward violence in literature was noted: George Orwell, in a famous essay called "Raffles and Miss Blandish," contrasted the gentility of the pre-1914 crime story with the sadism of the genre in the 1930s and 1940s. Of the often brilliant writers of this epoch, and of Fascism and Nazism, which attracted some writers but repelled more, as well as of the "nausea" experienced by sensitive souls in these years, something remains to be said in the ensuing sections of this chapter. They are the leading themes of the time.

LITERATURE AND THOUGHT BETWEEN THE WARS

The first solace of literate men after the shambles of 1914–1918 was an esthetic one. The literary revolution, whose roots lay in the prewar period, burst upon the general public in the 1920s. Graham Hough has placed "between 1910 and the Second World War" a "revolution in the literature of the English language as momentous as the Romantic one of a century before." Perhaps it came earlier in France. But so far as concerned the English-speaking world such names as Yeats, Joyce, Pound, Eliot, and Lawrence came to the fore after the war though they had begun their careers just before it. Wyndham Lewis called Ezra Pound, T. S. Eliot, James Joyce and himself "the men of 1914": this quartet who led the revolution in English literature emerged exactly as the war began. D. H. Lawrence's first major novel, *Sons and Lovers,* was completed in 1913; he wrote *The Rainbow* and *Women in Love* during the war. Joyce had *Ulysses* ready to launch on the world at the end of the war years. Elsewhere, too, buds of the prewar years burst into bloom. Paul Valéry and Marcel Proust in France may be instanced. The latter's great symphony of novels, *Remembrance of Things Past,* appeared between 1913 and 1927 though Proust died in 1922 at the age of fifty-one. The German master Thomas Mann reached the peak of his reputation in the 1920s as did the Frenchman André Gide.

Moreover the new art and music, associated with the names of Picasso and Stravinsky, predated the war in its origins but moved into the limelight once the guns were silenced. The year 1913 had seen those famous riots in Paris that accompanied the first performance of Stravinsky's *Rites of Spring,* and also the public tumult aroused by an exhibition of the new nonrepresentational art in the United States. A young American emigré named Gertrude Stein was already buying the paintings of her friend Picasso in Paris—for a song. Picasso was at that time living in poverty among a gloriously bohemian set in the attics of Montmartre. Cubism was born 1908–1910, but the paintings produced by this and other avant garde movements were as yet little more than the obscure eccentricities of certain social outcasts. But after the war, conditions became favorable for the reception of anything new, startling, revolutionary. An embittered "lost generation" of rebels against the purposeless slaughter of 1914–1918 had no interest in defending the values of their fathers, whether artistic, moral, or philosophical.

The Literary Revolution of the Twenties

Dadaism

In Paris in 1919 writers and artists launched their protest against everything; they named it Dada (a nonsense word). Everything seemed nonsense—literature, morality, civilization. Action is vain; art is vain; life is vain. All is absurd. Dada was a combination of literary and intellectual sophistication—all has been said, all ways have been used—with the despair of the years 1917–1919, years of slaughter and stupidity. Dada's activities were expression of its bitter derision; it held public meetings, well advertised by post-futurist posters, at which people made nonsensical speeches. Tzara, a Hungarian-Swiss who was one of its chief founders, wrote poems by clipping words from a newspaper article, putting them in a sack, shaking them up, and then taking them out one by one. If most Dadaist poems did not go quite so far, they specialized in incongruity:

> The aeroplane weaves telegraph wires
> and the fountain sings the same song.
> At the rendez-vous of the coachmen the aperitif is orange
> but the locomotive mechanics have blue eyes.
> The lady has lost her smile in the woods.

Which is not without charm though definitely without meaning.

Surrealism

Needless to say Dadaism was a thing of the moment, but its young literary leaders were to be found in the vanguard of other movements of the 1920s. Of these the most important was Surrealism. Something of Dada's wish to deliberately derange meaning appeared in Surrealism, and also some of its violently disruptive political protest, both however made a bit more constructive and coherent. Surrealism borrowed from Freud and Jung the idea that in dreams and semiconscious states the mind is freed from the tyranny of the rational and can produce fresh, authentic symbols. "Psychic automatism" was its method of writing poetry (suspend thought and let the words come). It may indeed be regarded as a continuation of prewar Symbolism with Freudian additions.

Underneath such extravagances there was a Romantic faith in the autonomy of the realm of art, which the poetic vision might contact beyond the realm of merely rational concepts. It was a kind of mysticism of art, philosophically an Idealism. Surrealism has continued to be the dominant force in French poetry. In addition, the Surrealists proclaimed themselves political activists and enemies of "bourgeois" society, which they held responsible for the unhappy divorce of art from life. At first they tended to join the Communists, who were the most vigorous foes of the "bourgeoisie," but later they grew disillusioned, along with others, with Communist tyranny and intolerance. Their sociology, like their politics, tended to be slapdash in the extreme, though occasionally inspired. It was in painting that Surrealism, Cubism, and related modernist modes had their greatest success. Gertrude Stein's attempt to duplicate in surrealist prose the success in painting of her friend Pablo Picasso did not really come off, though her personality made her one of the most celebrated women of the 1920s. Her mystifying style ("A rose is a rose is a rose"; "How do you do I forgive you everything and there is nothing to forgive") was perhaps not intended to be understood. ("Nobody knows what I am trying to do but I do and I know when I succeed," Gertrude declared.)

The greater writers of a great age of literature were not always incomprehensible. Of the trinity of major novelists, Joyce, Lawrence, and Proust, only the first departed from reasonably straightforward statement, and he only to any marked degree in his last work, *Finnegan's Wake.* The novels nevertheless included daring, experimental, and controversial elements. Joyce's *Ulysses* was banned before publication and stirred up one of the chief literary rows of the decade, matched only by Lawrence's *Lady Chatterley's Lover.* The difficulty lay in the frank approach to sex and the use of words heretofore not permitted in polite discourse. To Lawrence, return to a healthy primitive sexuality was important, not in itself but because he thought people who know how to live know how to love. Sex to him was the key to creativity: taproot of all energies, it is the source of beauty, religion, everything wonderful and vital. So far from being a mere hedonism, this resembled Romanticism's doorway of the senses to a transcendent realm of truth and beauty; a great deal bolder and buttressed by modern psychology, to be sure. Lawrence castigated the effete intellectualism as well as the timid bourgeois conventionality of the modern world, feeling acutely the need for something more sincere, more intense, more real. This neoprimitivism sent him back to the Etruscans and the Indians, or, if he had to live in the modern world, to Mediterranean peasants. It sent Arthur Koestler and other Communist converts to the strong, silent workers.

The integrity and "committedness" of Lawrence, as well as his tremendous creative vitality, made him one of the chief of the modern age's seers. Joyce's *Ulysses,* which then so shocked people, has since received wide recognition as one of the greatest literary achievements of modern times. Its "message," if any, was less clear. A vast allegory on the condition of man, a commentary on the futility of human existence, a great symphony in words, an affirmation like Nietzsche and Lawrence of the chaotic abundance of life? Like Eliot's poetry, it made use of startlingly modern techniques to recall modern man to his civilized heritage. Whatever else it meant, it was a triumph of art and meant that the artist shapes and gives reality to the world—a message similar to Proust's. These works were testimonies to the autonomy of art and pointed to a withdrawal of the artist—a withdrawal Joyce and Proust made quite explicit—from society, to go it alone.

The mood of the writers changed sharply in the 1930s with the coming of the great economic depression and the rise of Fascism. They wrote off the esthetes of the 1920s as irresponsibles. "But quite suddenly, in the

D. H. Lawrence

James Joyce

years of 1930–1935, something happens. The literary climate changes. A new group of writers . . . has made its appearance, and though technically these writers owe something to their predecessors, their 'tendency' is entirely different. Suddenly we have got out of the twilight of the gods into a sort of Boy Scout atmosphere of bare knees and community singing" (George Orwell). Writers became serious, political, almost social-messianic in the spirit of 1848. Conversion from gloom and alienation to hope and social purpose seemed a miracle at the time; only later did Orwell, who went through it, see it as he so wryly describes it above. Writers turned to social realism in the 1930s and pinned their hopes on red revolution. The English poets C. Day Lewis, Stephen Spender, and W. H. Auden, unlikely revolutionaries, wrote some things of which they were later rather embarrassed. So it went all over Europe.

The Turn to Social Realism

Arthur Koestler notes that actual entrance into the Communist party on an active basis, which was his experience, choked off literary expression, but that mild contact with Marxism as "fellow travellers" stimulated any number of writers in the 1930s. John Dos Passos and John Steinbeck wrote memorable works of "social realism" in the United States; Barbusse, Romains, and Malraux in France; Brecht and Seghers in Germany. Some of this mock-proletarianism later seemed ridiculous. The esthetes of the 1920s tried to become democratic "hearties" if not Communist revolutionaries; from the Kremlin, the real thing undoubtedly laughed at them, while making use of them as best it could. There was an Oxford Collective Poem made by Mass Observation, so far had the cycle swung from the intensely private art of the previous decade. But the intellectuals' hatred of the Nazi and Fascist dictatorships was real and worthy of respect. Why they thought the Stalinist dictatorship merited adulation is a question we shall postpone for a moment. This effort to regain a democratic and social content for literature was unquestionably significant and productive of much good literature. It tried to repair the relationship between writer and society sundered since the 1880s.

Novelties in Architecture, Music, Painting

The interwar years also brought a new architecture and a new music. Le Corbusier (Charles Édouard Jeanneret) led a whole school of architecture that denounced nineteenth-century eclecticism and demanded buildings for the machine age—"functional" and not traditional. Proclaiming that "the past must be destroyed," this architecture had affinities with Futurist art and literature. Walter Gropius headed a similar movement in Germany, where the ill-fated Weimar Republic, destined to succumb to Adolf Hitler's Nazis in 1933, experienced a brief renaissance in the mid-twenties, Munich rivalling Paris as a center of modern art and Berlin boasting the Bauhaus architectural and art school. There was perhaps more hope in this new style of building for modern man than there was in the novel.

Both Corbusier and Gropius, as well as the American genius, Frank

Lloyd Wright, had started their work just before 1914 but reached their creative period after the war. These dates correspond closely with those of the pioneer modernists in painting, music, and literature, and indeed Corbusier, who was also a painter, was deeply influenced by Cubism and Futurism. But almost no one had heard of Corbusier, Gropius, the Bauhaus, and "functionalism" before the 1920s, and then they were forced to do battle against outraged traditionalists. One of the larger engagements in this war took place in connection with the League of Nations building at Geneva, supposedly a great symbol of the postwar era, and it is significant that Le Corbusier's modernistic design lost out, even in his native Switzerland, to the sedate neoclassical edifice that still stands there in Geneva. Still, the new style was much discussed and won some triumphs. Dubbed "functionalist," it was in actuality never considered simply as utilitarian by its founders, but was intended to be a modern esthetic. Under Cubist influence it tended to be severely abstract-geometrical at first but came to include considerable poetic feeling.

In music, abandonment of tonality was the counterpart of abandonment of perspective in painting and the daring innovations of functionalist architecture; there were such superlative geniuses as Schoenberg and Bartók. There were infinite riches for the eye and ear in these immensely creative years, the years of Picasso, Kandinsky, Gropius, Corbusier, and all the others. Though traditionalists might suspect sheer anarchy in their art forms, actually the authentically modern mode in the arts was at work, transforming the way we look at things and hear them, just as it was at work in Einsteinian physics. It is small wonder that this was a revolutionary epoch in other ways too.

The remarkable developments in physics, previously referred to, continued after the war. The day of the signing of the Treaty of Versailles in 1919 brought news of an observation confirming Einstein's law of relativity, and throughout the 1920s the doings of the scientists made big if somewhat mystifying news. Einstein became a household word though the "man in the street" professed to find him as incomprehensible as Gertrude Stein or the Surrealists. In the 1920s through the work of Heisenberg and Broglie the startling implications of quantum theory became evident in the dual manifestations of the electrons: they behave sometimes as particles and sometimes as waves, breaking through barriers heretofore assumed to be absolute. It became necessary to resort to something like the "as if" philosophy of Vaihinger (1911) and say that all scientific terminology represents "useful fictions." Observations are real, but these observations can be extended to form such generalizations as electricity, energy, atoms, matter, etc., only as hypothetical mental constructs. Thus was positivism or phenomenalism extended to include warnings about our language, the new fashion in philosophy becoming "lin-

Mystifying Developments in Science

guistic analysis." When we use a word like *matter,* do we really mean anything verifiable? If not, "materialism" and with it a whole segment of philosophical argument disappears.

It became known, also, that the subatomic particles are subject only to probability and that the observer inevitably interferes with them preventing perfect observation; the limits of science had been reached because no one can step outside the universe, man being a part of it. One might make what one chose of all this, but clearly many old certainties were gone, and the new Einsteinian universe was less tidy: Bertrand Russell said it was more individualist, even anarchist, with no central government! There were more mysteries and probably less security and anchorage. Among the popular expounders of the new physics, Arthur Eddington adopted an Idealist position, pointing out that the scientist creates truth, the answers depending on what questions he asks. James Jeans spoke of the mysterious universe and found more room for God than Laplace or Darwin had left. Science was the new mysticism. Alfred North Whitehead explored the implications of the new science for Western metaphysics, showing that the mechanistic framework dominant since Newton no longer sufficed; he and others proposed a "pan-psychism" which saw the universe as composed of organisms; thus electrons and atoms became in a sense endowed with spirit, a return full circle to the Greek-medieval outlook on nature.

Because it was so closely related to the problems of the new science, the mode of philosophy that became dominant in England and some European countries may be introduced at this point. It was a veritable revolution in philosophy, keeping company with the other revolutions in thought of this period. Perhaps this revolution may be briefly described by saying that philosophy ceased to be a "search for wisdom" or a quest for absolute answers, and became instead just the logic of science or the clarifier of scientific methods and concepts. To those who protested that philosophy was abdicating its chief function and leaving modern man, who never so needed help with his values, high and dry, the answer given by philosophers of the new dispensation was that unfortunately this cannot be the philosopher's function. These philosophers were "Positivists," that is, they carried on the tradition, with a greater rigor and clarity, of regarding "metaphysics" (absolute being and value, transcendental reality) as not a true object of knowledge. We cannot really say anything rational about that. If someone, the poet or the seer, wants to speak to this question, let him;[3] this is not the realm of clear logical thought which is the philosopher's.

Revolution in Philosophy: Neopositivism

[3] Reproducing an argument among the nineteenth-century Positivists, some of the new Positivists said that statements beyond the realm of verifiable sense experience are merely beyond the competence of the philosopher, while others denied the right to talk about them at all.

The basic postulate was that philosophical method must be "scientific." Science is not only clear, logical, rational, analytical, but also "verifiable by sense experience." The application of these criteria suggested that for philosophy there is no specific end or content; its function must be to help the sciences—which alone can provide knowledge, since empirical investigation is the only sort of knowledge. "The business of philosophy is not to establish a set of philosophical propositions but to make other propositions clear." To clarify the meaning of words and statements might seem a modest goal but it can be most useful. If science experiments and verifies, philosophy defines and clarifies. Many meaningless problems and much nonsense may be removed by the rigorous analysis of words. Indeed the method might be extended to other fields, such as politics or ethics, to clear up confusions by defining terms, thus locating the problems.

Logical Positivism originated with a group of philosophers and mathematicians active at the University of Vienna from about 1920 until Nazism and war dispersed them in the 1930s, whereupon many of them went to Great Britain and the United States and exerted a considerable influence while blending with certain native traditions in these countries. These men included Schlick, Carnap, Neurath, and Wittgenstein, the latter going to Cambridge University early. They owed something to the prewar teaching at Vienna of Ernst Mach's "empirio-criticism," a careful analysis of the immediate data of experience based on the neo-Kantian view that only sense data exist and we cannot know the thing-in-itself. In Britain, the influence of Ludwig Wittgenstein (*Tractatus-Logico-Philosophicus*, 1921) blended with a somewhat related movement stemming from G. E. Moore and Bertrand Russell, Cambridge philosophers who broke with the dominant school of Idealism beginning about 1900. Their roots were plainly in British empiricism; this was the spirit of Bacon, Locke, and Hume, marked by a tendency to avoid all metaphysical flights, concentrate on careful analysis of actual experience, break problems down into their smallest components, watch out for the loose use of terms, and construct no "systems." The early Wittgenstein joined forces with Russell's "logical atomism"; the later Wittgenstein's keen interest in the logical structure of language reenforced Moore's influence to open up marvelous horizons of subtle inquiry to a generation of "linguistic analysts" and "semanticists."

The most extreme statement of the new school came from the English philosopher A. J. Ayer in the 1930s. No problems exist, Ayer suggested, except the factual ones of science. All the others can be shown by linguistic analysis to be nonexistent, pseudo-problems. Most of the things philosophers and theologians and moralists had been worrying about through the centuries—God, freedom, spirit, purpose, morals, etc.—were complete wastes of time. They can be shown to be either wrong state-

The Vienna Circle

A. J. Ayer

ments of the problem, or else purely personal or "emotive" projections of the feelings of the individual concerned, about which there can be no fruitful argument. Some of them we can reduce to empirical, testable statements, and these in principle can be solved, by the scientist (empirical investigator). The rest must be dismissed as so much empty wind.

Implications
of Logical
Positivism

The shock effect of this position is evident. As someone has remarked, theologians who were accustomed to being told they were wrong found themselves speechless at being told they were not saying anything at all! Applied to morality, Logical Positivism might be extremely subversive. Statements of value not being "empirically verifiable," they become mere expressions of preference. "I think adultery is wrong" is the same sort of statement as "I hate spinach" or "I dislike abstract art." (Though Hume had said something similar in the eighteenth century, he had been willing to fall back on custom and the consensus of mankind; twentieth century sceptics had scant respect for either.) It will be recalled that some of the bolder Enlightenment writers had equated right with pleasure and wrong with pain, the only categorical moral imperative being to satisfy one's urges. Sober academic philosophers now indirectly endorsed their hedonism. Strictly speaking, they only pointed out that logical thought can supply no sanctions for behavior; we must look elsewhere for values of this sort. It is open to us to find them in religion or in social utility. At the same time, the frank equation of moral tastes with other kinds of personal taste might be construed as issuing an invitation to moral libertinism. Presumably I should choose my conduct in the same sort of way I choose my neckties—all a matter of personal taste. And if I try to defend one sort of conduct against another by any sort of rational argument, I am talking nonsense.

What was one to make of this breathtaking dismissal of entire realms of intellectual experience? It is now generally agreed that Ayer was much too dogmatic; indeed he has admitted it himself. Logical Positivism or something similar has nevertheless remained, in a somewhat chastened form (and, recently, under increasing criticism), particularly in the British universities, as the only respectable kind of "philosophy." It has scarcely prevailed at all in the Latin countries. Clearly it represents a severe retrenchment or cutting back, intellectually and culturally, in order to get the advantages of clarity and certainty.[4] Like Locke, these modern *philosophes* advise us to consider only what the mind is fitted for and forgot all the rest. The method would seem to have great strengths and also the defects of its merits. It has clarified many questions but has resigned entirely in substantial areas of human experience where cer-

[4] Its popularity in the universities (not least American ones) seems to relate closely to a principle of rationalization in large professional institutions. This sort of philosophy is not vague, can be precisely graded, is even tinged with the prestige of "science."

tainty is impossible but which nonetheless are urgently important to mankind. Human culture would never have arisen at all, we may well believe, if people had always been as fastidious as these philosophers. An arid verbalism and a cloistered timidity mark their thought, some have felt. Moreover, it has been urged against them that their "verification principle" itself, their one test of truth, is an arbitrary, "metaphysical" assertion; how does one verify the verification principle?

But "the absence of any dogma or jargon, any universal method, any claim to finality" together with the keenness and closeness of its thought has impressed other observers of English philosophy. In the 1920s and 1930s, Logical Positivism's astringency, scepticism, and almost nihilistic tendencies recommended it. It was in part a kind of nose-thumbing at all the old pomposities; it was a paring back, a getting down to brass tacks preparatory to rebuilding the world of knowledge from the ground up. And in this respect it bore some resemblance to such other phenomena as the prose of Ernest Hemingway. We have only to read the first sentence of Ayer's "manifesto," *Language, Truth and Logic* (1935) to sense this mood: "The traditional disputes of philosophers are, for the most part, as unwarranted as they are unfruitful."

The astringent and analytical spirit appeared also in English literary criticism. The magazine *Scrutiny*, edited by Oxford professor F. R. Leavis, founded in the 1930s and published until 1953, encouraged what its title suggested, a meticulous line-by-line examination of poetry, in reaction against both the chatty sort of armchair talk about literature which had passed for criticism in Victorian times and against lack of clear literary standards. For somehow it was expected that close scrutiny would clarify standards. The Scrutinizers thought of themselves as cutting away large husks of sentimentality with a keen razor of critical analysis, in order to get down to the solid core of real literary value. Like the analytic philosophers, they were to be accused of aridity and pedantry; a fairly strong reaction against them set in after 1945. But they succeeded in introducing what seemed like a scientific expertness in the examination of the arts. Somehow this was bracing.

For science commanded great respect. Progress went on in numerous areas of science, though sometimes it seemed rather gloomy progress. It was at this time that genetics became a fashionable study. Psychology, in the universities, lay more under the influence of J. B. Watson, the "behaviorist," and the Russian, Pavlov, than of the more speculative theories of Freud and Jung. Eschewing any attempt to analyze interior states of mind, as unsuitable for the scientific method, the Behaviorists stuck to measurable observations of external behavior. This was an American school but for a time found considerable international favor. In its more dogmatic moods it was inclined to insist that human nature is determined by its environment in a mechanical sort of way, that life is made up of a

Behaviorist Psychology

series of "conditioned reflexes," and that "mind," as such, does not exist, there being only a pattern of electric reactions in brain tissue. Very Positivist, even eighteenth-century.

"Scientific humanism" was a term much in use; what it meant, roughly, was the possibility of raising mankind to new heights by the use of science alone, with heavy overtones of hostility to traditional religion. But to many the march of science threatened dehumanization. In his *Brave New World Revisited* (1959), written 27 years after his famous depiction of what might be the fate of man in a few centuries when he had been totally organized in accordance with scientific techniques, Aldous Huxley noted the use of Pavlovian theories in the "brainwashing" techniques practiced by the Chinese Communists. His *Brave New World*, he felt, had all but come true in a mere quarter of a century. Freedom and individuality would be sacrificed to the demands of the machine, large-scale organization, and technological progress. In the years since 1920 there has always gone on a lively controversy between those who hail science and technology as the liberator and savior of man, and those who fear he is being enslaved and spiritually destroyed by these terrible servants. With the spectacular advances in science and technology of these years, the issue became an urgent one. To raise it at the most urgent of all levels, nuclear fission was achieved in 1938 (following the work of Mme. Curie and M. Joliot in 1934 in inducing radioactivity by bombarding certain atoms with neutrons) and would be developed into the atomic bomb during the war that lay just ahead.

THE STRIFE OF IDEOLOGIES

In the 1920s and 1930s political themes became quite as exciting as literary and philosophical ones even for the intelligentsia. To an overwhelming extent these revolved around the revolutionary regimes that came out of the war in Russia and in Italy: Communism and Fascism.

Fascism   A result of the demoralization following the war and a disappointing peace, as well as of frustrated national pride, Italian Fascism was hardly a consistent doctrine, but rather a fusion of discontents, successful because of the near collapse of society. It owed something to the fierce strife between socialist trade unions and the industrial capitalists, and to the Socialist's paralysis of will in a divided mind, as well as to the continued failure of parliamentary democracy to function well. A mass movement, it appealed to various inchoate emotions. In part it was the nightmare of Ortega, of Spengler, of Lawrence, and of Huxley come true: a revolt of the dehumanized masses, who were then to be enslaved by the totalitarian state. But Fascism had its intellectual aspects, and made use of some interesting ideas. Its leader, Benito Mussolini, a man of humble birth, had been a left-wing socialist, and was a journalist with an inquisitive and somewhat intellectual turn of mind. He had absorbed at least superficially the advanced political ideas of the pre-1914 generation—from Nietzsche, Sorel, Bergson, and Pareto. He got from them the need for a complete revolution of values, to replace the decadent ones of bourgeois civilization, but also a contempt for materialistic socialism; a belief in elites rather than democracy; in the superiority of intuition over intellect.

Of the Fascist and Communist revolutions, much the same thing may be said as was said of the French Revolution earlier: ideas did not cause them, but they did guide and shape them. Discontents and the breakdown of order existed, the result of war and postwar problems (economic troubles, demobilization of soldiers). There was a host of other accumulated grievances. Italy had suffered from frustration ever since the rebirth of the nation in 1861, an event which was supposed to lead on to the glory befitting descendants of the Romans but instead brought only a series of humiliations. All this would in any case have brought on trouble, perhaps violence; but ideology helped shape this into a coherent, or more or less coherent, pattern of revolution.

The swashbuckling novelist and adventurer, Gabriel D'Annunzio, actually played a more creative part than Mussolini in setting the pattern. A man of ideas as well as of action was D'Annunzio, who put himself at the head of some exsoldiers and marched into the disputed city of Fiume in 1919, accompanying his seizure of it with flamboyant gestures of the sort soon copied by Mussolini—the uniformed private army, parades and mass meetings, the Leader addressing crowds from the balcony as they roared slogans back at him. The spirit of Fascism was very much this spirit of the romantic gesture, action for action's sake, and the mobilization of mass psychology. One may read here the whole mystique of the avant garde movement of the day: the Nietzschean incitement to embrace life and "live dangerously," the rebellion against bourgeois legality, the alienated artist's hatred of respectable society, the socialist and anarchist call to revolt. Despite the disreputable character of Mussolini, an intellectual charlatan, there were some ways in which Fascism was smartly up-to-date—more up-to-date than Lenin's Marxism, for it had absorbed the lessons of irrationalism and psychology. It stressed "charismatic" leadership and "superman" activism. The Fascists managed to project an image of dynamic leadership aimed at reviving the Italian nation, sorely distressed and apparently unable to do anything about its troubles. Their weakness was the weakness of the new irrationalism: no system or program, just action for the sake of action, belief in belief itself, creation of "myths" whatever they might be.

To supply the element of nationalism lacking in Nietzsche and Sorel (the latter repudiated Mussolini because of his statism), Mussolini invoked Hegelian strains, popular in Italy for some time. He confided the construction of Fascist philosophy to the distinguished neo-Hegelian

D'Annunzio

philosopher, Giovanni Gentile. The state represents the ethical ideal, and is superior to the individual, Gentile held. Both the individualism of bourgeois liberalism and the divisive class struggle of Marxian socialism are antisocial. Materialism was rejected as ignoble, and an organic conception of society approved. Claiming at first to stand for the individual against the state, Mussolini moved steadily toward more and more statism, a movement of the mind obviously not unaffected by the fact that Fascism had seized the state, and increasingly subordinated the individual to the community.

In addition to the above idea, Fascism seemed to revert to Jacobin conceptions of the general will, of which Il Duce, with his Grand Council of Fascism, was said to be the embodiment. Fascism represented itself as an answer to the degenerate liberalism of the parliamentary system. Also, the idea of the corporate state, developed in Catholic social thought and carried forward by Charles Maurras, became a part of Mussolini's system. Fascism thus appears, on its ideological side, as a pastiche of a number of ideas, with a heavy stress on statism, elitism, and irrationalism. Perhaps its marriage of statism (from Rousseau and Hegel) to the dynamic revolutionary romanticism of Nietzsche and Sorel may be regarded as its most striking achievement. (But the antiromantic conservative thought of Maurras was also somewhat in evidence.) One may argue with some plausibility that Fascism simply grabbed at various bits and pieces of ideas to justify its seizure of power. But it does not seem possible to dismiss its ideological aspects, for these were potent factors. It may be that this was why Fascism and Nazism had such startling success: their leaders were aware of the power of ideas, whereas the anemic liberalism of the time was not. Debased as it was, they offered a religion or faith to live by to modern man, who had need of it. For a few years Italy's most distinguished philosopher, Benedetto Croce, approved of Fascism because it had overcome traditional Italian indifference to politics and the state, revived national morale, and seemingly justified itself by its results.[5]

Mussolini strove to destroy the "lie of universal suffrage" and parliamentary democracy by substituting a strong, heroic elite; he only succeeded in putting Italy under the heel of a corrupt oligarchy. He broke the power of the trade unions but his "corporate state" scarcely provided any creative principle of economic cooperation. Fascism as a new religion was stamped on the mind of youth through control of the educational system and the organization of youth movements, but it soon ceased to interest anyone of intellectual quality. Mosca, the old proponent of elites, publicly regretted that he had ever criticized democracy, for the rule of the Fascists was worse yet. In brief, whatever promise there had been of

[5] An impressive number of notable Italian writers, artists, musicians, including Papini, Pareto, Pirandello, Puccini, Toscanini, praised the new Italian regime at first. Almost all became severely disillusioned within a few years after 1922.

a genuine new creed or spirit in Fascism soon vanished with only the old face of state tyranny in evidence, this time backed by the resources of modern technology. It is true that Mussolini for a while put on a reasonably convincing performance of the hero-leader, with some "charismatic" appeal. In many ways he was a genuinely talented man. But he wilted under the demands of the superman role and became rather ridiculous. Quite a few of Italy's better minds fled into exile. Others, like the great writer Ignazio Silone, were turned into Communists who fought the Fascist tyranny as best they could underground.

German National Socialism owed much to Fascism—Adolf Hitler idolized the Italian dictator—but included some distinctive elements. Like Mussolini, Hitler and his group hated democracy, preached a "national" socialism in place of the Marxist sort which they regarded as poisonous, and were fanatically nationalistic and statist. Nazism, too, thrived on defeat, national humiliation, and the disorders of the postwar era, which were very severe in Germany for several years after 1919. It owed a special debt to Richard Wagner and featured anti-Semitism, not conspicuous in Italian Fascism. It also opportunistically made appeal to all sorts of emotions. It denounced capitalism, Communism, the Jews, the traitors who had allegedly caused the defeat of Germany, the pacifists and liberals who continued to weaken her; it demanded a strongly led government capable of voicing the entire national will and leading Germany back to her place in the sun. Its brown-shirted gangs specialized in brutal violence. The Party, with its leadership-principle, borrowed heavily from Lenin's Russian Communist party in its organization. There were echoes of pre-1914 Pan-Germanism in Hitler's program of German expansion; there was also the "crude Darwinism" which caused the relatively ignorant Hitler to act consistently on the principle that life is a ruthless struggle in which the weak, the wounded, and the allegedly "biologically inferior" have to perish. Racism came from Wagner and a few other nineteenth-century writers, such as the Frenchman Gobineau, owing something, too, to the fashion for genetics, which sometimes took the form of belief in racial improvement by selective breeding.[6] From Nietzsche (selectively) the Nazis took slogans about supermen, heroic leadership, and the need to purge the old order ruthlessly.

In the crude thought of the demagogue Hitler, the Jew appears as a scapegoat, blamed for everything: among other things, for capitalism, democracy, socialism, decadent estheticism, modern art and literature,

Nazism

---

[6] Count Joseph Arthur de Gobineau, a friend of Tocqueville and a speculative sociologist in the tradition of Montesquieu, wrote his *Essay on the Inequality of the Races* (1853–1855), purporting to show that the white races and particularly the "Aryan" race alone created civilization. The work influenced Wagner. Flattering to the Germans because it found the highest concentration of pure "Aryanism" to exist in Germany, the theory was the work of a Frenchman anxious to show that the French aristocracy, originally Germanic, deserved its ascendancy.

modern scepticism and unbelief. In the slightly more sophisticated theorizing of the Nazi "philosopher" A. Rosenberg, the Jew is identified with intellectualism, which is related to internationalism, both to be set off against the sound instincts of a cultural people. Christianity has been corrupted by both Judaic and Mediterranean elements, but there is a sound "Aryan Christianity" which should be encouraged. Little of this barrage of vituperation could be dignified by calling it thought, yet it had an element of consistency. The decadent phenomena, blamed primarily on Jewish influence, are the internationalist, intellectualist, uprooted, atomistic ones; the sound things are rooted in the soil, national tradition, close group integration, intuition, and custom rather than abstract reason. It is easy to see in this sort of thinking many echoes of German and European thought, from early nineteenth-century conservatism and Romanticism, from Wagner and Nietzsche and German sociologists like Frederick Tönnies. They were not all disreputable ideas; perhaps they ought not to be blamed because they fell into the hands of the Nazis. The specifically Nazi contribution was the mysticism of race, which is generally considered to have been complete nonsense.

Talk about the "Nordic race" and its superiority was quite common and respectable in the later nineteenth and twentieth century, as may be seen, for example, in England's Cecil Rhodes, whose Anglo-American scholarships, still awarded annually and considered a high honor in the United States, were established for the purpose of knitting together "the Nordic race"; or in such Americans as Josiah Strong and John W. Burgess, a popular clergyman and a leading professor of political science. The United States rang with laments about the "mongrelization" of the native stock through immigration from "inferior" Slavs and Latins as well as Jews. Anti-Semitism was familiar in Great Britain: a recent writer has observed that "fifty years ago anti-Semitism was a political force in England that respectable people supported and with which honourable people sympathized." (Henry D'Avigdor-Goldsmid, *History Today*, April, 1964.) The Dreyfus case and the *Action Française* movement will be recalled as the first major appearance of modern anti-Semitism. Hitler learned his in Austria. There, the Germans as a minority in a sea of Slavs, Hungarians, and Jews developed an often hysterical Pan-Germanism as well as "master race" ideologies. Rosenberg was a Baltic German, again revealing the psychology of the colonist or resident alien. All this is to record the unhappy fact that racial prejudice and belief in racial or cultural superiority was hardly confined to Germany, or typical of it. German National Socialism was destined to write the most odious and detestable chapters of this disease in all history; the ideas were far from exclusively German.

The Nazi mysticism of race contained an echo of Jung's unconscious archetypes, alleged however to be a phenomena of *race:* each race has its soul, its symbols, its myths, which are carried in the blood. Jung like many Germans was evidently partly attracted to Nazism at first but later emphatically rejected it.

Hitler appropriated some of the ideas of the German conservative writers, a group that included Oswald Spengler, Ernst Jünger, and Moeller van den Bruck, though they did not much approve of him and after seizing power he persecuted this group as relentlessly as others. These thinkers responded to the defeat and humiliation of Germany in World War I by proposing a Spartan recovery program. Spengler and Moeller wrote of the need for strength of will, national resurgence, and a leader capable of embodying in himself the people's will. All weakening forces, such as democracy (alien to the "Prussian style"), liberalism, and class conflict must be eliminated. These ideologies stemming from the French Revolution were the virus poisoning Germany, which must return to conservative principles to regain unity and strength. Moeller and Spengler were the "conservative revolutionaries" who would use revolutionary means to bring about a conservative, that is, nationalistic, goal. But they were not racists and Hitler to them was a disreputable rabble-rouser. There are some striking affinities between these writers and Nazism, but not complete identity. German Neocon-servatism

Ernst Jünger was a spokesman of Germany's restless youth, who even before the war had created a Youth Movement expressing the urge to get back to nature and renew contact with elemental forces, a protest against the urbanized rationalism of modern life. Something similar existed in France and other countries. After the war, the "fatherless generation" or the embittered exsoldiers were revolutionary in spirit. This youth movement was intensely idealistic, yearning for something much better, earnestly if fuzzily convinced that the existing order—capitalist, mechanical, bourgeois, soulless—was bankrupt. The youth movement with its *Bünde* was separate from the National Socialists but often merged into it. Hitler took advantage of it; in the long run he did not represent its idealism, and it is clear that many young Germans who initially hailed Hitler soon became severely disillusioned with the new slavery his regime introduced. (By that time it was too late.) Radical, revolutionary as it was, young Germany was searching for something to believe in, something exalted and pure. The tragedy was that the figure it thought represented such revolutionary idealism turned out to believe in nothing.

The Nazi and Fascist movements were profoundly anti-intellectual. "When I hear the word 'culture' I reach for my gun," said Joseph Goebbels, Hitler's lieutenant. These movements came to be led by the brutal, the ignorant, and the criminal. They were extremely clever at exploiting the irrationality of the masses, for whom they often expressed great contempt. Keen students of propaganda, the Fascists and Nazis borrowed liberally from all the great mass movements of the past. They employed Anti-Intel-lectualism: Use of Propaganda the language of religious conversion, freely using such words as faith, deliverance, miracle, rebirth, sacrifice. Nineteenth-century nationalism did so too, as we may recall. They took much from the Communists, as well as from ritualistic orders such as Jesuits or Freemasons, and from the Army; it has been suggested that they also learned a good deal from American advertising. They played on symbols from the national past. Hitler and the Nazis "looked back into the stream of earlier German thinking and selected that which they found of value to them" (Otto Klineberg). All this was done cynically, in the sense that there was a deliberate use of "myth," a disparagement of objective truth, a frank acceptance of the need to lead the masses by techniques directed at the irrational mind. But all these ideas had been brought forth by such important prewar thinkers as Nietzsche, Sorel, Wallas. The war itself had exhibited the possibilities of nationalistic propaganda and helped undermine respect for truth, as governments resorted to what amounted to systematic lying. (In the postwar years, some civil servants confessed as much. See Arthur Ponsonby, *Falsehood in Wartime.*) Thus in many ways the Fascist and Nazi movements dredged up all the worst in prewar and war culture. They were the evil spirits of Western civilization, but they did not create the evil so much as exploit it. As nihilists, they were intellectual parasites, borrowing the ideas of others to use as tools of power.

Nihilism   Hermann Rauschning, himself a participant in the German neo-conservative movement, called Hitlerism "the revolution of nihilism" by which he meant to indicate that it had no doctrinal center at all, no belief in anything. It was an inherently destructive force, committed to eternal dynamism for the sake of dynamism. It was organized neuroticism, the sickness of a nation never quite soundly built and driven mad by the sufferings of war, defeat, and then economic collapse. This analysis itself may suffer from rhetorical exaggeration, but it does convey something of the deep corruption and moral bankruptcy of the Nazi state. Some intelligent Germans hailed it at first because they thought it might bring able leadership.[7] If it had produced a true elite able to govern well, one might have forgiven it its lack of democracy and even some ruthlessness. But it ended in war, the sickening slaughter of the Jews, defeat, and destruction. Thereby all that it had stood for or even suggested became repugnant to mankind.

The Fascist and Nazi creeds glorified war. "War alone brings all human energies to their highest state of tension," proclaimed Mussolini, "and stamps with the seal of nobility the nations which have to face it."

---

[7] The list of distinguished Germans who saw something in Hitler, at least for a time, has been found alarming (Gottfried Benn, Martin Heidegger, most of the universities' faculty). It could possibly be said in reply that the cloven hoof of the Nazis did not fully reveal itself at first and that few distinguished intellectuals stayed loyal to them. But some find this reply unconvincing.

The idea that war is a test of a people's moral fibre was an Hegelian one. Hitler believed that the decadent democracies would be incapable of waging war, because their people had been corrupted, softened, debauched. Under National Socialist discipline the German people must prove themselves worthy of history by facing war. Hitler plunged recklessly down a collision course that eventuated in war, a course obviously marked out by ideological elements in National Socialism, both in a negative and a positive way. Negatively, Hitler's ideology convinced him that the democracies with their materialism and un-*Völkisch* cultures were incapable of determined resistance; they would neither fight nor develop a firm national policy, because they believed in nothing, were led by internationalist Jews (apparently the Nazis even thought that Franklin D. Roosevelt was Jewish!), and were inefficiently democratic. Positively, Nazism implied the cult of virility, the test of war. Hitler expected Great Britain to ally with Germany and was prepared to allow the British to govern the seas and their colonial world. He had fallen under the sway of the "geo-political" ideas of MacKinder and Haushofer, which combined with his belief in Slavic inferiority to direct his ambitions toward a great Eurasian land empire, to be ruled over by Aryan supermen.

In the 1930s, reaction against Nazism, as we have previously suggested, provided a rallying point for the shattered morale of European intellectuals. At this same time, they were precipitated in large numbers into the camp of Communism. The "red decade," or at least the "pink" one, had begun.

Quite early, the new Communist government of the Soviet Union received significant support from Western intellectuals. "In this muddy age its ten years shine," wrote the American liberal magazine *The Nation* on the tenth birthday of the Russian Revolution in 1927, voicing orthodox liberal-left doctrine. Historians this side of the USSR are likely to find today that it shone mostly with blood. In 1932 the venerable Fabian Socialists, Mr. and Mrs. Webb, who had always stood for political democracy and personal liberty, heaped praise on "Soviet Civilization" in a substantial study; they praised it among other things for "liquidating the landlord and the capitalist." At just that time Stalin's ruthless war on the kulaks was driving peasants to starvation in a way one can hardly imagine the Webbs approving. What became almost a stampede of writers and intellectuals to the Communist bandwagon later appeared inexplicable, even to the people who joined it. There were, however, some reasons for it.

Bolsheviks and left socialists profited, first of all, by having none of the blood of the World War on their hands. Lenin and a few others, for example, Ramsay MacDonald in Great Britain, had denounced the

Soviet Communism and the Western Intellectuals

conflict from the beginning. As soon as the Bolsheviks fell heir to collapsing Russia in November, 1917, they issued an appeal to the workers of the world to lay down their arms. They continued to denounce the whole European state system as an iniquitous capitalist scheme and to cloak themselves in the garb of pacifism. Lenin provided a Marxist explanation of the great war—caused by imperialistic capitalism—and socialists alleged that universal peace would follow the extinction of the capitalist system. The unpopularity of the war, and the hatred of all war, that pervaded these years redounded to the credit of the Communists. A good deal of sympathy for the Russian Bolshevist government, also, was aroused by the shocked horror with which respectable circles regarded it; by their efforts to destroy it through military intervention in 1919–1920 (though these were feeble and half-hearted), and by their treatment of it as a pariah for some time after 1920.

Perhaps it is not quite possible to explain the pro-Soviet mood in a rational way. It became a symbol for all those who hated the "establishment." The disillusioned and the naturally rebellious, the unhappy young men and women of the "lost generation," saw here a successful revolution, led by a leader of genius and vision, which had overthrown a vicious and reactionary government in Russia. But whatever sympathy the Soviet "experiment" aroused before 1930, it was the impact of the great depression that caused the rush to Marxism. The Webbs, in the study mentioned above, praised especially the Russian "abandonment of the incentive of profit-making, its extinction of unemployment, its planned production for community consumption."[8] The Western democracies struggled almost hopelessly in the mire of economic depression in the 1930s, while in Russia things seemed to go forward with vigor and drive. "There is no unemployment in Russia": the explanation might be that there was economic slavery there, but in the grim atmosphere of the jobless thirties even that seemed better than unemployment. As a matter of fact, uncritical books by friends of the Soviet Union poured from the press, indicating that something like a paradise for the working man was being created, with all the old vices missing—vices such as greed, selfishness, prostitution, crime, ignorance. "Planned production for community consumption" had replaced the anarchy of capitalism.

The existence of Fascism and then Nazism polarized political attitudes and diminished the middle position. Mussolini and Hitler excoriated Bolshevism, as did all right-wing, conservative people; therefore if you attacked it you could be accused of being a Fascist, or as good as one.

---

[8] Fabian socialism was in considerable confusion because its solutions had seemingly not worked. In her diary, Mrs. Webb observed that "we went seriously wrong . . . in suggesting that we knew how to prevent unemployment. We did not." By 1931 there had been two Labour governments in Britain, yet the expected miracles had not come about. "I am beginning to doubt the inevitability of gradualness," Beatrice sighed.

(Marxist logic featured a method of reasoning by which "objectively" one could be a Fascist without even knowing it.) Some very intelligent people admitted that they backed Soviet Russia because it was attacked by those they disliked; they loved it for the enemies it made (*vide* André Gide). Communists did fight Fascism and Nazism; they led the way in the famous Spanish Civil War which pitted the two elements against each other. They showed outstanding courage in fighting as best they could the Fascist and Nazi dictatorships in Italy and Germany.

An additional attraction that may be suggested in explanation (if not extenuation) of the intellectuals' defection to Communism was Soviet literature and art, as Edmund Wilson, the distinguished American literary critic, has reminded us. The arts in Russia had not yet been placed in an official strait jacket, destroying their creativity and interest. They were still reasonably free, progressive, and graced by such names as Maxim Gorki, one of the greatest of living novelists in the 1930s (a holdover from the prewar era, but an enthusiastic convert to the Soviet regime); Eisenstein, the genius of the silent cinema; Prokofiev and Shostakovich, the composers. Culturally, today, the world of Communism has virtually nothing to attract the educated Westerner; this was not so true in the 1920s and early 1930s. Stalinization of all artistic and intellectual activity did not really get under way seriously until about 1935. After World War II it reached fantastic extremes during the reign of Zhdanov as Cultural Minister, when even music could be denounced as "ideologically incorrect" and scientists were persecuted for not paying sufficient heed to dialectical materialism. (Since the death of Stalin in 1953, there has been some slight relaxation of this rigorous censorship.)

The artists and intellectuals who rushed into the arms of Communism expected to find there greater freedom, greater creativity, a liberating force. Picasso said that he went to Communism as to a spring of fresh water. The great irony is that by 1931 Communism had become a system of slavery and an intellectual strait jacket, so that the intellectuals who entered it were condemned to frustration. The Communist party was being so organized as to destroy all intraparty democracy in the USSR and also so as to put the various other party units firmly under the control of Moscow. Communists in other countries were required to serve the Stalin-dictated party line blindly. In the name of Socialist unity they had to agree that the homeland of Socialism, the USSR, must be defended at all cost. They were led into the role of apologists for whatever might be done by Stalin, and in the middle thirties this included the astonishing reign of terror that "purged" almost all the old Bolsheviks along with hundreds of thousands of others as Stalin systematically destroyed all resistance to his dictatorship. In 1939 it included suddenly becoming the ally of Hitler. While a few agreed to submit their individuality entirely to the party and suspend all ethical considerations for the duration of the

Disillusionment with Communism

battle against capitalism, most found the conditions of intellectual servitude imposed on them intolerable and became disillusioned with the USSR. They might not abandon their revolutionary or Marxist views in leaving the party; they might claim (plausibly) that Stalin had betrayed the revolution and perverted Marx, as well as Lenin. But the exodus from the party that began about 1937 led most of the converts eventually away from the whole Marxist framework. They were led to reexamine Marxism and to see some of its defects, which could be regarded as having led to Stalinism.

Whatever their future destinations, the Left writers departed for them from their Red rendezvous at the end of the 1930s and later treated it for the most part as a mistake. A great deal was written by the one-time Communists about their odyssey in and out of the party. In his great novel *Darkness at Noon,* Arthur Koestler tried to depict the self-destroying psychology of the Communist who had given over his mind and soul to the Party. Koestler has described his own rather horrifying experience within the Party as a "spiritual discipline" that he would not wish to see expunged from his past, though he came to regard it as an intellectual error. (See *The Invisible Writing.*) A few, like Picasso and Bertold Brecht, remained; the latter faced and accepted with unusual clarity the decision to lose one's individuality in the party, to cease thinking and become nameless and faceless, "blank sheets on which the Revolution will write its orders," prepared to "sink into the mud" and "commit any vileness" in order that the cause might prosper. It was a decision any Communist had to make if he stayed in the Stalinist party. But it was a singular position for writers or artists to accept, and Brecht was one of the few great ones able to do so.

Leon Trotsky, Lenin's chief lieutenant in the Revolution, who was driven into exile and ultimately assassinated by Stalinists, provided a rallying point for some who wished to remain revolutionary Marxists while repudiating Soviet Communism under Stalin. Trostkyites regarded Stalinism as having perverted socialism by the errors of bureaucratization and the cult of personality. They were prone to criticize the lack of intra-party democracy and even the lack of personal freedom in the USSR, yet they remained attached to revolutionary Leninism including the rule of the party as "vanguard" or proletarian elite. On the whole, this group faded out too, after playing some part for a time as the resting place for those disillusioned with events in Russia but not prepared to abandon revolutionary socialism.

During World War II, wartime friendship between the Soviet Union and the Western democracies brought a temporary resurgence in Communism within the latter, but the strained relations between Russia and the West after 1945 had the opposite result. Dogmatic Marxism suffered a precipitate decline in Great Britain and the United States. It declined

Trotskyism

to a lesser degree in Italy and France, perhaps because of a curious affinity between its dogmatic and apocalyptic mood and that of Roman Catholic Christianity. Some of the French Existentialists, especially Sartre, were prepared to welcome a version of Marxism—not the obsolete dogmas, the absurd intellectual edifice, but the ethical protest against capitalism, the denunciation of the workers' alienation from his work and from society, which they regarded as the essence of Marx.

There were other "progressive" social movements in the decade of depression which were not Marxist but which assailed the existing order of "capitalism." The great economic depression caused a searching reappraisal of existing, "classical" economic theory. Among the revisers of economic orthodoxy the Englishman John Maynard Keynes stood out as an acute, penetrating, and incisive mind with a gift of literary expression. Keynes, who had challenged conventional public finance methods in the 1920s, came in the 1930s to put his views in the form of a general theory (1936). Pared down to its essentials, the Keynesian view was that contrary to the old theory there is no automatic tendency toward full employment in the free economy (Say's law); rather, there can be stagnation with unused human resources. This is because, among other things, the community's total savings are not necessarily invested in capital equipment. The interest rate, which is supposed to provide the automatic mechanism for insuring the investment of savings (the rate falling as savings rise), may not function effectively because liquidity preference (desire to keep funds in cash form easily obtainable) causes savers to accept a lower return on their money than they could get. Keynes stressed the propensity to over-save and under-invest in a mature capitalist economy; the result can be economic stagnation. The economy cannot be counted upon to right itself, as the older economics taught. It may have to be righted by the intervention of the government. Formerly the approved policy for dealing with depression was for the government to pare its expenditures and balance its budget, and governments did this during the early stage of the 1930s depression, with apparently ineffective results. The new economics called for an unbalanced budget, the government throwing its overspending into the economic stream to break the logjam.

Thus the new economics, as advocated by Keynes and his followers along with some others (the Swedish school was prominent), encouraged statism though not socialism (public ownership). The private economy can work effectively but it requires regulating with the great fiscal resources of the government used as a balance wheel. Interest rates can be manipulated by government action, the expenditures of the government can be varied, taxes raised or lowered according to the needs of the economy at any given time. The Keynesian view, roughly, prevailed, in

Keynes and the New Economics

that orthodox economic theory soon accepted a modicum of the new economics while governments, even conservative ones, accepted their responsibility to "maintain full employment" by use of a variety of powers such as those mentioned. This was an economic revolution and perhaps by implication a political and social one, if a mild one. It cast the "public sector" of the economy in a new and much more active role. It provided, as some saw it, a democratic alternative to Communist totalitarianism in the area of national economic planning. To others, the "Keynesian revolution" and the "welfare state" were steps on the "road to serfdom" (F. A. Hayek) only slightly less alarming than Red Bolshevism; they too reflected the coloration of the Pink Decade.

On any showing, the 1930s was a colorful time, with ideas or ideologies most prominently featured. It suffered subsequently from a severe reaction. That so many earnest writers and intellectuals had eaten of the bitter husks of Communism and thought, at least for a while, that it was good bread seemed an astonishing index of their gullibility, and has been one of the things responsible for a dismaying amount of anti-intellectualism in the post-1945 world. To be the victim of a merely political "ideology" marked one, later, as an innocent. The thrust of the Western mind toward basic social reform has not ended, but it was perhaps blunted and then diverted by the peculiar experiences of the 1930s.

The infatuation of creative writers with social issues in the 1930s left behind remarkable literary deposits, now somewhat out of style but bound to remain as landmarks for the historian to contemplate, some of them awe-inspiring in their sheer magnitude. For example, Jules Romains, the French novelist, wrote ten thousand pages in his mammoth multi-volume novel of social realism, *Men of Good Will*, outdoing Marcel Proust in length if not in quality, and intended to rival Balzac's great "Human Comedy" of a century earlier as a picture of the social world. Politicians, capitalists, industrialists, as well as intellectuals seeking to set the world right, fill these pages. The criticism made of Romains and other novels of this sort (the Englishman Robert Briffault and the American Upton Sinclair were among others addicted to it) is, for one thing, that they really had no first-hand knowledge of capitalists and politicians (or workers!), but invented stereotypes of what Marxist or Left-Liberal theory required them to believe of such men.[9] "Social Realism" was often wildly unrealistic. It was often enough the fruit of a blind ideological faith. Romains' huge opus is nevertheless a tribute to the moral earnestness of the writers of the thirties and their desire to bring life back into the scope of art and intellect.

[9] Romains was a Jaurès socialist, which is to say in American terms, roughly, a Norman Thomas socialist, or a Fabian: he had learned his socialism before 1914, in his youth. But the 1930s spawned the "Popular Front" idea, to bring all hues of the Left together.

Throughout everything, whatever their other disagreements, writers, intellectuals, political leftists, clergymen, and almost everybody else joined in one fervent sentiment: *nie wieder Krieg,* no more war. The war dominated literature. Romains' epic, just mentioned, paused for a whole volume at the battle of Verdun; Ernest Hemingway immortalized Caporetto; Henri Barbusse (*Le Feu*) showed life in the trenches; the most famous and poignant of all, Erich Maria Remarque's *All Quiet on the Western Front* (*Im Westen Nichts Neues*) cemented the postwar reconciliation of Germans and Frenchmen and Englishmen on the common sentiment of shuddering abhorrence of the whole grisly event. This mood had arisen indeed during the war, when the young English poet Wilfrid Owen, himself killed in 1918, wrote lines on the horror of a soldier's death and dismissed patriotism as a lie; or Siegfried Sassoon spoke the common soldier's resentment against "scarlet Majors at the base" who ordered youth to the slaughter and toddled home to die in bed. A miserable, bloody, and degrading war. This feeling was in good part responsible for the weakness of the Western democracies in the face of Hitler's post-1935 Nazi challenge; a generation fed on antiwar literature could not admit the thought of war even against the worst of evils. The final tragic irony of this generation was that it had to go back to war, which it hated, in order to destroy Fascism and Nazism, themselves products of the first war's brutalization of man.

EXISTENTIALISM

In the epoch of the world wars European intellectual man lived in a state of shock, in a nightmare world, such as one finds metaphorically projected in the fantasies of Franz Kafka (*The Trial, The Castle*). An unlucky enough man might have watched the mass slaughter at Verdun, seen the Bolshevik terror in Russia, observed the black-shirted and brown-shirted hysteria in Italy and Germany, the riots of starving workers during the great depression; fought in the Spanish Civil War, noted the appalling drift to world war again in the 1930s, and perhaps ended in a Nazi concentration camp, after having destroyed whole German or Japanese cities from the air. It was seemingly a world of terror and inhumanity, marked by the almost total breakdown of civilized processes and political rationality. On the other hand, he could have observed extraordinary wonders, too, not only scientific and technological but literary, philosophical, scholarly, suggesting a fund of creative energy in Western civilization that might yet save it. Evidently the chief problem was one of values: something to believe in that sophisticated modern man *could* believe in, something to serve as a directing principle for the aimless power of scientific technology, something to teach to the hundreds of millions of democratic citizens who, now "free," were slaves in their freedom for want of such values.

Sartre The serious concern for man as a being who must find values, amid the general wreckage of traditional ones, and act upon them in a nightmare world, is a theme that leads us to the group known roughly as Existentialists. Born between the wars chiefly in the writings of the German or German-Swiss academic philosophers Martin Heidegger and Karl Jaspers, "Existentialism" (Heidegger talked of his *Existenzphilosophie* while Jaspers used the term *Existentialismus*) did not become well known until just after World War II, when it leaped into international prominence largely owing to the brilliance of one of the outstanding writers and thinkers of modern times, Jean-Paul Sartre. Sartre, once a student of Heidegger's, has been novelist, playwright, editor, essayist, and political activist as well as philosopher (author of the long and difficult *Being and Nothingness*)—a combination of talents which, given the quantity and range of his writings and his role as moral and intellectual leader of a generation, makes him something of a modern Voltaire. Sartre fought in the French Resistance movement of World War II; postwar Existentialism received the flavor of the bitter and lonely experiences men went through in this war, whether in the *maquis* or the concentration camps. His fellow Frenchman, the Algerian-born essayist and novelist Albert Camus, killed in an accident in 1960, joined Sartre in leadership of the "second lost generation" after 1945. With all gods really dead now, nothing to believe in, the Existentialists quite remarkably turned to man himself to find new values.

Loneliness and Absurdity of Existence Existentialism drew on earlier ideas and indeed one of its attractive features was its absorption of much of the gropings of European thought and expression since 1800, or perhaps even earlier, into one structure; there is something here of a *philosophia perennia*. In one sense it is the ultimate Nietzscheanism. Sartre has written that "Existentialism is . . . an attempt to draw all the consequences from a consistent atheist position." "Dostoyevsky has written that if God did not exist, all would be permitted. That is Existentialism's starting point." If we really grasp the meaning of modern godless man's plight, we are at first reduced to nausea and despair. We must pass through the awful sense of depression that accompanies a real insight into man's condition. He is alone, for he cannot really communicate with others. He finds himself in a world to which he is utterly alien and which has no purpose or meaning. Society, too, is at work trying to depersonalize him, make him into a cog in the machine, make him play a role that crushes his individuality. But on the far side of this abyss (Existentialism is a "philosophy of the abyss," Emmanuel Mounier has said) there is one message of salvation, one ground of hope: man, the human consciousness, is after all left. He is somehow here, able to react; even in feeling despair, he shows the possibility of bestowing value on the meaningless world. As Camus noted, the world is absurd; but then it could not be absurd unless men judged it to be so; this feeling of the absurd itself is the start of philosophy. We are reminded of Pascal's "thinking reed."

Man is unique in the world; his own peculiar kind of being is radically different from all others. Heidegger, who called himself an ontologist, was preoccupied with the nature of Being—of what it means, in general, for anything to exist, and in particular what human existence is. For man, "Existence is prior to essence" Kierkegaard had already asserted. This striking idea found reenforcement in the naturalistic outlook of Darwin, as well as the psychology of Freud. Reason does not precede and determine man, but vice versa; man exists, and his will to exist leads him to invent "rational" systems, which are thus not ultimate but are a product of his drives, instincts, fears, hopes. It is of the nature of the human being to be unique, a concrete particular not to be understood by membership in a class or group, like other objects. True, insofar as a man is flesh he is the usual kind of being; moreover society is always at work trying to make him into a stereotyped object. But the human personality *ought* to be unique and free, not directed from outside or resembling an object. Heidegger's distinction between "authentic" personal existence and "being-in-the-world" became in Sartre's hands a distinction between being *en-soi* and *pour-soi*—in-itself and for-itself.

Being-in-itself is the mode of being for all things except man—for physical objects, anything that has objective identity. My own past, insofar as I look at it as something vanished and dead, is being of this sort, which is the normal kind of being. It is subject to essences, to generalizing; it is, we might say, the data of science; it is like Bergson's realm of the scientific intellect; it can be conceptualized. But human consciousness, as it exists in our minds every moment, *now,* is a radically different kind of thing—*pour-soi,* in Sartre's terminology. It is actually not being at all, but a kind of "hole in being"—a nothingness, in a sense. This striking analysis of human consciousness owed a great deal to the Viennese philosopher Edmund Husserl, who was writing around the turn of the century; and indeed Husserl, the mentor of Heidegger, ranks as a key figure in the emergence of Existentialism. It was prefigured even earlier in German Romantic philosophy.

Critics of Sartre (by no means lacking) have reproached him among other things for calling "nothing" what is patently something; but Sartre's general meaning seems reasonably clear. Our consciousness requires objects to respond to, we cannot have consciousness of consciousness. And our immediate conscious experience is not like anything we can think of; it is just conscious experience. If Sartre's analysis of this elusive substance is sometimes a bit fuzzy, it is a remarkably stimulating effort to examine what seldom has been examined.

Uniqueness of Human Consciousness

Being-For-Others

Sartre discusses a third sort of being, being-for-others, the realm of relations between people. I am an object to the other person, yet his characterization of me becomes part of my subjective consciousness and I become aware of his. I respond to and try to reject his objectivication of me. This mode of being is neither *en-soi* nor *pour-soi;* it is that which separates the *pour-sois,* a kind of polarization force between them. The whole of these subtle discussions should be read, of course, if one wishes to grasp the meaning of Sartre.

The nature of this protean nothingness, the *pour-soi* or human consciousness, is to be free, and to create itself. Defined only by his acts, man is free to assign values, to give his life meaning. Sartre and the Existentialists do not undertake to tell men what to believe in, how to act, for each of us must decide that himself; to be other-directed is to be unauthentic, to be guilty of "bad faith." Like the Postivists, so different from them in many ways, the Existentialists refuse to provide us with creeds and dogmas. Their function is to point out the importance of making choices, and the need to make them with utter integrity. One must win his way to authentic personal existence by refusing to be absorbed "in the world" or made an object. Man is an ambiguous creature; condemned to freedom, he has to act, but there is really no creed to tell him how to act (if he believes so, he is guilty of bad faith), and so he is anxious and forlorn. When he surmounts the crisis of feeling the absurdity of his situation, he acts in full understanding of his autonomy as free creator of his own values.

Ethical Message of Existentialism

Perhaps the elaborate and, to some people, somewhat mystifying Sartrean ontology is not so important as the ethical message, though it does provide an impressive foundation. The essential Existentialism is the message to be "authentic," to avoid "bad faith," to refuse to be "depersonalized." "Existentialism is the struggle to discover the human person in a depersonalized age," William Barrett has written. How can we be authentic individuals? Existentialists give us a few hints. We should reject intellectualism, or merely speculative knowledge; this does not speak to the human condition. We must presumably pass through the crisis wherein we see that there is no God, no meaning in the universe as such, nothing or no one to help us. Then we realize the uniqueness and wonder of man the creator of values. "This world is without importance, and whoever recognizes this fact wins his freedom," one of Camus' characters observes. When we realize that with each choice and act we not only make ourselves but give the whole universe what value it has, we have discovered the dignity of being human. Then we must be "committed," we must believe nothing that is merely idle opinion—what we believe must be for life. Like Nietzsche we must grasp it with our whole heart and soul not merely with the "cold prying tentacles" of conceptual thought.

By its own standards there cannot really be an "Existential*ism*," then; the whole idea is to escape *isms*. Each man's truth will presumably be different. In fact, the major figures of the school have disagreed with each other on various questions. Christian Existentialists are of course in basic disagreement with the atheistic ones. (To Gabriel Marcel, Sartre is "a degenerate disciple of Heidegger," and he disapproves of Heidegger!) Sartre has expressed much of himself in plays, Camus in novels; perhaps Existentialists have made their most striking contribution in the examination of various concrete life problems. Sartre on the nature of love, and why man is condemned to frustrate himself, a "useless passion"; Simone de Beauvoir on what it means to be a woman; Camus on man as rebel. These and other products of French Existentialism are classics of our time. Such plays as Sartre's *No Exit* seem clearly destined to be classed among the serious literary statements of our age.

Differences among Existentialists

There has come into existence, also, an interesting Existentialist approach to psychiatry. Existentialist psychiatry has spread rapidly and seems in some ways to offer better results than Freudian or Jungian approaches. It is fairly close in spirit to the latter. Still a bit fuzzy, Existential psychology, mostly based on Heidegger, shows keen insights into neurotic people by concentrating attention on their "ontological" situation, their need to define their own being.

The "phenomenological" study of subjective states has become a major concern under Existentialist influence. Phenomenology undertakes to make explicit a great deal of the contents of consciousness not previously examined. It is "the effort at a direct description of our experience just as it is . . ." (Merleau-Ponty). William James once remarked that "we ought to say a feeling of *and,* a feeling of *if,* a feeling of *but,* and a feeling of *by,* quite as readily as we say a feeling of blue or a feeling of cold." But we do not. Broadly speaking, Phenomenology may be said to be concerned with remedying this sort of deficiency, for reasons both of scientific clarity and psychological self-knowledge.

Phenomenology and Existential Psychiatry

Seen in this light, Existentialism is an aspect of the modern movement in literature and psychology, going back to Baudelaire and to James and Freud, with their keen interest in the inner world of man. Existentialism has been defined as "an attempt at philosophizing from the standpoint of the actor instead of, as has been customary, from that of the spectator" (E. L. Allen). It is a dimension of what Jung called "the undiscovered self." Subjectivism is the theme of the contemporary West.

Perhaps Existentialism may be understood by comparing its subjectivism to that of Kant. The Kantian revolution placed the focus of attention on the subject, the mind, rather than the object of knowledge, thus beginning something basic to modern philosophy. But Kant's subjectivism confined itself to the realm of logic, supposedly built into the human mind; it remained rational, merely transferring rationalism from

Subjectivism

outside to inside, as it were. Existentialism and Phenomenology go still further, behind rational thought, which is seen as the product of deeper experience, to a strange world of myth and symbol hardly yet explored. Kant's was a rational subjectivism, theirs an irrational, better infrarational. The rational is *not* the real, as Hegel taught. Existence is not rational, but even absurd; it simply is, and we cannot possibly reason about it—being it ourselves. Only some superhuman being could do that. Existence is a brute fact. We come to realize that men have invented reason to hide their fears or rationalize their desires. Baffled by this knowledge, we must nevertheless choose and act. As Yeats wrote, "We cannot know the truth but we can live it."

Existentialist Optimism   Existentialism may be regarded as itself absurd, or as the highest wisdom, as one chooses. Some misunderstandings, however, should be avoided. One of these, a vulgar but common misconstrual, is that Existentialists are gloomy people who have lost hope. Do they not say that the world is absurd, man is irrational, and there are no values, and do they not also talk about fear, forsakenness, dread, anxiety? But Existentialism is an answer to nihilism, not nihilism itself. Faced with absurdity, we do at first feel dread and anxiety, but then we rise above them to create values by squarely facing our situation and responsibilities. We choose, act, and thus win through to authentic existence thus endowing the universe with value. Existentialism is an optimistic and activist creed, leading us back to life and not leaving us in a Buddhist rejection of it. It is an expression of the defiant energy of the West in the teeth of all adversity. It is easy to accuse it of intellectual confusion or even charlatanry, but not of passivity and pessimism. It is not its fault that "God is dead"; that was the fault of modern science and rationalism. It tells us what we may do about this cruel death.

Christian Existentialism: Kierkegaard   Christian Existentialism may be regarded as still more optimistic. Soren Kierkegaard, who died in 1855, left little mark on his own time (outside his native Copenhagen) and was to remain largely unknown until he became a "discovery" of the Existentialists. He was a savage critic of Hegel's deterministic system, which makes man an automaton. (In this he owed something to the views of F. W. Schelling in his last years.) Such objective thinking—reasoning—destroys the individual, making him a part of the collective. Kierkegaard resisted this with all his being. In proclaiming that "existence is prior to essence," he asserted the primacy of the individual person over any abstraction. He complained that Hegel's system was not "for life" and demanded a faith that was. (Careful students of Hegel complain quite properly that this is unfair, for at times Hegel himself could be quite "existential." Still, the contours of his main system as widely understood doubtless conform to Kierkegaard's indictment.) This was the same thirst for absolute commitment, for a creed related to one's life situation, that we find in Nietzsche, who never read or heard of the obscure Danish parson. But Kierkegaard, unlike Nietzsche, was deeply religious, though his intense personalism caused him to attack the Church as a menace to real faith. Through anxiety and despair the individual must make his own way to God. The Dane's intense suspicion of conformism, the crowd, institutions, "phony" external substitutes for inward experience, remind us somewhat of certain of the esthetes, and it may be significant that he was a contemporary of Baudelaire (who in the end turned to religion himself).[10] But Kierkegaard, a pastor of the Lutheran Church, also pointed back to the great founder of his church, who demanded a faith based on personal experience and denounced sacramentalism along with the moralism of salvation via good works.

This intense stress on the inner life of the spirit, with its fierce assault on both intellectualized, philosophical Christianity *and* on liberal, moralistic Christianity, was scarcely suitable to nineteenth-century religion, which was going in exactly these latter directions. The "return to orthodoxy" in Continental theology was a post-World War I phenomenon. The Armageddon of 1914 shocked Christianity (also Judaism) out of its complacency and made possible a revival of apocalyptic moods. This reaction occurred in all the major churches. Among prominent individuals connected with this massive movement were Nicholas Berdyaev, a Russian of the Orthodox Church; Martin Buber, a Jew; Jacques Maritain, French Catholic; and the Protestants, Lutheran and Calvinist respectively, Karl Barth and Emil Brunner. Quite a few of these men owed something to Kierkegaard though they might disagree with him in particulars (see Martin Buber's well-known essay on Kierkegaard in which, from the viewpoint of Jewish Hasidic communalism, he reproached the Dane for being too antisocial, while testifying to the importance of *Fear and Trembling* in his own development).

Buber's *I and Thou* appeared in 1923; Berdyaev, who had known exile under the Tsar and had drifted close to Marxism before the war, hailed the Revolution of 1917 but found himself arrested and exiled by Lenin's dictatorship in 1920, after which he taught, lectured, and wrote in Berlin and Paris. Buber was born in 1878, Berdyaev in 1874, Maritain in 1882; all these men grew to intellectual maturity before World War I but then had their lives sharply altered by that event. As of the 1960s some of these sages were still living. The fame of Barth had spread so far that even *Time* magazine published an interview with the wise and witty old German theologian in May, 1963. Jacques Maritain at 80 is "widely recognized as the greatest living Catholic philosopher" (Will Herberg), Buber who died in 1965, as the greatest of modern Jewish philosophers of religion.

Varieties of Religious Existentialism

[10] According to Kierkegaard, spiritual development leads one through the aesthetic stage to the moral and finally to the religious. Only in immaturity is one content with mere literary form. But one infers that Kierkegaard had passed through such a phase.

Christian Existentialism touches closely on these imposing figures who have attempted to revive a somnolent religion in refutation of Nietzsche's and Sartre's claim that "God is dead." Maritain has tried to reconcile his neo-Thomism with Existentialism. The "crisis theology" of Barth comes close to it, as does the I-Thou experience described by Buber (a distinction between a person's relation to other persons and to things, with God as the "eternal Thou" to be encountered in a dialogue). Paul Tillich and Gabriel Marcel, from the Protestant and Catholic camps respectively, are more explicitly Existentialists.[11] We cannot here attempt to reproduce the many profound insights of recent theology; it can only be said that theology has been most active, justifying abundantly the claim of a religious renaissance. The trend has been decidedly away from a rationalized religion, a polite and moral one, an easy and conventional one. In dread and anxiety the soul realizes its dire predicament and then makes the "leap" to faith. The individual chooses and wins his existence by reaching out to a transcendent Being who is not "understood" but is encountered, addressed.

Certainly not all theologians have accepted Crisis or Existential ideas; but it is interesting and significant that there has been an earnest revival of theology, centering on such doctrines as original sin, the nature of Christ, and atonement, etc. Relegated at one time virtually to the scrap-heap of vanished dogmas, these issues have once again become important in an era when human pride leading to self-destruction has appeared as historic fact. Christian or Judaic thinkers can point out that we do not need to desert our basic Western traditions and embrace an anarchy of strange beliefs; it is possible to come to terms with the modern experience through the medium of an enlarged but basically traditional religious outlook. The Bible in the words of Rudolf Bultmann has been "de-mythologized"; the assaults of the Higher Criticism have become irrelevant, for it is not the literal truth but the Existential truth of this spiritual record that matters. Without God, or some transcendent source of value, man is condemned to destroy himself. He can sit in the wasteland and wait for the end or he can go forth to seek through the mists the God he has lost. (Heidegger, Simone Weill, and Samuel Beckett seem to prefer to "wait for God" to return.)

Modern Christian thinkers have tended to see in the totalitarian regimes and world wars of the unhappy twentieth century a consequence of the despiritualization of man through de-Christianization. Liberalism, capitalism, and materialistic socialism, reducing men to mere factors of production and atomizing them, prepared the way for the terrible explosions of Nazism and Communism, which these thinkers see not as

Totalitarianism a Result of Loss of Religious Belief?

[11] Practically all those who use the Existentialist approach wish to deny that they are "Existialists." Tillich has said that while "the existential element has a definite place" in his thought, "I would not call myself an existentialist."

products of the peculiar evil or misfortune of individual nations but as general cultural phenomena of modern Western civilization. ("Germany is not the sin of Europe, but of the entire modern world, the sin of a world so profoundly corrupted that peoples corrupt each other; and the last service rendered by the German people to the old civilization it formerly honored is to show to each nation, as in a monstrous mirror, the image of that which it perhaps is today without knowing it, and which it will surely be tomorrow." So wrote Georges Bernanos shortly after World War II.) Liberty and civilization depend on religious belief. The heroism of members of the Christian churches, Protestant and Catholic alike, in suffering martyrdom at the hands of Hitler's pagan totalitarianism advanced the prestige of religion in Europe; and subsequently the confrontation between the West and Soviet Russian Communism encouraged a definition of the former's position as historically Christian. Without question one must take seriously the revival of religion. Perhaps God is not dead after all. If not, it is singular that those who announced the death —the atheist existentialists—contributed not a little to the rebirth.

Existentialism has been introduced at this point because it was definitely born between the wars, when Martin Heidegger and Karl Jaspers were at work, and Heidegger's student Sartre began his literary career; when the revival of religion with overtones of an Existentialist nature took place, through Buber, Maritain, Barth, Niebuhr, Berdyaev. But during that feverish decade of political alarums and excursions, the 1930s, which began with the economic hammer blows of the Great Depression, moved on to Hitler's Nazi conquest of Germany, then to the war brought on by Nazi hatreds and aggressiveness, with Stalin's Five Year Plans and purge trials a part of the picture, little else gained much attention except these economic and political questions. Then came a war more dreadful than the last one, and more inhumane: the terror bombing of European cities by the Allies, the murder of the Jews by the Nazis, incredible and untold suffering, great and sometimes unrecorded heroism. This traumatic experience helped make relevant the insights of the Existentialists, and after the war this "philosophy" achieved large popularity.

It should not be supposed that antireligious rationalism totally disappeared. Especially after World War II and the decline of Marxism in the West, militant atheism wore a rather old-fashioned look, but it had many apostles. The Darwinism of a Julian Huxley or the free-thinking neo-Enlightenment anticlericalism of old Bertrand Russell seemed like carry-overs from the nineteenth century, but were not the less vigorously affirmed by these doughty warriors. In intellectual history as in other kinds of history the historian tends to talk about what is new, or what is in some sense typical of an era. He is in danger of overlooking the persistence of the old, especially at popular levels. Most great ideas take at least a generation to be understood and accepted. Freud, who gave the world his theories in the 1890s, did not become famous until the 1920s. Existentialism, a product of the 1920s, reached the average intellectual about 1946 and by 1960 was somewhat old hat to him; to the unintellectual, it may still have been wrapped in the impenetrable mystery of absolute novelty.

Julian
Huxley's
"Humanism"

At any rate British empiricism as represented by Lord Russell and others remained unconvinced of the merits of anything not founded on experimental verification and the critical reason. "As soon as it is held that any belief . . . is important for some other reason than that it is true, a whole host of evils is ready to spring up," Russell has remarked. And it is more than doubtful that he would regard the truths of Jung, of the Existentialists, and of the Crisis Theologians as demonstrable. Julian Huxley, for his part, has spoken at various times of "Scientific Humanism," "Evolutionary Humanism," and just "Humanism." The term suffered from considerable vagueness, but Huxley was clear enough about (a) his dislike of Christianity and other of the classic "religions," such as Buddhism, and (b) his conviction that Western man desperately needs some sort of substitute for religion, some kind of integrating and orienting idea-system, rooted in science yet able to supply values. (This feeling bears some relationship to the Russian-American social theorist P. A. Sorokin's call for an "integral" philosophy to combine the best of all of his alleged sociocultural modes, the idealist, sensate, and ideational—in other words to get the best of both the religious, philosophical, and scientific worlds. It may be suggested that second-range thinkers seem to feel they have solved the problem when they ask for an impossible combination of this sort.) So Huxley's Humanism comes to look very much like Comte's religion of humanity, as he abjures us in effect to worship human nature. In the view of Existentialist and religious critics, Sir Julian's man-worship leads to those very totalitarian systems he most abhors, to Nazism and Communism, which are the fruits of godlessness and "titanism." But this vigorous scientist, who later became the first director of UNESCO, would say that only through the scientific reason can man find his way to sanity in an age of irrationality.

There are many reasons for thinking that European man is raising his tents from off that modern soil where he has camped for three hundred years and is beginning a new exodus toward another historical ambit, another way of life.

JOSÉ ORTEGA Y GASSET

Man's existence is now nearing an absolute decision.

ROMANO GUARDINI

Contemporary Ideas in the West

7

SINCE 1945: THE POSTWAR CLIMATE OF OPINION AND TRENDS IN THOUGHT

As Europeans awoke from the nightmare of World War II to stand amid the ruins which assured them that the horrors had really happened, they were understandably tempted to reject all the old and start anew. If World War I damaged the respect felt for ancestral tradition, the second such cataclysm twenty years later seemed likely to destroy it. Gabriel Marcel, to quote but one example, has written of "the more than physical horror and anxiety I experienced in walking among the ruins of inner Vienna in 1946, or more recently in Caen, Rouen or Würzburg." Almost any European city between the Channel and the Dnieper could have qualified, though German cities suffered most, as a result of the incessant allied aerial bombings. He went on to note that for many the corollary was a total rejection of the European heritage (*The Decline of Wisdom*, 1954). These physical ruins were manifestations of the moral ruins displayed in Hitler's ghastly extermination of the Jews; the gas chambers of Auschwitz and Dachau brooded over a European atmosphere heavy with the smell of death.

Apart from the sheer physical and moral damages of the war, there had occurred what one historian phrased in the title of a book, *The Passing of the European Age*, or as the distinguished German, Alfred Weber, brother of Max, titled a little book of 1946, *Abschied von der Bisherigen*

Effects of the War

Geschichte, translated as *Farewell to European History.* In 1946 H. G. Wells, who had preached progress toward utopia for half a century, wrote *Mind at the End of Its Tether,* in which he decided that the end of civilization, of man, and perhaps of life on earth was rapidly approaching. A shattered and exhausted Europe was occupied by American and Russian soldiers, both of whom most Europeans looked upon as barbarians from outside. Before long it became evident that the Russians, at least, intended no liberation but a new enslavement to Communism. The Americans were to be looked upon as allies against the menace of Soviet power, and many Europeans were glad to clasp hands with the democratic land of the New World. The fact remains that quite a few bearers of the European culture continued to regard "Russia and America as the same," basically; as Martin Heidegger put it, "the same dreary technological frenzy, the same unrestricted organization of the average man" (*An Introduction to Metaphysics,* 1959).

For those who had expected brighter days with the Allied victory over Hitlerism, the coming of peace and the establishment of the United Nations, the years just after 1945 were deeply disappointing. As economic ruin engulfed Europe, a quarrel between the Soviet Union and the Western powers threatened a renewal of war—another war in the apparently self-perpetuating cycle of "wars in chain reaction," as a French writer (Raymond Aron) titled a book. The war had ended with the ghastly explosion of the atomic bomb over Hiroshima, wiping out an entire city; by 1954 far more destructive nuclear weapons carried by intercontinental missiles were available to guarantee that the seemingly inevitable next war would put a finish to much of the world. Pending this last apocalypse, the world was far from at peace, for there was war in Korea (1950–1953), in Indo-China, in Palestine, and elsewhere.

New
Perspectives
Whoever controlled Europe, Europe and the West no longer held the same monopoly of world power, prestige, and influence as formerly. The world had shrunk, and yet enlarged, as Weber noted: smaller because of modern transportation and communications, it was filled with all kinds of peoples formerly almost beyond the fringes of Europe's consciousness. For the peoples of Asia and Africa, too, in addition to the powerful United States of America, had arrived on the scene. They had gained or were about to gain their independence, they were "out of control" and demanding a place in the sun, and though as yet not powerful states they could no longer be ignored. Loosely united in attitudes shaped by their former vassalage to the West, they were a "third force" in world politics, of vast significance. Suddenly Europe became aware that she was after all a fairly diminutive peninsula on the huge land mass of Eurasia, and that what happened in Iran or the Indies, or even in the Congo and Algeria, was of some consequence. This was a revolution in geopolitical perspectives that announced a new epoch of world history, perhaps the first one since the fall of the ancient Oriental empires.

The other radically new perspective was a technological-scientific one, signalled by the explosion over Hiroshima. What the Atomic Age meant no one could foresee—whether the passing of the human race or its ascent to incomparably higher levels of material civilization. For the time being, it meant assuredly that military power rested overwhelmingly with those who held the capacity to make and deliver nuclear weapons, which included only the Americans and, soon, the Russians. Apart from this confirmation of weakness and dependency, atomic energy drastically transformed basic thought processes about the material world, driving home to all some of the implications of the new physics heretofore appreciated by only a few, such as the disappearance of "matter" in a sea of waves and electrical energy, the different laws of motion inside the atom, etc. After Hiroshima, no one could regard these things as just interesting theories.

On the other hand, there were countervailing tendencies working against the picture of bleak despair. The terrible war had at least purged Europe of much: of Nazism, anti-Semitism, and even, to a degree, of nationalism. The need to rehabilitate a culture drew men together. Survivors of the terrible experiences of the war, whether living under the nightly threat of terror and death from the skies, or in the hell of a Nazi concentration camp, or as fighters in the "underground," often testified to the strange kind of value in such experiences. Life was given more value by being precarious; simple objects acquired value. Such situations were at least a cure for empty complacency, a reminder of the tragic and serious nature of life, a precipitant of elemental human values. To come up against and face the absolute worst is a kind of purgative; this is the message that emerges from much of the postwar European writing.

Standing together against the Soviet threat, and then building a new Europe from the ashes, a Europe that might at last have learned to unify itself in a federation—these were goals that gave the common life some meaning. Europe began to make a spectacular economic recovery which swept on through much of the 1950s and brought to birth a unified European economy, the Common Market that resulted from the Rome Treaty of 1957 and was expected to lead on by stages to full political federation. Hope returned with the development of the NATO alliance between North America and the states of Western Europe, and with the avoidance of major war. Though life as always was filled with problems, many Europeans saw the light breaking through in the second decade after the war, with prospects even of Europe again assuming its place in world affairs—no "passing of the European age," despite the power of Russia and of America, and the arrival of the non-European peoples. The change between 1945 and 1963 was summed up by Raymond Aron: "In 1945, western Europe was a mass of ruins; today it is one of the most prosperous regions of the world."

Assessment of the very recent past is always a risky business, and what follows in this chapter must be offered with less confidence that what is selected for emphasis represents the enduringly significant themes of this period as posterity will see them. Nevertheless, it is most interesting and important to try to take stock of man's condition today as reflected in his philosophy, literature, his religious, social, and political thought—his world of ideas.

The Fear of Disaster

Unquestionably the postwar climate of opinion *has* been overshadowed by the sense of catastrophe and disaster, because of war, power, and the bomb. J. M. Cohen, in the concluding statements to his book *Poetry of This Age*, remarks that "events have dwarfed all possible comment" on public affairs and driven the poet to purely personal statement. "All that he can hope to rescue from an ever-imminent disaster will be a moment of love or insight or a clear conception of truth, which, having once been, can never be destroyed." It is possible to wonder whether this contingency of life is really so new. Every man's life is contingent every moment and always has been. Apart from that, earlier generations lived under the threat of starvation, disease, and other afflictions from which many moderns are by comparison almost free. In terms of the totality of human life, the modern world with its massive and longer-lived populations would be far ahead of any previous age even if it experienced a thermonuclear war. (The greatest world problem, according to many, is today *over*population.) Nevertheless, the reminder of man's contingent being, his constant confrontation with death, the possibility of centuries of "progress" being extinguished in a few moments (which might even be the result of an accident)—all this undoubtedly has undermined eighteenth- and nineteenth-century beliefs in a secular utopia or the progress of humanity toward perfection. The "boundary situations" about which Existentialists talk seem all too real in the world as it exists today.

Retreat from Ideologies

Thus the turn to "personal statement," to an insight of the moment and away from "ideologies" or total faiths. The retreat from ideologies has been a prominent theme since World War II. The political activism characteristic of the 1930s fell to low ebb in the 1950s. "Outside the Communists," a French writer observed in 1952, "French youth is almost totally disinterested in politics today." The same could be said for British youth, German youth, Italian youth. Heroic attitudes struck during the war, in the Resistance for example, had in the main turned sour. The Communist movement continued to attract a few, but not many[1]; the behavior of Stalin and his cohorts had destroyed it. There was a profound reaction against Marxism, which was a reaction basically against the tyrannical nature of Soviet Russia under the Stalinist dictatorship, a regime which

[1] The ability of the Communist Party to attract as high as 20 to 25 percent of the election votes in France and Italy must be set down more to the desire to register

sent millions of people to prison and labor camps without fair trial, showed itself willing to employ every sort of iniquity in the crudest "means justified by the end" credo, and threw international relations into chaos, while also destroying creative Russian thought and literature by a straitjacket of political control. In the sight of Western intellectuals, who had once seen it through a veil of illusions, the last of these was torn from the ugly face of Soviet Communism by the enslavement through military force of the peoples of eastern Europe. And it was seen that this moral bankruptcy was implicit in revolutionary Marxism, because of its deification of the historical process, its fanatical faith in a future utopia held to justify any amount of death and crime now.

To some extent, too, the "end of ideology" has been facilitated by the failure of ideology in the Soviet Union itself. In Stalin's era the high priests of the Communist Party, charged with the zeal and dogmatism of the Marxist faith, made decisions. In the Khrushchev era (1953–1964) this power tended to gravitate toward bureaucracy and expertise, a process summed up by one student[2] as a "transition from charismatics to mathematics." This trend seems likely to continue. In general, the element of breathless, apocalyptic exaltation in Russia that was a legacy of the great Revolution and was perpetuated in the Party, tended steadily to wane as rationalization and normality took over. Not even the charisma of Lenin is safe from the corrosions of time and life. If Stalinization debased it, the post-Stalin era completely destroyed it; the New Jerusalem of Marx and Lenin has become just another managerial and bureaucratic society. At the same time, of course, monolithic unity ceased to be a characteristic of world Communism because of the split between Chinese and Russian leadership as well as the general decay of Soviet evangelicalism. Chinese Communism remained much more highly emotional and aggressively ideological, but for the Western world its appeal cannot be as strong as was once the case with the Russian movement.

Despite its intellectual bankruptcy, the hold of Marxism on certain young intellectuals perhaps ought not to be underestimated. It seems to be the only system providing both intellectual synthesis and defiant rebelliousness, things much prized by youth, so flagrant errors may be overlooked. Such Marxists often accuse everyone else of deliberately concealing the truth.[3] They still believe the proletariat is growing steadily

---

a protest against the dominant parties, usually involved in a coalition government, than to any real enthusiasm for the doctrine. In the German Federal Republic, Communism virtually ceased to exist, a reaction against the subjugation of eastern Germany by the Communists. It is almost nonexistent in Great Britain.

[2] Leon Smolenski, "What Next in Soviet Planning?" *Foreign Affairs*, July, 1964.

[3] See, for example, a review of such a work in the *American Historical Review*, July 1963, p. 1049, where it is pointed out that Ranke, Stadelman, Clapham, and Jouvenel, among other well-known historians past and present known for their relative objectivity, are accused of such deliberate falsehood.

more miserable (and has been ever since 1789!) in the "capitalist" societies. It is vain to apply evidence or logical argumentation to such a faith;
we are in the presence of a will to believe hardly matched since the days
of the early Christians, and perhaps this will, like that one, may become,
almost miraculously, a central fact in the modern world. But it seems more
likely that it can survive only as a recourse of the very young or the very
unlettered.

Gaullism
If Marxism was generally rejected (except in an Existentialized
form, attempted by some French writers), any other fervent sort of
political mystique was equally suspect. There was little enthusiasm for
democracy—two cheers for it, as E. M. Forster wrote, but not three; it is
the worst of all forms·of government except for all the others, as Winston
Churchill had put it; one accepted it as the elimination of ideologies,
not as an ideology. In France, the Fourth Republic set up immediately
after the liberation of 1944–1945 was more democratic than the Third had
been, but gave way in 1958 to the considerably less democratic (or at least
less parliamentary) Fifth. The latter, headed by national leader Charles
de Gaulle, leader of the Free French forces in World War II, embodied
a transfer of power from Legislature to Executive, the latter presumably
expressing the general will, in a way reminiscent of both Jacobinism
and Bonapartism. But this change signalled the death of older political
ideologies in France, too, and the search for fresh new forms, shaped
out of national and European traditions but departing from the more
familiar mold of parliamentary democracy as it had grown up in the Third
and Fourth Republic. The new French state bore some of the marks of a
Saint-Simonian technocracy, managed by a bureaucratic expertise or
brains trust. Politically, the Existentialists seem to have proved a failure.
Intensely emotional and naively moralistic, they overlook all the real
problems of politics, an art where emotionalism is almost fatal and mere
"commitment" cannot take one far—an art of adjusting conflicting claims
and values not all of which can possibly be satisfied, and of appraising
immensely complex situations. Existentialism is a personal faith, politics
a social art—things as far apart as possible. Indeed, by its own criteria
Existentialism seems almost forced to exclude politics, in any sense but
that of one's own personal wishes, as a form of "unauthentic" behavior.

In place of total solutions, political theorists suggested piecemeal
solutions (Karl Popper). "Rationalism in politics" is a snare (M. Oakeshott); the art of politics is an adjustment of differences in pragmatic
ways. After experiencing all those "cruel or fierce political ideologies
[which] have played havoc with human welfare," wrote famed British
historian L. B. Namier, the mature political community learns to do
without them altogether. Namier gave his approval to the condition
described with some degree of alarm by philosopher Stuart Hampshire:

"There is a tired lull in English politics, and argument on general principles has largely died. . . . Both political parties are now in this sense conservative, tied to day-to-day expedients." Political writing took the form of close analysis of actual political behavior (such as voting), which often left few romantic illusions about the rationality and responsibility of "the people," or ordinary citizens. Analyses in any wider sense were apt to bypass ideology, too. Bertrand de Jouvenel, writing *On Power* (*Du Pouvoir*), found the most significant aspect of political evolution to lie not in the forms of government, aristocratic or democratic, but in the steady growth of the apparatus of coercion, regardless of forms—the growth of Power.

Similarly in economic thought, argument and analysis was likely to transcend the old issues between "capitalism" and "socialism." For example the discussion of economic growth, carried on in such books as those of W. Arthur Lewis, Colin Clark (*The Conditions of Economic Progress*), and W. W. Rostow, who subtitled his *Stages of Economic Growth* "a non-communist manifesto," noted among other things that ownership of property is not as such a vital factor. Neither David Ricardo nor Karl Marx is very relevant to twentieth-century economic problems, whether those of the "affluent societies" of the Western democracies or the youthful near-primitive economies of new African and Asian nations trying to find a short cut to affluence. Even in the Soviet Union, realism began to prevail over Marxian dogma: in the future it seemed likely to do so more and more.[4]

The Socialist parties that survived changed their outlook considerably; while the German Social Democrats had almost ceased to be recognizably socialist at all, British Labourites (carried into office right after the war and at all times a powerful political party in Great Britain) quietly abandoned nationalization of industry and a planned economy, in their earlier dogmatic forms, as panaceas for the evils of capitalism. Their experience in the 1945–1951 period of power helped move the British Socialists away from these dogmas; for (as Labour leader Hugh Gaitskell himself pointed out) state ownership did not seem to make any significant difference in the condition of the workers, nor did it solve the economic problems with which Britain was faced. Thinking hard, the intellectuals of Labour struggled to find a new rationale for the party, with not much agreement and often some strange conclusions. Labour theorist W. Arthur Lewis, for example, appeared to opt for a more vigorous kind of entre-

Changes in Socialism

---

[4] In order to make the Soviet system of state-planned socialism work, an illegal "shadow economy" of private enterprise grew up, comprising perhaps as much as 25 percent of the economy, and winked at most of the time by the authorities. And in 1965 Soviet policy seemed to be turning in the direction of more decentralization and scope for managerial initiative.

preneur capitalism—a program that would have appealed more to Nassau Senior than to Karl Marx, one imagines. Increasingly, the Socialist party became as flexible and opportunistic as its rival, the Conservatives; less ideological and more "practical," it simply found *ad hoc* answers to particular problems. It was a participant in the game of democratic politics, the stakes of which were political power; the means to power, wooing a diverse and changeable electorate.

Concern with
Question of
Power

The study of power has been an outstanding feature of recent political and social thought. "We have all become intensely aware of power as the major phenomenon in all societies," Raymond Aron has written. In addition to Jouvenel's brilliant book, the works of the Heidelberg sociologist A. Rustöw, writing in the shadow of Max Weber, may be instanced among the general theoretical studies. The theme comes through in any number of more specific studies of foreign policy and international relations.[5] George Orwell's *1984* gave expression to the frightening possibilities of power in the modern state to enslave its citizenry. This popular fantasy-satire described a condition in which the government disseminates all knowledge. Technology enables the state to control everything, even to read thoughts; "Big Brother" is everywhere. Thought control has become accomplished so thoroughly that men have ceased to think, they have been brainwashed into automatons by their government. This fear for liberty under the conditions of moderi life has been a pervasive theme. Here it may be noted that it runs counter to prewar progressivism in that the latter whether Marxist or Keynesian tended to be statist. The new political thought has been "conservative" in that it has shown a greater mistrust of the power of the state, whoever may be in charge of the state. It has returned to Lord Acton's motto that all power tends to corrupt and absolute power corrupts absolutely.

"The mighty invasion of government into economic life," it has been often noted, constitutes "one of the most fundamental contrasts between the twentieth century and the nineteenth." The depression of the 1930s frightened men into accepting large measures of government regulation, a trend aided by the new economic theories of Keynes, while World War II brought total war and with it, of necessity, total organization under government control. It is obvious that modern industrial society is too complex and specialized to be run by the laissez-faire rules of the nineteenth century. Since 1945, a continuing vast military defense program and a "space" program of gigantic dimensions have meant an expanding role of government in most countries. This increasing statism, while

---

[5] See also the studies of "power elites" within nations by such sociologists as Theodore Geiger and C. Wright Mills, or such historians as Sir Lewis Namier and his disciples (a very important school in England) or, in France, Jean Lhomme (*La grande bourgeoisie au pouvoir*).

ardently defended by a variety of collectivists, including neoliberals as well as socialists, aroused protests against it in the name of the sovereign individual, of spiritual autonomy, and of esthetic and moral values opposed to the reign of bureaucracy and the rule of the machine. Orwell's *1984* may be regarded as representative of such protests. (See also Huxley's *Brave New World Revisited*.)[6]

"Utopianism," based on optimistic views of human nature, became most unfashionable. A quotation from the distinguished American theologian Reinhold Niebuhr may suffice: "No cumulation of contradictory evidence seems to disturb modern man's good opinion of himself. He considers himself the victim of corrupting institutions, which he is about to destroy or reconstruct, or of the confusion and ignorance which an adequate education is about to overcome. Yet he continues to regard himself as essentially harmless and virtuous." Against this Enlightenment outlook Niebuhr and other contemporaries reacted with ferocity. "It is necessary not to believe in human nature." Carried on by such internationally famous men as Paul Tillich and Rudolf Bultmann, the German neo-Protestant message that originated with Barth and Brunner continued to attract attention. Existentialists of all varieties told the individual that he is responsible for his own being, cannot put off blame for his actions on "society" or anyone else, and cannot find salvation in social utopias.

Many in the modern world continue to fear more than anything else the eclipse of liberty and of the free personality under the exorbitant encroachment of statism and mass society. They may differ in their terms, or in the exact identification of the enemy: is it the state, or the democratic mass-man, or machine technology, or all of these? But there is broad agreement about the nature of the problem. "Personality is losing all along the line against power," J. B. Priestley wrote in 1955 ("The Gentle Anarchists"); the popular British author added that the younger generation "takes regimentation for granted" having become accustomed to the loss of liberties which everyone enjoyed until a few decades ago.

This deep concern about the authentic individual in an age that seems to conspire to destroy him has been a leading cause of the Existentialist fad, as we have already noted. It may also be found in the vogue for Zen Buddhism. The message of Zen, insofar as one exists, is to annihilate reflective thought and become natural by bathing in the waters of pure spontaneity, to make oneself a ball floating down the stream, an animal with instincts and not ideas. This state of cheerful empty blessed-

Reaction against Utopianism

Zen Buddhism

---

[6] In his acute book *The Liberal Mind* (1963), Kenneth Minogue pointed out that liberalism suffers from, among other things, the contradiction of wishing both to enlarge the individual's freedom by diminishing state action and to promote his welfare by increasing state action. Basically individualist, the liberal seeks to harness the state to serve individual purposes, yet finds himself sanctioning an ever-growing network of statist restrictions on personal liberty.

ness is to be attained by certain exercises. Zen Buddhism is an exceptional blend of cynical hedonism with vague spiritual strivings for release from social conformism and rationalization. Its popularity in certain circles of European and American intellectuals is doubtless a temporary thing, but it is significant for the spirit of the times. Its message is not dissimilar from that persistent individualist reaction to an overly rationalized world which the West has known ever since Rousseau; at the same time it includes an exotic appeal, fitting in with the era of minglings and mixtures between East and West in this modern counterpart of the Hellenistic Age of ancient times.

Christian Democracy

Christian Socialism or Christian Democracy emerged temporarily after the war as a promising substitute for the older political ideologies. It had the advantage of being nondogmatic and dedicated to the spiritual individual. Under strong leadership (in Italy, De Gasperi was the leading statesmen of the postwar decades), Christian Democrats showed concern for the welfare of worker and peasant and emerged as the strongest political party in France, Italy, and Germany soon after the war. They tended, however, to dissipate from vagueness of doctrine. While political parties bearing their name might continue to exist, these lacked any very specific ideological content. This was natural, for the Christian position is not positively political and may be turned in any number of different directions. Under Existential influence, Christianity in the postwar world undeniably carried on its post-1919 revival; but often it meant only the imperative of "commitment" and involvement, a personalism that cared deeply for the individual and his inner life but did not stand for any very clear dogmatic position.

Decay of the Esthetic Revolt

European intellectuals in the prosperous 1950s and 1960s often complained of modern materialism, in a society still predominantly "bourgeois," led by the quest for money and pleasure, a society meretricious, corrupt, and without values. The Freudian and Lorenzian revolutions had succeeded all too well, for sexual restraints had almost ceased to exist in some circles. The formerly avant garde movements in art and music had become respectable; bankers invested in abstract art and Picasso was a millionaire. Old "Bohemian" might have become new "beatnik" but as a symbol the disreputable life was considerably worm-eaten. ("Beatnik" and "hippie" carried, much more, the connotation of juvenile insecurity; see pages 259–260, on contemporary esthetic revolt.) In brief, the old methods of sneering at an insensitive society had worn out and it was difficult to invent new ones. Even the erstwhile rebels seemed to have given up and settled for hedonism. They might continue to castigate the Western tradition in general and the modern Puritanical bourgeoisie in particular for the sin of repressing sexual pleasure; they might continue to accuse "capitalism" or the acquisitive society of vulgarity and hard-heartedness. But in fact these attacks had lost their savor.

With the old Left in general disarray, there have been vague stirrings toward a "New Left." In England a number of diverse motivations coalesced to create something of the sort. After 1956, the remnant of the British Communist party mostly cut loose at long last from Moscow's moorings and sailed off on its own toward some kind of neo-Communism. At about the same time a strong pacifist movement emerged influenced among others by the nonagenarian philosopher Bertrand Russell, culminating in the Campaign for Nuclear Disarmament along with attacks on American foreign policy and demands to take Great Britain out of the NATO alliance—"neutralism." (Suez, along with Hungary, exerted a potent influence in 1956.) Stung by defeats in the elections of 1955 and 1959, the Labour Party subjected itself to a searching reappraisal which found some recommending less socialism but others more. A younger generation of "angry young men"—angry perhaps at Britain's declining power, at the "caste system" of a still somewhat snobbish society, or just angry, with the natural rebelliousness of youth—began to strike out in various directions: from 1956, also, dates the curiously significant play by Mr. John Osborne, *Look Back in Anger*. "Angries" who attacked "the Establishment" in a rather sophomoric way, marchers protesting against nuclear weapons and American bases in Britain, Labourite politicians searching for a new formula—these somewhat unpromising elements have been joined by a few writers of real note in the "New Left." There has been some influence from French Existentialism. From time to time these leftward rumblings erupt in manifestoes and new magazines, which have their significance on the cultural scene; but thus far at least it is hard to find anything to raise them above the ephemeral. They might as readily be construed as the death throes of the older Leftism as the birth of a new one. Certainly they testify to an uneasiness among the younger intellectuals, but this mood is perennial and can hardly be considered significant unless it creates a doctrine or movement of real distinction.

In France, too, despite some absorption of Marxist elements into an Existentialist ethic with the approval of Sartre, the leftism of the 1930s is no more and can only arouse occasional echoes, among the aging or among rather immature and provincial intellectuals.[7] "Vegetating in the utopias of the last century," as a recent French writer (Jean Duvignaud) has put it, seems futile; "new dreams must be invented for a new world." Raymond Aron has written of "the end of the socialist myth." A new "myth" would seem to be urgently required, but to cast it in the shopworn images of "capitalism" versus "socialism," "proletariat" versus "bour-

[7] A *Union de la Gauche Socialiste*, created in 1957, experimented in a more eclectic socialism drawing on Proudhon, Jaurès, and the Christian socialism of Lamennais and Sangnier. It dreamed of defanaticizing the Communists and undogmatizing Marx, in order to fit them into this "Popular Front." It does not seem to have gotten very far.

geoisie," etc., is no longer helpful. For most European intellectuals—even those east of the disintegrating Iron Curtain, in the post-Stalinist era of Soviet Communism—the way forward politically seems fully open, as yet largely undetermined, but reasonably certain to demand fresh formulations.

The Italian Communist party in recent years has moved far away from the rigid dogmatism of Stalin's day to become almost an open-minded party of the Left, willing to discard Marxian shibboleths and seek altogether fresh formulations. One of the most remarkable phenomena of recent Italian history is the "dialogue between Catholicism and Communism"—rather startling testimony to the liberation from dogma on both sides. From the Catholic side, Pope John XXIII's extraordinary 1963 encyclical "Pacem in Terris" issued a call to the spirit of liberal thought and social action in the Church, opening the door to communication with other groups. Nothing is more symbolic of the new spirit in Europe than this, and this willingness to explore radically new avenues and keep open the dialogue between all men of good will seems hopeful.

The Peace Corps Impulse

Social consciousness and political activism cannot be written off as an interest of Western man, and these suspicions of old ideologies are but a preparation for the fashioning of more efficient tools with which to tackle social problems. Much of the non-European world faces desperate problems of conquering abysmal poverty and raising the general material and cultural level. By comparison Europe as well as the United States luxuriates in an "affluent society." It is difficult for the conscience of the West to justify this relative affluence unless aid is given to less fortunate peoples, who today stand in the forefront of world history asking for their place in the sun. Considerable intellectual activity has already been directed toward these problems of economic development, by economists and sociologists, historians and students of political behavior. If this activity embraces no grand dogma but is rather concrete and piecemeal, it is not the less intense. What might be called the "Peace Corps complex" has been a European as well as an American phenomenon, serving as an outlet for youthful idealism and search for adventure. Young people wish to go to the "emergent countries" of Africa as educators, technicians. But a considerable store of new knowledge is required if this purpose is to succeed at all.

European Unification

If aiding the less affluent peoples of the world was perhaps one of those "new dreams for the new world," another was the unification of Europe, excitingly begun in the 1950s with the Treaty of Rome (1957) as a landmark.[8] Economic integration, it was hoped, would lead on to

[8] In an address of March 25, 1959, French President Charles de Gaulle tied these two things together, European community and aid to other peoples, adding to it the possibility of healing the breach between Russia and the West, in a vision

eventual political union in a federation or United States of Europe. The latter step had yet to prove its possibility and there was disagreement about the means to get there; but the progress toward economic unity in a single Common Market area of France, Germany, Italy, Belgium, Netherlands, and Luxembourg, despite disappointing failure to bring in Great Britain, encouraged hopes. The healing of the old feud between France and Germany was especially heartening. Conceivably this goal which Nietzsche and Ortega had dreamed of, along with so many others, could provide an outlet for the idealism of European man. United rather than divided into hostile national units, western Europe might then regain its place in the world and give leadership toward even larger areas of co-operation. A slow and painful process which had to overcome ancient prejudices, unification had acquired considerable dynamism, but whether as an idea it could exert the same force as nationalism remained to be demonstrated. French President Charles de Gaulle, at least, believed that it would be necessary for a time to work through the existing nationalisms, the first step being a "Europe of the Fatherlands," a European superstructure based on the nations of Europe; he disagreed with those who thought it best to bypass the existing states to set up European institutions now, allowing them slowly to expand their powers (the "functional" approach).

European thought is not all of a piece, needless to say, despite trends toward economic integration. Apart from the gulf between Soviet and West European thought, with the Soviet "satellites" uneasily in between, there are other differences between country and country, region and region, within western Europe. One significant one may here be noted. "Anyone who has attended international congresses," Gabriel Marcel has recently written, "is aware that, even putting aside Marxism and its derivatives, there exist in the modern world two distinct types of philosophy, without any living communication between them: there is on the one hand logico-mathematical neopositivism which predominates in the Anglo-Saxon countries and in parts of Scandinavia, and, on the other, there are the doctrines of metaphysical inspiration, whether existentialist or not, current in Germany, France, Italy, Spain and in the countries of

Contrast between British and Continental Philosophy

close to the heart of present-day Europe's political idealism:

> We, who live between the Atlantic and the Urals, we, who are Europe, possessing with Europe's daughter, America, the principal sources and resources of civilization . . . why do we not pool a percentage of our raw materials, our manufactured goods, our food products, some of our scientists, technologists, economists . . . in order to vanquish misery, develop the resources . . . of less developed peoples? Let us do this not that they should be the pawns of our policies, but to improve the chances of life and peace. How much more worthwhile that would be than the territorial demands, ideological claims, imperialist ambitions which are leading the world to its death!

South America." Within the latter camp, he might have added, there are lesser differences of accent between, say, French and German Existentialism. But the one he notes is surely the notable contrast. We have already had our attention drawn to this. The geographical line of demarcation seems peculiar, for while the sources of Existentialism are chiefly Protestant (Kierkegaard and Jaspers come to mind) it is in the Roman Catholic countries that it has tended to prevail. (Moreover, British Positivism owes a debt to imports from Catholic Vienna.) One might suggest a tradition of thought in the Catholic world that is more metaphysical and esthetic, less empirical and less "nominalist."[9] However it may be explained, the contrast of which Marcel speaks exists as one of the singular phenomena of the modern intellectual world. A distinguished British intellectual, Alan Pryce-Jones, has written humorously of Englishmen out of place at European intellectual assemblies dominated by broodingly profound Italians or Frenchmen—the Englishmen looking "small, pink and cheerful." Britain's divorce from the Continental economic community seems reflected in this differing climate of philosophical opinion. Politically, the French departure from parliamentary democracy has introduced a further distinction, for Parliament remains the center of the British system (albeit some have detected a shift here, too, toward more power in the Cabinet at the expense of the House of Commons).

There are other regional and national differences. The novel and
poetry are especially susceptible to national divergence. Surrealism has
dominated French poetry, but exerted only a slight influence in England.
The British novel, subtle and sensitive, agrees with the British philosophy of recent years in avoiding big moral and metaphysical issues, but in France the "novel of ideas" ranks first. But no country can be pigeonholed save at the expense of some distortion; neither British, French, German, nor Italian intellectual life is monolithic. For example, some of the younger British writers, as Ernest Gellner and Iris Murdoch, have rebelled against the Positivist orthodoxy, by now suspected of being part of the "Establishment." Only in the Communist half of Europe—and perhaps also in Spain[10]—has monolithic orthodoxy prevailed—at the cost of

Diversity of European Thought

[9] When George Santayana, the Spanish-American philosopher who studied at Harvard University under William James, came to a break with the school of American Pragmatism headed by James, he gave expression to feelings of roughly this sort, equating Pragmatism with a Protestant mode that affronted his Catholic, "humanist" outlook. Santayana fled from the United States to spend his later years in Italy. Englishmen like D. H. Lawrence who rejected the native soil for something vaguely Existentialist also, it may be recalled, chose to live in Italy.

[10] Spain has been dominated by memories of the terrible civil war of 1936–1939 and governed by the right-wing victors of that war, who tend to identify liberal and democratic forces with Communism and Anarchism. Free thought has not existed, for the censorship finds a danger to the state in any sort of nonconformist or critical thinking. But this intellectual deep freeze seemed to be slowly dissolving under the warmth of economic good times and international contacts during the sixties.

sterility. And this seems to be dissolving in the 1960s. Since about 1958, names such as Pasternak, Yevtushenko, and Solzhenitzyn symbolize a dramatic revolution against Communist authoritarianism in the USSR. European writers and philosophers have visited the USSR and lectured without censorship for the first time since the 1920s. One goal of the Pan-Europeans is to assist in the drawing of Russia back into the major stream of Western Civilization, as her Communist-led alienation wanes and she becomes more like the West economically and socially. It seems a reasonable hope.

As an added note on the diversity of European intellectual life, one may add that French, German, and English domination of intellectual life may be less today. Italy, at least, can claim a small renaissance, as witness the novelists Moravia and Lampedusa, the prestige of the Italian cinema, of Italian fashions, design, architecture. At least in social science and economic theory, the same might be said for the Scandinavian countries. In addition, Europe reads American writers as never before.

The post-1945 climate of opinion might be summed up as a profound revulsion against all that came before, especially the immediate prewar period in its Marxist and statist aspects; followed by a probing for new values, slogans, and modes of thought which have not yet emerged clearly; the leading discernible theme being a mistrust of all ideologies and absolutes, a concern for the individual existent person against abstractions and pressures to conform as well as against the awful power of the state; with social, economic, and political inquiry reflecting this mood in being concrete and piecemeal. In modern times European thought is too complex to submit to any such summation without all kinds of qualifications, however. As it emerged into what seemed the somewhat clearer daylight of the 1960s following a time of fogs and smokes, obviously it confronted a number of conflicts and dilemmas that threatened its future. The next section will attempt to formulate some of these.

DILEMMAS OF MODERN MAN

In the east of Europe, the great Soviet State has conducted since 1917 an experiment in the monist or monolithic society built on a single ideology. There are advantages in having one faith, but also disadvantages. It is tidier, but it involves suppression, and in the long run one cannot achieve unity except at a terrible price in tyranny. This is the medieval experience all over again. In the modern world, it must in any case fail, as is indicated by the trend in the USSR since the death of Stalin. Those who reproach Western civilization for its chaotic lack of unity are undoubtedly right in part, but they may be forgetting that for the last several hundred years that civilization—modern European civilization—has been committed to pluralism and freedom. "Monolithic social ends," as Karl Popper writes, "would mean the death of freedom: of the freedom of thought, of the free search for truth, and with it, of the rationality and dignity of man." The case for European liberalism rests on the value of the "open society" as well as on the hatefulness of persecution for conscience's sake. It rests on the belief that only through the free inquiry of many minds working in many ways can we hope to find solutions to our manifold human problems, still so numerous as almost to stagger the mind. The retreat to an island of dogmatism enforced by the sword is a shallow, superficial, erroneous answer—really an abdication.

Divergence between Soviet Russian and Western Thought

The divergence between Soviet and Western thought may be illustrated by some exchanges to be found in the *History of Mankind* published under the auspices of UNESCO (United Nations Educational, Scientific and Cultural Organization). In the first volume, *Prehistory and the Beginnings of Civilization,* written by two British historians (1963), Soviet historians dissented frequently, the general grounds of their dissent being that the Western historians present history as "no more than a kaleidoscopic change of whimsical patterns with no inner consistency and no principle in their development" (page 508), and more particularly that they fail to put the facts in the Marxian framework of concepts and stages. (All societies must involve "exploitation" by a bad ruling class, all history must exhibit an evolution from slavery to feudalism to capitalism, etc.) The reply of Sir Leonard Woolley to Professor I. M. Diakonoff and his Russian colleagues was of course that to represent history as the latter desire would be to misrepresent it, since the facts exposed by empirical investigation reveal no such neat agreement with the Marxist categories. The frequent exchanges between Diakonoff and Woolley recorded in the notes for each chapter leave the impression of a doctrinaire *a priori* approach on the Russian side which Western historians could only regard as naive, but which the Russians obviously consider to be the only way of rendering history intelligible at all. (Purely factual matters were often in question, but clearly the bias or presuppositions of the historians helped decide what they thought the "facts" were.) And it must be admitted that the Soviet historians could have written a better organized, more lucid account than is contained in the more than 800 large pages of this volume, replete with suspended or uncertain judgements and revealing as it does the enormous complexity of ancient history. Their history would have been clearer; but it could not have passed critical scrutiny by the eyes of knowledgeable experts in the West.

The pluralism and sophistication of the Western intellect create difficulties, though they are a source of strength. The Western intellectual tradition is doubtless the most complex ever known. It is now an old roué of civilization, which has experienced everything and seen through all myths. It now finds it difficult to believe in anything; it tries, but it is too self-conscious, it knows that its faith will be a myth. Modern achievement in every field is marked by great technical mastery. But the specialist has taken over at the expense of a general culture; and amid a wealth of specialized techniques for unearthing scientific, factual knowledge, modern man has the greatest difficulties finding values. These are among the leading dilemmas of modern man, who struggles to integrate all his intellectual subcultures into something like a single culture, and to find something his logic will let him believe in. Contemporary culture lacks unity and lacks faith; yet in some degree men want and seek these things.

Specialization, with technical competence in a high degree but compensating losses in range, depth, and linkage with other fields, is found wherever we look. It has infected philosophy itself, no longer queen of the intellect but largely content to be a specialized branch of experimental science. Economics, also, has fallen victim to specialization, as has sociology, in that the grand classical syntheses have been abandoned in favor of micro-analysis, the examination of particular situations rather than the whole of society. It would be impossible to find a branch of learning not afflicted with this sort of "crisis," examined in a recent symposium called *Crisis in the Humanities*. There is far more knowledge; it is far less meaningful because less integrated. This dilemma has also appeared in other disciplines formerly more "humanistic." Much literary criticism in recent times has spurned the historical, biographical, or moral aspects for strict and close verbal analysis of the work of literature itself—a sort of literary linguistic analysis. The branches of creative literature themselves have shown a similar pattern. A distinguished contemporary English literary critic (Graham Hough) has spoken of the enormous gains in "technical competence, sheer skill in handling the tools" in the last forty years or so—of the conquering, among other things, of a whole new realm, the unconscious—and yet accompanying this a "loss of authority," a loss also of range and substance, a tendency to deal with the "ripples on the surface" of life.[11] The recent French novel, too, exhibits an almost dismaying variety of technical tricks, regarded as necessary to be up-to-date. Poetry too, of course, has become ultrasophisticated in technique—subtle, oblique, capable of saying anything and saying it stylishly, but finding nothing very memorable to say—consisting of "private" rather than "public" statements.

Though these generalizations, indicative of a triumph of technique over life, are subject to exceptions, they seem broadly descriptive of an important trend. Technique has brought precision, has eliminated much untidiness and cleared up errors, but it would seem to have entailed a loss of vitality, and to have fragmented thought and culture into unrelated

Historical Research

[11] BBC broadcast talks, printed in *The Listener*, January, 13, 20, 27, and February 3, 1955.

pieces.[12] Historical writing, too, often today takes the form of well-researched, technically accomplished studies, making use of archival material—the sacred emblem of the historian's guild—but lacking the literary skill, the grand manner, the sweep of older historians. George M. Trevelyan's eloquent plea, written in 1913, for Clio as essentially a literary muse, belonging to the humanities and not to the sciences, has scarcely prevailed; Trevelyan was *passé* before he died, hopelessly dilettantish by the standards of the Lewis Namier school in Great Britain. It is true that since 1900 historians have moved away from the Positivistic conception of history as capable of yielding laws on the analogy of the physical sciences, a view then very strong. (Witness J. B. Bury, Foustel de Coulanges.) They have rather tended to follow the line indicated by the German Wilhelm Dilthey, or by Benedetto Croce the great Italian historian and philosopher, a position well expressed in R. G. Collingwood's book, *The Idea of History* (1946). On this view history is neither the handmaiden of science nor a branch of *belles-lettres*, but is autonomous, its function being to recreate the past from the perspective of present thought and in so doing clarify the present. "The science of the particular," its job is not to search for general laws, but to explore unique past experiences in depth, choosing the ones most relevant to present experience. Such a view corresponds roughly to the professional historian's instinctive idea of what he does when he writes history. It is a defensible one; but it opens the door to a great deal of aimless and not very important research done just for the sake of doing—because it is "there," meaning by "it" all too often some archival sources.[13]

Toynbee   Arnold J. Toynbee's vast tapestry of universal history with its sweeping claim to unearth the laws governing the rise and fall of civilizations has not been favorably received by most professional historians. Yet the literate public eagerly bought and read it, indicating a thirst for "philosophical" history, not assuaged by most historical writing today. With vast erudition and an appropriately grave and classical style, Toynbee set forth on the somewhat Romantic quest of finding in history the secret of the sickness of Western civilization. He offered a study in comparative civilizations, identifying twenty-one different civilizations in human his-

---

[12] The same is true of psychology, as previously noted. Academically respectable are behavioristic studies which present the exact reactions of rats and men to a variety of external stimuli, all very carefully done. Freud, McDougall, and other speculators about the mysterious dynamics of the inner mind are dismissed as unscientific. This is truer in Great Britain and the United States than on the Continent. For a commentary, see Arthur Koestler's *The Act of Creation*, 1964.

[13] A much discussed review in the famous London *Times Literary Supplement* for June 28, 1963, registered violent protest against the "Ph.D. pestilence" which requires or encourages useless and graceless pedantry in the humanities, in this case, not in history but literature. The institutional necessity of writing theses and dissertations, under conditions of contemporary mass education, may be blamed for some degeneration in research.

tory and seeking to show the common pattern of their inception, growth, decline, and disintegration—some, on his view, having perished completely. A meditative if sometimes platitudinous style, a deeply spiritual outlook, an awareness of an amazing range of ideas as well as historic facts, lends to Toynbee's leisurely *Study of History* (altogether in twelve volumes, the substance of it abridged by D. S. Somervell in two volumes) a great appeal. His conclusions are not regarded by most of his competent critics as having much validity. "Laws" turn out to be truisms; there is doubt about the neat isolating of civilizations as separate units; comparisons mean little when stripped of Toynbeean rhetoric. Nevertheless the large amount of discussion aroused by Toynbee has been a stimulus to historical thinking. A landmark of our times, Toynbee's massive work testifies to the global perspective and to the technical resources of the modern historian—the historian of no previous generation could have assembled so much knowledge from all over the world—and to the perennial interest in the great question, whither mankind? But it has scarcely provided an answer.

In reality, Toynbee's opus was the product of his feeling that modern Europe had fallen into decay and was headed for death, a feeling aroused by World War I, intensified by the rise of Communism and Nazism and the depression of the 1930s, and seemingly confirmed by the truly suicidal violence of World War II. He turned to history to try to find an answer to the causes, and thus possibly the cure, of such declines and falls, just as Thucydides had done when faced with the suicide of Periclean Greece in the Peloponnesian War, and Machiavelli had done in the twilight of Renaissance Italy. When a sophisticated civilization falls on bad times it will produce brilliant diagnoses. But it is not clear that the diagnosis helps. Toynbee seems to know what qualities civilizations have when they are at their creative zenith, and what symptoms they exhibit when in trouble—not a difficult thing to describe. But in the end he can only exhort Western civilization to be more creative and cease having troubles. His scheme of science, purporting to show that many other civilizations have gone through similar patterns, and his effort to find useful laws of the secular movements of whole civilizations, are too vague and subjective to command assent or have much meaning. So Toynbee's masterpiece turns out to be less the scientific analysis he thought it to be than a kind of vast prose poem lamenting the sickness of a civilization. This is not to say it is useless; on the contrary, less as science than as rhetoric, it has worked on literally millions of minds. No other serious work of such length has been so widely read in our time. History can console us as well as inspire us.

Toynbee protested against too much narrow specialization, but fell afoul of specialists. Most historians seem content to plough well their own narrow furrow, each building his own separate tunnel to the past, as one historian has recently put it (J. H. Hexter). This is the tendency in all branches of knowledge. Martin Heidegger wrote in 1929, in one of his searching criticisms of modern civilization, that "the scientific fields are far apart. Their subjects are treated in fundamentally different ways. Today this hodgepodge of disciplines is held together only by the technical organization of the universities and faculties, and preserves what meaning it has only through the practical aims of the different branches." The modern American university is an excellent cultural mirror of this sprawling disunity.[14] Scientist-novelist C. P. Snow, in *The Two Cultures*, a book much discussed in England, drew attention to the gulf developing between scientists and humanists in an age of specialization, even in the English universities with their traditions of a broad liberal education.

Overspecialization is a particular danger because it may cut off that cross-fertilization of the disciplines that has so often proved stimulating in the past. Students of intellectual history are especially aware of those cases, in which Darwin received vital stimulation and critical ideas from Malthus, Kant from Rousseau, Kepler from Pythagorean mysticism, etc.[15] If the disciplines—or even worse, small sections within each discipline, as seems to be the case today—are cut off from each other and from a matrix of general ideas common to all, we have a formula for scientific desiccation. Our sciences as well as our general culture will dry up, humanity itself will shrivel, the human personality lose itself in a wilderness of jargon and pettiness. This is the fear, and it seems well-grounded. Gabriel Marcel (*The Philosophy of Existence,* Chapter 1) has pointed out that the individual in modern specialized society loses his human personality to become "an agglomeration of functions." This destruction of his sense of whole being seems to be what the Existentialist psychotherapists (such as the German Binswanger) have in mind as the basic cause of neurosis and psychosis in the individual.

It may be noted that this complexity and specialization defeats the

---

[14] In this respect one might consider as significant what happened to the General Education program established at Harvard College in 1945 following the report published (and widely read) as *General Education in a Free Society.* The idea of this educational program was, in substance, to counteract specialization by giving to all students a small number of basic courses which would set forth in broad terms the common cultural heritage. In practice, the idea never worked, and in 1964 another Harvard committee confessed failure and in effect gave up the broad courses and common-heritage approach. Its justification for doing so was largely that existing academic patterns simply will not support the 1945 program. Good faculty is not interested in teaching the general courses; they are therefore neglected and badly taught, while the better professors put their energy into specialized research and teaching. This is at a great institution of learning which has long dedicated itself especially to the liberal arts and the humane studies.

[15] One may urge on behalf of intellectual history that it attempts to combat this cultural chaos of isolated fields, this "hodgepodge of disciplines," by putting the various areas of thought in a common context and seeing the relations between them. It is one of the very few academic disciplines today trying to perform this task, so desperately needed if our civilization is to recover its sanity and balance.

dreams of the individual's mental power and thus ends a long epoch in modern history. The realm of knowledge becomes far too vast for any one mind to grasp, even in the most general terms, and one gives up the quest, resigning oneself to being at the most a cog in some incomprehensible machine. Renaissance, Enlightenment, and Romantic man all thought it possible to understand everything. In the sixteenth century, Walter Ralegh observed casually that he bought *every* book that was published! In the eighteenth, a Voltaire, a Hume, a Jefferson kept abreast of just about all branches of knowledge, also without impeding their numerous other activities. The last of those who still sought omniscience were the great nineteenth-century synthesizers, Hegel, Marx, and Spencer, but their schemes broke down. Synthesis is beyond the grasp of anyone today, evidently. Such virtuosi of erudition as Toynbee and Teilhard reach toward it, but even these are far from achieving it. This dream must be abandoned; and if so, the failure would seem to entail a fundamental alteration in Western man's outlook: a defeat for individualism, for rationalism in the older sense. The assault on what David Knowles calls "a single reasoned and intelligible explanation of the universe on the natural level, and a single analysis of man and his powers . . . valid for all men and final within its sphere" came under attack as early as the fourteenth century with the scepticism of Ockham, and was further eroded in the Reformation. And yet, as Knowles adds, this scepticism "was never wholly victorious, and never finally accepted": European man clung to his dramatic belief in an ultimate knowledge accessible to the enlightened mind. Doubtless both Hegelianism and Darwinism in their different ways undermined it; doubtless no one had ever really been omniscient; and yet the great Victorians did continue to believe in the unity of knowledge, and the individual's ability to grasp in a general way this unity. If we are driven to complete fragmentation, we are at the end of rational individualism. Perhaps we are at the end of personality, as well as philosophy—condemned to be interchangeable with computers, or to be intellectual drones who heap up useless knowledge.

Another consequence of overspecialization, or at least a related cultural phenomenon, is the gulf between the average man and the expert or adept. There is no audience, no common ground. The complexity and diversity of thought, breeding a situation in which a few experts in any area communicate only with each other, leaves a vacuum in the "popular" mind which must be filled largely by rubbish. While the popular market for fiction and nonfiction alike is mostly satisfied by low-quality journalism, serious thought and advanced expression go on among isolated and esoteric minorities. Cultural distance between popular and advanced thought has always existed and perhaps always will; but there have been cultures wherein a general consensus or forum was closer to a possibility than in the vast democratic nations of today. This is sometimes blamed on their being vast, or their being democratic; but the true culprit, in the main, would seem to be the intellectual fragmentation we have been discussing.

The truly appalling shoddiness and silliness of this popular culture—American television or the average run of movie—is responsible for the alienation, to the point of insanity, of many people sensitive to beauty and human dignity, as it is also the source of opinions about the "degradation of the democratic era" or the abject decadence of modern man. The truth is that democracy arrived at the same time as specialization, doubling the dimensions of the problem. To absorb and civilize the millions who had heretofore lived beneath civilization would have been a challenging enough task at best. But simultaneously civilization itself has encountered the crisis of modern complexity and scepticism, and above all, the fragmentation of which we have been speaking.

Democracy and Culture

It is far from clear that democracy is *responsible* for cultural anarchy. It is certainly not responsible for the cultural degradation of the common man, for this of course preceded it; Tocqueville had observed that "the common people is more uncivilized in aristocratic countries than any others." Matthew Arnold, in his sane appraisal a century ago, pointed out that democracy represented a striving of the common folk after whatsoever the reigning society affirmed as valuable. When democracy came to Athenian Greeks, the common folk sought after wisdom. If it comes to a military barbarism, they will want to be plundering soldiers. In Japan they write *hokku* poems. If democracy comes to an acquisitive capitalism, the people want to acquire. Arnold at least distributed the blame equally: "At the very moment when democracy becomes less and less disposed to follow and to admire, aristocracy becomes less and less qualified to command and to captivate."[16] Those qualities of "lofty spirit, commanding character, exquisite culture" which Arnold thought the eighteenth-century aristocracy possessed had ceased to be evident. In brief, cultural failure must not be blamed altogether on the mass, but on society for not holding up high values as a beacon to it.

The Need for Values

Another major dilemma of modern man obviously is this need for life-giving values, which can evidently come only from some sort of religious faith (religious in the widest sense), while his heritage of scepticism prevents any such belief. This dilemma is substantially that expressed by a Shavian character who cried that "we have outgrown our religion, outgrown our political system, outgrown our strength of mind and character. The fatal word NOT has been miraculously inscribed in all our creeds."[17] "I've been looking for something to believe in," says Alan Squier in Robert Sherwood's *Petrified Forest* (1936). "I've been

[16] "Democracy," in *Mixed Essays,* 1879, first published 1861.
[17] *Too True to Be Good,* 1934.

hoping to find something that's worth living for—and dying for." Modern poets, novelists, dramatists, philosophers, preachers have now and again found things worth living and dying for. They found it in the 1930s and 1940s in the struggle against Nazism, and after that possibly in the fight against Communism. These were negative crusades—against something evil that had appeared, something itself the result of modern spiritual illness—and it is not clear that they provided the basis for a positive structure of value. Plainly many men believe in and struggle for such things as social justice, racial equality, honest government, the elimination of extreme poverty, national self-government for peoples who do not have it, etc. The questions remain, freedom for what? (Georges Bernanos, *La liberté pour quoi faire?*, 1953). A higher standard of life to what end? Can liberty, equality, and democracy really be ends in themselves, or are they not rather the means through which men can achieve some goals and values of life? If so, does not achievement of the former without the latter lead only to an ignoble materialism, an affluent society with vulgar tastes, the spiritual deserts of suburbia so often seen today in the United States?

In this dilemma there are signs of a yearning to return to traditional creeds. The great Italian writer and former Communist, Ignazio Silone, has declared that "the rediscovery of a Christian heritage in the revolution of our time remains the most important gain that has been made in these last years for the conscience of our generation" (1946). Both World Wars I and II quickened interest in religion. Silone has joined W. H. Auden, the late T. S. Eliot, Graham Greene, François Mauriac, and many another distinguished elder statesman of the literary world in embracing a Christian creed, sometimes after having followed strange gods earlier. This is a movement of the greatest significance. Others have been led to such exotic shores of faith as India and Japan in their search for a tenable religion for modern man; still others explore the possibility of a higher religious synthesis between East and West. Jung directed attention to the universal symbols or archetypes underlying all religious experience. Zaehner, Kerenyi, and others are engaged in a massive exploration of the domain of comparative religions. Never has there been greater interest in historical and theological studies of the Christian past. Outstanding in the Christian world in recent times has been the ecumenical movement, the quest for unity. Breaching the walls between sects and churches erected in Reformation times (or earlier, in the case of the Greek-Roman schism) has made some progress, and given rise to searching reexamination of church history and doctrine. The recent pontificate of John XXIII in the Roman Catholic Church was epochal for its turn in this direction. Many exciting world conferences have made what seem promising gains for ecumenicalism.

The Search for Religion

Yet though there is keen interest in religion, there is little assurance of what religion it is we are to hold to. If Christianity, it must evidently be "de-mythologized." A recent series of books titled "Religious Perspectives," issued by a leading American publisher, dedicated to "dealing with basic spiritual concerns in the hope of defining a doctrine of man," illustrates some of the uncertainties. It distinguishes religion from theology, defining the former as "the feelings and aspirations of men . . . a sense of the sacred and the transcendent." "*Religious Perspectives* is an effort launched by informed and learned world leaders to guide us toward the spiritual serenity which is nowhere found amidst the mechanical triumphs of the rocket century," a distinguished scientist and historian wrote in the prospectus. Men hope, somehow, for "spiritual serenity" (which reminds us of the Stoic's quest during the period of the decline of the Roman Empire in ancient times) or for "feelings and aspirations." Granted the need and the sincerity of those who express it, one wonders if this vague yearning can possibly bear fruit in real religion. The miscellaneous tracts which have appeared in the above-mentioned series, excellent as some are, do not encourage one to believe that a religious renaissance is upon us. This one example is not of course conclusive. There are without question many earnest Christians in the world today, and many others who have adopted Zen Buddhism or something similar with equal sincerity. But there also appear to be modern Western intellectuals who are shopping for a good myth, and who cannot really believe in any except as a pose.

Nihilism in Philosophy

As has previously been suggested, there is (it is alleged) a degree of moral nihilism about the dominant mode of academic philosophy in the Anglo-Saxon world. If Existentialism urges us to believe in something, no matter what, just so we believe, Logical Positivism tells us that no sort of moral belief has any rational defense and so one belief is as good as another—or perhaps none at all is best. C. E. M. Joad, in his book *A Critique of Logical Positivism* (1950), made the point eloquently. No community can survive, he pointed out, without a vigorous belief that some things are wrong (killing, cruelty, lying, faithlessness, etc.), yet our philosophers tell us these cannot be shown to be wrong but are merely subjective expressions of emotional preference. Nor can any civilization be vigorous unless its members are energized to action by their conviction that to do something is important, whether this be painting pictures, building steel mills, or raising food; yet contemporary philosophy declares all "values" unverifiable and thus implies that they are hardly worth holding. "Communism and Fascism," Joad added, "are the natural by-products of scepticism and nihilism. Most men need a creed and there is nothing in the empirical world upon which a creed can be based." If this indictment of our philosophers is overdrawn, as doubtless it is, it yet contains some truth.

Philosophy such as that of the analytical school would seem to be in danger of suffering the same fate as that which overtook the medieval philosophers. "Thought divorced from life must always wither, and the philosopher of the fourteenth century withdrew more and more into his own world, in which definitions and conclusions were no longer controlled by all other kinds of human experiences. . . . Thought preyed upon itself, and suffered fragmentation." David Knowles' comment on the Schoolmen might be applied with equal force to the contemporary academics. If so, it is suggestive of decadence and the end-of-an-age, despite the subtlety of contemporary philosophical analysis. The late Middle Ages had their subtle doctors, too, but they were swept aside in the revolution of Renaissance and Reformation.

The reply of the philosophers would be that it cannot be wrong to apply intelligence and reason to moral and political questions, where irrational nonsense has reigned. The philosophers really assert a value, at bottom; it is the value of rational, critical, analytical thought. Now few in the West are prepared to deny this value. With it, however, it becomes impossible to accept in the fullest sense—and religions are not much good if half-hearted—any religious affirmation of values. Modern Western man, at least at the top intellectual level, is ultrasophisticated and disabused. He can find nothing to believe in. Despairingly, he may try to believe in belief itself, telling himself that there is something heroic in making up values. This is the path of Existentialism from Nietzsche to Sartre. Academic philosophy seems content to show how irrational the whole process of value-making is and dismiss it from the list of problems to be tackled by logic and reason. It is, at least, not *their* business.

Looked at in this light, contemporary thought might be seen as a study in frustration in which myths are set up for logical analysis to demolish. In one corner of the ring is the positivistic philosopher, descended from Hume and possessing all the keen-edged weapons of modern logic, prepared to knock down anything that can be said about values, purpose, God, etc. He will allow us to believe in nothing except observed facts. Seconding him are hosts of scientists and scientific naturalists. In the other corner appear all kinds of myths, some imported from the Orient or even from the primitive world, some dredged up from the European past, some newly created; often they are violent and irrational, and they seek to overcome the sharp jabs of the analysts by the sheer force of their affirmations. Desperately needing a religion, modern man cannot really believe in any.[18]

[18] As a footnote, it may be noted again how often men look to history for a clue to what they should believe. Thus the very intelligent Frenchman Bertrand de Jouvenel urges as an argument for economic expansion: "If we look at the history of Man since the Stone Age, we find that men have always been altering their processes; this,

If religious need is, as C. E. M. Joad has written, "a product of man's consciousness of his loneliness and helplessness in an alien and indifferent universe," then this need has never been greater than it is today; for with all his technological apparatus modern man must realize as never before how frightening are the cosmic forces he confronts. Hopefully launching his rockets at the moon, he cannot but be aware, if he reflects, what strange and terrifying adventures may await him if he probes into the incalculable vastness of the universe with its other possible worlds. At home, he suffers from the paralyzing fear of a nuclear war that would cause the most ghastly suffering in his history, while he continues to be plagued by political conflicts suggesting that he has hardly advanced much in this area since Thucydides and Plato tried to fathom the causes and cure of war and civil strife. Moreover all his economic "affluence" has not given him happiness.

The
Dilemma of
Modern Man

"The spirit of man in the present age has been under a gray pall of uncertainty, insecurity, scepticism," a well-known British philosophical writer, Lord Samuel, remarked a few years ago. In the present age, it has also exhibited unconquerable vitality, defying a hostile universe to assert new values, in a truly Promethean gesture. But there remains a deep schism in the soul of the West which it is hard to see being altogether cured, so long as it retains the knowledge and subtlety of which scepticism is the natural fruit. This dilemma has haunted the most sensitive and creative minds of the twentieth century. *The Castle,* Franz Kafka's symbolic novel, depicted modern man frantically and unsuccessfully searching for those who will tell him what to do and to be. This feeling lies behind the desperate evocation of the primitive (back to the Etruscans or the blond beasts) which some of the most profound moderns have so strangely attempted. Fascism, Nazism, and Communism may be seen as equally desperate reactions against the cultural crisis of a civilization built on scepticism, on freedom to do—what?[19] And this dilemma may explain why intelligent non-Westerners have been puzzled by the West's apparent lack of faith in itself. (Dr. Malik, the Arab philosopher, remarked a few years ago that "the Western mind . . . has been softened

---

then, pertains to our species; as a believer I must conclude that we were meant to do so and therefore that it is good" (*Listener,* December 15, 1955). "Just because it has always been so" may seem a doubtful argument, but it *is* an argument, of consequence when others are missing. It is based on fact. It rather resembles Carlyle's Victorian recipe for overcoming doubt: up and work.

[19] Erich Fromm, *Escape From Freedom* (1941): freedom, so long striven for, turned to ashes in the mouth of modern man and brought a terrible loneliness, from which he flees, because of the absence of values. Lewis Mumford, *A Faith for Living* (1940): "Fascism . . . reveals certain obdurate truths about life itself which never entered the doctrines of those who believed in automatic progress." Robert S. Lynd, *Knowledge for What?* (1939): the source of fascism is "in the human soul, not in economics."

and undermined from within and without. The effect of this softening has been for this mind to lose faith in itself. . . .")

Despite signs of revival and of a toughness that defies disaster, one must surely concede extensive evidence of decadence in contemporary Europe. As a final dilemma, we may suggest that the European world shows signs of having exhausted its usable traditions. Paradoxically, in the midst of so rich an inheritance it finds no gesture that gives satisfaction, but compulsively repeats stale ones that have lost their magic.

One of the most pathetic reiterative gestures is the esthetic-experimental. Rimbaud, Verlaine, the Surrealists, and the Dadaists did it once; but one cannot add to them, one can only repeat them in ever more violent and therefore feebler ways. In the 1960s the "little magazines" continue to flourish, bearing such names as Gong, Howl, Yowl, Nomad.[20] But for the most part they contain only obscene echoes of the great age of European experimental literature and esthetic revolt. No doubt the gesture is soothing to the souls of the men and women who fling these notes of defiance at an obtuse world. But the notes have gone sour, and the gesture is so stale it can have no significance. When not highly derivative in form, aping Tzara, Appolinaire, Rimbaud, etc., these writings tend to be formless. The French have produced the antinovel. Others like to let computers write poems. The content of this literature is a kind of parody of the Decadents; the theme is not so much decay as putrefaction. A critic has spoken of "the charnel house flavor" of William Burroughs' novel *Naked Lunch*, a bible of the bedraggled avant garde of the 1960s. American "beats" and "hippies" write of drug addiction, and other degraded states. Nihilistic in form and content alike to the last degree of nothingness, this is literature not of revolt nor even of despair, it seems beyond despair. Writing of the contemporary avant garde Ken Baynes remarks that "the artist's brave cry of freedom has turned into the shout of a buffoon."

It is hard, though, to deny the human need at the root of these pathetic gestures. Literature is a purgative; novels are written out of the urgent necessity for the individual to somehow make coherent his experiences—a need for wholeness. Whole categories of American novels, coming from the most chaotic of modern Western societies, speak of this need. They are typically written by lost, lonely, isolated souls, condemned to existence in some provincial outpost (Southern town, prairie village) or urban slum-jungle. They are remarkable achievements, and often lead their authors to fame and fortune, perhaps to Hollywood. Usually they lead nowhere, creatively: having purged his soul of loneliness, bitterness, and confusion in one extraordinary outburst, the author typically subsides

Avant Garde Gestures

[20] Two special issues of the London *Times Literary Supplement* in August, 1964, surveyed this field with extraordinary perceptiveness.

and becomes a "disappointment" to the critics.[21] (Names such as Mailer, Salinger, Ellison and others will come to mind.) No sustained vision or philosophy lies behind them. The American "novels of the absurd" seem not to rise to an Existential surmounting of the absurd; they simply display it. Certainly they are interesting, and Europe has been very interested in them. Intellectually, they seem to testify mostly to the anarchy of the modern world. They testify also to the fierce integrity of the creative individual and his remarkable capacity to use literature as a means of extracting, *creating* value and meaning for his world, and also to a surprising public interest in this literature. But in their intellectual confusion they are a dismaying reminder of how little unity the modern world has; it seems to be a collection of unattached monads desperately reaching out to make contact with something else.

A typical desperate gesture comes from the "Situationists" who, founded in 1957, quickly split into factions, one in Germany and one in Sweden. They combine execrations against bombs, politicians, conformity (both Communist and capitalist varieties) with strange esthetic experiments, pornography, and unconventional town planning. Vaguely Sartrean and post-Surrealist, they are rather incoherently experimental in all directions, and it is not clear that they even take themselves very seriously. Their violently extremist attitudes toward modern society, politics, and art mark them as post-Decadents and post-Communists.

In political and social thought, the present age would seem to be equally at the mercy of sterile formulae from the past. Fallen out of favor, in some degree, is the old socialism-progressivism with its oversimplified dogmatic stereotypes and its overtones of religious evangelicalism. Some of the new thought is hard-headed, piecemeal, disabused, unwilling to anticipate utopia, essentially Benthamite in its practicality and to a degree Saint-Simonian in its use of specialist expertise. But the old dies hard, and young intellectuals still talk vaguely of "Establishments" they are against, the need for total social reconstruction, the wickedness of the existing political order. In fact, as we have noted, a serious interest in politics is rare among today's intellectuals; and their own anger is the angrier for lacking clear formulation or even a clear target.[22] (The vague word *Establishment* as a label for an alleged "ruling class" of a few sinister people pulling all the strings is a scapegoat term, indicative of

[21] "The blighted career, the arrested career, the diverted career are, with us, the rule," Van Wyck Brooks complained in 1922. "The chronic state of our literature is that of a youthful promise which is never redeemed." It does not look as if this has changed much.

[22] One might read, in this connection, the essay-review by Alan Pryce-Jones of a manifesto of the younger British writers, published in 1957 (see *The Listener*, November 7, 1957). The essay is entitled "The Messiahs of the Milk Bars?" and gives vent to the distinguished English editor's shrewd suspicion that these young "angries" really have no clear idea what they are angry about.

intellectual bankruptcy, rather like the Jewish Conspiracy of the Nazis in this respect. There is no such monolithic ruling circle in today's Western democracies.) Mouthing the tattered phrases of yesterday's Marxism, they are not really happy with these phrases but have not learned any others.

A recent study of André Malraux by William Righter finds the clue to that extraordinary Frenchman in a restless search for a cause. In turn revolutionary, novelist, art critic, and politician, this modern Chateaubriand, child of Nietzsche, Spengler, and Pascal, with a sense of modern man's tragic predicament has tried to escape it by finding a worthy goal to pursue. Though he has tried many, it is not clear that Malraux ever settled on one, and so rather like Baroque man he has simply been a man in movement. It would be possible, with Heraclitus and Montaigne, to rest content with an ephemeral and illusory world, seeing change itself as the only value. But European man obviously is not happy with such a solution; he must find some absolute. Yet he seems unable to do so.

THE NEXT STAGE?

Having pointed out some notable areas of tension afflicting our common civilization today—between technology and humanism, reason and faith—and some signs of decadence, it would be wrong not to add that every civilization confronts similar conflicts, along with others, and that Western civilization possesses terrific resources of vitality with which to encounter them. It is not amiss to include a tribute to Europe and the West. Coming home from a trip to the Orient in which he investigated aspects of Indian and Japanese thought, Arthur Koestler in his interesting book *The Lotus and the Robot* tells how

> I started my journey in a sackcloth and ashes and
> came back rather proud of being a European.

With the return of confidence after being shaken badly by the two horrible fratricidal wars of this century, Europe is likely to return to the fountains of its own traditions more and more. Western civilization has revealed powers of renewal and regeneration many times before. Its history is a history of renaissance, of which *the* Renaissance, the post-medieval renewal based on rediscovery of the ancient classics, was only one. Battered by the terrific crisis of the Reformation, Europe came up with the scientific and intellectual renaissance of the seventeenth century, a renewal based on the creative use of older materials. Shaken by the French Revolution and its wars, Europe integrated this revolution into its traditional culture in the nineteenth century. Mass democracy, specialization, and industrial technology today present a challenge that Western civilization may be able to meet.

Creative and Dynamic Qualities of Western Civilization

The somewhat tentative and inconclusive quality of this final chapter testifies principally to the historian's inevitable uncertainly in the present. Tomorrow is necessary to understand today. That is the very reason for writing history: with the passage of time, the past falls into perspective— into various perspectives, indeed—and events or ideas which then seemed chaotic reveal their meaning. The historian is at a loss to predict the future. "Historicisms" of the past which claimed that they had found the key to all history, past, present, and future, stand forever discredited; we can no longer believe in this particular brand of theology disguised as science. Evolution creates ever fresh forms which are outgrowths of the past but could not have been predicted; lucky guesses are possible, but systematic prediction and control is not. If one knew only the seed one could hardly foretell the plant. In history, too, we are in the position of not knowing what the final result, if there is any, will be. We can see where we have been, and from this suggest some possibilities for the future, but possibilities only. Of all people, indeed, the historian is probably most aware of diversity and contingency in man's affairs.

One guess, often risked today, which seems very nearly a certainty in a broad sense, is that the West must and inevitably will make fruitful contacts with non-Western peoples' including not only the richly developed Oriental civilizations but also peoples much closer to the primitive than ourselves. Asia and Africa have entered into history, and the world has taken on new dimensions for European man. A typical comment is this one by Mireas Eliade: "Western culture will be in danger of a decline into a sterilizing provincialism if it despises or neglects the dialogue with the other cultures. . . . The West will have to know and to understand the existential situations and the cultural universe of the non-Western peoples. . . . Furthermore, this confrontation with 'the others' helps Western man better to understand himself." The last point is an illustration of the familiar fact that we as individuals or as social units commonly define ourselves, in good part, through our relation to others and to a larger organism consisting of ourselves and these others.

Professor Eliade, a leading student of comparative religions, adds that some recent developments in Western thought have prepared us for this task. Depth psychology, including Jung's interest in the world of myth as related to the dynamism of the psyche, is one; and in general that discovery of the unconscious irrational which came to Europe in the age of Nietzsche and Freud, and of the Symbolists in art. *Myths, Dreams and Mysteries: The Encounter Between Contemporary Faiths and Archaic Realities* is the title of Eliade's book from which the above quotation came. Cultural anthropologists have been at work, ever since the later nineteenth century, probing the psychology of contemporary primitive man and suggesting theories of the role of myth and religion. A good deal of what Christian Europe and Rationalist Europe formerly dismissed

Dialogues
with Other
Cultures

as simply superstitious nonsense now has become of deep interest, because it reveals the primordial workings of the human mind, and insofar as it probes the religious element, it can be of more than clinical interest.

This "dialogue between East and West," or between civilized and primitive, need not submerge Western civilization in a syncretic world culture, though it might. It could result in more sharply defining and discovering the West's own being, as effective dialogue can do. It might wake that old civilization up and save it from its weary scepticism.[23] It can remove misunderstandings between civilizations thus helping to reduce conflicts and wars. There is a great deal of mixing and mingling going on today, as everyone knows. Americans assist in the founding of African universities; people from all over the world come to American, British, French, and Russian universities; thousands of scholars annually exploit the lavish subsidization of international intellectual exchange.

The outcome of all this is most problematical; but no one would deny that it must eventually entail some sort of a revolution in the mental outlook of all men. What sort, it is impossible to predict. Wyndham Lewis spoke of "cosmic man," denationalized and made into a common mold; he thought the Americans represented this process, having no particular national culture but being products of the modern machine age, and that the rest of the world would sooner or later be "Americanized." It is a fate many European intellectuals would regard as worse than death, yet there may be something in it. Their own lands are in fact being to a degree "Americanized," though this is not really Americanization at all but the penetration of modern technology and its by-products (business methods, etc.) and of cultural democracy. Neither machine technology nor democracy was invented by the Americans, they only arrived at their full fruition earliest in the United States. Television and the cinema are "cosmic" cultural forces, along with the business and industry of a world increasingly knit together commercially. The "international style" in architecture may be as depressing as most motion pictures made on the French Riviera by American producers using Italian actresses; it may be equally depressing to some to watch Tokyo change from a Japanese city to a kind of exotic imitation of New York. Fads for Zen or for African art may seem the shallow pretensions of pseudointellectuals. But all this happened once before in history, at the time of the Alexandrian and then Roman Empire. And perhaps out of this vast process of syncretization will emerge new civilizations, as Western Europe emerged from the decay of the ancient world.

At any rate this dialogue and this mixing go on, and must surely hold

"Cosmic Man"

[23] It is perhaps significant that one of the outstanding influences on French thought in recent years has come from a brilliant anthropologist, Claude Lévi-Strauss, whose highly sophisticated, technically accomplished analyses of primitive societies seem to offer deep insights into all human cultures.

one of the keys to our future. The process underscores the radical change that is taking place in the world of ideas. It looks very much as though this is a critical stage in man's long journey, and that what comes next, perhaps in the next century, must decide the question of his future on earth.

Apart from such larger issues, there are many potentialities of thought that may be provisionally projected, and some are outgrowths of more familiar Western preoccupations. Though the old ideologies may be in disarray, the drive toward social reform and amelioration continues. There are many dreadfully urgent evils to be assailed. Things are drastically wrong with society, culture, and the economy. Poverty needs to be remedied, labor made more creative, leisure more rewarding, urban living less bleak. Automation and overpopulation challenge industrial society to adapt or choke to death on its own products.

Neo-Marxism   The influence of Marx in a more sophisticated and perhaps fruitful way appears in recent sociology: the work of Raymond Aron in France, of Rolf Dahrendorf (*Class and Conflict in Industrial Society*), or the volume of *Marxismus Studien* recently sent out from the University of Tübingen, edited by Dr. I. Fetscher, can be instanced. Marx is here corrected and expanded beyond the toleration of any dogmatic Marxian ideologist, but the problems to which he pointed and many of his concepts remain. Industrial society with its classes, conflicts, and frustrations is still after all fundamental to Western civilization. Despite what was said about the apparent poverty of "new Left" movements, this quest for fresh formulations will go on, making judicious use of old materials. The crisis consists in the decadence of nineteenth-century social ideologies which were apocalyptic religions, essentially Romantic faiths embracing historicism, messianic expectations, total solutions, and total explanations. These myths have been seen through, and have proved disastrous failures. The task consists in harnessing social reform to a different vehicle. Can it be a neutral science, or is this a sterile notion?

Foreign policy is another area beset by myths and goblins, never really reduced to a rational science, and in grave need of much high-level conceptualization that must involve historian and political scientist.[24] The public mind must then be educated to accept more sophisticated views and analyses. This involves a better journalism and a more highly educated public. The whole vast undertaking of making democracy work by adjusting a complex, mass society to the individual's understanding looms before us. The old Matthew Arnold-Alexis de Tocqueville questions still

[24] See among other works Roland N. Stromberg, *Collective Security and American Foreign Policy*, 1963, a study in mythology and reality in the realm of foreign policy.

demand an answer: can democracy be intelligent, produce a higher culture, and solve its problems effectively?

The crisis of literature is the need to socialize the rebellious artist, the lonely individual and defier of conventions, alienated from society. A recent perceptive study of American literature bears the title *After Alienation*. Must the creative writer always stand in opposition to the crowd? If so, need he stand quite so far away? And *after* alienation, *after* estheticism, what indeed? The desperation of recent bohemian gestures, referred to above, suggests that this can hardly go on. The Baudelaire-Rimbaud effect was grand, but it cannot forever be repeated. The future of literature, like the future of religion, is an open and an urgent question.

It is wrapped up with the broader question of the future of culture itself. Quite a few European historians and intellectuals in the past century have evoked the picture of the traditional European culture, rooted in the classics and carried by a literate elite, being borne under by a tide of mass-men which has increasingly thinned and degraded the great traditions. It is a familiar picture, and from Kierkegaard and Nietzsche to Jaspers and Ortega y Gasset it has inspired poignant lament. Its implication that what has ruined modern man is democracy repels the socialist left; and insofar as it blames the decline on machinery and industrialization, it is obviously a vain lament. But the concern to preserve culture—conceived of broadly as a power of serious, sustained thinking within a context of accepted knowledge—against the modern barbarism of "mass media" and on the other hand overspecialization, must be the enduring mission of those whom Mr. Henry Mencken liked to call the "civilized minority"—the clerks, the intellectuals, the teachers, writers, and readers. On the one hand lie the comic book, the tabloid newspapers, advertising, paperback sex, the average television program, opening up horizons of mental degeneracy never before known, not even by primitive man who had more dignity and content in his myths than this. These things represent a negation of all the high ideals of life in favor of a kind of least common denominator of the consciousness; they reflect the condition of people cut off from contact with any accepted and orderly body of expression and learning.

On the other hand is a vision of mountain ranges, reaching back through the centuries, of the poets, philosophers, and Great Thinkers, ultimately back in the far distance to Plato, Aristotle, and Homer; nearer lie high peaks called Shakespeare, Milton, Montaigne, Rousseau, and an incredible number of other hills. It has now become too formidable a terrain to be entered for most people; perhaps it always was. But it constitutes the West's spiritual home. Today the citizens of this mighty realm live in mud huts on the plain nearby, fearing to enter the magic land that was their home. They seem to have lost the map.

EPILOGUE

Madame Sevigné, celebrated seventeenth-century wit, once remarked that Cartesianism, like coffee, would prove a temporary fashion. She was wrong (doubly!). There have been temporary fashions often enough in the world of ideas, now largely forgotten; but even the most obscure left some stamp on the human race, and Madame Sevigné's ghastly error reminds us that some leave a very heavy impress indeed. They shape our civilization, it is not too much to say. At least they shape the way we conceive and describe it, which comes to very nearly the same thing. We can hardly escape them.

Taking stock of Western civilization after World War II, Georges Bernanos opined that its future would have to be Cartesian or Hegelian (perhaps, as E. Morot-Sir has rejoined, it must manage to combine the two). Others, like Sartre, declare that we cannot escape coming to terms with Marxism, the "unsurpassable" ideological statement for our age. Still others would suggest that it is the Enlightenment, especially as summed up by Rousseau, that must be digested or thoroughly regurgitated, the central problem of our civilization.

Without pausing to examine or explain such statements, we can surely see roughly what they mean and in what sense they are valid. Ideas sum up epochs, generalize whole realms of individual human experience. "Cartesianism" is shorthand for the challenge of technological power and a scientific culture; Hegelianism for nationalism and secular messianism; Marxism for the problem of creativity in an industrial age, etc. Ideas, the ones that survive, have their roots in social reality and express urgent human needs. They enable us to think about these needs and so to begin to meet them. As an aid to such thinking, they need to be studied with the utmost care, and by more people; for as John Locke said, "in truth the ideas and images in men's minds are the invisible powers that constantly govern them."

This is the realm of what Father Teilhard de Chardin has named the "noösphere," the realm of the mind and all its products. Here, as Julian Huxley has written, man finds "floating in this noösphere . . . for his taking, the daring speculations and aspiring ideals of men long dead, the organized knowledge of science, the hoary wisdom of the ancients, the creative imaginings of all the world's poets and artists"— all this and much more too. The organization of the noösphere, as both these great modern biologists suggest, is the great task of the future and one which has scarcely yet begun. Huxley has noted how much of the vast amount of knowledge presently being accumulated, in the various special branches of learning, is "lying around unused" because "not integrated into fruitful concepts and principles, not brought into relevance to human life and its problems" (*The Humanist Frame*, 1961).

If the most urgent task confronting man is the organization of his ideas so that they may be creatively used, and if these ideas indeed are "the invisible powers that govern men," then the systematic study of ideas, in relation to life, that is, the social and historical context, would seem to be not the least important of the many studies currently pursued. A great deal of work remains to be done.

Suggested Reading

GENERAL WORKS

John H. Randall, Jr., *The Career of Philosophy*, Vol. 2 (1965) deals with the nineteenth century; as a history of philosophy with broader cultural perspectives it may be supplemented by Vol. 7 of *Frederick Copleston, A History of Philosophy* (1963). General intellectual histories include *J. Bronowski and B. Mazlish, *The Western Intellectual Tradition: Leonardo to Hegel* (1960), and W. H. Coates, H. V. White, and J. S. Schapiro, *The Emergence of Liberal Humanism* (2 vols., 1966–1967). *Crane Brinton, *The Shaping of Modern Thought* (1950) is slighter but suggestive. *Raymond Williams, *Culture and Society 1780–1950* (1958) contains stimulating essays on writers in relation to their times. *W. Warren Wagar (ed.), *European Intellectual History since Darwin and Marx* (1966) consists of essays on various subjects by a number of scholars. *Albert Salomon, *In Praise of Enlightenment: Essays in the History of Ideas* (1963), contains essays written over many years by a leading student of ideas. *Gerhard Masur, *Prophets of Yesterday* (1966) chiefly concerns the 1890–1914 generation but is generally useful. *Josef L. Altholz, *The Churches in the Nineteenth Century* (1967); H. T. Overton, *Social Ideals and Economic Theories from Quesnay to Keynes* (1962); George H. Sabine, *A History of Political Theory* (3rd ed., 1961); W. P. D. Wightman, *The Growth of Scientific Ideas* (1950); and Emory S. Bogardus, *The Development of Social Thought* (4th ed., 1960), are useful works of reference in their respective fields. So, too, are the following: *Arnold Hauser, *Social History of Art* (Vol. II, 1951); *G. P. Gooch, *History and Historians in the Nineteenth Century* (2nd ed., 1952); *The Pelican History of Music*, edited by Alec Robertson and Denis Stevens (1962); the several volumes of *The Pelican Guide to English Literature*, edited by Boris Ford (Vols. 5, 6, 7); Rene Wellek, *A History of Modern Criticism* (to be completed in 4 vols., 1955 ——); William Boyd, *The History of Western Education* (7th ed., 1964); *Nikolaus Pevsner, *An Outline of European Architecture* (5th ed., 1957).

The historical background can be found in Vols. 9–12 of the *New Cam-*

* Starred books available in paperback edition.

bridge Modern History, but less forbidding general histories, stressing social and cultural processes, include, for the pre-1848 period, °J. L. Talmon, *Romanticism and Revolt: Europe 1815–1848* (1967) and °E. J. Hobsbawm, *The Age of Revolution 1789–1848* (1962); for later periods as well, Gordon Wright, *France in Modern Times* (1960); George L. Mosse, *The Culture of Western Europe* (1961). An excellent all-around textbook is Gordon A. Craig, *Europe since 1815* (2nd ed., 1966).

An excellent selection of source readings is Franklin Le Van Baumer, *Main Currents of Western Thought* (rev. ed., 1964), of which Part III is most relevant here. So too is Eugene Black's *Posture of Europe, 1814–1940* (1964), which stresses social and political thought; °Eugen Weber's *Paths to the Present* (1962) will be found useful for literary and artistic movements, as also will °Elizabeth G. Holt (ed.), *From the Classicists to the Impressionists* (1966). The two nineteenth century volumes in *The Pelican Book of English Prose,* general editor Kenneth Allott, are worth recommending as a convenient place to find a picture of the age as mirrored in its writing. See also °Roland Stromberg (ed.), *Realism, Naturalism, Symbolism,* 1848–1914 (1968), one of a multi-volume documentary series.

CHAPTER 1

°Church, *Influence of the Enlightenment on the French Revolution* and °Talmon, *Origins of Totalitarian Democracy* (1960), provide insights into the ideology of the French Revolution; see also Renée Waldinger, *Voltaire and Reform in the Light of the French Revolution* (1959). Jacques Godechot, *La Pensée Revolutionaire en France et en Europe 1780–1799* (1964) and *Le Contre-revolution 1789–1804* (1961) are by the outstanding French historian of the Revolution today; in English, one can consult such authorities as Crane Brinton, *The Jacobins* (1930); and Paul H. Beik, *The French Revolution Seen from the Right* (1956). Elizabeth Eisenstein, *The First Professional Revolutionary: Buonarroti* (1959) brings out the Revolution's socialist Left, on which the classic study was probably Jean Jaurès' old *Histoire Socialiste de la Revolution* (1901–1904). °Burke's *Reflections on the Revolution in France* and °Tom Paine's *Rights of Man* are often reprinted; see also °A. Cobban (ed.), *The Debate on the French Revolution* (1949) and Ronald W. Harris, *Political Ideas 1760–1792* (1963). The large and growing literature on Burke includes biographies by Philip Magnus, *Edmund Burke: A Life* (1939) and Carl B. Cone, *Burke and the Nature of Politics* (2 vols., 1957–1963); Charles Parkin, *The Moral Basis of Burke's Political Thought* (1956); Francis Canavan, *The Political Reason of Edmund Burke* (1959); other studies by Peter Stanlis and Ross J. S. Hoffman. Stanlis has edited some essays by American Burke scholars under the title *The Relevance of Edmund Burke* (1964); Hoffman with Paul Levack edited *Burke's Politics* (1949). Burke's *Correspondence* is being edited and published at the University of Chicago under the direction of Thomas W. Copeland and others.

Another interesting book is Bernard N. Schilling, *Conservative England and the Case against Voltaire 1789–1800* (1950). °Christopher Herold (ed.), *The Mind of Napoleon* (1955) reveals the revolutionary emperor's often fascinating thought processes; a recent study of considerable interest is F. C. Healey, *Rousseau et Napoleon* (1957). Herold has also authored an engaging biography of Mme. de Staël, *Mistress to an Age* (1958). Equally delightful is the old H. N. Brailsford classic, *Shelley, Godwin and Their Circle* (1913, often repr.). There is an exploration of *William Godwin and His World* by Rosalie Grylls (1953).

Kant's philosophy may be approached through °Volume 6 of Copleston's *History of Philosophy* (1960); Volume 7 (1963) is from Fichte to Nietzsche. °H. D. Aiken (ed.), *The Age of Ideology* (Mentor series Vol. 4, 1956) contains a brief introduction with selections from Kant. *The Critique of Pure Reason, The Critique of Practical Reason, Religion within the Limits of Reason Alone,* and others of Kant's writings are available in recent paperback reprints. °Lewis W. Beck, *Commentary on Kant's Critique of Practical Reason* (1960) and °Norman Kemp Smith, *Kant's Critique of Pure Reason* (2nd ed., 1962) are expert guides. Richard Kroner, *Kant's Weltanschauung* (1956) sees the philosopher in a broader framework; Leonard Krieger, *The German Idea of Freedom* (1957) finds the political influence of Kant less liberal than usually indicated. A symposium, *The Heritage of Kant,* edited by G. T. Whitney and D. F. Bowers (1962), can be recommended for the philosophically sophisticated. The outstanding work on Fichte for the intellectual historian is in French: Xavier Leon, *Fichte et Son Temps* (3 vols., 1922–1924, 1958). °Fichte's *Addresses to the German Nation* have often been reprinted. Light on the setting of German thought in this great age comes from J. H. Bruford, *Culture and Society in Classical Weimar, 1775–1806* (1962) and Henri Brunschwig, *Le Crise de l'Etat Prussien á la Fin du 18e Siècle et le Genèse de la Mentalité Romantique* (1947). Among other German worthies of the grand epoch, Herder found an outstanding American student in Robert T. Clark, *Herder, His Life and Thought* (1955) as well as in A. Gillies, *Herder* (1945) and more recently F. M. Barnard, *Herder's Social and Political Thought* (1965). René Wellek, *Kant in England* (1931) and John H. Muirhead, *Coleridge as Philosopher* (1938) reveal the effect of the German philosophy on the English; for France, see George Boas, *French Philosophy of the Romantic Period* (1925).

Jacques Barzun in *Romanticism and the Modern Ego* (1944) (paperback edition titled *Classic, Romantic, and Modern*) provides a broadly cultural and historical introduction to the subject of Romanticism. Northrop Frye (ed.), *Romanticism Reconsidered* (1963) contains essays in definition and reevaluation of which the one by René Wellek is a particularly useful survey of recent writings on the subject. Lovejoy's celebrated essay is reprinted in his °*Essays in the History of Ideas* (1948), but compare his treatment in *The Great Chain of Being,* pp. 228–314. Meyer H. Abrams, *The Mirror and the Lamp* (1953) is a perceptive literary study, as is also (despite some eccentricities) G. Wilson Knight's *The Starlit Dome* (1959). These, along with Frank Kermode, *The Romantic Image* (1957), may be singled out from a vast amount of work in literary criticism or exegesis, to which, as usual, the *Pelican Guide* (Vol. 5, *From Blake to Byron*) is a good guide, in English literature. °Graham Hough, *The Romantic Poets* (1953) is a thoughtful summation by one of today's outstanding British critics. °Maurice Bowra, *The Romantic Imagination* (1961) and °Walter J. Bate, *From Classic to Romantic* (1946) are worth inclusion on any list on the Romantic movement for the general reader. The endless number of more specialized studies include such regional examinations as E. Allison Peers, *A History of the Romantic Movement in Spain* (1940) and Roger Duhamel, *Aux Sources du Romantisme Français* (1964). Max Dufner (ed.), *Romantics: Kleist, Novalis, Tieck, Schlegel* (1964) reprints some of the works of the Germans. Kathleen Coburn (ed.), *Inquiring Spirit* (1951) is a carefully selected and arranged introduction to the thought and expression of Samuel Taylor Coleridge, most philosophical of the English Romantic poets; compare °E. D. Hirsch, Jr., *Wordsworth and Schelling* (1960). J. D. Boulger, *Coleridge as Religious Thinker* (1961) and Richard B. Brandt, *The Philosophy of Schleiermacher* (1945) suggest the relationship between religion and Romanticism. See also Raymond Schwab, *La Renaissance Orientale* (1950). On political aspects, see Crane Brinton, *Political Thought of the English Romantics* (1926); John Colmer, *Coleridge, Critic of Society* (1959); R. Aris, *History of Political Thought in Germany from 1789 to 1815* (repr. 1965); H. S. Reiss (ed.), *Political Thought of the German Romantics 1793–1815* (1956); and R. J. White (ed.), *Political Tracts of Wordsworth, Coleridge, and Shelley* (1953). André Maurois, *Chateaubriand* (1958) is a dazzling portrait of one of the greatest of Romantic personalities, the same popular biographer having also limned George Sand and Alexander Dumas. Chateaubriand's *Memoirs* (*Memoirs d'Outre-tombe*) were edited in 1961 by Robert Baldick. Walter Friedlaender, *David to Delacroix* (1952) deals with Romantic painting with attention to the social background. There are, finally, Howard Hugo (ed.), *The Portable Romantic Reader* (1957), and in the Heath *Problems* series, John B. Halsted (ed.), °*Romanticism: Definition, Explanation, and Evaluation* (1965).

CHAPTER 2

Studies of Burke and Coleridge, already cited, are applicable to the conservative ideology; general surveys, somewhat useful, are °Russell Kirk, *The Conservative Mind: Burke to Santayana* (1953) and Réne Rémond, *The Right Wing in France from 1815 to DeGaulle* (English tr. 1965), as well as a recent compilation edited by Hans Rogger and Eugen Weber, *The European Right* (1965). E. L. Woodward, *Three Studies in European Conservatism* (repr. 1963), and Douglas Johnson, *Guizot* (1963), are closer looks at conservative statesmen. Works on Bonald, Maistre, and Savigny are surprisingly few in English, but recently Jack Lively has selected from *The Works of Joseph De-Maistre* (1965), supplying a long introduction. John Morley's essay in his *Biographical Studies* (1923) remains useful on "The Champion of Social Reaction." See also Elisha Greifer's article on Maistre in *American Political Science Review* (September, 1961). °John Stuart Mill's essay *On Bentham and Coleridge* has been reprinted with an introduction by F. R. Leavis (1950).

Leslie Stephen, *The English Utilitarians* (repr. 1950) still may be the best, though °E. Halévy, *The Growth of Philosophical Radicalism* (repr. 1955) is more prolix, and there is a recent major work on Bentham by Mary P. Mack, the first volume of which, *Jeremy Bentham: An Odyssey of Ideas* (1962) carries the founder of the Utilitarian school down to 1792. Many of Bentham's writings have been reprinted in popular editions, for example, Harold A. Larrabee (ed.), *The Handbook of Political Fallacies* (1962). Graham Wallas' classic biography of *Francis Place* (1919) affords insight into Radicals in action. John L. Clive, *Scotch Reviewers: The Edinburgh Review 1802–1815* (1957) provides a picture of the Radical intelligentsia, and incidentally carries on the study of "the Scottish inquiry." William C. Havard, *Henry Sidgwick and Later Utilitarian Philosophy* (1959) carries on the story of the Benthamite tradition in thought, while an interesting sidelight is Eric T. Stokes, *The English Utilitarians and India* (1959). On the Political Economists, in addition to histories of economic thought previously cited, see °Marc Blaug, *Ricardian Economics* (1958); Kenneth Smith, *The Malthusian Controversy* (1951); Lionel Robbins, *Robert Torrens and the Evolution of Classical Economics* (1958); and, in view of its modern importance, John Maynard Keynes' essay on Malthus (among other economists) in *Essays in Biography* (1951). The advanced student of Economics might explore the acute contemporary criticism of Utilitarian assumptions offered by I. M. D. Little in °*A Critique of Welfare Economics* (1956). The rejoinder of one who then rejected "the dismal science" is presented in W. F. Kennedy, *Humanist versus Economist: The Economic Thought of Samuel Taylor Coleridge* (1958).

Jack Lively, *The Social and Political Thought of Alexis de Tocqueville* (1962) authoritatively considers the ideas of one of the great nineteenth-century liberals. On liberalism generally, see °L. T. Hobhouse, *Liberalism* (1934); Harry K. Girvetz, *From Wealth to Welfare: The Evolution of Liberalism* (1950); G. de Ruggiero, *History of European Liberalism* (English transl. 1959); and Harold J. Laski, *The Rise of Liberalism* (1936), a Marxist interpretation. The French liberal *Prévost-Paradol* (1955) has been treated by Pierre Guiral. Richard H. Thomas, *Liberalism, Nationalism, and the German Intellectuals 1822–1847* (1951) is more restricted than the title suggests but offers revealing insights into some German circles.

G. D. H. Cole's multivolume *History of Socialist Thought* begins with a volume on *The Forerunners* (1953). Another comprehensive history is Carl Landauer, *European Socialism* (2 vols., 1960). More critical of all the manufacturers of utopias, J. L. Talmon's *Political Messianism: The Romantic Phase* (1960) covers them capably. The first three volumes of M. Leroy's monumental *Histoire des Idées Sociales en France* (Volume 3 was published in 1954, covering the 1848–1871 period) are a mine of information. Books on individual socialists include °Frank E. Manuel, *The New World of Henri Saint-Simon* (1956), by an outstanding American intellectual historian; G. G. Iggers, *The Cult of Authority: Political Philosophy of the Saint-Simonians* (1958); Leo A. Loubère, *Louis Blanc* (1961), the life of a participant in politics as well as a framer of social ideas, one of the great nineteenth-century democratic socialists; and Henri Lubac, *The Un-Marxian Socialist: Proudhon* (1948), a more thorough study than the summary by °J. Hampden Jackson in *Marx, Proudhon, and European Socialism* (1957). See also Alan B. Spitzer, *The Revolutionary Theories of Blanqui* (1957). Among those who have written about Robert Owen, the Scottish socialist, are Margaret Cole, *Robert Owen of New Lanark* (1953) and Rowland H. Harvey, *Robert Owen, Social Idealist* (1949). °Crane Brinton, *English Political Thought in the Nineteenth Century* (1949) includes the British socialists and liberals. E. H. Carr, *Bakunin* (1937) is a life of the great Anarchist; Eugene Lampert in *Studies in Rebellion* (1957) offers sympathetic portraits of the Russians, Bakunin, Herzen, and Belinsky. Herzen has recently been treated by °Martin Malia, *Alexander Herzen and the Birth of Russian Socialism* (1961). (For additional references on the socialists see under next chapter.)

On Hegel, see Copleston's seventh volume (1963); J. N. Findlay, *Hegel, A Re-examination* (1957), which may be compared with the hostile °Karl Popper, *The Open Society and Its Enemies: Hegel and Marx*, Vol. 2 (4th ed., 1962); °Herbert Marcuse, *Reason and Revolution: Hegel and the Rise of Social Theory* (1941), very much to be recommended; and F. Engel-Jánosi, *The Growth of German Historicism* (1944). The German historical school is also closely considered in chapters of °Herbert Butterfield, *Man on His Past* (1955). Hegel's own writings are readily available in selections such as °*Reason in History.*

D. O. Evans, *Social Romanticism in France 1830–1848* (1951) is a valuable little book; wider in range is the work of °E. J. Hobsbawn, *The Age of Revolution 1789–1848* (1962). Jean Lhomme's *La Grande Bourgeoisie au Pouvoir* (1960) is, for those who can read French, a work of originality and deep insight into the class that dominated this era. One of the leading prophets of the 1848 period is well handled by G. Salvemini, *Mazzini* (1957). °Lewis Namier, one of the greatest of modern historians in Great Britain, wrote a stimulating appraisal of *1848: The Revolution of the Intellectuals* (1948).

CHAPTER 3

On the Victorian era generally, °Walter E. Houghton, *The Victorian Frame of Mind* (1957) rounds up a good deal of the age's thought and °Asa Briggs, *Victorian People* (1955) has considerable interest for the intellectual historian; °*Those Earnest Victorians* (1935) by Esmé Wingfield-Stratford is slighter but a pleasurable introduction, while G. M. Young, *Victorian England: Portrait of an Age* (1936) is becoming a classic. °*Victorian Prose*, edited by Kenneth Allott, is Volume 5 of *The Pelican Book of English Prose* (1956). The crowded and brilliant Victorian intellectual scene can only partially be reflected in the following outstanding books: Mario Praz, *The Hero in Eclipse* (1956), a study of the Victorian novelists; Owen Chadwick, *The Mind of the Oxford Movement* (1960) and °Geoffrey Faber, *The Oxford Apostles* (1936); Benjamin Lippincott, *Victorian Critics of Democracy* (repr. 1964). *Walter Bagehot* (1959) has been edited by Norman St. John Stevas and described by Alastair Buchan, *The Spare Chancellor* (1960); his °*The English Constitution* (1867) is available. Lionel Trilling, *Matthew Arnold* (1949) is perhaps the outstanding book on another eminent Victorian; a useful selection of Arnold's poetry and prose has been edited by John Bryson for the Reynard Library (Rupert Hart-Davis, 1954), which also has a Macaulay edited by G. M.

Young. Recent Ruskin anthologizing reflects the tremendous interest in this formerly underrated Victorian; there are volumes selected by Joan Evans, *The Lamp of Beauty* (1959), John D. Rosenberg, *The Genius of John Ruskin: Selections from His Writings* (1963), and Kenneth Clark, *Ruskin Today* (1964). Rosenberg has written one of the best books about Ruskin, *The Darkening Glass* (1961). G. M. Trevelyan, the famous historian, edited a one-volume *Thomas Carlyle* (1954). On Victorian literature, *The Pelican Guide*, Volume 6, is *Dickens to Hardy*. The mid-Victorian feast can be reluctantly brought to a close by noting two recent studies of historians, Giles St. Aubyn of Henry Thomas Buckle—*Victorian Eminence* (1958)— and W. H. Dunn of *James Anthony Froude* (2 vols., 1961–1964).

John Stuart Mill best introduces himself in the famous and oft-reprinted *°Autobiography*, but a superb modern biography is that by Michael St. John Packe, *Life of John Stuart Mill* (1954). Karl Britton writes on Mill in the Penguin series (1953); a recent and rather controversial interpretation is Maurice Cowling, *Mill and Liberalism* (1963). Two valuable studies are R. K. P. Pankhurst, *The Saint-Simonians: Mill and Carlyle* (1957) and Iris W. Mueller, *John Stuart Mill and French Thought* (1956). A good selection from Mill's political writings was made by editor Bernard Wishy under the title *°Prefaces to Liberty* (1959). The complete works are being edited and published at the University of Toronto, ultimately to reach some 20 volumes.

Mill himself wrote on *°August Comte and Positivism*, an essay recently (1961) reprinted. Among recent scholars, D. G. Charlton, *Positivist Thought in France 1852–1870* (1959) deals with the second generation Positivists in the heyday of the creed; Walter M. Simon, *European Positivism in the Nineteenth Century* (1963), a major work of scholarship, ranges far and deep in the Positivist vein. One of the few studies of Ernest Renan in English is R. M. Chadbourne, *Ernest Renan as Essayist* (1957). Basil Willey, *More Nineteenth Century Studies: A Group of Honest Doubters* (1957) detects the influence of Comte but it was much overshadowed in England by that of Darwin. On the latter there is of course a large literature, including the very scholarly *Forerunners of Darwin* (1959), edited by Bentley Glass; Milton Millhauser, *Just before Darwin: Robert Chambers and His "Vestiges"* (1959); *°G. G. Gillispie, Genesis and Geology* (1951); *°Loren Eiseley, Darwin's Century* (1958); *°Gertrude Himmelfarb, Darwin and the Darwinian Revolution* (1959), an extremely useful and attractive summary of the impact on ideas; and *°W. Irvine, Apes, Angels, and Victorians* (1955). Alvar Ellegard has carefully studied the reception of Darwin's theory in the British press 1859–1872 in his *Darwin and the General Reader* (1958). In addition to various editions of *°The Origin of Species*, of great interest is Darwin's *Autobiography* which must be read in the 1958 edition, edited by Nora Barlow, the first complete one published. (See article by Maurice Mandelbaum, "Darwin's Religious Views," *Journal of the History of Ideas*, June, 1958.) For the influence of Darwin, see J. Herman Randall, Jr., "The Impact of Darwin on Philosophy," *Journal of the History of Ideas* (October, 1961); Walter J. Ong (ed.), *Darwin's Vision and Christian Perspectives* (1960); Basil Willey, *Darwin and Butler* (1960); L. J. Henkin, *Darwinism and the English Novel 1860–1910* (repr. 1963); and especially John Dewey, *The Influence of Darwin on Philosophy* (1960) and *Reconstruction in Philosophy* (1937).

*Talcott Parsons (ed.), *Spencer's Study of Sociology* (1961) may be used as an entrance to the thought of this Victorian oracle, who needs more study than he has received in recent years. Cyril Bibby, *T. H. Huxley: Scientist, Humanist, Educator* (1959), deals sympathetically with "Darwin's bulldog."

CHAPTER 4

* T. B. Bottomore (ed.), *Early Writings of Karl Marx* (1963); *Bottomore and M. Rubel (ed.), *Karl Marx: Selected Writings in Sociology and Social Philosophy* (1956); and *Robert Freedman (ed.), *Marx on Economics* (1961) make up a good selection of basic texts. *H. B. Mayo, *Introduction to Marxist Theory* (1960) supplies a systematic critique, as does H. B. Acton, *The Illusion of the Epoch* (1954) on basic philosophy and also Gustav A. Wetter, *Dialectical Materialism* (1958) and *Karl Popper, *The Open Society*, II. (Popper is less severe on Marx than on Hegel.) More sympathetic are *R. G. Tucker, *Philosophy and Myth in Karl Marx* (1961) and *G. D. H. Cole, *The Meaning of Marxism* (1950). One can profitably add to a shelf on Marxism the following: *George Lichtheim, *Marxism: An Historical and Critical Study* (1961); A. Cornu, *The Origins of Marxian Thought* (1957); *M. M. Bober, *Karl Marx's Interpretation of History* (2nd ed., 1948); *R. N. Carew Hunt, *Marxism Past and Present* (1954); and the essentially biographical studies of Marx by *Franz Mehring, *Karl Marx* (1948); *E. H. Carr, *Karl Marx, a Study in Fanaticism* (1935); and *Isaiah Berlin, *Karl Marx, His Life and Environment* (3rd ed., 1963). Gustav Mayer has written the best life of Friedrich Engels (1935). About the "Young Hegelians" who paralleled Marx, see Isaiah Berlin, *Life and Opinions of Moses Hadas* (1960) and *Sidney Hook, *From Hegel to Marx* (1950). *Ludwig Feuerbach's *The Essence of Christianity* has been recently reprinted.

While some later versions of Marxism are discussed in portions of the next chapter, we may conveniently mention here books on some disciples and followers of Marx: *Peter Gay, *The Dilemma of Democratic Socialism: Bernstein's Challenge to Marx* (1952) and *Eduard Bernstein, *Evolutionary Socialism* (1909) present the most important "revisionist" among the German Socialists; Samuel H. Baron, *Plekhanov: The Father of Russian Marxism* (1963) and *A. G. Meyer, *Leninism* (1957), a most perceptive essay, introduce the Russian school, to which one might add Donald W. Treadgold, *Lenin and His Rivals 1889–1906* (1955). Harvey Goldberg's recent life of *Jean Jaurès* (1962) and Aaron Noland, *The Founding of the French Socialist Party 1893–1905* (1956) are among the best books on the French socialists. R. Hostetter, *The Italian Socialist Movement 1860–1882* (1960) is to be followed by another volume. G. D. H. Cole's two volumes on *The Second International* in his *History of Socialist Thought* (1956) are good. David Footman has written a life of Ferdinand Lassalle, Marx's early rival within German Socialism under the title *Ferdinand Lassalle, Romantic Revolutionary* (1947).

On other than Marxian socialism: A. M. MacBriar, *Fabian Socialism and English Politics 1884—1914* (1962) is the latest and best work on its subject, but can be supplemented by Margaret Cole, *Story of Fabian Socialism* (1961); the Beatrice Webb *Diaries* (Vol. I, 1952); and the reprinted *Fabian Essays* of 1887, the manifesto of the movement. S. Maccoby, *English Radicalism, 1886–1914* (1955) deals with left-wing liberals in the British Isles. T. H. Green has recently found a biographer in Melvin Richter, under the title *The Politics of Conscience* (1963). Daniel Roberts, *Victorian Origins of the Welfare State* (1960) and Herman Ausubel, *In Hard Times: Reformers among the Late Victorians* (1960) are among a plethora of books in this area. A. R. Vidler, *A Century of Social Catholicism 1820–1920* (1964) and Josef L. Altholz, *The Liberal Catholic Movement in England 1848–1864* (1960) are among recent works on this subject in English; there is a considerable library in French, including a lengthy survey by Emmanuel Barbier, *Histoire du Catholicisme Liberal et du Catholicisme Social en France 1870–1914* (5 vols., 1924). Charles A. Barker's excellent study of *Henry George* (1956) and L. W. Eshleman, *A Victorian Rebel: The Life of William Morris* (1940) present two diverse but equally important figures in late nineteenth-century socialism. *George Woodcock, biographer of Proudhon, has a book on *Anarchism* (1962), as does James Joll, *The Anarchists* (1964). A brilliant work of intellectual history, Franco Venturi's *Roots of Revolution* (1960) explores the Russian populist movement, on which see also James H. Billington, *Mikhailovsky and Russian Populism* (1958).

To put Marx in the perspective of other nineteenth-century "historicisms," see again Butterfield's *Man on His Past;* Engel-Jánosi, *Rise of German Historicism;* and in addition *G. P. Gooch, *History and Historians in the Nineteenth Century* (1935) and Friedrich Meinecke, *Die Enstehung des Historismus* (Munich, 1936). On specific historians, Gertrude Himmelfarb, *Lord Acton* (1952); Theodore von Laue, *Ranke: The Formative Years* (1950).

CHAPTER 5

Students of nineteenth-century nationalism include *Hans Kohn, *The Idea of Nationalism* (1944), *Pan-Slavism* (1953), and other works; Carlton J. H. Hayes, *The Historical Evolution of Modern Nationalism* (1931) and others including *Nationalism: A Religion* (1960); and Elie Kedourie, *Nationalism* (1960). Among more specialized works are M. B. Petrovich, *The Emergence of Russian Pan-Slavism 1856–1870* (1956); Frank Fadner, *Seventy Years of Pan-Slavism in Russia* (1962); and Eugen Weber, *The Nationalist Revival in France 1905–1914* (1959). Weber has also written on the *Action Française* (1962), while Robert Byrnes in *Anti-Semitism in Modern France* (1950) presents the anti-Dreyfusards. A. P. Thornton, *The Imperial Idea and Its Enemies* (1959) is a brilliant book by a leading student of British imperialism. Mildred Wertheimer (1924) and, in German, Alfred Kruck (1954) have examined *The Pan-German League (Alldeutscher Verband)* (see also under National Socialism, next chapter). Salo W. Baron's *Modern Nationalism and Religion* (1947) was a stimulating group of lectures by a notable contemporary scholar. The interesting *Diaries* (1958) of Theodore Herzl throw light on the mind of the founder of modern Jewish nationalism. While an immense number of books touch on the subject, a work synthesizing European nationalism and nationalistic ideologies on the eve of 1914 seems to be lacking.

On Nietzsche see °Walter Kaufmann, *Nietzsche* (1956), an excellent and sympathetic study; F. C. Lea, *The Tragic Philosopher* (1957), evocative and penetrating, conceivably the best book on Nietzsche; °George A. Morgan, *What Nietzsche Means* (1943), one of the first to rescue Nietzsche from misunderstanding in the English-speaking world; William D. Williams, *Nietzsche and the French* (1952), a study in intellectual influences; A. Manthey-Zorn, *Dionysus* (1956), a sensitive appreciation. Two of the high priests of Existentialism have written formidable works on Nietzsche: Karl Jaspers, *Nietzsche: An Introduction to the Understanding of His Philosophical Activity* (English tr. 1965) and Martin Heidegger, *Nietzsche* (1961). Kaufmann edits *The Portable Nietzsche* (1954), a good selection from the often reprinted writings. Again one may consult Copleston, Volume 7. The acute eccentric who influenced Nietzsche and so many others is introduced by °Patrick Gardiner in the Penguin series—*Schopenhauer*.

°L. L. Whyte, *The Unconscious before Freud* (1960) is a splendid work of scholarship. The vast literature on the founder of psychoanalysis must begin with Ernest Jones' 3-volume *Life and Work of Sigmund Freud* (1953–1955), abridged in paperback edition (1956). Otherwise, a generally stimulating and high-quality symposium is °Benjamin Nelson (ed), *Freud and the Twentieth Century* (1957); °J. A. C. Brown, *Freud and the Post-Freudians* (1961) is one of the best books; Frederick J. Hoffman, *Freudianism and the Literary Mind* (1957) is a distinguished essay. The writings of Freud himself are the best source, including in paperback editions °*On Dreams,* °*Ego and Id,* °*The Future of an Illusion,* °*Civilization and Its Discontents,* and others. For Carl Jung, °Frieda Fordham, *Introduction to Jung's Psychology* (1956); °Joland Jacobi, *The Psychology of C. G. Jung* (1942); Avis M. Dry, *The Psychology of Jung* (1961); and the many writings of Jung himself, which are being published in an edition of his collected works (18 volumes when complete). A general history is °Walter Bromberg, *The Mind of Man: A History of Psychotherapy and Psychoanalysis* (1963).

°Ian W. Alexander, *Bergson* (1957), one of the Bowes and Bowes series of *Studies in Modern European Literature and Thought,* is a concise introduction. Ben Ami Scharfstein, *The Roots of Bergson's Philosophy* (1943) finds many anticipations. Thomas Hanna (ed.), *The Bergsonian Heritage* (1962) is a recent reappraisal. A helpful short Bergson readings book is H. A. Larrabee (ed.), *Selections from Bergson* (1947).

The impact of the new physics can be discerned through the writings of the chief innovators themselves, for example, Max Planck, *The New Science* (1959), and Albert Einstein, *The Meaning of Relativity* (5th ed., 1955), or °*Relativity* (1924). Successful in making the new concepts comprehensible and significant to the public were °James Jeans, *The New Background of Science* (1934) and *Physics and Philosophy* (1942); and °Arthur Eddington, *Space, Time, and Gravitation* (1920).

°Walter Kaufmann (ed.), *Religion from Tolstoy to Camus* (1961) is a convenient anthology. Other books illustrative of religious currents at the end of the century are °Robert M. Grant, *A Short History of the Interpretation of the Bible* (1963), the Higher Criticism; Edward T. Gargan, *Leo XIII and the Modern World* (1961), the Pope whose personality wrought a change in the Roman Catholic Church; J. H. Miller, *The Disappearance of God* (1963), the theme of dying faith traced in five nineteenth-century English writers; Adrien Dansette, *The Religious History of Modern France* (2 vols., 1961); S. R. Hopper (ed.), *Lift Up Your Eyes: The Religious Writings of Leo Tolstoy* (1960), the leading Prophet of the age; and Marjorie Villiers, *Charles Péguy, A Study in Integrity* (1965), an introduction to the many-sided writer whose outstanding characteristic was perhaps the expression of a new religious consciousness. Donald Attwater, *Modern Christian Revolutionaries* (1947) is interesting.

The enormous and revolutionary activity in literature and the arts can be partly apprehended through the following works: °Eugen Weber (ed.), *Paths to the Present* (1962), an anthology featuring literary movements; °Enid Starkie, *From Gautier to Eliot* (1960, 1962), concerned with the French influence on British literature and shedding light on both; °Arthur Symons, *The Symbolist Movement in Literature* (1919) and °Edmund Wilson, *Axel's Castle* (1936), classic accounts of the literary revolution of the 1880's, to which can be added °C. M. Bowra, *The Heritage of Symbolism* (1943), a thoughtful commentary; °Mario Praz, *The Romantic Agony* (2nd ed., 1954), a work of fabulous erudition which looks on the Decadents with unfriendly but penetrating eyes; °Graham Hough, *The Last Romantics;* David Daiches, *The Novel in the Modern World* (1939) and *Poetry in the Modern World* (1941); °Holbrook Jackson, *The 1890's* (1913), a classic account of the Oscar Wilde-*Yellow Book* era in Britain; and, as a revelation of the social foundations of the literary revolt, C. Grana, *Bohemian versus Bourgeois: French Society and the French Man of Letters in the Nineteenth Century* (1964). J. I. M. Stewart, *Eight Modern English Writers* (1963) is Volume XII of the *Oxford History of English Literature,* and includes Hardy, Henry James, Joyce, Shaw, Lawrence, Yeats. °Ernest J. Simmons, *Leo Tolstoy* (2 vols., 1960); E. H. Carr, *Dostoyevsky* (1962); André Billy, *The Goncourt Brothers* (1960); and Martin Meisel, *Shaw and the Nineteenth Century Theater* (1963) are all outstanding but only suggestive of the large number of books on individual writers. John Rewald has a good book on the *History of Impressionism* (1961). Roger Shattuck, *The Banquet Years: The Arts in France 1858–1918* (1958) and H. M. Barzun, *Orpheus: Modern Culture and the 1913 Renaissance* (1960) are worth reading on the whole artistic scene in the prewar years. On the Ibsen affair, °Shaw, *The Quintessence of Ibsenism* (1891) has been reprinted recently. An almost classic study is N. Pevsner, *Pioneers of the Modern Design from William Morris to Walter Gropius* (1936).

Political and social thought: for the socialists, see preceding chapter. °H Stuart Hughes, *Consciousness and Society: European Social Thought 1890–1930* (1958) is generally useful. Michael Curtis, *Three against the Third Republic* (1959) ably and interestingly presents the outlook of Sorel, Maurras, and Barrès. Sorel is also the subject of a first-rate book by J. H. Meisel, *The Genesis of Georges Sorel* (1951) and one by I. L. Horowitz, *Radicalism and the Revolt against Reason* (1961). Meisel also edited and commented on Gaetano Mosca's *The Myth of the Ruling Class*, in a 1958 edition of this pre-1914 classic. That the Third Republic had at least a few intellectual defenders is indicated by J. A. Scott in *Republican Ideas and the Liberal Tradition in France 1870–1914* (1951), the chief of these being Charles Renouvier. Vilfredo Pareto's magnum opus has been translated into English as *The Mind and Society*, recently reprinted (2 vols., 1963); *From Max Weber* (1946), edited by C. Wright Mills and H. H. Garth is a fine selection from the great German sociologist, with accompanying introduction. Much light on German political attitudes is shed by Harry F. Young's excellent biography of *Maximilien Harden* (1959), a noted German editor and publicist. The Italy of Pareto, Mosca, and Croce is capably chronicled in an excellent book by A. W. Salomone, *Italian Democracy in the Making 1900–1914: Italy in the Giolittian Era* (1960), as well as in portions of a recent book by John A. Thayer, *Italy and the Great War: Politics and Culture 1870–1914* (1964). Classics of political thought from this era, reprinted in popular editions, are *Robert Michels, Political Parties* (1915) and *Graham Wallas, Human Nature in Politics* (1908). Bernard Semmel, *Imperialism and Social Reform: English Social-Reform Thought 1895–1914* (1960) discusses a significant British theme.

CHAPTER 6

Henry R. Winkler, *The League of Nations Movement in Great Britain, 1914–1919* (1952) may be singled out from a large literature on this wartime subject. An intellectual history of the 1914–1918 years is lacking, and no books on the subject will be cited here, except that such memoirs as Leonard Woolf, *Beginning Again: An Autobiography of the Years 1911–1918* (1964), one volume of several he has written about himself, will supply the basic materials for such an account. There have been anthologies of wartime literature, such as the recent *Up the Line to Death* (1965), edited by Brian Gardner, a selection of war poetry.

*H. Stuart Hughes, *Oswald Spengler: A Critical Estimate* (rev. ed., 1962) is a commentary on the author of *The Decline of the West* (repr. 1961), a most celebrated expression of war and postwar pessimism. Among Aldous Huxley's works, *Brave New World* (1932) has been reprinted along with his later comments, *Brave New World Revisited* (1958). Among other period pieces of the 1920s, *J. Ortega Y Gasset, *The Revolt of the Masses* (English ed., 1932) is a classic, while Montgomery Belgion, *Our Present Philosophy of Life* was a 1929 commentary; *The Long Weekend* (1941) by Robert Graves and Alan Hodge examined popular culture in Britain between the wars. Beatrice Webb's *Diaries*, Volume 2, 1924–1932 (1956) edited by Margaret Cole are among the more interesting sources. Another outstanding personal record may be found in the fascinating memoirs of *Arthur Koestler, *Arrow in the Blue* (1952) and *The Invisible Writing* (1954). T. S. Eliot's *The Waste Land* appeared in 1922. A solid intellectual history of the 1920s decade appears also to be lacking as yet.

Of the many works on the literary renaissance of the times, such general surveys as Germain Bree and Margaret Guiton, *An Age of Fiction: The*

French Novel from Gide to Camus (1958) and *Walter Allen, *Tradition and Dream* (Amer. ed., 1964, titled *The Modern Novel in Britain and the United States*) supply guides, and more intensive investigation can be carried on, pleasurably, in the many excellent biographical and critical studies of writers, for example, *Harry T. Moore, *The Intelligent Heart* (1954) on D. H. Lawrence; *Richard Ellman, *Yeats: The Man and the Masks* (1948); *Marvin Magalaner and Richard M. Kain, *Joyce: The Man, the Work, The Reputation* (1956); or, also on Lawrence, the perceptive essay of Graham Hough, *The Dark Sun* (1956). The most exhaustive investigation of Marcel Proust in English is being carried on by George D. Painter (2 vols. thus far, 1959, 1965). Henri Clouard, *Histoire de la Litterature Française du Symbolisme a Nos Jours*, Vol. II, 1915–1940 (1949) is a good handbook for French writing of all sorts. *Wallace Fowlie, *The Age of Surrealism* (1950) is a lively and penetrating approach to its subject, embracing the activities of poets, dramatists, painters, and novelists. *Peter Blake, *Le Corbusier* (1964), succeeds brilliantly in conveying the life, times, and art of the great modernist, in short space. The other artists in the age of Picasso and Kandinsky are too numerous to record, but Herbert Read, *Concise History of Modern Painting* (1959), effectively illustrated, is a guide which does not ignore intellectual implications. John M. Brinnin's life of Gertrude Stein, *The Third Rose* (1959) takes us into the heart of the artistic world of the 1920s.

Many of the themes introduced in the last chapter carry over into the 1920s and the same bibliography applies (Freud, Jung, Bergson, the new science). C. E. M. Joad, *Guide to Modern Thought,* first published in 1933, found modern physics, psychoanalysis, and Bergsonian vitalism among the doctrines most in need of explaining to the general public. Joad tried his hand in *Philosophical Aspects of Modern Science* (repr. 1959) at illuminating the revolution in physics; so did many others in this decade, and in addition to those previously mentioned, one might call attention to *Werner Heisenberg, *Physics and Philosophy: The Revolution in Modern Science* (1959) and *Louis de Broglie, *Physics and Microphysics* (1955), both by great scientists associated with the revolution. Karl Heim, *The Transformation of the Scientific World View* (English tr. 1953) is a remarkable essay by a German theologian.

The new political ideology, Italian Fascism, can be approached via the excellent general historical survey in Denis Mack Smith, *Italy: A Modern History* (1959). A really good account of Fascist ideology, or even of Mussolini, seems lacking in English. The only thorough study of Il Duce is Renzo de Felice, *Mussolini il Rivoluzionaria 1883–1920,* the first of a projected three volumes (1964), which among other things confirms the influence of Nietzsche. Federico Chabod's distinguished *A History of Italian Fascism* has been translated (1963) and H. S. Harris, *The Social Philosophy of Giovanni Gentile* (1960), has examined the leading philosopher of Fascism. *S. William Halperin, *Mussolini and Italian Fascism* (1965) may prove helpful. On the related ideology of German National Socialism, there is good background in *Fritz Stern, *The Politics of Cultural Despair* (1961), dealing with three representatives of an alleged "Germanic ideology" including the postwar ideologist of the Right, Moeller van den Bruck, whom he claims to be proto-Nazis. Compare K. von Klemperer, *Germany's New Conservatism* (1957). Walter Laqueur, *Young Germany* (1962) deals with the Youth Movement which the Nazis exploited. Peter Viereck, *Metapolitics: The Roots of the Nazi Mind* (rev. ed., 1961) is interesting and important but should be read critically; another recent effort to chart the intellectual origins of the Third Reich is °George L. Mosse, *The Crisis of German Ideology* (1964). The symposium sponsored by UNESCO and published under the title of *The Third Reich* (1955), to which twenty-seven German, French, American and British experts contributed, contains a number of discerning essays on the intellectual origins and affinities of the Nazi period. Hitler's own writings, of course, including °*Mein Kampf* and his speeches—see Gordon W. Prange (ed.), *Hitler's Words* (1944)—as well as *Hitler's Table Talk* (1953), and °Telford Taylor (ed.), *Hitler's Secret Book* (1961), have been widely publicized. As Alan Bullock points out, Hitler was primarily a man of ideas, crude though these ideas may have been. No really adequate intellectual history of Hitler and the Nazi Revolution seems yet to have appeared. Bullock's °*Hitler, A Study in Tyranny* (1952 and subsequent revisions) is the standard life in English, but rather lacks depth for the intellectual historian. Herman Rauschning, *The Revolution of Nihilism* (1939) remains uniquely valuable as a record of Hitler's mind, along with the same German author's *Hitler Speaks* (1939). Many books have appeared which throw light on one corner or another of the Nazi mind, among these several notable volumes recently on the Austrian background of Hitler's youth: see Andrew G. Whiteside, *Austrian National Socialism before 1918* (1962) and William A. Jenks, *Vienna and the Young Hitler* (1960), revealing Viennese anti-Semitism and pan-Germanism of the pre-1914 years as represented by such Austrians as Karl Lueger and George von Schoenerer. R. L. G. Waite, *Vanguard of Nazism* (1952), a very scholarly study of the immediate postwar years of confusion and freebooters, indicates some of the circumstances out of which Germany's sickness arose. Lewis Hertzman, *DNVP: Right-wing Opposition in the Weimar Republic 1918–1924* (1964) is a recent addition to the growing list of well-researched monographs in English. Outstanding among German scholars is Karl D. Bracher, while H. Heiber's *Adolf Hitler* has been translated (1962). Ernst Nolte, *Three Faces of Fascism* (1966), is an excellent treatment of French, Italian, and German fascism, giving full attention to the intellectual elements—the translation of a work that first appeared in Germany in 1963. Stanley G. Payne, *Falange* (1962) is a thorough analysis of Spanish Fascism, if such it was.

Julian Symons has written a lively book on *The 1930's* (1960). Neal Wood, *Communism and the British Intellectuals* (1959) and David Caute, *Communism and the French Intellectuals* (1964), supplement such popular books as °R. H. S. Crossman (ed.), *The God That Failed* (1950) and °Raymond Aron, *The Opium of the Intellectuals* (1962) on a subject that has not lacked attention, the seduction of the intellectuals by Communism. Autobiographical material such as that in Arthur Koestler's previously cited books is relevant (Koestler and Ignazio Silone wrote the best of the self-analyses in *The God That Failed*). George Orwell, in °*Collected Essays* (1954) and

Homage to Catalonia (American ed. 1952) contributed notable insights here. Such novels as Thomas Mann, *The Magic Mountain* (1930); Ignazio Silone, *Fontamara* (1934); and Arthur Koestler's *Darkness at Noon* (1941) provide deeper clues to this haunted decade than may be found in more formal history. G. D. H. Cole's Volume 5 of his *History of Socialist Thought* is *Socialism and Fascism 1931–1939* (1960). Louise E. Dalby, *Leon Blum: Evolution of a Socialist* (1963) tells the rather tragic story of an intellectual in politics caught in the murderous pattern of the pre-World War II years.

Philosophy: Logical Positivism and Linguistic Analysis can be studied in Viktor Kraft, *The Vienna Circle* (1953); J. O. Urmson, *Philosophical Analysis: Its Development between the Two World Wars* (1956); °A. J. Ayer *et. al., The Revolution in Philosophy* (1956); and °Copleston, *Contemporary Philosophy* (1956), which divides its attention between the analytical and existential schools. °I. M. Bochenski, *Contemporary European Philosophy* (1956) is also a sound and lucid guide. A. J. Ayer (ed.), *Logical Positivism* (1959) is a fairly technical recent symposium. Existentialism has given rise to a battery of books; any selection must be somewhat arbitrary. °H. J. Blackham, *Six Existentialist Thinkers* (1952), one of the first and best, though rather compressed; °Walter Kaufmann, *Existentialism from Dostoyevsky to Sartre* (1960); °William Barrett, *Irrational Man* (1958), a popular book; °Norman N. Greene, *Jean-Paul Sartre: The Existentialist Ethic* (1960) are all excellent commentaries. °Martin Heidegger's *Existence and Being* (*Sein und Zeit*, 1927), Gabriel Marcel, *The Philosophy of Existence* (1949) and other writings, and °Jean-Paul Sartre, *Being and Nothingness* (tr. 1956) are texts of the Fathers, along with the writings of Kierkegaard from which a selection has been made by Lee H. Hollander (1960). For biography, see °Walter Lowrie, *A Short Life of Kierkegaard* (1951). °David E. Roberts, *Existentialism and Religious Belief* (1963) suggests the relationship which many others have explored; for example, °John Macquarrie, *An Existentialist Theology: A Comparison of Heidegger and Bultmann* (1955). °Rudolf Bultmann, *Existence and Faith* (tr. 1960) is a collection of writings by the German scholar who has exercised so great an influence on Protestant religious thought. William J. Richardson, *Heidegger* (1965) is a valiant survey of the Existentialist in all his phases, by a Roman Catholic priest.

The neo-orthodox religious revival may be grasped through the writings of its chief practitioners, among them °Karl Barth, *Credo* (1936); °Martin Buber, *I and Thou* (1923) and *The Eclipse of God* (1952) [a convenient anthology, edited by Will Herberg, is °*The Writings of Martin Buber*, (1956)]; °Jacques Maritain, *St. Thomas Aquinas* (1946) and other writings; and °Paul Tillich, *The Dynamics of Faith* (1958). See also C. G. Jung, *Psychology and Religion* (1938); R. Hostie, *Religion and the Psychology of Jung* (1957); and °Will Herberg, *Four Existentialist Theologians* (1958). Arnold Nash (ed.), *Protestant Thought in the Twentieth Century* (1951) is a good general survey. Walter M. Horton, *Contemporary British Theology* (1936) indicates that the English reaction was milder; compare William Temple, the leading Anglican theologian.

CHAPTER 7

Europe in the shadow of catastrophe was mirrored in a library of poignant laments right after the war. [One or two of the optimistic Anglo-Saxon utterances of the war years might be mentioned; perhaps Julian Huxley, *Democracy Marches* (1941) and *On Living in a Revolution* (1944) will do.] Alfred Weber, *Abschied von der Bisherigen Geschichte* (1946) was translated as *Farewell to European History*, perhaps a trifle inaccurately. Georges Bernanos, *La Liberté pour Quoi Faire?* (1953), a series of essays on the European spirit written 1946-1947, expressed the mood of hope amid despair that is found in many Existentialist tracts. J. Ortega y Gasset, *The Modern Theme* (English tr. 1961) and Gabriel Marcel, *Man against Mass Society* (1952) are examples of the latter. Among the broader comments on the human or European situation since 1945, in addition to some previously cited under Chapter 12, the following may be singled out: Julian Huxley, *The Human Crisis* (1963); °Lionel Trilling, *Freud and the Crisis of Our Culture* (1955); and R. Guardini, *The End of the Modern World* (1957). Adrienne Koch has collected a number of significant statements from various moderns in °*Philosophy for a Time of Crisis* (1959). Richard M. Weaver, *Visions of Order: The Cultural Crisis of Our Time* (1965) is the statement of an American traditionalist.

The continuing Existentialist impulse can be followed in F. H. Heinemann, *Existentialism and the Modern Predicament* (1954); J. von Rintelen, *Beyond Existentialism* (1961); °Paul Roubiczek, *Existentialism: For and Against* (1964); H. M. Ruitenbeek (ed.), *Psychoanalysis and Existential Psychology* (1962); and Jean-Paul Sartre, *Marxisme et Existentialisme* (1962). °Pierre Thevanez, *What is Phenomenology?* (1962) and Herbert Spiegelberg *The Phenomenological Movement: An Introduction* (1960) can serve to introduce this important philosophical trend, which has given rise to an increasing number of books. The debate about Logical Positivism and Analytical philosophy also has continued: thus C. E. M. Joad, *A Critique of Logical Positivism* (1950); Barrows Dunham, *Man Against Myth* (1948); Ernest Gellner, *Words and Things* (1959); H. D. Lewis (ed.), *Clarity Is Not Enough* (1963); and D. J. B. Hawkins, *Critical Problems of Modern Philosophy* (1958), the latter from a Thomist perspective. Colin Smith, *Contemporary French Philosophy: A Study in Norms and Values* (1964) ranges widely over French thinkers by way of demonstrating that Sartre and Marcel are by no means the only ones of interest. °L. Reinisch (ed.), *Theologians of Our Time* (1964) is an exciting overview of themes already referred to under the previous chapter's bibliography (Barth, Buber, Maritain, Heidegger, Bultmann, etc.).

Several compilations of some value attempt to encompass *Political Thought since World War II* (1965)—the title of a book edited by W. J. Stankiewicz; see also T. E. Utley and J. S. Maclure (ed.), *Documents of Modern Political Thought* (1957) and for its area R. A. Butler (ed.), *The New Conservatism: An Anthology of Postwar Thought* (1964). Representative of postwar trends are Michael Oakeshott, *Rationalism in Politics* (1962), with its hostility to dogma and utopia, and Bertrand de Jouvenel, *Power: The Natural History of Its*

Growth (English trs. 1948, 1949); and more popularly, *George Orwell, 1984* (1949) and *Animal Farm* (1954), tracts against totalitarianism. Hannah Arendt, in *Origins of Modern Totalitarianism* (1958) and *Between Past and Future: Six Exercises in Political Thought* (1961), offered flashily written tracts for the times. *Leopold Labedz (ed.), *Revisionism: Essays on the History of Marxist Ideas* (1962) includes some perceptive essays on the "new Left," as does Gilles Martinet, *Le Marxisme de Notre Temps* (1962). One of the notable efforts to redefine socialism in Great Britain was Douglas Jay, *Socialism in the New Society* (1961). A somewhat uncertain trumpet call of the younger British writers was heard in the 1957 symposium titled *Declaration.* *Milovan Djilas, *The New Class* (1957), became a significant political document through the martyrdom suffered by its author, a Yugoslav revisionist Communist. Kenneth Minogue, *The Liberal Mind* (1963) is a penetrating critique of the modern "liberal" as trapped in the contradiction of statism versus individual liberty. Bibliographical help may be found in an article by Roy C. Macridis and Bernard E. Brown in *American Political Science Review* (September, 1957), "The Study of Politics in France since the Liberation: A Critical Bibliography." Stephen R. Graubard (ed.), *A New Europe?* (1964) contains a wealth of interesting material on social, cultural, and political as well as intellectual trends. Henry S. Kariel, *In Search of Authority: Twentieth Century Political Thought* (1964) discusses one significant theme.

Literature: see again Bree and Guiton, *An Age of Fiction,* Walter Allen, *Tradition and Dream,* and other works cited under Chapter 12. Richard Ell man and Charles Feidelson have recently edited an interesting collection of statements under the title *The Modern Tradition: Backgrounds of Modern Literature* (1965). *J. M. Cohen, *Poetry of This Age* (1959) is a wide-ranging collection with a fine introduction. *John Cruickshank, *Albert Camus and the Literature of Revolt* (1959); Henri Peyre, *The Contemporary French Novel* (1955); and *Victor Brombert, *The Intellectual Hero: Studies in the French Novel 1880–1955* (1961), are among outstanding studies in this significant area. A most interesting document is *S. R. Hopper (ed.), *Spiritual Problems in Contemporary Literature* (1952). André Rousseaux, *Litterature du Vingtième Siècle* (1939 ——) is a multivolume series dealing with some English and American as well as French writers. Marcus Klein, *After Alienation* (1962, 1964) discusses the American novelists. Special issues of the London Times *Literary Supplement,* such as the two issues of August, 1964, on "Avant Garde" literature, are of exceptional merit.

On various branches of academic thought see Joseph S. Roucek (ed.), *Contemporary Sociology* (1958); T. H. Marshall, *Sociology at the Crossroads* (1963); *H. M. Ruitenbeek (ed.), *Varieties of Modern Social Theory* (1963); *R. C. and G. J. Hinkle, *The Development of Modern Sociology* (1954); *H. R. Hays, *From Ape to Angel: An Informal History of Social Anthropology* (1958); D. E. Butler, *The Study of Political Behavior* (1955); Harold Lasswell, *The Future of Political Science* (1964), a somewhat amazing prospect; John Sutherland (ed.), *Psychoanalysis and Contemporary Thought* (1958); H. P. R. Finberg, *Approaches to History* (1962); and Joan Robinson, *Economic Philosophy: An Essay on the Progress of Economic Thought* (1964).

For the perplexed modern who wants to "keep up" with all the branches of learning in an age when this is impossible, Alan Pryce-Jones has bravely edited *The New Outline of Modern Knowledge* (1956), a unique one-volume guide. Jacques Ellul, *The Technological Society* (1965) is a good example of the kind of book that deals with the impact of scientific and technological change on modern life and thought. *C. P. Snow, *The Two Cultures and the Scientific Revolution* (1959), a celebrated essay, opened up the question of hyper-specialization and loss of contact between minds; among the few writings addressed to this significant question, Owen Barfield, *Worlds Apart: A Dialogue of the 1960s* (1963) deserves note.

Europe's expanding cultural relationship to the non-Western world has been handled in a variety of ways. See William E. Hocking, *The Coming World Civilization* (1956); Arnold J. Toynbee, *The World and the West* (1953); and F. S. C. Northrup, *The Meeting of East and West* (1946). Arthur Koestler, *The Lotus and the Robot* (1960) finds no reason to believe that the Orient has any "spiritual cure to offer for the evils of Western civilization"; but the large literature on Zen Buddhism, on which see for example C. Humphreys, *Zen Comes West* (1960), may testify to the opposite. *R. C. Zaehner, *The Comparison of Religions* (1958); R. H. L. Slater, *World Religions and World Community* (1963); and *Paul Tillich, *Christianity and the Encounter of the World Religions* (1963) speak of the growing dialogue between the world's religions, as does *Mircea Eliade, *Patterns in Comparative Religion* (1958). Eliade's interest in the primitive world is expressed in his *Myths, Dreams and Mysteries* (1960). But patterns of accommodation and communication are also evident in relationships between national and religious units within the Western world. René Wellek, *Confrontations* (1965) deals with this theme, while for the ecumenical debate within world Christianity, see among others Augustin Cardinal Bea, *Unity in Freedom* (1965). Finally, Arnold J. Toynbee's massive *A Study of History* (12 vols., 1939–1963), the bulk of it abridged by D. C. Somervell in two volumes (1946, 1957) may be the most significant commentary of our times, unless this be Fr. Teilhard de Chardin, *The Future of Man* (1964).

ADDITIONAL SUGGESTED READING †

Joan McDonald, *Rousseau and the French Revolution* (1965)

Klaus Epstein, *The Genesis of German Conservatism 1770–1806* (1966)

Richard Herr and Harold T. Parker (ed.), *Ideas in History* (1965)

Franklin L. Baumer, *Religion and the Rise of Scepticism* (1960)

*Marc Raeff (ed.), *Russian Intellectual History: An Anthology* (1966)

*B. M. G. Reardon (ed.), *Religious Thought in the Nineteenth Century* (1966)

David P. Calleo, *Coleridge and the Idea of the Modern State* (1966)

Peter M. Stearns, *Priest and Revolutionary: Lamennais and the Dilemma of French Catholicism* (1967)

Alexander Altmann (ed.), *Studies in Nineteenth Century Jewish Intellectual History* (1964)

Karl J. Weintraub, *Visions of Culture* (1966)

† Listing is according to subject matter.

Walter A. Kaufmann, *Hegel: Reinterpretation, Texts, and Commentary* (1965)

Edward J. Brown, *Stankevich and His Moscow Circle 1830–1840* (1967)

Walter L. Arnstein, *The Bradlaugh Case* (1965)

Joseph Hamburger, *Intellectuals in Politics: John Stuart Mill and the Philosophical Radicals* (1966)

Henry Collins, *Karl Marx and the British Labour Movement* (1965)

H. W. Wardman, *Ernst Renan: A Critical Biography* (1964)

Malcolm Easton, *Artist and Writer in Paris: The Bohemian Idea* (1964)

Shirley R. Letwin, *The Pursuit of Certainty: David Hume, Jeremy Bentham, John Stuart Mill, Beatrice Webb* (1965)

Edward Alexander, *Matthew Arnold and John Stuart Mill* (1965)

F. W. J. Hemmings, *Zola* (2nd ed., 1966)

Ellen Moers, *The Dandy: Brummell to Beerbohm* (1960)

Morse Peckham, *Beyond the Tragic Vision* (1962)

R. J. Hollingdale, *Nietzsche: The Man and His Philosophy* (1965)

*Gerhard Masur, *Prophets of Yesterday: Studies in European Culture 1890–1914* (1961)

Reinhard Bendix, *Max Weber: An Intellectual Portrait* (1960)

W. Warren Wagar, *H. G. Wells and the World State* (1961)

*W. Warren Wagar (ed.), *European Intellectual History since Darwin and Marx* (1967)

Arthur Marwick, *The Deluge: British Society and the First World War* (1965)

John A. Thayer, *Italy and the Great War: Politics and Culture 1870–1915* (1965)

Matthew H. Elbow, *French Corporative Theory 1789–1948: A Chapter in the History of Ideas* (1953)

Julius Braunthal, *History of the International* (2 vols., English tr., 1967)

Joel Colton, *Leon Blum: Intellectual in Politics* (1966)

George L. Mosse (ed.), *Nazi Culture* (1966)

Peter G. J. Pulzer, *The Rise of Political Anti-Semitism in Germany and Austria* (1965)

R. G. Colodny (ed.), *Frontiers of Science and Philosophy* (1965)

Roy Pierce, *Contemporary French Political Thought* (1966)

George Lichtheim, *Marxism in Modern France* (1966)

*Donald A. Lowrie (ed.), *Christian Existentialism: A Berdyaev Synthesis* (1965)

*J. H. Plumb (ed.), *Crisis in the Humanities* (1964)

Judith Sklar, *After Utopia: The Decline of Political Faith* (1957)

Raymond Williams, *Modern Tragedy* (1966)

LOCATING ADDITIONAL BOOKS AND ARTICLES

The foregoing suggestions being but a highly selective listing, any student doing a serious research paper must have recourse to bibliographical aids to assist him in locating books and articles on his subject, a need that becomes greater as the volume of publication grows. Of such aids, perhaps the best within its range is the four-volume bibliography, *English Literature 1660–1800* (1926–1962), edited by R. S. Crane, Louis Landa, and others, taken from the periodical *Philological Quarterly*—extensive, frequently annotated, and actually going much beyond strictly literary studies and beyond England. William D. Templeman and others have edited a similar *Bibliography of Studies in Victorian Literature 1932–1944* (1945), based on *Modern Philology*, with a photoduplicated supplement by Austin Wright, *Bibliographies of Studies in Victorian Literature 1945–1954* (1956); for the remaining years, consult the journal. Annual bibliographies are supplied by the Modern Humanities Research Association, *Annual Bibliography of English Language and Literature* (1920 ––); the English Association (London), *The Year's Work in English Studies* (1920 ––); and The Modern Language Association, *Annual Bibliography* (1955 ––). Also helpful are °F. W. Bateson, *A Guide to English Literature* (1965), and °Donald F. Bond, *A Reference Guide to English Studies* (1962). Thomas R. Palfrey, *A Bibliographical Guide to the Romance Languages and Literature* (1963), and Jethro Bithell (ed.), *Germany: A Companion to German Studies* (5th ed., 1955) help with other European countries; also *The Oxford Companion to French Literature* (1959), and others in this series.

The periodical *Isis* prints a bibliography every year for the history of science, and A. C. Crombie and M. A. Hoskin are editing an annual bibliographical review, *History of Science: An Annual Review of Literature, Research, and Teaching* (1962 ––). For philosophy there are the International Institute of Philosophy, *Bibliography of Philosophy*, annually (1954 ––); G. A. De Brie (ed.), *Bibliographica Philosophica 1934–1945* (2 vols.). *The International Bibliography of the Social Sciences* is published periodically by UNESCO. The American Historical Association's *Guide to Historical Literature* (1961), edited by George F. Howe *et al.;* the French series, *Nouvelle Clio,* now replacing the older *Clio* series (1963 ––); the Royal Historical Society's annual *Writings on British History,* and the Historical Association (London), *Annual Bulletin of Historical Literature;* the German *Handbuch der Deutschen Geschichte* (1954) edited by Bruno Gebhart are among the leading aids to students of history. There are numerous bibliographies for special periods or areas, and a good guide in general is °Wood Gray, *The Historian's Handbook* (2nd ed., 1964).

Among the more valuable research tools of a general nature are Constance Winchell, *Guide to Reference Books,* °Jean K. Gates, *Guide to the Use of Books and Libraries;* Theodore Besterman, *A World Bibliography of Bibliographies* (5 vol., 1965–1966); and °John W. Spargo, *A Bibliographical Manual* (3rd ed., 1956). Spargo, Wood Gray, and Bateson should be in the personal library of every student doing research.

Serious students should know the leading learned journals, which are usually a source of bibliographies in their area. *Historical Abstracts* and *Political Science Abstracts* help locate journal articles, as also do the standard guides to periodical literature such as *Reader's Guide.* Following are some of the leading journals for the student of ideas: *Journal of the History of Ideas;*

for the history of Science, *Isis, Osiris, Annals of Science;* for Literature, *Modern Philology, Philological Quarterly, Studies in Philology, Modern Language Review, Publications of the Modern Language Association; French Studies, German Studies, Comparative Literature;* for Philosophy, *Journal of Philosophy, Mind, Thought, Journal of the History of Philosophy;* for Religion, *Journal of Religion, Church History, Harvard Theological Review, Theology;* for History and Politics, *American Political Science Review, Review of Politics, Journal of Politics, American Historical Review, Journal of Modern History, English Historical Review, History, Revue Historique, International Review of Social History, Victorian Studies, French Historical Studies.* There are many others of possible value.

Index